You're Going to Be Dead One Day

You're Going to be Dead One Day

a love story

David Horowitz

REGNERY
PUBLISHING
A Division of Salem Media Group

Regnery® is a registered trademark of Salem Communications Holding Corporation

Cataloging-in-Publication data on file with the Library of Congress

ISBN 978-1-62157-379-1

Published in the United States by
Regnery Publishing
A Division of Salem Media Group
300 New Jersey Ave NW
Washington, DC 20001
www.Regnery.com

Manufactured in the United States of America

10 9 8 7 6 5 4 3 2 1

Books are available in quantity for promotional or premium use. For information on discounts and terms, please visit our website: www.Regnery.com.

Distributed to the trade by
Perseus Distribution
250 West 57th Street
New York, NY 10107

To my Mom and Dad

wherever you are

CONTENTS

one

May

I generally have a soft spot for family occasions and warm weather, which is an obvious reason for my contentment today. Not only is the sun shining down on a brilliant spring morning, it is also Mother's Day, and my wife, April, and her sisters have planned a small gathering at our house to celebrate. At this moment I am off by myself in a corner of the sitting room where the windows meet, contemplating how occasions like this inevitably bring bittersweet memories to the surface, and looking forward to them.

Since it is still early, I have settled into a luxurious leather chair that my wife bought for me recently. The new chair is also elaborate with stainless steel rails and machinery that electronically tilts the user back and raises the legs to an optimal therapeutic point. It is equipped with a glass holder and a retractable desk that allows me to write with the least discomfort. The manufacturer calls my catbird seat "The Perfect Chair," and from where I am perched I would not argue. Its price, if you were curious, has been set accordingly and would discourage many people from even considering the option. It certainly would have discouraged me if the decision had been mine. But it was a surprise from April on my release from Los Robles Hospital's acute physical therapy unit, where I was laid up for two weeks for reasons I will divulge shortly. It is one of many gifts that bear the imprint of a wifely concern for my well-being, which is a healing balm in itself.

Along with the chair, she has set up a new movable desk by my bed, and these two pieces of furniture are where I spend most of my time now, since I am no longer mobile. A little over a month ago, I went into the hospital for what I thought was a routine hip replacement, but while I was under the anesthetic the surgeon slipped up and damaged my sciatic nerve, leaving me with a paralyzed left foot and a reservoir of neuropathic pain. Until this mishap, like most people I took my limbs for granted and had no idea how a useless foot and damaged nerves could take a person down.

My wife is understandably upset about my condition and pressing me to sue. I have contacted an attorney but am skeptical about securing any positive result. In the litigious environment of the medical profession, doctors have availed themselves of elaborate defenses that are difficult to breach. Only time will tell whether I will ever recover the use of my limb or whether the courts will deliver me a modicum of satisfaction.

When I signed up for the operation, I had not the slightest inkling that a calamity like this might be awaiting me. I had undergone a similar procedure on my right hip ten years earlier, after which I was out of the hospital in a day, and functioning reasonably well within a few weeks. This encouraged me to follow my normal approach to problems: just get them out of the way and get back to work. But when I awoke from this procedure in my hospital bed, I knew immediately that something was very wrong. My foot was hanging lifeless from the ankle, a syndrome known as "drop foot," and instead of my release papers the hospital had provided me with a morphine pump. I could not move my toes. I could not *feel* my toes, and barely the foot itself.

My doctors have told me that my present condition is not hopeless and some sort of recovery is likely. But they remain evasive as to when this might materialize and what it might be like. Nerves apparently have their own schedule and manner of repair. Whether they will heal enough to restore what I once took for granted remains disconcertingly uncertain. Nonetheless, I have accepted the ambivalent prognoses and canceled engagements for the next several months, at not a little personal cost. Two of the speeches I was scheduled to give would have been before thousands of people and carried with them honorariums I now have plenty of use for. I have accepted this setback with as much philosophical attitude as I can muster, having found in the course of many lost battles that it is better not to fight the inevitable when it is staring you in the face.

It is also wise to try to enjoy the life you have before the gates begin to close. In the years before sixty, I led a physically robust existence and never paid much attention to matters of health. But in 2001, as the country reeled under the attacks of 9/11, I was diagnosed with a prostate cancer and underwent a radical prostatectomy to remove it. I seem to have been battling significant ailments ever since. I don't wish to exaggerate these trials, because until my present unfortunate case, I have managed each of the problems without too much disruption of my activities and accepted the new limits my body has laid on me.

Entering this new world naturally prompts thoughts about "last things." I have written three philosophical memoirs about the lessons to be drawn from our brief journeys on this earth, and this is undoubtedly the beginning of a fourth. I began them with a book called *The End of Time*, a title with dual meanings since the "end of time" can refer either to the purpose that we give to our lives or the purpose our limited allotment of time imparts to them. In this book, I also included observations on the utopian quest for a perfect world, which is a secular religion for many, and has been the focus of most of my thinking life. This quest is really an attempt to deny the permanence of injustice, of which death is the exemplary case.

The second memoir, *A Cracking of the Heart*, was about the admirable life and untimely demise of my daughter Sarah. You do not really know death until you have lost someone you love, and lost her forever. Writing about my child was a way of salving my grief, and the book has been helpful to others dealing with irreparable loss. The third volume, *A Point in Time*, while slim like the others, is actually a *summa* of my life's work. Its focus is again the social redeemers who want to escape the meaninglessness of life by pursuing the fantasy of a heaven on earth, while sewing the seeds of catastrophes along the way.

While I am awaiting the family's arrival, I can enjoy an interlude of undisturbed solitude in which to consider these matters. Of course I could fill my head with happier reflections, but I won't. Thinking about our mortal condition, and the way it affects how we live in the here and now, remains as seductive to me as ever. It provides my old age with the *frisson* of youthful discovery and has been the inspiration for some of my most satisfying work. Others may suppose that so morbid a preoccupation on a bright spring morning could only be inspired by the fact that in a week I have a long-standing appointment to see my oncologist. But I can assure you this is not the case. After all, I have lived with the same cancer for thirteen of the most productive years of my life. And who isn't facing a death sentence?

Nonetheless, my reflections on mortality are disturbing to those like my wife who are immersed in the life around them and instinctively understand the utility of fresh air and sunshine to the human spirit. I appreciate and respect this attitude, which is why I choose to conduct my ruminations in a corner by myself.

Family Matters

Mother's Day has not always been a tradition in the Horowitz family. As a reflex of his communist politics my father dismissed the occasion as a "greeting card holiday" designed to make profits for Hallmark. I was long influenced by his view until a Mother's Day came along when April said we should buy a helium-filled party balloon shaped like a heart and send it to my mother Blanche with our prayers. The idea was pretty alien to me. My mother had been dead for twenty years, and the idea that we could communicate with her through a plastic balloon sent skyward seemed ridiculous. But the little ceremony April contrived and put her heart into brought tears to my eyes, because her thoughts for my mother were so sincere and put me in reverent mind of the woman who was once such a towering presence in my life.

It is April's family who will be joining us this morning. Her younger sister, Kim, is already here, and has been staying in the house since April's accident (which I will come to shortly), taking only a few days off now and then to attend to her own household in Huntington Beach. This has been a great help in our family crisis, as Kim does the cleaning and cooking, and, equally important since we are both on medications, drives us to our respective doctor's visits.

April and Kim were the youngest pair in a brood of ten, but were separated twenty years ago when Kim and her husband, Jim, were forced to move to Indiana because of a work-related problem. On their return to California, they settled two hours down the coast and kept to themselves. It was only when April's mishap occurred that the two were reunited and began to resurrect the tomfoolery of the times they had together when they were young.

Now their laughter rings about the house, triggered more often than not by April's manic impersonations and pranks. The two women are on the back porch attending to our yelping canines. When the dogs have finished their breakfast, they exit the kitchen door to romp about the sprawling lawn at the back of our house. There are four Chihuahuas and two Boxers in the menagerie. One of the Boxers, named Max, belongs to Kim, the other, named Merry, to us.

We will not be a large group this Mother's Day, but sufficiently entwined to make the occasion work. April's older sister Cherri will be driving up from West Covina with her husband, Wendell, a Vietnam veteran. Kim's husband is coming up from the beach, while their son, Ryan, will arrive separately to complete the gathering.

Unanswered Questions

My solitude has begun at the far end of the house from the women's laughter and the dogs' happy cries, and I am deep into my head and the dark thoughts that preoccupy me. A stream of light pouring through the living room windows has brightened this pleasant interval of not so pleasant concerns, making them even more incongruous. But press on I will.

All questions about death begin with observations that only a religious faith can answer. I have no such faith, and therefore my posing of these questions is without a hope that life eternal awaits us where all will become clear. Consequently, I am left to grapple with these stark facts: there is no one to tell you when you will be gone from this life, and no one to tell you why you are here and waiting to be gone in the first place; and there is no one to tell you what happens then—whether you will be nothing at all with every memory of you vanished. These questions at the heart of our existence are formidable loose ends of our earthly stay that threaten to undermine it at every turn. It is remarkable to consider that even though they are central to our lives, we are no closer to answering them now than when Pythagoras discovered that musical notes could be translated into mathematical equations.

The dialogue that goes on in my head in response to our dilemma is the product of a lifelong conviction that we should strive to understand the existence into which we have been cast and not merely endure it as we would a case of drop foot or a dose of bad weather. Is there something peculiar about this? Or is the subject averted because it might ruin our day?

A Hidden God

At seventy-five I have reached what would once have seemed to me a formidable age; but it hardly feels that way now that I am here. Having begun to understand how the game is played, I am ready for a second round. However, for reasons unexplained, the game was not set up that way. One and done. After years of reflection on this fate, I have grown used to it and to a surprising degree accepted it. Yet the finality of a cosmic emptiness still rankles, like a puzzle missing its central piece. There is just no satisfying way to comprehend the possibility that everything one has lived and worked for and loved will simply disappear.

The seventeenth-century French scientist and religious thinker Blaise Pascal, whose poignant life ended when he was only thirty-nine, devised his own approach to these questions. He explained the darkness at the heart of our existence by the paradox of a Hidden God. Only God could fill the emptiness we face but chooses not to. He will not even reveal to us that He is there.

In this season of medical ordeals I have encountered my own paradox, which is fortuitously temporal and happy. It fills the only life I have and thus trumps Pascal's angst. April and I have been together for twenty years and age has overtaken us, but in the midst of our medical woes I find myself in the throes of a passion that I would have thought reserved only for the young and innocent. And these feelings marvelously are shared. I ask myself, how can adults schooled by time and aware of each other's inoperable flaws fall again so deeply in love? As with so many other important things I cannot explain this, but it has brought a happiness to my physical suffering that has made me perversely apprehensive of its ending.

Two Sensibilities

Over the years, April has made many concessions to my intellectual distractions but has never reconciled herself to the morbid reflections of my late memoirs. Perhaps this intolerance derives from the age gap between us, which prompts her to visualize the emptiness I will leave when I am gone. She, the optimist, is a pessimist about this, which might account for her near panic when she hears me utter phrases like "the end of time." She is instinctively apprehensive that tomorrow may turn dark, while I, the pessimist, am upbeat about my prospects and rarely see disasters coming. How do I reconcile these contradictions? I don't. Like Walt Whitman I could respond that I contain multitudes, but probably my heart is simply incapable of following my head.

When I look for a cause of my optimism, all I can come up with is this: I was brought up in a quasi-religious environment whose members had set out to "change the world." From a very young age I was taught that despite all improbabilities, despite the fact that our community of communist believers was tiny and hunted, the brave new world we were seeking was just beyond the horizon. History was on our side. Tragic experience has taught me the destructive folly of this faith, but habit and instinct continue to say otherwise.

Asking how a pessimist about humanity and its prospects can still be optimistic about his own is no different from asking how an atheist can be moral. Obviously this is possible, unless one believes that all atheists are criminals. There is a dimension to our lives, finite as they are, which contains possibilities that are not. So there is nothing strange in agnostics like me embracing them.

Our different outlooks also affect the way April and I view my current benighted state. April agonizes over the details of my new life—the pitiful sight of me hobbling across the floor with my walker and therapeutic boot, the agonies I suffer when the pain is severe, my return to a childlike dependence, requiring her assistance with such simple tasks as putting on my clothes, bathing, or getting in and out of the wheelchair we take on outings. How utterly transformed my life has become. How it has shrunk under the knife of an incompetent hand. Such thoughts roll into a rage inside her, which can be assuaged only by thoughts of retribution.

I, on the other hand, have few of these feelings. Of course I can see her point, and am touched by the way she assumes the role of my defender. But unlike her I do not dwell on these circumstances or rail against the forces that have brought me low. My opening bout with prostate cancer was also my first stoic lesson, and my daughter Sarah's untimely death seven years later provided a brutal completion of the course. What they said to me was this: *you are not an exception*. This is my code. It is not something I think about; it is the *way* I think.

I can say with confidence, therefore, that I haven't spent any time agonizing over the injustice of this bungled operation or imagining scenarios in which it never happened. Unfairness is part of the genome of our existence. Therefore, accept it and move on. What I focus on is getting through these days and figuring out how a recovery might take place. When the stabs of pain threaten to lift me out of my chair, I tell myself these are the nerves re-firing, and that augurs well. I have no idea if this is the truth, but I am encouraged by my doctors to think it is, and thinking so certainly helps me to get by. I have disciplined myself to be patient, having learned through experience that improvement is not going to proceed according to any schedule of mine.

Principally, I focus on the daily satisfactions that are within my reach. These lie in what I can accomplish with my brain, and the perfect chair April has provided. I am preparing the text and publicity plan for a book called *Take No Prisoners*, which will be published on July 28, 2014, which is two months from now. I also have a larger literary project in the editing and completion of a ten-volume edition of my collected writings called *The Black Book of the American Left*. Yet another concern is an organization I created nearly three decades ago called the David Horowitz Freedom Center, which is on the cusp of an expansion. Communicating with my staff and board by e-mail, I have been able to see to fruition several projects that bring a special satisfaction to me because they are all the brainchildren of the young team I have hired, which will one day replace me.

Finally, there is the task that I do for the sheer pleasure, posting photos of beautiful equines on the Facebook page "Heart of a Horse." Several years ago I hired my grandson Jules to assist me and with his help I was able to put up the page every day I was in the hospital. The Facebook page is the public face of the Heart of a Horse Foundation, which April created to rescue horses. It was designed to promote her work, and the images posted are provided by world-class equine photographers and artists. In the course of time the Heart of a Horse page has attracted six hundred thousand viewers from Iceland to Australia and Poland to Argentina. I usually sit down to post the images in the early hours before breakfast, and am drawn into a zone of calm, which refreshes me for the more combative agendas of the day ahead.

The general optimism I have referred to, which seems stubbornly innate, is regularly confounded by the law of unintended consequences. For the same outlook that has seen me through predicaments that might daunt others can also be a kind of denial, leading to personal setbacks like my hip surgery. Why was I so sure this operation would be as easy as the last one? Why didn't I conduct a diligent search for a surgeon who had consistently good results? Why did I pick one off the Internet? The answer is I was too eager to get the procedure out of the way so I could get on with more important tasks, too confident there was no danger in rushing ahead.

Unfortunately, the hard knocks I have received throughout my life have never fully overcome my instincts and taught me the lessons they should have. Though chastened, I still catch myself attempting to barrel my way through the ordeal of this recovery as though the paralysis of my foot was something to be over and done with like mumps.

I would not be candid if I did not admit that sometimes my optimism fails, and I run into a wall that nearly flattens me. The day April surprised me with what she called a "get-along scooter," one of those electrical go-carts you see the disabled go about on, I was forced to confront the dark side of the equation. Settling into the small vehicle and riding it up to the mailbox at the end of our driveway, I had a vision of the emptiness that might lie before me—a state in which I was permanently crippled. The prospect was overwhelming and, though I was able to hide them from others, I could not hold back the tears.

In an ironic turn, however, the get-along scooter soon proved a great convenience and even pleasure. It allowed me to move around the house with ease, especially on days when the pain was so great I could not bear to put my foot on the floor. The very next time I took the cart outside for a spin, the boyish thrill of wheeling around the driveway at what seemed like reckless speeds was exhilarating. April, who had a great time riding on it herself, said it was the first time in weeks she had seen me smile.

Faith

I try to honor April's wish not to thrust the darkest of my thoughts in her direction and to keep a lid on them when company is around. I do this not only because I love her but because her own vibrant conviction that there is indeed a God and a place beyond death where we will reunite provides my home with a comforting, inspirational light. Nor do I dismiss her faith out of hand. I am continually impressed by the unsolved mysteries of our existence and by our inability to understand them—how the inexplicable persists despite the advance of knowledge, and how it is all around us; how science, as advanced as it has become, has no clue as to how the universe was created and cannot explain how life on earth began.

And there is, too, the undeniable fact that I am not without faith myself. I have lived my life as though my actions meant something and everything would add up in the end. Without thinking about it, I have had a conviction so deep it might have been encoded in my genes—that while there may not be providence in the fall of a sparrow, as Hamlet supposed, there is nonetheless a purpose to our ends. Though I cannot articulate it, this purpose causes me to conduct myself as though my wife, not I, were right.

A Near Fatal Incident

Nine months before Mother's Day, while I was home working, April was in a terrifying car accident that almost took her life. In an instant of dizziness at the wheel of her truck, she slid off the soft shoulder, went through a flimsy fence, and plunged down a steep incline. Within seconds she had glided off the rim of an agricultural drainage pipe and gone airborne before crashing into the steel of its inner wall. The impact at the end of her thirty-foot drop was so powerful that it demolished the new Ford. The vehicle landed on its side, leaving her suspended by her seat belt, and the airbag failed to open. Only the strength of the cab remaining intact saved her.

For what seemed an interminable interval, April hung in mid-air, passing in and out of consciousness. Fortunately, the accident had occurred during rush hour, and commuters came down the hillside to locate her and call the paramedics. When the rescue workers arrived they pried her from the wreck and rushed her to the Los Robles Hospital emergency room, and then to the intensive care unit. There she was diagnosed with a contused heart, a collapsed lung, a broken clavicle, and six broken ribs.

I had no idea this was happening until two hours later when I received a call from a nurse saying my wife had been in an accident but was all right, by which she meant alive. It took me fifteen minutes to get there to see April hooked up to monitors and IVs with a drain in her side. She was in a semi-drugged state and kept repeating "I was airborne" and then "I was hanging almost upside down and screaming your name." I held her hand and told her I loved her and assured her she was going to get better, and tried to listen to the fragments of her tale. I was so glad to see her alive I never quite took in the fact that I had nearly lost her or that she was not out of danger yet.

Because of the contusion and collapsed lung, the hospital held her in the intensive care unit for over a week, while doctors kept coming in to monitor her condition and to worry about her heart. The doctor in charge told her, "You're lucky. If that contusion had filled your heart with blood, you would be dead. As it is, you can be thankful to be here." Every day I came to reassure her about her recovery and refused to consider the possibility of life without her. From the beginning I dealt with this as I did bad news generally. She was going to be all right and nothing in our lives would change.

But of course they already had. I cannot adequately describe the physical agonies she went through over the next nine months or the aftereffects of the injuries she is still dealing with even as she tries to nurse me back to health. The psychological impact of the accident was almost equal to the physical—the acute sense of being brushed by death, the exaggerated fears that ordinary incidents now provoked, the anxiety that she would never be able to raise her arm again and never ride her horses. It was crystallized for her one day in her tack room at the upper end of our ranch when she picked her lunge whip off its hook and swung it weakly. There was no way she was going to be able to crack it. She thought: "My body is broken and my life is changed forever." Feelings like this continued for seven months until a day came when her frozen shoulder began to thaw and, seemingly at that moment, my own trauma reversed our roles.

Mother's Day

When everyone finally arrived at the house, the sun was overhead. We had been hosting brunches for the same crowd almost every other Sunday, so it was going to be hard to make Mother's Day seem special. But with three mothers present we were ready to give it a try. April and Kim had made up a quiz with which they hoped to embarrass the others. The first question was, "How did Mother's Day begin?" Cherri drew the question and surprised us by saying confidently that it began as a holiday to celebrate military mothers who had lost their sons in World War I. Everyone agreed that was the right answer and complimented her. But in fact we all had the wrong answer and so embarrassed ourselves. According to Wikipedia, a peace activist named Anna Jarvis invented

Mother's Day in 1905 to commemorate the death of her mother that same year. It had nothing to do with the military.

With everybody talking at once, the conversation quickly shifted to anecdotes of the sisters' childhood, as it usually did in this group, focusing on rivalries and jealousies they tried to carry into the present. Kim was claiming that Cherri had stabbed her brother Joe when she was twelve and he was thirteen. Kim was three at the time. Such a bone of contention was not unusual in a household that had been run by siblings whose parents were frequently absent, and often for long stretches. Cherri, who was clearly hurt, defended herself as though she had been publicly defamed. Although the incident had taken place nearly fifty years ago, this quarrel was a regular feature of family get-togethers, thanks to Kim's persistence.

About two weeks later, on Memorial Day, Kim and April and I made a visit to brother Joe's house and then to the Queen of Heaven cemetery to lay flowers on the grave of their mother, Mary. Before departing for the cemetery we asked Joe if Cherri had actually stabbed him. He explained that the reverse would be closer to the truth. Cherri had been slapping him in a fight while he was cooking and holding one of those large forks used to lift a roast. One of her slaps had poked a prong of the fork into her own forearm. He smiled at the way the canard had a life almost as long as theirs.

The Heart Has Reasons

It is odd that April can have such dark worries about my life expectancy but is unnerved by my reflections on the emptiness toward which we all are headed. It is all the more puzzling because I have no intention of letting these dark views influence my actions. If one were to act on the opinion that we are nothing and nothing matters, one could end up a nihilist or sociopath. Instead my stoicism tells me to cherish what I have and to make the world within my reach a little better. I accept the contradiction—that my head might tell me one thing and my heart another—and listen to my heart.

I am not ashamed to admit that I don't know the answers to life's most important questions. There is even an advantage to a perspective that accepts the insoluble contradictions at the center of our being. It allows one to keep one's mind open, and that in turn can open new worlds.

I am going to relate two stories with which I hope to illuminate this observation. One is about two people and a dog, and the other about an incident that happened to me, which science cannot explain and you will probably not believe yourself. To forestall any unwarranted assumptions about my gullibility, let me begin by saying that I have never had experiences of the kind that lead others to claim with confidence that they have touched unseen worlds. When I am told of such experiences, I am inclined not to believe them, though I have seen enough acts of improbable intuition not to dismiss them entirely either.

The Stories

The first story concerns my late daughter, Sarah. Or perhaps it does not concern her at all. That is one of the mysteries I cannot resolve and that typifies the enigmas that surround the meanings of our lives.

I cannot capture in a paragraph or two the amazing life of my daughter Sarah, which ended at the age of forty-three from the effects of a birth condition known as Turner Syndrome. I have written a book about her life and death and called it *A Cracking of the Heart*. The title refers to the humbling one must go through to let knowledge in but also to the effect of her passing on me, which has left a wound that cannot be healed.

My daughter lifted every soul she touched and opened hearts wherever she went. The first chapter of my book was titled "You Resurrect the Dead," which is a line from the Jewish funeral prayer to promote the ascension of the souls of the departed. She recited this prayer every day over her morning coffee. She did not herself believe in a corporeal resurrection, but she did believe in a resurrection of the spirit. She found such a concept—called "a rolling of the souls"—in Judaism. She was not afraid of death and was in this as in all she did an example for the rest of us.

Two days before the incident I am about to relate, April was rummaging among the shelves in my office searching for a copy of *A Cracking of the Heart* to give to her sister. When she found it, she handed it to her sister, and as she did so two black-and-white photographs fell from between the pages. One was a picture of Sarah, still an infant, sitting on the grass in our backyard in England, where she was born. The other was a picture of me as a young father. When the two women saw the photos fall from the book, they gasped, perhaps not realizing that it was I who had put them there.

Two days later April awoke in the early morning hours and went to the adjacent bedroom so that she could retrieve some of the sleep she had lost because of the snoring by our Chihuahuas and me. When she was settled in the other room, she fell into a deep dream state in which she suddenly saw Sarah's face, and was then bathed in such a warm light that she felt utterly at peace. When she awoke, she came to me and told me about her dream. By then it was six in the morning, and I was sitting up staring at my computer where a photo of Sarah had suddenly come up on the screen. When April looked at it and saw how sad I was, she said, "Let's get out into the morning air, and while we're at it let's find a place to eat."

Without much thinking about it, we agreed to have breakfast at a Jewish deli in a local strip mall where we had eaten once or twice before. We sat down on their wooden chairs and April ordered matzo ball soup and I potato latkes. While we were waiting for our orders, we took some plastic plates and utensils from a general counter and put them on our table. April's soup came first and I availed myself of one of her bagel crusts and began opening a small package of marmalade with the idea of applying it. But at just that moment, in the swiftest motion and without any warning my plastic plate lifted off the table and struck me in the lower chest.

We both saw and were taken aback by this impossible movement. "What just happened?" April said, and then asked me if I thought it was Sarah trying to contact me. Later when we were in the car she asked me again. She remembers me assenting but I can't imagine I did. On the other hand, I did toy with the idea of seeing Sarah again, and an immense wave of pleasure swept over me when I did. But it didn't alter my view that my daughter was gone.

There was no way I could explain what had happened. No door was open to allow a sudden gust of wind to blow the plate into my chest. The table was anchored by a heavy metal base. What we both saw was inexplicable.

April, on the other hand, would not let go of the incident. Several times she brought up the episodes that had put Sarah's energy into our lives that day: the book and photos, her dream, the fact that I had been thinking about her too. But although I was at a loss to explain what had happened, and even though I *wanted* the cause to be Sarah and continued to mentally explore the happy possibilities if it were, I could not make myself believe.

If someone else told me this story, I would reject it out of hand, probably with a slight roll of the eyes. Things like this just don't happen; plates do not fly off tables. But it happened to me. And therefore I am forced to file it as one of those mysteries that I cannot explain. And of course each of us has encountered the inexplicable at some point, and probably dismissed it as something that science could explain if called upon to do so. But there are probably an equally large number of people like April, who don't dismiss these experiences, who resurrect the dead. I am grateful to her because her belief brought my daughter close to me and set me to thinking about her and wondering if I would ever see her again.

Waiting to Be Picked Up

It would probably be hard to contrive two people more different from each other than April and myself, and not just in regard to existential issues. When we first met I was immersed in politics, but when I invited her to a house meeting with Pete Wilson, the governor of our state, she had no idea who he was and begged off for lack of interest. Of course this changed as we became a couple, and eventually she hosted New York's Governor George Pataki and other political notables in our home. I do not pretend to understand how the chemistry between us works, but it has. And just as I have brought her into my worlds, she has taken me on journeys I would never have embarked on if we hadn't met.

I would never have owned a dog, for example, if she had not dropped one on my doorstep, and then another and another and another. People whose hearts are not open to animals could never understand how these acquisitions came to affect me. One of my friends, a retired attorney, is a smart man but overly cerebral. When the dikes failed during Hurricane Katrina and thousands of people were threatened with drowning, he said to me, "Can you believe that there are people in the middle of this flood who won't get out because they don't want to leave their pets behind?" My friend is generally a caring person, but he said this with a smile big enough to let me know he thought such people absurd. But to a dog person it is *his* attitude that is absurd. Someone like my friend could never understand what these relationships bring to us, or the feelings that would make it difficult if not impossible for us to leave our companions behind.

Now for the second story. At Christmastime two and a half years ago, April and I were out for a drive. We had gone to Calabasas to have lunch and were heading back home. April was at the wheel when she began taking roads that steered us somewhat out of our way and to the Agoura Hills animal pound. This was a partially hidden complex of buildings constructed unceremoniously with large blocks of concrete painted grey. Later she observed that she had passed this pound many times before and never gone in. The only way she could describe what had come over her on this trip was that she felt as though someone was waiting for her.

As you would expect, the pound was an indescribably sad place. There were maybe seventy dogs, some young and spirited, some old and passive, all waiting for someone to pick them up, and all destined to be put down if no one showed up to do so. The woman who greeted us was friendly and solicitous. As she led us through the holding pens, she explained that this was the final stop for the dogs that animal control had captured. They had all come from other facilities, where no one had adopted them. If they weren't taken this time, within a few weeks they would be gone.

April asked the lady to show us the ones who were running out of time. In the very first stall she took us to, there was a coffee brown Chihuahua with very short legs, a white bib at her throat, and white accents over her eyes. The plate on the stall said her name was "Coco," and the lady told us they thought she was thirteen years old. Coco was standing on her hind legs and pressing her little body against the cage netting, and wagging her tail as though she and April knew each other. The tip of her tongue hung from the side of her mouth where some teeth were missing, giving her a goofy look, and April commented later that her little black eyes called to her in a way that said, "Please take me. I may be old but I'm a very good girl." To this imagined appeal, April replied, "Hello, Coco, you've got a silly little tongue," and got the goofy look back.

When April reached into the cage and picked Coco up she detected a putrid odor coming from her mouth indicating it was infected. The woman told her that Coco had been found along with a pack of other dogs in a house in Belmont, which they suspected was a breeding kennel. The owner had died and the dogs were removed to another pound where they were held for several months. No one had taken Coco, probably because of her age and the odor, so she was shipped to Agoura.

It was obvious why Coco would be used for breeding Chihuahua puppies. Her markings were beautiful and her expression precious, and she had a spirit that made her disregard her circumstances and, instead of cowering in a corner, rush to the front of her cage, stand up on her hind legs, and try to catch our attention. It was also clear from the state of her teeth that no one had looked after her health for years, probably forever. Her beautiful coat had also been marred by two large teeth marks on her rump, probably the result of an attack by a bigger dog. The fur that had overgrown them was gray rather than brown and looked like splotches on her otherwise sable-like coat. Perhaps it was also her goofy tongue drag that spoiled the image for some prospective adopters, causing them to leave her behind.

For us, Coco's flair sealed the deal. As April described it to me later, when she saw Coco run to the front of her cage it was as if she was saying, "Hey *me*, adopt *me*. I have lots of love for you, and if you look at me with kinder eyes you'll see how cute I am." Of course dogs don't talk. But on the other hand we don't know how they think or what they are trying to communicate either. Whatever the cause, a bond was struck between April and Coco that was to be the little dog's salvation.

We asked the woman to open the cage, and Coco came right over. April picked her up, and gave her a kiss, and said "Boy, Coco, your mouth smells really bad." She put her fingers on either side of Coco's jaw and opened it and said, "Oh my God, your teeth are discolored and infected. That must really hurt. I am going to take you to the vet right away." After paying our $50 pound fee, that is just what we did. As soon as we were outside the pound, April dialed her friend Dr. Kevin Smith, a large-animal vet, who said an infection such as she was describing could easily be fatal and advised her to take Coco directly to a small-animal vet he knew in Ventura.

The vet's name was Lori, who, after inspecting Coco, said it was the worst mouth infection she had ever seen. There was a hole in Coco's nasal cavity, her jawbone was eaten away, and her teeth were so far gone that if she didn't have immediate surgery to remove them the infection would most certainly kill her. "I can't imagine the pain this dog has been in," Lori said. "Do anything it takes to save her," replied April.

The operation took four hours and cost $1,000, which gave me a little jolt. But since Coco was ours, I could hardly deny her anything that would keep her alive. Coco's teeth were so rotten that they crumbled when Lori began to remove them. Eventually, she had to take out all but two and sew up the hole in Coco's nasal cavity. When it was over, Lori told

April that if she had brought her in a little later it would have been too late but, as it was, she was going to be fine. April picked Coco up and kissed her all over, and said, "Coco, I'm your new mommy, and now I'm going to take you home."

Coco proved to be an exceptional addition to our household. Despite her age, she was full of curiosity and energy and warbled and made other funny sounds as she explored her new home. At night, she immediately took a place in our bed near our heads, and nestled up close to me so I could stroke her fur until one of us fell asleep. Coco also had a growl, melodramatic to say the least, which was hilarious to us but intimidated all the other animals, including Winnie, our very large Bernese Mountain Dog. We wondered whether the drama queen was an inborn personality or had developed out of the hard life she had lived in the breeding mill and the battles she had been forced to fight in order to survive. We worried about her age and what we had been told was her enlarged heart. We didn't know if she had only months to live.

But she fooled us all. She ran with the pack, sometimes tumbling over herself when she tried with her little legs to keep up. She was relentless about getting the most out of life, setting an example for everyone else. Her antics amused all who encountered her, and it could be said that, with all the love that was showered on her, these last years were truly golden. Recalling them afterwards gave April and me the warmest feelings, and a tremendous lift every time we thought of how a fortuitous stop along the way had given Coco a new life.

When we took her in, we hoped that Coco would go on at least for a year, and when she passed that milestone we came to wish that she would live forever. But as she neared the end of the second year she was struck by an illness the vet never quite identified. It put her in intense pain that did not respond to the drugs the vet provided. When the pain continued for weeks so that she no longer ran in the yard but crawled under the furniture, hiding as animals do when they are ready to die, we visited the vet again to take her out of her misery. The vet had a place for the euthanasia, which she called the Rainbow Room. I have a vivid image of Coco, cradled in the vet's arms looking at me with almost a wink of peace as the drug took her out of her pain and she slipped away from us for good.

We buried her in a little graveyard along the outer fence near the upper yard where our horse arena and stables are. The lone occupant of the gravesite until then was Winnie, who was with us for nine years and whom we had put to sleep in the same Rainbow Room a few months earlier. She had lost the use of her legs and any quality of life. It was as terrible to see this sweet and loving dog in such pain as it was to lose her forever. April laid hearts and flowers at the graves and set two kneeling angels to watch over them.

You can call these feelings sentimental and the intuitions and compassion that bonded Coco to us delusional. Dogs don't talk, and Coco's "thoughts" were likely what April projected onto her. But what of it? Whatever the source of the feelings that had created the bond, they had led to great pleasure for us and a new life for Coco. How would a stark "realism" affect the passion to rescue little creatures like Coco and share the unforgettable lives they give us? In the end, all that really matters is the presence of that passion, born of whatever faith will foster it, that inspires us to step forward to save a little life, and to give and receive the pleasures that come from such a bond.

two

June

The Paradoxes of Youth

I have framed this memoir as a meditation on age and as a result am in danger of obscuring the work of younger years when I was nurturing a generation that would one day replace me. As we all grow older there is a bittersweet quality to parenthood and to the reflections on days that are past. In a perverse way our children's successes become a measure of our own decline as their exciting steps lead to a future without us.

On Mother's Day my thoughts turned to April's twenty-eight-year-old son, Jon Jason, who could not be present, and to what his upbringing reflected about her. From the year of

Jon's birth, April found herself on her own, a single mother working a full-time job to support them both. Her own mother, Mary, who had been absent for long stretches of April's childhood, was home for Jon's, and took care of him daily from the end of school until his mother returned from her job doing skin care in a plastic surgeon's office. Although April had never gone to college herself, she recognized the intelligence of her son and encouraged high ambitions for him. She put him in a Montessori school and supplied him with the books he wanted, and encouraged his interests, which from an early age were scientific. And she took care to give him the stability and security in his young life that she had lacked in her own.

One of the first things that made me realize that April was someone I could trust in marriage was, paradoxically, the way she hid Jon's existence from me for months after we began seeing each other. I was so impressed by this that I wrote about it when I told the story of our romance in *The End of Time*. When she finally did reveal that she had a son, she was visibly nervous about how I might react to her deception. But she could have saved her worries. As I wrote: "Even before she began explaining, I understood that hiding her son was a way to keep from me an intimate and vulnerable part of herself when our relationship was still fresh and she didn't know me that well. Far from alarming me, her secret was reassuring. The lengths she had gone to protect her child's love told me how careful she would be with mine. I had already given her my own hostage. Who can hurt you more than someone who has your heart?"

Jon was eight when I met him, a sensitive, shy boy and, as time proved, an exceptionally good son. I don't remember a day in the twenty years we have known each other that I had cause to raise my voice or speak a word in anger to him. His biological father, "Big Jon," is a craftsman who builds custom cars and trucks for journeymen and municipal governments. I quickly saw that he had imparted to his son a respect for work and a deep sense of integrity. Over time Big Jon showed his son the love he had found so hard to give to their infant family at the beginning.

But it was five years before Big Jon agreed to meet or even talk to me. This was because April's brother Patrick, a fellow of jealous instincts, had planted dark thoughts in his head. *He's going to make your son a Jew and a Black Panther and get him killed.* That kept Big Jon away until the thirteenth birthday party April and I held for his son at a local eatery. The atmosphere between us was cool at first, but then I made a point of letting him know that I admired the good work ethic and the honesty he had instilled in his son. I would always respect, I said, the fact that Jon was *his* son, and would always welcome him in our home. From that moment there was no tension between us, and over the next fourteen years we became better and better friends, until at Jon's wedding on our back lawn in 2012, Big Jon and I hugged each other with tears in our eyes.

Although April and I were passionate about each other within months of our meeting, it took two years of wooing to get her to move in with me, and another two before we were married. This caution on her part was the perfect antidote to my reckless disregard, which had caused me such trouble, including two absurd marriages whose embarrassing details I have reported in *Radical Son*. The first was actually agreed to within six weeks of my meeting the prospective bride. Not surprisingly it was over within three months of the wedding vows. April put restraints on this rashness, which I confused at the time with adventurousness and courage. She has provided a welcome discipline to such impulses ever since.

I had never said a political word to Jon J, whom I had only recently met, when April showed me a "Letter to Santa" he had written as an exercise in his Montessori school. This was during the Clinton administration and its sexual scandals.

Dear Santa,

I wish I had these things. I wish I had a new president. I wish that people would help them-selves. I wish that people would respect America. I wish that people would think twice before having baby's [sic] that they can not love and care for. I wish that all Americans, black, white and brown would be proud to be Americans together as one. I wish that I could have a bike. And new stuff for my computer.

Love,

Jon J

I sent the letter to Rush Limbaugh who read it on air, causing a little stir of pride in the family.

In 1996, the three of us moved into a fixer-upper in the Pacific Palisades. At first Jon J didn't want to move in because he was scared of the big hole that our renovations had tem-porarily left in the living room floor. We tried to address his insecurity by having an artist paint a mural of an astronaut and spaceship on his bedroom wall. It proved to be the initial step in winning him over. For the first two weeks in our new home he insisted that April sleep in his bed, until one night as he became more comfortable with his new life he said to her, "You don't have to sleep with me anymore. You should be sleeping with David."

Jon was now in the fifth grade and had to face life in a new school. Although it was a charter elementary school in an upscale neighborhood, it had the same problems as schools everywhere. The schoolyard was terrorized by a bully who systematically singled out kids in the yard for torment. Finally, Jon's turn came. For days the bully taunted and jabbed at Jon, who was still very shy but physically much bigger. When the day came that this troubled youngster decided to attack, instead of pummeling him and paying him back for the blows he had inflicted, Jon just held him down until the adults came over and pulled them apart. Later he explained to his mother that he didn't want to hurt him. Jon was just that kind of kid.

April was a force for stability and promise in her son's life. She never allowed him to get down on himself or set his sights low, and she shone a constant light of love on him. My own mother stood behind me much as April stood behind Jon but could not handle the intensity of feeling contained in the word "love." As a result it was mostly absent from the Horowitz household. Not so from April's. The son was constantly washed in his mother's affection. I had never witnessed so much frank exchange between a mother and her child before. I am sure that this played a role in inspiring his compassion for others and in encouraging him to have dreams and pursue them. I am sure that it planted in him the most important confidence of all—that he had the power to make his dreams become real.

But this confidence did not flower overnight. There was a daunting shyness in him that I took upon myself to help him overcome by including kids from the local playground in basketball games I played with him. The most peculiar manifestation of the anxieties that festered inside him were severe stomach pains, which caused him to throw up nearly every day he had to go to school or when he had an exam. It was particularly hard to fathom because he was such a good student. Nonetheless for as long as these symptoms persisted, which was until he entered college, he was only a good student, not the extraordinary one he became.

As he grew older, Jon became a spiritual person, like his mother. But in his case it had an institutional dimension as well. We had pulled him from a disastrous public middle school and put him in a Lutheran one. When he was ready for high school, we enrolled him in St. Monica's, a Catholic school where the religious instruction was Jesuitical and also Marxist. At St. Monica's John came under the influence of a benevolent priest who recognized his talents and converted him to Catholicism. He went on to Loyola Marymount University, another Jesuit school, where he majored in biology and the level of his studies became too erudite for me to follow.

During these years it was one of my great pleasures to engage Jon in intellectual conversation and try to offer guidance drawn from what had suddenly become a considerable accumulation of life experience. The most important advice I ever gave him, I think, was that he had to look after himself, because no one else would, which sounds a lot colder than it is. No matter how dearly we loved him, we could not live his life for him. We could never keep abreast of all the details of what was going on in his world and affecting him. In the end he was going to have to make the crucial assessments and decisions for himself. I have no idea whether this advice ever made an impression, but I was gratified that as he grew older and was faced with difficult, life-affecting decisions about what graduate school to apply to and what career to pursue, he took hold of them like a man and made them himself.

During these years, I was writing my philosophical memoirs about mortality and faith with which Jon was familiar. Consequently, we had occasion to explore some of these questions together, which gave me a chance to find out what he thought. I knew that he had a sober attitude toward the church and its fallibility and a healthy concern about the corruption to which even "men of God" were prone. It was the time of the molestation revelations in the Catholic Church, where priests who preyed on young boys were protected at the highest ecclesiastical levels, revealing the moral rot that is endemic to human institutions and reminding us that in the end, *we* are the problem—one of the prominent themes of my books. For Jon, faith was a personal matter rather than an institutional one. He attended church regularly and participated in its social activities. But in the matter of belief he was and would always be his own man.

In June 2009, Jon graduated from Loyola Marymount. That Father's Day he gave me a card that provided me all the satisfaction for the years we spent together that I could ever wish for. It was one of those corny greeting cards with a cover that said "Dad You Rock." But it was the words inside that got to me: "From the beginning of our relationship some sixteen years ago, you instilled values in me that I am forever grateful for. You helped show me how to be a great husband with the support and unfailing love you gave my mother throughout your marriage. You exposed me to the beauties of classical music, opera and literature, as well as encouraged me in my intellectual pursuits. Most importantly, you did all of this happily and with warmth and love. I may not be your son by blood, but you have loved me like one of your own."

Jon was admitted into the master's program at UCLA with a research appointment that helped finance his education and in 2012 was awarded a master of science degree in microbiology, immunology, and molecular genetics with a thesis titled "Polarization of the endothelium governs monocyte differentiation and function." There was no way I could have helped him along this path, which was beyond my intellectual reach. I had the same experience with my biological sons, Jonathan and Ben, and my daughter Anne. There was a time when I had a sense of where they were going and could maybe give them advice along the way. Then, with such swiftness that I didn't see it coming, there came a moment when their knowledge and careers accelerated at light speed and left me in another building with my nose pressed against the glass.

We had crossed a Rubicon in our relationships. I was no longer their mentor, no longer drawing them out of their shyness, worrying about the directions they were taking. No longer a parent in the sense I had been. A whole world that had been mine was gone. Now they were independent, and my relationship with them was as an equal, and in their areas of expertise a pupil at best. Being a parent is an awesome power and responsibility, but my tide had run out. I was now a helpmate with experience to share. There was satisfaction in that, but it was also a diminishment, as great or even greater than the one apparent in the weakening sinews of my aging frame.

While he was still at Loyola Marymount, Jon met a young Filipina woman named Kathleen Alejandro and fell in love with her. Their engagement lasted through all of Jon's years in graduate school until September 2012, when they finally tied the knot. April and I offered them our house for the wedding, but by the time April got finished re-landscaping the half-acre that was our back lawn, filling it with rose bushes, and building a gazebo to serve as a chapel it was more accurate to say that we offered them a new addition to our house. When the day came and the guests arrived two hundred strong, it proved to be a memorable event. Jon had strung lights through our trees making the evening celebration magical. All the guests danced on a floor that was laid out on the lawn, including Kathleen's family, my family, and April's. If I live to be a hundred (as April insists I must) I don't think I will ever see a celebration like it again.

Jon had entered and won a competition to be one of only twenty students who would attend the University of Colorado as both an M.D. and Ph.D. candidate (MudPhuds as they were called), with the National Institutes of Health funding his education and support, worth roughly $700,000. It was a long way from the broken home he had come from.

In his first year in the program he was told to come up with a research project that could be submitted to the NIH or some other funding agency. This was merely an exercise for new students and not for actual submission. Jon had done most of his graduate work in immunology and was aware of the link between psoriasis and cardiovascular disease. His proposal was a project to identify the gene that linked the two diseases and open the door to alleviating the cardiovascular consequences for psoriasis sufferers.

Jon looked at his detailed research project and thought that it could and should be funded. So he sent his paper to a husband-and-wife team on the Colorado faculty who were heading a large research program on the link between psoriasis and heart disease. They agreed with him, submitted the proposal to a funding agency, and offered to make him the head of the research project he had designed.

Jon told us this in a phone call a week before our Mother's Day gathering. I was immediately interested in his project because five years earlier I had had an angina. My "widow maker artery" was almost completely clogged, yet I had no history of heart disease in my family and for years had been on Lipitor, the drug that controls cholesterol. But I did have psoriasis, and this link seemed now to explain it.

Jon's call from a distant location underscored the irony of families. Your children are dependent on you and inseparable, and then one day they are grown and largely gone. April shed many tears when Jon went off with his bride to explore their new horizons. She felt she was losing a big part of her life and her identity as a mother. But at the same time there were also tears of joy at what a remarkable young man her baby had become.

Adventures with the Foot

While I was still in the hospital after the botched operation, a man came to my bedside and took a mold of my calf and foot. Days later an AFO boot was brought to my bedside. AFO stands for "ankle foot orthosis," and the idea is that this hard plastic boot will brace the ankle and also raise the foot the paralysis has dropped. When I tried it out in the hospital, it worked pretty well. But then a day came when it caused me such pain I had to hop around and pull it off. After this experience, I switched to the clunky therapeutic boot that April brought home when she broke her navicular bone. You see skiers with these devices all the time. The clunky boot was serviceable for a while, but then I began to get medical advice that I needed to wear the AFO because it is designed for patients with drop foot. The advice came first from a nurse who didn't have much experience with the problem. But then I went to a podiatrist, who insisted that I wear it. If your AFO hurts, he said, it needs an adjustment. You must go to the manufacturer and they will do it.

So I called the hospital and found the manufacturer and made an appointment. I went in and a seemingly knowledge-able man took my AFO and adjusted it. He put a pad in the arch and reshaped it a bit, and put it back on my foot. Again the pain was excruciating and I had to take it off immediately. He said, "You are suffering from neuropathic pain. It's not the boot. It's you." When someone with expertise is so deci-sive you don't want to challenge him, and I didn't, even though I had my doubts. I returned home and put on the therapeutic boot, and my doubts were confirmed. I experi-enced nothing like the pain from the AFO. I could walk with the clunky boot, so I did.

It seemed at the time as though I had a medical appoint-ment every day. Shortly after my unsuccessful visit to the AFO maker, I had an appointment with Dr. Vimal Lala of the Advanced Pain Medical Group. On my way to see Dr. Lala, I began to visualize a sandal that would keep my foot close to the ground, and unlike the boot would be flexible.

At this point, I wanted to feel the ground because I sensed that my foot was actually coming back. It was two months since my operation in April, and I had been trying to move my toes for weeks. Then one day they did move, if only a few millimeters. I kept on trying to flex them, until one day I could move my whole foot, and move it up and down, and the toes as well. I no longer had drop foot, or if I did have it, my case was much improved.

I showed Dr. Lala my foot and the movement I had achieved and explained my problem with the boot pain. Dr. Lala practically pounced on the sentence I had just uttered. I shouldn't be wearing any therapeutic boot and certainly not an AFO, he said. These boots were braces for people with broken bones. What I needed was to restore the muscles and nerves that were not working. Ideally, I should be walking around barefoot.

On hearing these words, my desire for a sandal became irresistible, and with April as my escort and the get-along scooter as my transportation, I went to the mall and I bought a pair of leather sandals that were just about perfect. When I put them on I felt like I was walking on air. Hobbling on air would be more precise. My foot was still weak and also swollen, which caused enough pain, especially in the morning when I woke up, to keep me on Percocet, an opiate, for the early part of the day.

At this juncture April started oiling and massaging the damaged limb. It was an idea suggested by the podiatrist, who had his assistant do just that. Despite the odd nerve reactions in my foot, which felt uncomfortably electric, these manipulations felt good enough that I asked April if she would do it regularly for me. We figured that lymph was causing the painful swelling. April had had a case of lymphedema, so she knew what she had to do to bring the swelling down. The results were dramatic. She brought the swelling down, and for the first time in months I could see veins on the top of my foot, which had begun to look like an actual foot again. The movement I could achieve with it was now even greater than before.

Just How Much She Loved Me

Just as this partial recovery was taking place, I was faced with a dilemma that put April and me in conflict. I had been invited to an event that involved a dinner and discussion in a hotel suite in Los Angeles followed by an all-day meeting. It would be my first venture into the outside world in the two months since my operation. I wanted very much to go to this meeting, but April was against it. She felt I was not physically ready, and under her pressure I canceled it. But then I received a call from Dr. Bob Shillman, the sponsor of the meeting and a member of the executive committee of my board, urging me to go. I was deeply committed to the purposes of the meeting and didn't want to let Bob down. I also felt that it would be psychologically important for my recovery if I went. So I raised the issue with April again, but she was still opposed, unmoved in her conviction that I was not ready for such exertions and would suffer a setback if I went. She was also concerned about how I would look to the others attending, given the medication I was taking, and worried that it would damage me if I didn't do well. And she was concerned that under the stress I might fall and injure myself, not an unreasonable concern given how wobbly I became when tired.

The event was a private meeting of five leaders of organizations who were dedicated to combatting the anti-Semitic campaign that had been launched on college campuses by front groups for terrorist organizations. The goal of these organizations was the destruction of the Jewish state, and they were making disturbing progress. It was, in fact, remarkable how these groups, which were offshoots of the Muslim Brotherhood, had received the tacit support of college administrators and become a prominent and intimidating force on American campuses.

These Islamist groups had teamed up with the anti-Semitic left and were conducting anti-Israel demonstrations across the country, spreading two genocidal lies that the uninformed found persuasive. The first was that the Jews had stolen Arab land to create the state of Israel. The second was that Israel was not a democracy but an "apartheid" state. Actually Israel, along with Syria, Lebanon, Jordan, and Iraq were all created from land that had belonged to the Turks— who were not Arabs—for four hundred years. In other words, the Arabs had a weaker claim on the land around the Jordan than the Indians had on the United States. Equally malicious was the lie that Israel was an "apartheid state." Israel is actually the only state in the Middle East that is tolerant toward its minorities. Although the claim was laughable, its effect on the ignorant was to delegitimize Israel and make it easier for the terrorist armies of Fatah, Hamas, and Iran to destroy the Jewish state.

I was not a Zionist and had never been to Israel, but I believed Israel's tiny democracy was the frontline state in the war that Islamic Nazis had declared against the West. Their special message for the Jews: *In the name of Allah, we will exterminate you.* Each year for several years my Freedom Center had conducted campaigns on more than a hundred campuses to combat these malignant forces, which had the protection not only of college administrators but also the Jewish campus groups—in particular Hillel, which was afraid to offend Muslims and was extending them an olive branch by attacking their critics.

April was familiar with my efforts but was not swayed from her view that I should not attend the meeting. I had been engaged in political battles forever, and one meeting was not going to change the world. She continued to fear for my health and for my public persona. She also feared for my safety and hers. The left had put itself in the service of the Islamic holy war and was personally vicious toward me. Because I opposed them, they had identified me as "the godfather of the modern anti-Muslim movement." Calling opponents of Jew-haters and terrorists "anti-Muslim" is a typical leftist tactic. The Southern Poverty Law Center, which was responsible for this libel, couldn't (and didn't) point to a single statement among the millions of words I had written and uttered that could be described as "anti-Muslim."

Another factor in April's thinking, which went unmentioned, was that the Islamists I opposed were terrorists, supported by the left, and no one could dismiss the possibility they would seek retribution for my stands. We had always lived with this possibility, first from the Black Panthers and now, with the "report" identifying me as the anti-Muslim "godfather" fresh in mind, from the Islamists.

But in the end, despite her fears and despite her concerns about my health, she saw how much I wanted to go, and she agreed to take me to the Century Plaza Hotel, an hour's drive away, and stay with me for the times I needed her. Not for the first time in our embattled life together, I was grateful for her support.

Then, as fate would have it, on the day of the meeting I had a serious mishap. I was in the bathroom shaving and my feet were bare. As I was exiting the room I stubbed the big toe of my good foot on the doorsill and lost my balance. As I was falling, I grabbed for something to stabilize me, but it turned out to be the handle of an upright vacuum cleaner, which immediately folded under my weight, and I went tumbling down. During the fall, I managed to flip myself over to my right side, protecting my injured foot and the new hip, as I went down with a thud. Our cleaning lady, who was close by, called out in horror to April just as I uttered the words "Don't tell my wife." Soon everybody was standing over me, while I tried to explain that my left leg was okay, even as I felt a pain in the calf, and could see no one believed me.

I was able to rest for a few hours until the pain subsided, although my big toe continued to throb and I had a tender bruise on my right buttock. I told April as firmly as I could manage that I still wanted to go, and disturbed as she was by what had happened, she consented. We put the get-along scooter in the bed of the black Ford F-150 I had bought her after her accident and got into the cab. But as soon as we started driving, I could see that she was disturbed, although the apparent focus of her distress was the automobile. We had hardly left the driveway when she noticed a message on her dashboard that said "Off Road," indicating that the truck was in four-wheel-drive mode. She couldn't stop fretting about this as we drove down the Santa Rosa Road. Would the car break down if we drove it on the freeway? Would the engine be ruined? Would it explode?

As she turned the truck onto Moorpark Road, the very stretch of highway where she had had her accident, she became so panicked that she began to ask if we should go back and get my car. I told her to stop the truck and call the Ford dealership and ask them about the message. The service manager told her to look for a toggle switch and move it back to the two-wheel mode, but she couldn't locate it. He then assured her that she could use the four-wheel drive for the freeway and it would just mean greater wear on the tires and poorer gas mileage. When she had a chance, she could take the truck to any Ford dealer, and they would fix the problem. And so she decided to push on.

But as she drove and we talked I could see that she was still agitated and it was getting worse. Finally it poured out of her. "You are reckless and you are not aware of how reckless you are. When you drive the get-along you bump into things. The other day you almost ran over a child in the mall. Even when you are walking you don't notice how wobbly you are, and how you bump into people." As she unloaded on me, it was not her words that I focused on so much as her expression, the anguish in her voice, and the fear in her eyes. "I'm so frightened for you," she said. She was shaking and in tears. "You don't realize what you do." She didn't have to articulate the next words because I knew what was coming: "You are thinking only of yourself. You don't consider what you put me through."

I may be dense and in denial sometimes, but I am a feeling person, and I love this woman with a fierce passion. It didn't take me a heartbeat to see what I had done. It was not just the bravado, which made me want to ignore my drugged and crippled state, drive a little recklessly on the scooter, and take on more than I should. It was my life that was pressing down on her. This was a person who had not been brought up to do battle in the world of political savagery that she had inadvertently entered when she fell in love with me. As a result of her injuries she was in physical pain herself and psychologically raw. I could not dismiss what she had said. I did bump into walls and people. Because of the drugs I was taking I was not myself, but pretended I was. I did have enemies who hated me enough to want to see me dead. And I had not taken her anxieties or her warnings seriously enough. She knew how much my political causes meant to me, and because she loved me, she had been ready to put herself through hell. She was driving me to the meeting to which she did not want me to go, and to which I could not have driven myself. She was fighting through her fears because she wanted me to be who I was. She loved me that much. It did not matter if her fears were fully justified. It mattered how she felt. It was how at this moment what I was doing was torturing her, and I had to man up to it.

I was silent as these thoughts ran through my head, reflecting on how this moment had been repeated many times in the twenty years our destinies had been tied together. I thought of how she had stood by me through crises and trials when others might not. How she helped me to live a life she would never have chosen for herself. As we reached the hotel room, I let the dam break. I told her how deeply sorry I was for putting her through this, how much I appreciated what she had done, and that I would try to be more attentive to her concerns. The tears were running down my cheeks as

I thanked her for what she was doing for me, and how appreciative I was at her understanding that while I could try to change some things, I could not change who I was, and how grateful I was that she loved and supported me anyway.

We lay in each other's arms in the hotel room for a while. My words had calmed her, and her concern was now for me and for how I would pull myself together for the meeting. She didn't want me in tears, didn't want me feeling guilty. She just wanted us to be one and at peace. And then it was time for me to go upstairs, where the meeting was about to begin. We had planned that she would spend the night with me at the hotel and help me to get ready in the morning. Then she would go back home to take care of the animals and maybe oversee some of the construction projects she had undertaken around the house. She would return in the evening to pick me up.

I mounted the get-along scooter, which saved me from having to hobble down the long halls with my cane. When I arrived at the meeting everyone was solicitous, as people usually are with someone in my condition, and we began our talks. I felt my powers returning as I spoke, mindful about slurring my words (as April had cautioned me) and trying to appear less injured than I was. The next day I made it through the all-day meeting, gratified by the influence I was able to exert and surprised by the stamina my body had shown.

When the meeting concluded I returned to the room, and April and I ordered room service and a salmon dinner, with capers for her. The time we had spent together had been good for us both. She was pleased that things had gone well at the meeting and that I had come through it better than she feared I would. We were both somewhat chastened and happy to be on track again. I knew I could never eliminate her concerns about me or the pressures my life brought to bear on her. But I was certainly going to try harder to do just that.

A Harrowing Call

On Mother's Day, when we were all gathered together, I received a phone call from Elissa, the mother of my children. Elissa and I were married for nineteen years and have been divorced for thirty-six, but we have remained close—first through our children and grandchildren and then as two people who had cared deeply for each other through life's trials, particularly the untimely death of our daughter Sarah. I am grateful to her for opening her heart to me after the divorce, which was my doing and never her wish. Instead of being divided into two mutually exclusive parts, my life is reasonably whole thanks to her and also to April, who would have happily included her in our Mother's Day celebration if she had been able to come.

When I answered the call, Elissa told me that our oldest son, Jonathan, who was only fifty-three, had just had a heart attack and was in intensive care. It was hard for me to hear her say, "I feel like I've been a bad mother. I'm not supposed to outlive my children." Then she corrected herself—"But Jon's not dying." Yet she, more than anyone else in the family, understood that we all are.

Fortunately, Jonathan's episode was not as serious as we feared, and he was able to leave the hospital within a day or two. As soon as I learned of his condition, I attempted to phone him to see how he was doing, but I couldn't find the hospital he was in and had to wait a day to reach him. I left a message for Renee, the woman he had lived with and loved for twenty-five years, and soon heard back that he was doing all right. Even before I received this news, I called my other son, Ben, who was in Israel on business. He and Jon were very close, and Ben had become a man of considerable influence. My shortsightedness in choosing an orthopedic surgeon was weighing on me, and I didn't want Jon taking any chances, so I asked Ben to see if he could get him a good cardiologist. I knew he would have contacts at Columbia University Medical Center because he had recently been made a trustee of the school and his mentor and friend Bill Campbell was chairman of the board. In a few days, Ben was able to get the head of the Columbia Medical Center to call Jon and fix him up with excellent care.

When I finally spoke to him, I was much relieved. The doctors had performed an angiogram and inserted a stent, just as they had in my case. I told him of my own experience and not to worry, he was going to be all right. There was a little anxiety in his voice, but over the next few days, the cheerful, take-it-in-stride character I knew so well was back. And I also learned that he had put himself on a dietary regimen that would help his condition, and that he had already lost weight, and that relieved me too.

The Divide

Years before, my labors in the vineyard of parenthood had been upended by the crime that shattered my political faith. Perhaps there were other forces that would have sundered my marriage, but the depression that then overtook me and lingered for seven long years sealed its fate. My divorce from Elissa in 1978 was a continental divide in my life and, to a lesser extent, in my relations with my children. Jonathan was seventeen when the marriage unraveled and well on his independent way. But the other three were still at home. I stayed close by and tried to maintain the family whose bonds I had broken, but a significant part of my authority was gone, and there were many times in the years that followed when I feared I might lose my children. They never turned their backs on me, but an internal space opened up where we would meet as strangers, a space that without their permission I could not cross.

My Musical Son

Elissa and I always knew that our first child had a musical aptitude. When Jonathan was ten months old he would stand in his diapers at the front of one of my speakers, which was as big as he was, hold on with one hand, and bounce his knee to the beat of the music. Before he was two he could identify every instrument in the orchestra by its sound, a trick he learned from listening raptly to Benjamin Britten's *Young Person's Guide to the Orchestra*. When he was an adolescent I asked him what instrument he liked and bought him a saxophone. When he was seventeen and just out of high school, he moved to Los Angeles and formed a band. Although he had played the sax in his high school bands, he was now playing the bass. He was always a quick study like that. Better yet, he also wrote the songs—both lyrics and music. I went to Los Angeles to see him play at a club called the Lingerie and was warmed all over by what I heard. It brought out the youngster still in me, and the lyrical quality of his music was almost as old-fashioned as I was. As his dad, of course, it did occur to me to ask him how he managed to do the band and also his classes at UCLA. "Oh, I only go to class when there's a test," he replied. I might have reprimanded him, but he was an honor student, so how could I argue?

I will always remember his graduation from UCLA, even though I couldn't make him out among the ten thousand graduates who were packed into a sports stadium for the ceremony. When we did meet in the parking lot, he was easily identified by his bouffant, black-dyed rock-and-roll hair and the pink high-heeled boot poking out from under his academic gown.

He was a remarkably talented songwriter. Granted, I am his father, but in my opinion he is up there with the best professional lyricists. On the other hand he is so much a limelight avoider that it's hard to find a trace of him or his songs on the Internet, even if you know where to look. He has long been something of a cult figure among the music crowd, and that's the way he prefers it, mysterious and hidden. When I asked him if he had copies of his lyrics he e-mailed back, "I don't; they may be online somewhere. That record was a long time ago—pre me having a computer." I'm not sure I understand this casual attitude toward his work. He doesn't seem bitter that he is not better known or that the albums he produced were not the hits they deserved to be. Far from it. He will give you a dozen good reasons why celebrity is a prison and a curse. Shortly after the e-mail, on the other hand, he was able to locate some of his lyrics.

Quoting a couple of them can't justify the claim I made, but it can give you a taste of how intelligent and clever and musical they are. He started out with a band called Candy, and this was one of his refrains:

> What if every time was like the first time
> Then all those things I told you would come true
> Because if every time were like the first time
> Girl I'd never walk away from you.

In his third album, which featured a band called The Loveless, the lyrics grew melancholy and bitter:

> Staring at the holes in the wall,
> Where your pictures used to hang.
> Reading your old letters
> Listening to the rhythm of the rain.

> And I'm wondering if I'm on board your train of
>   thought.

And I'm laughing 'cause I can't remember why we
   ever fought.

And it's times like these I almost miss you.
And it's times like these I almost wish you were here.
And it's times like these I almost miss you.
Wish that your ghost would disappear.

I always wondered what wound had caused him to produce such lyrics, and was even concerned about it for awhile.
But then he had such a cheerful demeanor generally and was
so creative that I stopped worrying.

Unfortunately, Jonathan had chosen to enter an industry
that was on its deathbed. I already knew from his first album,
which he had written when he was in his early twenties, that
the music world was a bad news business. In those days there
were MTV shows that featured "countdowns" of the hits.
Candy's first video debuted at number eleven in the Los
Angeles market. But there were no Candy albums in the
stores. The reason? Just before release, the record company
that made the album was bought by PolyGram, and the
PolyGram executives didn't want the A&R executive who had
been responsible for Jon's album to have a success and gain
a leg up on them. So they killed the record.

This turned out to be a business norm. In another incident the megahit band KISS stole one of Jon's lyrics. One of the KISS musicians used to hang around Jon's gigs at Madam Wong's and other L.A. clubs. Jon had written a song with a clever refrain: "You put the X in Sex." Without so much as a word of explanation or request, KISS changed the lyric to "She puts the X in Sex" and made it a hit. Although they were multi-millionaires, they didn't even throw a bone to the youngsters whose work they had pilfered. I was furious, but my son just took it in stride, as he did many other adversities, and went on to the next challenge.

Because of my concerns about the effect of the divorce on my children, it came as a surprise and a grace to me in 1984 when Jonathan asked me if I would like to move to Los Angeles and share an apartment with him. The four members of his band had been living in a flat together but had broken up the household when some of them decided to move in with their girlfriends. I was still in Berkeley, living in a cottage-like house that I bought after the divorce. But I didn't hesitate to say yes. I sold the house, packed up my things and joined my son in a one-bedroom apartment I rented in West Hollywood.

My internal disorder was not over, however, and the joint domicile with Jonathan lasted only a few months as I was busy making one of the many mistakes it would take before I was able to find my balance again. Within six weeks of moving to Los Angeles I was engaged to a woman I barely knew and who barely knew me, with the result that I was soon single again. None of this turmoil interrupted the post-divorce connection I had with my son. It was part of Jon's easy-going nature that he was able to take in stride events that might feel like earthquakes to others.

In anticipation of my new marriage, I had bought a house in Griffith Park. Jonathan's band played from the roof of my garage at the ill-fated wedding. After the breakup, I offered him a small room with a private entrance in my new home. Excited by the prospect of having him live with me, I began building him a beautiful apartment on the garage roof with a wood-beamed cathedral ceiling. But when it was completed, he didn't move in. Instead he left Los Angeles to pursue new musical horizons in New York. I was disappointed by the move. But I wanted him to succeed in the musical career he had chosen, and he thought he could do this better in the "Big Apple," as he liked to refer to it.

In New York he formed a new band and put out his second and third albums but soon came up against the brute facts of an industry that was on life support. He struggled for several years until a day came when a company called Napster destroyed the record business and put the biggest challenge of all in his path. Napster was an Internet swap site where recordings could be lifted off the page for free, effectively killing the ability of the artists to make money from record sales. In retrospect, Jon described the challenge this way: "For me Napster was a new punk rock. Punk rock was why I got into the music business in the first place. It had a do-it-yourself spirit and an anything-is-possible/no rules attitude. Napster had the same charge for me."

To succeed in the music world now became a test of ingenuity and industry savvy, which, it so happened, Jon had in abundance. So much so that he was sought after by the record companies over the next years as he used his fertile brain to find a way to succeed in a mortally wounded business and eventually to make his way to the top. To make ends meet he had gone to work for the Sony Corporation as an accountant and was so good at what he did they offered him a job running the department, which he turned down. It was no mystery to me why after I visited him in the Sony headquarters, which reminded me of the nightmare corporate future portrayed in the film *Rollerball*. As I've already noted, one of the things I've always loved in my son was the way he enjoyed life, and always seemed to be nursing a silent chuckle. But when I visited him at Sony I was shocked to see how depressed he was. His shoulders were slumped and there was no sparkle in his eyes. I was happy when he quit Sony and went to work for a music publishing company called Fiction.

It was the end of the 1990s, and the money stream of the record companies with their giant overheads had dried up. In his typically casual way, Jonathan summarized how the new environment affected him: "the Internet happened and I got interested in music online." What he meant was that he saw in the Internet a way to promote bands without the record companies. His insights were so keen and the strategies he devised so effective that one day in the not too distant future, a major record company would ask him to come and run it. He turned that offer down too.

In 2001 Jonathan formed Crush Management, a company that would publish music, manage bands, and most importantly figure out a way to make them popular and profitable. He likes to describe Crush as "a futuristic music company." Since Jonathan was a cult figure, people came to him with ideas and bands looking for management. One of the early bands he picked up was called Fall Out Boy. He explained to me why he liked them: "The lyrics to a song they had called 'Dead on Arrival' stood out to me: 'This is side one / flip me over / I know I'm not your favorite record.' It seemed like they came from someone with a great mind." Great mind or no, they were certainly original, which is a scarce commodity in any corner of the popular culture. The problem, however, was how to make a name for Fall Out Boy so they could sell records, attract crowds on tour, and make money. When I asked my son how he did it, he said, "The wizard never steps from behind the curtain." So I can't tell you more about his secrets than he has been willing to share with the public, which is not much.

He and his partner, Bob McLynn, who joined him in 2002, worked for three years on making a name for Fall Out Boy. In 2005 they succeeded. Fall Out Boy's album *From Under the Cork Tree* sold three million copies, unheard of for a new band in the desert that Napster had created. Crush had also signed another band, Panic! at the Disco, which was selling two million albums. Both bands were on the cover of *Rolling Stone*, and Jonathan's charges were so popular they were able to sell out venues like Dodger Stadium.

When I had just finished setting these words down, I turned on the *Today* show, and there was Fall Out Boy, promoting their latest album, *Save Rock and Roll*. This was ten years after Jonathan had helped them launch their careers, and as Matt Lauer explained to the television audience, their new album was already number one on iTunes in twenty-seven countries.

My son had worked a musical miracle that would not stop. By Father's Day 2014, the twenty-one groups and artists he signed had sold seventy-seven million albums, had collected $165 million in touring receipts, and had 730 million YouTube views. His clients include the hottest songwriter in the business—Sia—who has written hits for Beyoncé, Rihanna, Eminem, Katy Perry, Jennifer Lopez, and herself. On accepting the Songwriter of the Year award in 2014 Sia thanked my son, the "best manager in the world," and her new album, *1000 Forms of Fear*, went to number one on the charts and number one worldwide. Jon and his partner also resurrected the band Train, which in 2012 had the number-one single of the year and the biggest single in *Billboard*'s history. That same year, a song by his group Gym Class Heroes was chosen to be the official song of the Olympics, and another of the group's works became the official song of the New York Giants.

I am proud of my son's achievements, and particularly pleased with the way he continues to be such a happy and thoughtful person, despite the pressures that go with his success. He wears all this lightly, as he should. One thing that intrigues me is that although I remember him as a voluble youngster, he has grown into a pretty reticent adult, no doubt part of his business strategy. Although I don't want to exaggerate his diffidence, you sometimes have to pry his thoughts from him, and even then he likes to remain, as he puts it, behind the curtain. Perhaps this is a reaction to his preachy old man. I don't know if it is, and it wouldn't bother me if it were.

Because of his reticence there are a number of things we don't bother to discuss. Among these is politics, except obliquely. I've already mentioned how the divorce made me cautious around my children for many years, although that's now no longer an issue. Another factor affecting our communication has been the public attacks on me from my opponents. From the moment I broke with the left my enemies regularly took positions of mine and turned them upside down or inside out until they had no relation to anything I had ever believed or said. They would claim, for example, that I supported slavery or was a Torquemada intent on suppressing ideas I disagreed with, which were both the opposite of the truth. In an uglier vein, they said I was a racist and a bigot, and wanted the poor to suffer. It was patently ludicrous, but that didn't stop them from spreading their malice across the Internet and other public media.

When I was approached by people, even friends, who were not familiar with what I had said or done recently, I never knew what opinion they might have of me. The attacks had a similar effect on my relations with my family, who were dispersed across the country and out of touch with my current thinking and public actions. How did they view me? What did they think of me? For several years I could not make facile assumptions about the answers, although over time through many conversations and books written by me that changed.

Jonathan is not a political person. I enjoy this feature of his personality. He is in touch with what I would call the normal world that looks askance at politics and politicians and is busy taking advantage of the amazing opportunities that America has to offer. My talks with Jonathan have the effect of bringing me back to earth. He probably voted for Obama, at least the first time, but I don't really know or care. I've avoided this area in our conversations because I didn't want my conflicts to burden him. His bands have played the White House and Kennedy birthday parties. The entertainment community doesn't spend a lot of time thinking about political issues but reflexively embraces leftwing opinions because it finds them "cool." My son does not share this shallowness, but there is no need for him to confront it either. I didn't want to create a situation where he might feel put on the spot, caught between his father and the world he moves in. I wanted him to enjoy his success. Even more important, I didn't want my enemies to become his. So I just bypassed the political in our conversations—if he wasn't interested in discussing politics, neither was I. In the talks we did have, however, we were quite close in our outlooks and our assessments of people, and that was a comfort I could live with.

Jonathan's observations are always interesting to me. He is a shrewd judge of character, as you would expect a man of his achievements to be. I enjoy the times I am able to spend with him and always feel sad when they are over and he has to leave. This is a problem that stems from our geographical separation and his success. I have to be content feeling close to him in my heart and enjoying our phone conversations and the times when we are able to sit down together in Los Angeles or New York.

Like my other children, Jonathan has his own life and his own world now. They are a mirror that shows me my own limitations and makes me wonder about the different paths I might have taken, and whether they would have turned out better for me, or worse—who knows? Parenthood, it turns out, teaches you about yourself, and not always in a reassuring way. You see your failings starkly, and hardest of all you have to accept the distances that the dance of life creates. My connection with my son is different from what it was when he was in the bosom of the family that Elissa and I created. The loss is painful to me, but it is the course of life and I accept it. I also left my parents behind when I ventured out into the world. Now I understand their case.

Father's Day

While I have been writing this, another holiday has crept up on me. The third Sunday in June is Father's Day, and while there is no family gathering scheduled, the occasion is nonetheless having an emotional effect on me, not least because of the vulnerability I am feeling as a result of my slow recovery and continuing pain. It has been two and a half months since the operation, and I still feel weak and dependent and unsteady when upright. This is unsettling, especially in the way it makes me feel much older and feebler than I am.

My first present is from Jonathan and Renee—a bottle of Silver Oak cabernet with a note that says, "Hey pops. Happy Father's Day." They send me a present of fruit or cheese or wine on every calendar occasion. Perhaps I am overly sentimental, but it invariably puts me in mind of how Jonathan opened his door to me after the divorce now more than thirty years past. The cabernet came in a leather case, and April and I gathered it up and set off for a local Italian restaurant. I hobbled in, uncorked the cab and ordered a dinner of filet mignon with a mushroom risotto. April's preference was salmon and a white chardonnay. Then we topped off the evening with a latte and tiramisu. When I reported the menu to Jonathan, he said I should have been the one to have the salmon. I explained to him that the surgeon who crippled me had also caused me to lose a third of my blood and I was on a diet of red meat to harvest iron and restore my red blood cell count. Besides, steak goes better with a cab.

Jon Jason and Kathleen have sent me two jars of marmalade, a favorite of mine going back to when my grandmother used to read me poems of A. A. Milne, especially the one in which the king wanted butter for his bread but the queen and all his servants offered him marmalade instead. As a marmalade man, I found the Wilkin & Sons "orange with malt whiskey" a particular treat.

Ben and Felicia have sent me orchids, as they always do on occasions like this. But it is the note in Felicia's hand that justifies the good feelings I have despite the trials of my seventy-fifth year: "Happy Father's Day! Although we are far away across the Atlantic, we are thinking of you on this special day. And we want to let you know that we love and treasure you in our lives."

My Onetime Friend Florence

Two weeks earlier, unbeknownst to me, Elissa took another blow in a life that seemed too filled with them. Her best and oldest friend, Florence Roberts, expired at home in New York after a three-year battle with leukemia. Florence had been one of four particularly important women in Elissa's life, including my daughter, Anne, who is thankfully still with us. The others—Elissa's sister Barbara and our daughter Sarah—were also taken from her in untimely fashion, Barbara by a cerebral hemorrhage, Sarah by causes unknown but probably connected to her birth condition.

Elissa and Florence were inseparable girlhood friends. In fact, it was through their friendship that Elissa and I met, when she was only sixteen and I but two years older. At the time, Florence was seeing a friend of mine named Michael who asked me if I would like to double up with him on a blind date. I said yes, and Elissa and I immediately became a couple. Florence was not too happy with Michael, so we introduced her to one of my college classmates, Moss Roberts, with whom I was also close and had encouraged to become politically radical. When I graduated from college, Elissa and I married and moved to Berkeley, where I was admitted to graduate school. Moss and Florence soon followed so that he could pursue his own studies at the university, and then they too married, beginning an odyssey in which our families grew together. Eventually Moss secured a teaching position in Oriental languages at New

York University, but he and Florence continued to summer on the West Coast.

It was politics that eventually separated us—or rather separated me from Moss and Florence. In 1974 the Black Panthers murdered an innocent woman named Betty Van Patter, whom I had recruited to help them. When I confided to Moss what had happened, he shocked me by defending the murderers because they shared our progressive views. Like the rest of our leftist friends, he blamed the "power structure" for the crime—not because the "power structure" had anything actually to do with Betty's murder but because in the radical playbook blacks were oppressed and therefore innocent, while whites constituted a "power structure" and were therefore guilty of whatever transpired that was bad. I do not know what Florence's reaction was, but it had to be close to her husband's. Shortly after the murder my marriage began to unravel, and Moss and Florence aligned themselves against me.

A few years after these events, the wounds of the divorce began to heal, and Elissa and I grew close again. It wasn't only time that made it possible for us to come together, or the love we shared for our children and grandchildren. It was also maturity: a recognition that we were two people who loved each other but wanted different things out of life. We had raised four beautiful and creative children, and we shared a pride in that. But we could not delude ourselves into thinking that when they had grown up and no longer needed our direct care we could continue to live side by side. This was my view at the time, not Elissa's, but I believe she came to accept it.

It is strange how life works this way—you begin it with great gambles you are completely unprepared to make, and then you must painfully undo the messes you create for yourself and others along the way. I have no regrets about marrying Elissa who has been a wonderful mother to our children and whom I still love as family. I cannot speak for her, but despite the pain of the divorce, it finally worked out for me. One could say I have had two lives. Not that I am schizoid. I went through rivers of pain to change my understanding of myself and others, and become what I am today.

As the years progressed, and Moss and I grew older, I made some attempts to see if the relationship that had been torn apart could be repaired. This was quixotic no doubt, since I had dedicated the second half of my life to combatting the malignant delusions of the left, while Moss and Florence had marched along the same communist lines they had grown up in. I did not want to turn my back on the non-political dimensions of our lives or the bonds we once had, but the weight of our commitments proved too great.

I have never considered all or even a majority of leftists to be bad people. The historical narrative has a diabolical twist in which destructive illusions about the future seduce good people into the arms of evil. Consequently, when people of the left relate to me in a decent way—however rare that may be—I am ready despite all differences to reciprocate. An Irishman named Ernie Tate was a friend of mine in the days I worked for Bertrand Russell in London. Ernie had little formal education and was schooled instead by his comrades in the Fourth International, a Trotskyist sect. I was a leftist not of his persuasion and I noticed that he never got angry when I challenged a view he held but just smiled at me as though I were a child unable to grasp the arcane wisdom of his Trotskyist faith. After I left England, fifty years went by during which we did not see each other. Then I was contacted by someone writing a book about the events we both participated in who told me Ernie had written a memoir called *Revolutionary Activism*, in which he treated me kindly. When I read the book I was no more surprised by the fact that his political views had not changed at all, than I was to see that he did treat generously a one-time friend whom his fellow leftists now regarded as a monster. He was that kind of person. I wrote and thanked him and he replied. But even as we exchanged pleasantries about the past, I knew that there could be no future in the relationship we had resumed because our conflicts now were in the present and he could not forgive me that.

I think Florence had some of Ernie's openness. She was naturally curious and could see more sides to an issue than perhaps she allowed herself to concede. Some fifteen years ago when I spoke at New York University, she came to hear me, even though my subject was the malignant effects of the left to which she was so wedded. Afterwards, she came up to me and if she was hostile concealed it well. I was happy to see her, remembering the days of our friendship. But when I sent her a copy of *Radical Son* and inscribed it "For the good times," she told Elissa, "There were no good times." She had that kind of capacity for righteous anger, which in my experience is generally shared by people convinced that they can make a better world.

When a person dies, you get to look over the life and assess it as a whole. I tried to do that with Florence. Her work had been as an attorney practicing family law. While her political activities involved a constant war against the enemies of the left, in her daily routines she had dedicated herself to helping the poor and the outcast. I would be remiss if I were to overlook these admirable efforts.

When she died two Sundays before Father's Day, an obituary appeared in the *New York Law Journal*. My sister, Ruth,

sent me an e-mail from Nova Scotia with the link. The obituary said that Florence had headed up two family units for the
Legal Services Corporation in Brooklyn and Queens and had
"spent much of her career... serving low-income families,
incarcerated women and victims of domestic violence." Even
in retirement Florence was active, volunteering with the
Incarcerated Mothers Law Project, "often visiting women in
prison to advise them on their parental rights. She also served
on the advisory board of the New York Asian Women's Center, which helps women and children escape domestic abuse."

This was worthy work. In the larger scale of things, this
counts. Florence was a good wife and mother and raised two
fine children, and that counts too. And she was a best friend
to Elissa for more than sixty years, right to the unhappy end.
And for me that counts a lot. I'm sorry that her political
engagement—and no doubt mine too—created a wall
between us that was insurmountable. That was a loss for both
of us.

My Wilderness Sister Ruth

I have mentioned my younger sister, Ruth, without introducing her, so let me repair the oversight. Like offspring,
siblings are with you always and measure the distances you
have come, and therefore all that you have left behind.

I know Ruth would have liked to be with us on Mother's Day. She is a family-oriented person and in years gone by visited us whenever she could. I think this is why she was thoughtful enough to send me Florence's obituary. Ruth keeps up a correspondence with several members of the family, including me, which she fills with descriptions of her environment and daily routines, giving us a picture of how she lives. I am grateful for these updates, and they have helped us to grow closer over the years. For a long time there was a sea of tension between us, mainly the result of political frictions, but obviously reflecting other issues that neither of us was good at bringing to the surface.

Despite her intentions, Ruth made a decision forty years ago that causes family occasions with us to be so rare they are practically non-existent. In the early 1970s she moved to the remote northeastern tip of Nova Scotia, a thousand miles east of Maine. The weather there is so raw and unpredictable that her house is equipped with a barometer to warn of incoming storms. The only time I was able to visit—more than twenty years ago—it took me longer to get from Toronto to her home in Nova Scotia than it did to get from Los Angeles to Toronto. When I was ready to return to California, she had to drive me to the airport in Sydney, a hundred miles away, through a snowstorm so intense there were complete whiteouts along the way. The only occasion when she has been able to visit us was our wedding, and I was grateful that she did.

When she moved to Nova Scotia, Ruth met and married a Vietnam War resister named Ian Sherman. He is a visual artist who works in wood and marble, and in his day job has built and maintained coastal hiking trails around Inverness. Now retired, he volunteers time to the trail organization he founded and also to a local human rights group. In 2007, Ruth also retired from her job as the librarian at the local high school, where she had worked for twenty years. Recently, they became grandparents for the first time.

Ruth has made a quiet and satisfying life in Nova Scotia, a place of imposing natural beauty. It doesn't snow there all the time, and in the months when it doesn't she is a devoted gardener. Her move to this remote setting has a philosophical underpinning which she summarized in a letter to me: "Our life here is about tending the land, being more or less self-sufficient and living in harmony with the natural world. We are back-to-the-landers." As a Sixties person, she incorporates this modest ambition into a comprehensive worldview: "We take a real, deep, and complete interest in global issues, our local community issues and our day-to-day life in our valley, which we see as entirely inter-connected."

My sister is a private person, which is one reason she moved to the wilderness. She did not like even the small mention I made of her in *Radical Son*, so I am trying to be respectful of her privacy now. When *Radical Son* was published, there was still a political gulf between us—she had remained on the left as I gravitated right. But this rift eventually healed itself and is long since gone. I'm not sure how it happened, but we don't talk politics anymore, and both of us are grateful for that. I love my sister. Life is impossibly short, and if you are lucky enough to have a sibling who loves you and can travel through time with you to your beginnings, you don't want to lose her. I miss my sister, and wish she had been able to join us on Mother's Day, and hope that if the opportunity presents itself in the future, she will.

My Business Son

My third child, Ben, began life as a shy, neurasthenic child, physically small and thin, almost afraid of his own shadow. I remember watching him have a meltdown during an egg-and-spoon race at a local camp as I looked skyward and silently pleaded, "How is my son going to survive in this rough world?" Those days are long gone. I am certain that the transformation took place around his fifteenth year, after my departure from the household, when he joined the Berkeley

High football team to play as its center. My reaction to this—
he was the first Horowitz ever to put on a football uniform—
was to worry that he might be crippled by an injury. But there
was no way I was going to stand between him and his desire.
Fortunately, my fears proved overwrought as he bulked himself up and became a man.

When he came of age to go to college, I urged him to
apply to Columbia University rather than UCLA like his
brother. I didn't like the size of UCLA, and for reasons that
don't seem so compelling to me now, I wanted him to be
exposed to Columbia's core curriculum, which introduced
students to the great texts of Western Civilization and had
a big impact on my romantic self forty years before. Columbia was an expensive school and I was by no means rich, but
I put together every extra dollar I had to pay for his tuition.
There was an irony in this. Both my sons are shrewd with
money, and both are somewhat bemused and not a little
critical of the way I manage my accounts. For whatever
reasons, I have always spent what I had. I wanted the best
for him and didn't think twice about my decision even
though it would drain my account. I know Ben shakes his
head at what he regards as my prodigal ways, but, as it happened, paying for his Columbia education was one of the
best investments I ever made.

The core curriculum in Western Civilization proved to be a minor aspect of Ben's study. He was drawn instead to the school's computer science program and on graduation took a master's in the field at UCLA. Then he went out for job interviews, and I was able to help him get an appointment at Silicon Graphics, the cutting-edge company in the field, through a Berkeley friend who had married its CEO. I couldn't get him the job, only the interview, but that was enough. He was immediately hired, and that became the first step in what was to become a remarkable career.

I was also able to be of service to him in another way. That apartment I had built for Jonathan, which he never occupied, came in handy for Ben. While still at UCLA, he married a USC grad named Felicia Wiley, the youngest child of an African American family whose parents had migrated to Los Angeles from Shreveport, Louisiana. Felicia was the first member of her family to go to college, and when Ben met her was a supervisor in the complaint department at Toyota. I offered the couple my house for their wedding reception and the freshly built apartment over my garage to live in.

As soon as Ben was hired at Silicon Graphics, he and Felicia and their first-born child, Jules, moved north. The next years were stressful for their family as Ben transitioned through jobs at NetLabs, Lotus, and Netscape. I gave him some fatherly advice, advising him to be aware that the demands of his career were stressful for his wife and family and therefore to pay attention to what was going on in his household. Years later he wrote a number-one bestselling business book called *The Hard Thing About Hard Things*, which gained such an impressive reputation that Rupert Murdoch bought a thousand copies to distribute to his managers. In telling the story of the company he created, Ben included some autobiographical details among which was the advice I had given him. At the time he was not making that much money and was reluctant to invest in an air conditioning system despite a heat wave that was distressing his wife. As he related it, the anecdote sounded a little bizarre but was probably accurate. "Son, do you know what's cheap?" I apparently asked him. "Flowers. Flowers are really cheap. But do you know what's expensive? ... *Divorce*." Or so he recorded it. He got the message and the air conditioning, and he and Felicia have been inseparable now for twenty-five years.

This was the last useful advice I was able to give Ben for many years, as he was moving in a world that was not only foreign to me but involved such complex decisions that I wouldn't have had a clue what to tell him had he asked me. At Netscape he met and became friends with Marc Andreessen, co-inventor of the browser. When Netscape was bought by AOL, the two of them put in their required year and then launched a company they called Loudcloud, with Ben as CEO. In an incredibly adverse economic environment, which came close to bankrupting the company, he changed the name to Opsware and the company mission to software, and in the course of a dramatic white-knuckle saga made it an amazing corporate triumph. Less than seven years after he created the company he sold it to Hewlett-Packard for $1.6 billion, forty times its value only a few years before.

Ben's story has become a Silicon Valley legend. He has told it in gripping prose in his book, and told it so well that I would be foolish to try to duplicate any part of it here. Reading about his travails as he battled market crashes, dealt with corporate rivalries, and coped with the unexpected to prevail in the end by the skin of his teeth, I was taken by a thought that I wanted to shout from the rooftops. The thought was this: If leftists were to read this book with half-open minds and see what the life of a real CEO is like—the judgments he has to make, the risks he has to take, the personnel issues he has to handle, the corporate puzzles he has to solve, the adversities he has to soldier through—they would instantly see the folly of their beliefs, and abandon their delusions about "surplus value" and corporate exploitation and capitalist enemies. They would throw their socialist texts in the trash where they belong and be awed at what it takes to create an enterprise and steer it to success through "the gale of creative destruction," as Schumpeter once described the turbulent weather of the economic marketplace. But this will never happen. Even if leftists were to read Ben's book, they would not believe what they read because it would shake the foundations of their moral being. This is why ignorance rules the political world, and always will.

Ben's account of the challenges he faced and met filled me with a paternal glow and also with wonder at where all that brilliance and sharp-eyed character assessment came from. When I put this question to him, he said that it came the hard way, by learning from his mistakes as he went along and (as he left out) by not making the same mistakes again.

Reading his book made me marvel at the differences between him and his old man. For I was driven—one might say obsessively—by a mission that blinded me to many things at the periphery of my sight. The mission was to "change the world" and, when that came to grief, to confront those who refused to give up this misguided quest. I was so absorbed in pursuing these wars that I didn't pay proper attention to things I should have. As a result I didn't have the breadth of vision of either of my sons, and consequently, unlike them, did repeat my mistakes and paid the price.

A parallel difference was my confrontational attitude, born of my upbringing in a communist family. Ben was not unaware of this and made his own observations about it in his book. He recalled how he started out in the corporate world following my example but quickly found that it led to dead ends. And so he changed. Both he and Jonathan were able to locate grooves in the system they could run along, outwitting their opponents and finding ways to succeed. I have the greatest admiration for both of them for this ingenuity in working their way out of the family mold.

Reading Ben's description of the crises he faced, I experienced shivers of regret over the fact that I was unaware at the time and had failed to provide him a shoulder to lean on. Where was I indeed? And then I remembered: I was facing my own crisis with a prostate cancer and the efforts to get on my feet again. But there was more to it than that. A point comes—sooner than we think—when our children set out on their independent courses, and the possibility of influencing them or giving them the shoulder they once had is all but gone. Still I can't help wishing that circumstances had allowed me to give my son help in those dark years.

Today Ben is riding the crest of his success. After selling Opsware as part of the corporate deal he had made, he was required to spend a year of what he regarded as indentured servitude running Hewlett-Packard's two-billion-dollar global software division. The day he was liberated, he began implementing his next career step, the creation of a venture capital company called Andreessen Horowitz, which in less than five years has grown to be a $4.3 billion company at the top of the Silicon Valley food chain. His appearance on the cover of *Fortune* in March 2014 confirmed that he had taken his place with the titans of the digital world.

Ben has instincts very much like those of his brother, Jon, with whom he is close. They are generous souls and often join in efforts like building a library for Uganda's Abayudaya tribe in the name of their sister Sarah, who spent a summer teaching the tribal children. Ben has a son, Jules, and two daughters, Mariah and Sophia. Mariah was born with a severe autism, which requires around-the-clock care, and autistic charities are naturally an important Horowitz family philanthropy. Although Sarah and Mariah were the inspirations for these efforts, the real force behind them is Ben's wife, Felicia, who has grown from the anxious and pressured young mother I first got to know into a gracious hostess, social organizer, fund-raiser, and philanthropist. She is also a talented quilter whose works are auctioned for tens of thousands of dollars to help her worthy causes. Ben and Felicia have provided scholarship funds for African American students at Columbia and equally munificent sums to American Jewish World Service, which is the organization through which Sarah worked and which focuses on helping abused women all over the world.

The cause of oppressed women is a passion for Ben, as he explained on the Internet in an article called, "Why I Will Give 100% of My Book Earnings to Women in the Struggle." You can find that at bhorowitz.com, his business blog with ten million followers. He begins every column of business advice with an illustrative quotation from some rap artist. As a result, Ben has become fairly famous as an enthusiast of the genre—not to mention a rebel in the business advice column world—and has become friends with Kanye West, Nas, and other hip-hop figures. Nas's iconic album *Illmatic* draws on his growing up in the Queensbridge projects where, ironically, as a twelve-year-old I once distributed communist literature. Ben's advocacy of hip-hop led to an invitation from Henry Louis Gates to give a seminar on the subject at Harvard. When I queried him about all this he said, "Dad, you have to understand that rock and roll is communism, hip-hop is capitalism." I said, "Are you going to tell them that at Harvard?" He said, "Yes I will." And he did.

As you can see there is a bit of chip-off-the-old-block here, which is immensely gratifying to me. I am struck by how different Ben's career (like Jonathan's) is from mine yet how close we are in outlook and understanding. I feel very much at home when I am with Ben and Felicia and enjoy the large extended family that Felicia's parents, sisters, aunts, and uncles have brought into my life. I gave a eulogy for Felicia's father, John, at his funeral, which was inspired by my son's great love for him. John Wiley was a good man, with little formal education but with a shrewd mind and gentle instincts. As a young father he worked on oil pipelines and followed them to California. Before he died Ben gave him a present of a ride around the track in a Formula One with Mario Andretti at the wheel. His widow, Loretta, is a ray of sunshine, always looking to the bright side even though her life has had its share of heart-breaking tragedies. "My attitude," she says, "is it's one time here. Be grateful for what you get. That's all there is." And so it is.

It's an odd experience watching your children take over and render you fairly useless and old hat. It accelerates the sense of diminishing horizons at the same time it ignites fires of love, and feelings that despite your shortcomings you did things well and you can look back on the life that is vanishing and feel good.

Healing

While savoring these family passages I still have to cope with my daily condition, which continues to weigh on me. When I wake in the mornings my leg feels like lead, and there is pain shooting through my foot, and I'm wondering how I will be able to walk or make it through the next hours. When I finally roll out of bed, the first thing I reach for is my cane, which will help to take the pressure off. But even with this support, shuffling along I feel a hundred years old, and can't see how I will ever be whole again. On the TV the talking heads are droning on reminding me that I will not be part of that dialogue again soon if at all, nor will I be traveling cross country to deliver the speeches that have been an important part of my work. I have practically dropped out of a debate in which I have been engaged for half a century. The younger bodies and livelier brains of my children's generation are taking over and leaving me behind. I am not unaware that these thoughts of oblivion are premature and somewhat overwrought. When my foot is better and the pain subsides, I will probably come back in some semblance of myself and get in a few more rounds. But then I will be gone with John Wiley and all the rest.

My Rebel Daughter

Of all my children, my youngest, Anne, appears to be the one who picked up the confrontational gene that shaped so much of my life. Anne and I share fundamental traits, and yet despite our similarities, so obvious to others, there is a distance between us, which I cannot fully explain. I long attributed it to the divorce, since she was only nine at the time. When she and Sarah came to my foredoomed wedding in Los Angeles, she insisted that they both wear black and be rude to my bride. I don't know how to assess what goes on inside the heads and hearts of others, but her rebel streak was there from the outset and has not been directed only at me. She is the one child in the family to have dyed her hair purple when that was a teenage fad, and the only one to elope and get married in Tahoe with no family members present. Both episodes were far more disturbing to her mother than to me. She made amends after the elopement by having a reception many months later in Berkeley, which we all attended.

The following anecdote provides a flavor of her character. Shortly after the divorce, Elissa and I attended a parents' night at Martin Luther King Junior High, where she was a student. We gathered in one of the classrooms with a group of other parents and children and listened to Anne's teacher talk about the class and his students. Toward the end of his remarks, he complained that our children weren't always attentive, and it bothered him that they talked among themselves while he was trying to teach them. No sooner had these words left his lips than a voice that I immediately recognized as my daughter's shouted, "If you weren't so boring maybe we would want to listen to you."

I was appalled by this embarrassing outburst and show of disrespect. When we left the room, I scolded my daughter, much to the disapproval of my now ex-wife, who was understandably angry with me for other reasons. In retrospect I can see how a distraught father would react the way I did, worrying that a thirteen-year-old should show more deference to her elders. But I also see how bold my daughter was in speaking up for herself and her classmates against a form of abuse from tedious instructors that was not uncommon in classrooms. On another occasion, I had to go into her school to confront a teacher who should never have been in a classroom and who failed her on an exam because she wrote her answers in orange ink. Another incident that enraged me was her high school college adviser telling her she "wasn't college material."

My daughter went to UC Riverside and then to UCLA, where she received her RN degree, and went immediately to work in an abortion clinic. Anne has never been a political person, but she soaked up many Berkeley attitudes and felt both that women should have the choice whether to abort their babies, and also quality healthcare if the choice was to do that. But she soon found she didn't like nursing because once she had mastered the routines, the job was "boring." She went back to school, this time to the UC San Francisco Medical Center where she earned a Nurse Practitioner's degree, which gave her more authority and flexibility than her previous credential.

Her first job was in a community clinic, where she was left on her own since there were no other pediatric specialists. After a year there, she took a job at another community clinic, where 95 percent of the patients were Spanish-speaking. She already had some facility in the language and quickly brought herself up to speed. At the clinic she worked with foster children, who she discovered had a level of sophistication that other children didn't. She decided she wanted to develop an assessment tool that could be used to evaluate the maturity of a foster child who desired emancipation. It was the rebel at work. She went back to school and entered a Ph.D. program but as school started she got pregnant and left. She hated the program in any case because of its extreme academic focus. "No one really was interested in my wanting to create something practical."

In the millennium year she delivered a son named Elvis, and sent out a notification to the family that said, "The King has arrived." When Elvis was about a year and a half she went to work at La Clínica de la Raza in Oakland, where she worked for seven years, ministering to families and providing quality care for their children. But in 2007 she took a new job in the pediatric clinic at the Juvenile Justice Hall in Alameda County. While she was there, she still maintained a position at La Clinica as an after-hours triage clinician, and also as a laser clinician in a program to remove gang tattoos from youngsters who wanted to start a new life.

I have to confess that her work with criminals, even though they were youngsters, bothered me. It took me back to my experience with the Black Panthers and made me nervous for her safety. I discussed this with Anne more than once, but if I have conveyed here anything of the spirit of my daughter, you will understand why I could never rest assured she had listened to me or, if she had listened, heeded my advice. I was afraid that in befriending these criminal youngsters she would cross invisible lines that might make them mistake her kindnesses and come after her for more than she was prepared to give. I was also fearful for my grandson Elvis, a precocious and good-natured child who might become a target if Anne wasn't careful.

As it has turned out, my fears have so far been unfounded, and so perhaps my bad example did have an impact. Meanwhile my daughter has been a Good Samaritan to many troubled youngsters. I will confine myself to two examples.

E., a Juvenile Hall inmate, started getting arrested when he was eleven. He had sickle cell anemia, but all he knew about sickle cell was that sometimes he had priapism—a painful erection that lasts for more than six hours at a time. He had other pain and was supposed to take antibiotics daily, which he refused. Anne asked him point blank if he knew what sickle cell anemia was. He said he didn't really know but that he knew he would die by the age of twenty-five from it. He was fifteen at the time.

So Anne talked about it to him. To explain the importance of hydration she used the example of Cheerios in milk. She made a plan for keeping him hydrated so he wouldn't get priapism. Eventually he got to a point where he wanted to try daily medication to avoid crises. This required frequent blood work and adjustments to the dose, but he agreed and stuck with it. E. told Anne that he wanted to be an astronaut. "Ninety percent of my kids tell me they want to play pro football or basketball, and I am pretty sure that they won't, but an astronaut I had never heard before." She didn't tell him that he would never qualify because of the sickle cell, since even a normal plane ride requires oxygen for so-called "sicklers." So she told him if he completed his next program, she would send him to space camp at Stanford. With that as an inspiration, he completed the program. But while she was trying to raise the money for him to go to space camp, he got arrested again. He was placed back in the same program, and they made the same deal. Anne was having trouble raising the money, so she decided she would just pay for the space camp herself. Unfortunately, she never got to make the payment. E. ran away from the program and was murdered shortly after his eighteenth birthday.

Anne is philosophical about her work. "I don't think I can save anyone. I don't think I can really change anything," she told me. I was struck by how she had come to the same conclusions it took me so long and cost me so dearly to arrive at; how different her attitude was than mine had been for the first half of my life. Then she told me about one of her successes:

"B. was a very shady character, full of stories that I think he himself believes. He had been in and out of the Hall for a few years on different types of theft charges. Then he came in and we got a call from a doctor at his school health center. He had a positive HIV test but had not returned for follow up. In trying to locate him, we found out he was in Juvenile Hall. One of the most awkward conversations I have ever had was trying to tell this fifteen-year-old boy that I knew he was HIV positive and I knew he knew and I knew he didn't want me to know. He was in some of the most amazing denial I had ever seen. He got released and disappeared, no meds, no follow up.

"Then he got picked up again. We got to know each other well over many discussions regarding whether or not he would be compliant with treatment, where he would go for treatment, where he was going to live, etc. I remember one day he looked at me, almost startled, and said, 'I really have this, don't I?' When he got released again, a lot of disasters followed. During his final detention we requested the judge keep him past his eighteenth birthday so we could stabilize him and complete therapy for a secondary condition. During this time we created a team of outside and inside people who would continue to support him in the community. While this is not unusual, most kids don't get to sit with their entire team and help dictate the plan of care.

"B. is about twenty now, and even though I cannot continue to provide him healthcare, I provide him the support of a knowledgeable friend whom he trusts. So he will call the clinic when he knows I am there to ask what to do about a rash or that his meds are running out or that someone asked him to get a TB test and do I know what he needs to tell them. I get great satisfaction out of being B.'s friend, and there to help."

My daughter helps a lot of people. She also has the ability to anger people, including members of her family. I love my daughter and am proud of the good she does, but I wish the rebel in her would mellow and settle down, even though its progenitor is probably me.

Max

The dogs in our household are its life. They are the children one can actually handle after reaching middle age, which is one reason we miss them so fiercely when they are gone. About midway between Mother's Day and Father's Day, Kim's brindle boxer, Max, died. This was accompanied by days of mourning in our household. Boxers are prone to cancers, and Max, who was almost ten, had a tumor as big as his stomach pressing down on his spleen. Max had large black eyes and a fearsome look, which scared strangers. But to those of us who knew him he was a sweetheart.

There is another reason the passing of our pets affects us, and that has to do with what I call the happiness of dogs. They are happy to see us, whenever that is, and happy when we acknowledge them, if only by a look or a scratch behind the ears. In the morning all I have to do is stir from my slumbers and my Chihuahuas will set up a yowling and a cackling, a yipping and a yapping, as though Gabriel had sounded the trumpet summoning us to Judgment and a life of eternal bliss. It is no great mystery why we miss them when they leave.

Max was Kim's shadow in the same way Jake, my white Chihuahua with black cow patches and bubble eyes, is mine. Jake has been with me thirteen years and has kept watch over me all that time—through the prostatectomy, the first hip replacement, and now in my present hobbled state. When I get up, he will follow me from room to room as if spotting my position and checking to see that I am all right. He shadows me so closely that sometimes I will look around for him only to discover he is underfoot.

It is Lucy, our auburn with the Flying Nun ears that April is sure will be the next to go. Age has slackened the flesh around her mouth and turned many of her hairs white. She is twelve and overweight and has a heart murmur and a wheeze, and is prone to laze around the house. But she has been doing this for some time. I take my hope from that.

The short lives of dogs offer lessons to us. They teach us the evanescence of life and get us used to the fact that everything we love will be lost. Not that the next passing will be any easier than the previous one. It never will be. But in raising our awareness that what we have is temporary these passings teach us to embrace it while it is still here.

Max was put to sleep in the same Rainbow Room where we said goodbye to our little Coco. The rainbow idea seems to have originated among horse people. In a legend of loss and reunion, horses, when they die, are said to pause at the foot of a "Rainbow Bridge" to wait for their owners to follow them. An unknown author has written a poem about the bridge that every horse person knows.

> By the edge of a woods, at the foot of a hill,
>> Is a lush, green meadow where time stands still.
>
> Where the friends of man and woman do run,
>> When their time on earth is over and done.
>
> For here, between this world and the next,
>> Is a place where beloved creatures find rest....
>
> Their limbs are restored, their health renewed,
>> Their bodies have healed, with strength imbued....
>
> Then all of a sudden, one breaks from the herd.
>
> For just at that second, there's no room for remorse,
>> As they see each other... one person... one horse.

So they run to each other, these friends from long
past.
    The time of their parting is over at last.

The sadness they felt while they were apart
    Has turned to joy once more in each heart.

They nuzzle with a love that will last forever.
    And then, side by side, they cross over…together.

This is the statement of what I call a creative faith. The
secular and skeptical will dismiss it as merely a saccharine
fantasy to salve the wounds of a bruised heart. But that is
precisely its utility. For those who believe it provides a healing
hope. Does it matter if there is such a bridge or not? This is a
question no different from whether there is life after death.
Or whether there is a God. No one knows the answers to
these questions and no one can know. Therefore both
answers—yes and no—are expressions of faith. The only
question then is how these faiths affect the life we are in.

My wife is a believer. When I asked her about the Rainbow Bridge, she said, "To me the Rainbow Bridge means
peace. I thank God for the Rainbow Bridge because it will
guide my loved one to the other side, and one day to a

reunion. I hope so, because I want to see Coco, and I hope to see the ones I failed so I can make it up to them." As she said this her voice cracked and there were tears in her eyes, which is the way she responds whenever she thinks of losing Coco. But it is this same passion that caused her to save Coco.

Faiths

There is only faith to guide us when we are confronted by final questions. Atheism is no less a faith than theism because we cannot know the answers to the questions it raises. But not all faiths are the same. What I call "creative faiths" are those that look to another life to resolve the contradictions of this one, and offer consolation for irreparable loss. But there are also destructive faiths whose consolation for the flaws in this one is a mission to transform the world we inhabit into one they desire. They are destructive faiths because their goals are impossible. To succeed they must confer extraordinary powers on ordinary beings. Moreover, those who resist them—the non-believers—must be regarded as enemies of the good, and therefore the party of the damned. Consequently, the real product of destructive faiths is hate. Jihadist Islam is such a faith and so is Marxism and so are all quests for a perfect world.

The first half of my life was devoted to this kind of faith. It inspired and guided me for many years but in the end it broke my heart. I came by it innocently, having been born into a family of progressives who found meaning for their lives in a redemptive mission. Their hope was to establish "social justice" enforced through the power of the state. But the only way to accomplish this was to change human beings—to make them different from what they have been since the beginning of time. And that could only be accomplished by stifling human freedom, and thus destroying the hope itself. The religion I was born to was communism. Its adherents desired justice, but their practice inevitably was the totalitarian state.

I embraced the progressive illusion as an unspoken condition of parental love. That may sound brutal, but as a child of loving parents I wasn't conscious of the coercion. Instead I was lifted by my parents' passion to heights of righteousness and self-regard. It was intoxicating to be tasked with saving the world and having your family and community applaud you for every step you took along the path to the goal.

Secular faiths are difficult to relinquish since they have all the comforts of a religious calling—the consolation for what we suffer, the power that flows from serving a cause. Millions are wedded to the progressive idea no matter how many catastrophes it produces. These are not mistakes as progressives maintain. They are the predictable consequence of ascribing powers of salvation to self-centered, needy human beings, who are prone to treachery and deceit.

In mid-life my commitment to the faith confronted me with a crime I could not ignore. When my political comrades murdered Betty Van Patter, I could no longer close my eyes to the way revolutionary vanguards behaved as though they were sanctified by a law higher than the one that governed everyone else. I could not ignore how the faithful refused to challenge the crime because they were afraid to jeopardize the beautiful dream. For the first time in my life I no longer felt righteous. For the first time I was able to listen to the voices of others who did not share my faith, and which I had previously dismissed as voices of the damned.

Now I had a debt to pay and justice to seek. It was not the social justice of progressives, which denies the rights of individuals in the name of a greater good. The justice I now sought was for individuals like Betty, who were victims of the progressive faith.

Divergent Paths

It probably hasn't escaped your attention that none of my children have pursued political careers like their father's.

Even my daughter Sarah, who took up many political causes, did so within the framework of a deeply felt Judaism. Her religious philosophy guided her politics, not the other way around. When the writer Walter Isaacson read an earlier version of this manuscript he raised the following questions: Why were my children not political? Why, on the other hand, was I so passionately political, and why did I continue to be political throughout my life, even when I moved to the other side? How do my children's choices and mine reflect on the general human desire to extract meaning from this life?

Here are my answers:

I relayed Isaacson's question to my son Jonathan and asked him about his choice of a musical career. His response was immediate: "Children normally run away from their parents. Only dummies go into the family business." It was a characteristically wry reflection of Jonathan's own attitude but a bit too facile as a general observation. The desire to establish an individual identity is indeed strong but so is the dynastic pull, and many worthy offspring follow in their parents' footsteps. Philip was the king of Macedonia, but his son Alexander conquered the world. Leopold Mozart was an accomplished composer; his son Wolfgang was a voice for the ages. The reason Jonathan chose music as his own career was because that was his first love. He never gave politics or

any other profession a second thought. This was true of each
of my children: they loved what they pursued and found in
their pursuits a meaningful direction for their lives.

I was one of the dummies Jonathan referred to, entering
the family business. It was less a business actually than a
religious calling, a passion that informed the moral life of
everyone who was part of it. My decision was dictated not
only by my parents' devotion to the progressive cause but also
by the fact that the members of our entire community were
committed followers of that cause. It was not only a *worldview* that enveloped me but a *world*. I don't remember ever
thinking I was free to pursue a different course. If I had done
so, it would have been seen not as an alternative but a betrayal.
The lesson I eventually took from this was to avoid raising
my own children as I had been raised, which was to enter the
family business. I didn't want to narrow their choices by
making their approval of my work or my political opinions
seem to be conditions of my affection. If Jonathan had been
raised in my father's household, to make the point, he would
have faced daunting opposition to his rock-and-roll career,
while the opposition to the religious and business careers that
Sarah and Ben pursued would have been even stiffer.

The decision to set my children free was made easier
because as they were entering adolescence I was increasingly

plagued by doubts about the wisdom of the path I had chosen—or that had chosen me. But why, when those doubts were finally overwhelming—when I was able to see that the political movement to which I had dedicated myself produced sinister results—did I not just quit the field? The lessons I had learned from my experience I had already recorded in my autobiography, *Radical Son*, which was my declaration of independence from the cause I had been born to. Why not end it there and find a less combative world to enter?

Would that matters had been so simple. But a light did not go on to suddenly illuminate everything wrong about the past that had engulfed me. From the time of Betty's murder, it was twenty years before I reached the point where I could actually write a book like *Radical Son*. Before I could understand a movement so deeply inscribed in the psyches of its followers and formulate a response to it, I had to free myself from an outlook that was inseparable (or so I thought) from my identity and being. Those two decades were years of gut-wrenching self-interrogation and discovery. The process was ongoing and made it impossible for me to end the odyssey I had begun as a very young man with the book I had written.

Having been inside one perspective and now looking at things through very different eyes, I was able to understand—

to *see*—how the best intentions led to evil results. I even managed to capture this sense of foreseeing the future when I created a motto for the online magazine I came to publish: "Inside every liberal is a totalitarian screaming to get out." Of course, I meant by this that every progressive who imagines that a beautiful future is possible will be tempted by its very beauty to go along with any means necessary to achieve it. Out of good intentions, therefore, dreadful results. To confront the siren song of the left and warn of its consequences became my calling.

As for Walter's final question—what meaning do efforts like mine impart to a life?—they don't. They provide the satisfaction of contributing to a good cause and in that sense could be said to make a life seem meaningful. But I don't believe, as progressives do, that the moral arc of the universe is bent toward justice. Therefore, in the long run, the battles I have fought and the many volumes written have as good a chance of adding up to nothing as they do of contributing to a happy ending. In the long run, history does not move in a positive direction. Or any direction. If I entertain a hope of historical progress, it is limited to this: that my children and theirs will live in a freer, less threatened, and more humane environment than I did. I cannot engage the future any further or more widely than that.

Yet we all seek a larger purpose to our lives, and this quest for meaning is inescapable; it is part of our genome. How should we deal with the desire to make the world whole, and to make it make sense? My advice is this: Keep a wary eye on such urges, which cannot be satisfied. Be careful about what you seek. Where large matters are involved, a modest ambition is usually the prudent one. Tend your garden. Cherish friends and family. Our lives are enlarged and our sense of who we are is enhanced when our children turn out well, and when we can be of help to others. Find satisfaction in this and in completing the tasks you undertake and in fulfilling the responsibilities that are yours. Bear always in mind that only a religious faith can impart meaning to our existence. It does so through the vision of a life hereafter that repairs the irreparable flaws in ours and makes us whole. Now we see through a glass darkly, only then face to face. This is the only faith that has a chance—and it is only a chance—to work without destructive consequences.

By contrast, the bad faiths—the faiths that seek to change *this* world and purge it of evil—lead inexorably to passions that are themselves evil: the desire to take away freedom and to suppress those who resist. That is why missions to redeem the world by making it just are the source of the great calamities of our times.

This is what I have concluded through bitter experience and what I feel called on to testify to others, and will continue to do so until my final breath.

three

July–August

Karma

April and I began living together in 1996, and once we were under the same roof, animals began appearing. I use this construction advisedly because I was not involved in their coming. First a dog named Barney; then a Maltese named Buddy, whom we called "Fat Man"; and a Shih Tzu named Molly, who rode in my lap to and from my radiation treatments for the prostate cancer that had leaked into my system. Then came Jake and Lucy and Lucky, who are with us still; and Winnie and Coco, who have only recently passed.

In the eighth year of our marriage we were living in Cala-basas. April had begun riding a gorgeous paint named Alvin, who was boarded at a ranch in Agoura Hills, about twenty minutes away. Soon she was buying the horse, and then we were buying an acre-and-a-half ranch in the Santa Maria Valley so that Alvin could be with us all the time. As soon as we had acquired the ranch, April bought another horse named Diddy to be Alvin's companion. No sooner had we settled into our new home than April began rescuing horses that people had abandoned. To help her, I used the Internet to set up a foundation, which she named Heart of a Horse, to raise money to fund her rescues. It did not take me long to realize that there was a powerful karma at work here that was changing our lives.

One day April took her mother, Mary, to the Saddle Rock Ranch where Alvin was boarded before we bought our home-stead. While they were there, Mary told April a story she had never heard before. It was about a chestnut quarter horse named Brownie that Mary had been given as a little girl and whom she loved with a little girl's passion. Her parents first sat her on the horse when she was only two years old, and as she grew she could be seen riding him all around the farm where they lived. One day when Mary was ten, she and her sisters were playing about the barn when Brownie turned her head suddenly and struck Mary in the face. A horse's head is very hard and the blow knocked the child out. It was completely unintentional, but when her father found out he flew into an alcoholic rage and took the horse out in the field with his shotgun and killed her.

When the deed was done, Mary's father refused to bury Brownie, and the carcass lay in the field for days. The next morning Mary went to sit with her dead friend. She sat there all day and cried. No one could get her to leave. Finally night came and the family went out and dragged her in. The next day she was out there again, hugging Brownie and crying. This went on until Mary's mother finally forced her father to get the tractor and drag Brownie's body to a far part of the field and bury her.

April was shocked to hear the story. Reflecting on it afterwards, she thought Mary never really recovered from the tragedy. "When Brownie died," she said, "her death seemed to take a piece of my mother's heart with her to the grave."

Mary grew up to have ten children of her own, the first when she was only fifteen. There were six girls and four boys, of whom nine survived. April was the next to the youngest, five years behind her next older sister. They all lived in a one-story ranch style house with a big back yard in Bakersfield. Her parents had a troubled marriage, and her father was often gone for long periods. On several occasions her mother threw up her hands and abandoned the household too, leaving the children to fend for themselves. When April was three, she was sent to live for a year with her Aunt Perky and Uncle Gene until her mother came back. She didn't know why she had been sent away, but her uncle and aunt were very kind to her.

At home, she spent a lot of time in the care of her sisters, who often regarded her as a drag on their teenage activities. "I found myself alone a lot, wishing that someone would come to pick me up," she remembers. There were lots of kids in the house and lots of pets, including six or seven dogs that lived in the backyard. One of the dogs was April's, a mutt named Sammy Davis Jr., to whom she was devoted. One afternoon she came home from school and the house was unusually quiet. Only two dogs were inside, and she didn't hear the usual barking from the backyard. So she went through the kitchen and opened the sliding door to look in on the dogs. But when she got to the yard they were gone. She went around the side of the house to see if the gate was open, but it wasn't. Then she heard a door slam and someone moving about inside the house and knew it was her mother.

She went in, found her mother, and told her she couldn't locate Sammy or the other dogs. She saw that her mother had been drinking and was upset. "Where are the dogs, I can't find them," April said. Then her mother told her she had called the pound and the officers had come and taken them all away. She tried to reassure her daughter that it was for the best, but April was already beside herself. She cried and cried and ran out into the backyard to Sammy's doghouse as though he might be there. But there was no Sammy. She went back inside the house and through her tears begged her mother to let her go to the pound to get Sammy back. But her mother said no, that wasn't going to happen. Sammy would not be coming back. April was eight or nine at the time.

When April told this story to me, she said, "My mother had done it because she was angry. She had been drinking and was mad at my father because he had left her. All those dogs and children must have seemed too much for her to cope with. I guess her father had set an example for her that she could not break free from. But in that moment, I knew for myself and in my own heart that my path was going to be different."

Back from the Dead

And so it was. As soon as we were set up on our new ranch, with Alvin and Diddy in the stalls, April began rescuing abandoned and neglected horses. One day the Ventura

County humane officer called to tell her about an abandoned horse in a stall near Lake Casitas. The horse had not had anything to eat for a long while and was in very poor condition. He was going to be removed from the property. The humane officer asked April, who was becoming known in the area as the "Heart of a Horse Lady," if she would take the horse, rehabilitate him, and then find him a home. April agreed to meet her at the site in Ojai.

The abandoned horse, an Arabian, had been owned by an illegal immigrant who had been arrested on a criminal charge and sent back to Mexico. Several other horses were stabled in the same location, but none of the owners had bothered to feed the Arab who had been left behind. April drove her truck to the site. It was a dry field, parched and dusty. There were only a few trees to break the harsh rays of the sun overhead.

Across from the entrance, April saw a cluster of semi-open shacks that served as stalls. The stalls had no water. April glanced at her dashboard and saw that it was 108 degrees outside. She got out of her truck, walked over to the edge of the stall, and looked in at the abandoned horse. "I saw a bay colored skeleton that appeared to be an Arab," she told me later, "although he was so emaciated and his body so distorted that I had to look twice to make sure. His flesh was shrunken from lack of food and seemed to hang from his spine, making his head, which was down, seem exceptionally large. His flanks were sunken and instead of being rounded his rump was all angles where the flesh had receded, bringing his bones to the surface. He had a tattered black mane and a ragged tail, and, most heartbreaking of all, he was on his knees in the manure, as though he had given up hope and was simply waiting for his misery to end. I thought to myself, *this poor fellow is ready to die.* But the moment I stepped into the muck inside the stall, he lifted his head and looked up at me."

When he did, April began talking to him. She said, "I don't know your name, or who you are, and you don't know me. But I'm going to help you. Just hold on sweetheart. I will rescue you and find you a home." Outside the stall there was a bucket filled with empty beer cans. The humane officer and April dumped the cans out, rinsed the bucket clean, filled it with water, and brought it into the stall for the Arab to drink. Then April went over to her truck and pulled out a twenty-five-pound bag of alfalfa pellets. She poured the pellets into a container and put it near the Arab, and he immediately began to eat. He chewed very slowly and with great effort. "He was so weak it was pitiful," she remembers, "and the air was so hot. My heart went out to him."

Once they had provided the Arab with water and food, there was nothing more they could do for him at the moment. They needed to get a vet out to look at him and then remove him from the site to a place where he could be rehabilitated. Before April could call the vet, she needed to leave the place. She did not want to be there by the stables alone. Men with hardened faces and hostile looks were standing around. They were day laborers, who owned the horses in the stalls next to the starving Arab, but had not fed or watered him. They had been warned that the law was looking into the case, and they were standing around sullenly, as though making up their minds as to what kind of trouble they might be in and what they were going to do about it. April mounted the cab of her truck and drove off.

When she got back on the freeway, she dialed Dr. Smith, her vet, and filled him in on what she had seen. They agreed to meet later in the day and drive together in his vet truck to the field in Ojai. When she returned, even though it was only about four or five hours since she had been there, April could already see a change in the emaciated little Arab who still had no name. He had drunk more of the water and devoured more of the feed, and the nourishment had begun to revive him. When she looked over the wall of his stall, he was standing and holding his head up and looking back at her. His eyes had begun to have a flicker of life in them, and she imagined him saying, "Hey you're back, the lady that gave me something to eat. I didn't think I'd see you again."

They entered the filthy stall, and April helped Dr. Smith place a halter over the Arab's head. This gave them enough control so that he could administer the medication he had brought to ease the Arab's discomfort. When this was done they attempted to walk him out, but he had been confined to the stall for so many months that he was hardly able to walk. April was a little worried that he might pass out. The two of them rubbed his body all over, then they walked him over to the wash rack across from the stalls and hosed him down and tried to flush off the dirt, which was caked on his back and flanks and legs. His head was now up and his eyes alert, but he also extended his neck toward them and seemed to want them next to him. As they put him back in his stall, April kissed him goodbye and said, "I promise I will be back tomorrow."

As Dr. Smith and April headed for the vet truck, two men came toward them and began talking in broken English about the owner who had been sent back to Mexico. One of the men asked April, "Are we going to get in trouble for this horse?" Her first concern was to avoid any possible scene that might compromise the Arab's removal, so she said, "No.

There is not going to be any trouble, because the horse is leaving with me on Monday." Then she asked him as unthreateningly as she could, "Why has this horse had no food and water for so long?"

He looked at April and said, "I don't want no trouble." Holding up two fingers he pointed at the starving Arab and lied, "I give this horse two flakes of hay every day." A flake is a normal meal for a horse, and two meals is a normal portion for a day. If the Arab had been fed that much hay, there was no way he would have been in the skeletal condition he was in.

"You gave this horse two flakes of hay a day?" said Dr. Smith. "*Si.*" Dr. Smith did not bother to conceal his anger: "You gave this horse two flakes of hay a day and he's three hundred pounds underweight? That's a miracle. I've never seen anything like it in my practice. This horse is skin and bones and getting ready to die. How is that possible?"

"Maybe he got cancer," the man said.

The next day April could not stop thinking about the Arab with no name. She had some business to take care of before she could see him, but when her tasks were done, she drove back to the scorched field off the freeway in Ojai. She pulled up, jumped out of her truck, and ran to his stall. There he was, and he was standing up straight. He looked right in her direction, and his body language said, "Wow you came back for me."

"Yes, I came back," she said out loud; "I've brought you some treats and some fly spray to get those nasty things off you." She fed him some horse cookies and began to apply the spray. Some horses shy at the sound of the aerosol, and the Arab turned out to be one of them. He probably had never encountered fly spray before or heard the aerosol whoosh. So April sprayed her hand instead and rubbed it over him. As she worked her way down from his face, and over his withers to his flanks she could feel every bone sticking out. It made her sad to be touching his skeleton like that, but she also saw he was loving the touch. As she rubbed and soothed him, he turned his head and his big brown eyes looked at her as if to say *thank you*. "You are going to be coming with me Monday to start a new life," she said. Then she realized his new life had already begun.

Before driving away, she asked the men who were still hanging around what the horse's name was, but no one would tell her. On the way home, she decided she would call him Lazarus. "God put a conscience into the person who phoned the Humane Society and alerted the officer who then called me," she said. "If that person had just passed the Arab the way everyone else had, he would soon have been dead. The name Lazarus means, 'God is my help.' That phone call was the first link in the chain that brought Lazarus back from the dead." When Monday came, she returned with a hauler to transport him to the ranch, where she had rented a stall to start him on the path to rehabilitation.

In the months that followed, a trainer worked Lazarus, and a sports therapist massaged his muscles and stretched his joints. Dr. Smith provided him with vaccines and other medications, and a farrier shoed him properly. April organized a group of young girls to give him baths and ride him and shower him with affection. When the rehabilitation was complete, this horse that had looked like a concentration camp survivor could easily be mistaken for a show animal— he was that beautiful.

And talented too. One day the Mexicans at the ranch were playing their mariachi music, and Lazarus suddenly began to dance. It turned out that he was a *charro* horse, used in the Mexican rodeos which are held all over California, although the general public is hardly aware they exist. Lazarus was so full of energy and life. He would take off on a run and fly across the arena as Arabs do, making leaps in which all four of his hooves left the ground. It was a display of joy expressing his happiness in his new life, and it lit up April's heart to watch him. She knew, however, that she would have to part with him soon. In the end, the goal of rescue is always to find the abandoned animal a "forever home."

Sure enough, after several months a man from a nearby horse canyon came to adopt Lazarus. April was cautious because she did not want Lazarus to be abused again. But her concerns were allayed by the kind character of the man. He already had a white Arabian and wanted to make Lazarus his companion. When Lazarus finally left, April's emotions were a mixture of joy at his rejuvenation and sadness that he would be leaving her. She cried for a long time. She had come to love him so much, as she did all her horses.

I am in awe of my wife for the devotion she has shown to these abandoned creatures. A spiritual heart breeds compassion for the vulnerable, as the story of Lazarus illustrates. But why have I told this story in detail and at length? It says something about the cruelty of men toward any creature they consider weaker or unable to retaliate. As a critic of messianic illusions, I see it as a lesson in the irredeemable aspect of the human condition, the casual cruelty and normal deceitfulness of human beings, which will always frustrate hopes for a better world.

It is also a lesson in the possibility of redemption for an individual life. Each time you bring someone back from the doors of death, each time you restore them to health, you see how fragile life is and how glorious it can be. My heart is warmed every time I think of the skeletal figure April came upon and the magnificent creature that emerged through the love and care that she and her volunteers showered on him.

The story of Lazarus is also the story of a creative faith. Do horses have thoughts and emotions similar to ours? If you talk to a horse, does he understand you? Can you inspire his will to live? Does God watch over his creatures and arrange phone calls leading to rescues like this? Does it matter? What matters is a heart that is open, that connects you to the voiceless; what is important is a faith that inspires you to see to their care and revival. Without these, none of what April did—and not only for Lazarus—would be possible.

In my view, the good deeds that are done in this world are performed by people of faith who love and are not daunted by the ordinary cruelty of others. They are performed by people who act on the belief that our lives are connected and that we are placed here for a reason, whether by a divinity or not. My wife's belief is the source of immense good to those who might never have received it. And I am its chief, if not always deserving, beneficiary.

Is it necessary to believe in a God to have this faith? I do not think so, although it is certain that belief in God and an ordered universe can be a powerful inspiration to good deeds.

There are many sources of creative faiths, but what they have in common is this: they are born of humility and love; their adherents do not presume to act like gods and try to recreate the world.

Bury the Bad and Embrace the Good

During the days of my glacial convalescence, one thing on my mind was a book-signing party I had set in motion for July 26, which would be four months after my mishap. It was going to be held at our home, and its ostensible purpose was to celebrate the publication of *Take No Prisoners*, a book I had written about how to fight a bad faith. We were expecting two hundred people and had prepared entertainments to make the occasion memorable, with a band, a disk jockey, and a barbecue. The theme was western and we were hoping everyone would come decked out in ten-gallon hats and cowboy boots, and ready to have fun.

The real energy behind the event was April's, who had a very different view of what this party would mean. "This is a celebration for us of our return to the world, to life," she said to me. "We've been buried for so long now with our medical problems, this is a chance to see our friends and your supporters all at once. We're going to get a great lift out of this, and maybe, even, it will put you back on your feet."

While immersed in preparations for the party, we were visited by a branch of April's large family that was missing from our Mother's Day gathering. Jim and Kim were there along with Cherri and Wendell. But the guests of the day were their sister Ramona's children, Race and Jackie O, and their families that included five children. For this festivity, April had bought the children a store full of toys, including a stable and horse for one of Race's little girls. Afterward I asked April if these weren't the kind of toys she would have liked to have when she was a little girl, though I knew the answer before she gave it.

In the evening, when the younger generation had departed, a little gathering formed around the table under our Jacaranda trees. It included Kim and Jim and April and their former sister-in-law Cindy. The conversation turned to their childhood and to stories out of school about April's parents. When Kim and Jim began talking in a mocking tone about alleged sexual improprieties by April's father and mother, they triggered an angry reaction. April was a fierce defender of the good she remembered in her parents and would not tolerate the disrespect Kim in particular was showing for their memories.

Nothing struck me more forcefully than April's defense of her father, who had psychologically abused her, disowning her to her face and taunting her verbally on many occasions throughout her childhood. It was only as a young adult that she acquired the psychological fortitude to fight back. Yet at the end she had gone to his sick bed and wiped the sweat from his brow and bathed him and let him know that she forgave him. She wanted to keep only the memories of the kindnesses he had done to her and her siblings and to bury the bad memories with him. She had the same attitude toward her mother. "It is best," she said, "to remember the good. It is best for one's own heart to be at peace."

When I thought about this attitude of hers, so different from her sister's, I realized that it had played a central role in our marriage as well. Every marriage faces formidable obstacles in the fact that two people with different sensibilities must live together under one roof. Consequently in every marriage there are conflicts, which generate strong emotions. Sometimes when they rise to the surface they may even seem to preclude a life together. These conflicts are somehow resolved in marriages that work, and not in those that don't. In mine it has more often been the readiness of my wife to embrace the good and bury the bad that has released us from these moments and reunited us on the other side.

A Partial Remission

While all the party preparations were going on, our home continued to have the feel of an *hôpital des invalides*. An x-ray had shown that April's clavicle had still not healed, and the broken bones were pressing down on her axillary nerve, causing the pain to run down her arm to her fingertips. As if that were not enough, she had also developed a case of chondromalacia, an inflammation of the underside of the knee, which was also quite painful and required physical therapy to correct. At the same time, I was going through a phase of recovery (to put the best face on it) where there were hours in the day, and especially at night, when I was besieged by waves of eye-rolling pain. These episodes prevented me from concentrating on my work and had to be medicated. From where I sat, the recovery was going so slowly I was beginning to give up hope that I would be back to a semblance of the normal by the time of the party.

Then, quite suddenly, I had a remission. The foot massages April was giving me were having an effect, as were, no doubt, the exercises I was doing and the passage of time. Where I was sometimes taking two or three pills a night to deal with the pain, I was now going days without needing even one. It was an amazing pleasure to walk without pain and not to feel the soreness that I had become used to along the sciatic ridge of my foot. I was still hobbling because of the frozen ankle and would tire easily as the foot swelled under the pressure of my exertions. But there was no denying the trend was positive. Twice a week I was attending rigorous physical therapy sessions, which focused on the muscles that were weak and the sinews that were still locked. It was now the middle of July, and the party was only a week away. The therapy had given me increased flexibility, and I was beginning to think I would attend as a semi-recovered case. I was looking forward to that.

A Romance of Age

When the day finally arrived, the party proved to be just the celebration of life and return that April had predicted. Our friends and neighbors came, and my co-workers at the Center. It was the largest gathering of April's family outside of funerals that anyone could remember. Her sisters were there, her brother Joe, and members of her extended family including Big Jon, who thanked her for putting the reunion together. There were about two hundred in all, and they seemed to be having an exceptionally good time.

The festive atmosphere was heightened by the talent we assembled. My friend Joel Gilbert brought his Dylan tribute band, Highway 61 Revisited, to play a forty-five-minute program. Another friend, screen actor Steven Bauer, brought his guitar and performed a solo set of songs by McCartney, Elton John, and others. But for me the high point of the afternoon came when the DJ announced he was playing "April's and David's wedding song" and April and I stepped onto the temporary floor that had been laid over the grass and began to dance.

April was in a blue and white flower print dress, stunning as her blonde hair caught highlights from the sun. The misters we had put in place because the day was hot elevated the dreamlike effect, enveloping us in a gauzy vapor. Like newlyweds, we drew each other closer and kissed.

Our friend Arrik Weathers had indeed sung the song at our wedding sixteen years before, but I had first given it to April when I had not yet proposed but knew I was about to. I knew, too, that she would have worries about what she might be getting into, since I was coming from such a different world from hers. The song I gave to her was called "I Swear," and was sentimental and over the top in the way that pop tunes often are ("I swear by the moon and the stars in the sky"). But it fit the occasion and what I wanted her to hear:

> I see the questions in your eyes
> I know what's weighing on your mind ...
> I'll stand beside you through the years ...
> And though I'll make mistakes

I'll never break your heart
I'll give you everything I can
I'll build your dreams with these two hands
We'll hang some memories on the walls
And when just the two of us are there
You won't have to ask if I still care
'Cause as time turns the page
My love won't age at all

The moments we danced to this song were enchanted, not with the romance of youth, which is a romance of promises, but the more difficult romance of age—of achievement. For twenty years I had kept these promises and would keep them to the grave. I could not say that about my whole life, but I could say it about the life I shared with April.

We were among friends, and our dance struck a chord with many, even moving some to tears. The day after the party we received a note from one: "I want to thank you for including me in your party yesterday. Of all the enjoyable conversations I had and food I ate, what touched me most was watching you two dance your anniversary dance. I am truly grateful for the angel that came to you, April, in your moment of death and brought you back for David and the rest of us."

Amen.

Inspiration

I have already observed how the short lives of canines impart an important discipline to the mortals who own and love them. Their stoicism in the face of life's adversities set benchmarks for us all.

April and I have adopted two rescue dogs who are missing legs—a condition that didn't have the same relevance for me when we rescued them as it does now. Lucky was the first to become part of our household. At five pounds he is a little snip of a dog with a white coat and brilliant black eyes. We call him "knucklehead" because the abuse he experienced sometimes triggers emotional squalls when he feels threatened. His right front leg was already shriveled when April came upon him in a Petco adoption center and was drawn to his bereft look. When she inquired about him, she was told that Lucky had been there a year. "Nobody wants him." When April heard these words she picked him up and said, "Lucky, you're coming home with me," and we have had him ever since.

The vet thought Lucky's withered leg posed a hazard and advised us to remove it, which we did. The absence of the front limb has given him a sort of hippity-hop gait, like a rabbit's. "My little jumping jelly bean" is the affectionate way April refers to him. One of my pleasures is to watch him race after the other dogs as they scamper across the lawn. Because of his handicap, he occasionally stumbles, rolls over, and picks himself up to bound after them again. This all reminds me of Coco, who used to fall into a roll when she pursued the chase faster than her little legs could handle.

Abby is a deer Chihuahua with a silken black patch on her back and a brown underbelly and markings to frame it. She was found by some students hiding under a pile of wood in downtown Los Angeles. Her hind leg was broken and dangled at her side, and she barked hysterically, darting away when anyone approached. The students left her scraps to feed on until they finally had the idea to bring her to us. When she arrived at our house, she was screaming in pain and fear, which continued without stopping for three days.

As soon as she arrived we took her to the vet, who worked hours to save her leg but finally had to give up. There was just too much scar tissue to make the limb workable, and she removed it entirely. I can identify with Abby for the nights of pain she went through. She is still frightened of car lights and still screams every now and then, but she is a sweet and loving dog, and because it is her hind leg that is missing can outrun any of the four-legged Chihuahuas in the house.

What impresses me is how both these dogs have picked themselves up out of tragedy and created new lives. For them, three legs, however cumbersome at times, is who they are, and they accept it. This is worth the effort we made to save them and puts a smile on my face whenever I think about it.

four

September

Testosterone

In the idle time that an extended convalescence offers, I have had occasion to think about the fact that this is the first book I have written without any testosterone in my system. This odd fact is a consequence of the hormone therapy I began last January under the guidance of my oncologist. My PSA levels had spiked to nine, which is a lot for someone without a prostate. Fortunately, scans revealed there was no metastasis into my bones or lymph system. Nonetheless, to be safe my doctor put me on a program of Lupron shots, which reduced my testosterone levels to about zero.

I don't think what I have written here marks a dramatic departure, either in tone or sensibility, from what I have written before. But I have to admit that I have been a bit watery of late, and sometimes the slightest setback in my general condition, or even something as innocuous as watching a YouTube video of Train receiving the Group of the Year Grammy and thanking my son Jon for "saving their careers," can set off crying jags as uncontrollable as that of any female on her period.

Admittedly I am on a cocktail of other drugs, like Neurontin, which may account for these mood swings. But I don't think the medications are behind all the reactions. After all, why should tears be inappropriate when you think about how your children have gone into the world and realize that all those days you shared are gone with them?

As a result of this hormone-induced testosterone deficiency, I was even experiencing the kinds of hot flashes that are familiar to women during menopause. At first I resisted when my wife urged me to take a drug to eliminate them. This was a bit of male bravado, and pretty quickly I had to concede that I had overreached. The hot flashes proved to be bothersome enough that I wanted to be rid of them. "At last," my wife exclaimed, "you know what it's like to be a woman!"

Maybe—but not so much a woman that my passion for her has dimmed. Though I have known April for twenty years and despite the fact that my loins have been lifeless since starting the treatments, there are moments every day when I see her face, or her flesh, or her form relaxed or at some task, and my chest flushes and I want to go over and kiss her just as when we were younger and my loins were alive.

In September I had another appointment with my oncologist. My PSA had dropped to 0.1, close enough to zero, and I was told that I could discontinue the Lupron treatments, at least temporarily until we could assess the result. This meant that my body would now be creating testosterone again and the missing sexual feelings would return. I look at the whole experience of their absence as a useful way of measuring the passions of the heart.

Setback

For more than a month my bad leg had felt unusually swollen and painful, bad enough that I made appointments with my primary care doctor and my neurologist, Michael Wienir, who is also a good friend. The first appointment was on a Monday, but my primary care doctor was so busy I had to see one of his associates. She introduced herself by saying she was not actually a doctor but a "physician's assistant," which immediately undermined my confidence in the advice she was about to give. After examining my leg, she said I probably had a blood clot (not unusual after operations like mine) and should go directly to a hospital emergency room and get an ultrasound to see if I actually did. But this was not something I wanted to do, having spent many hours in emergency rooms waiting for attention. Moreover, I had an appointment with the primary care doctor the next day, and Dr. Wienir the day after that.

When I saw the primary care doctor and he examined my leg he said with authority, "You do not have a blood clot," and sent me home. The following day I went to see Dr. Wienir and he was not so sure. He made an appointment for me with a vascular surgeon for the following day. The appointment was in the medical center adjacent to Providence Hospital. After examining me the vascular surgeon ordered an ultrasound, which showed that I had an "acute" blood clot extending from my ankle up through my groin. I was immediately put on a gurney and taken upstairs to a bed in the hospital where they ran an IV and put me on anticoagulants. I remained in the hospital for five days, during which I had time to think about all the physical therapies I had been through, the massages of my swollen leg, which put me in a lot of pain, and the exercises I had performed with similar results. I was lucky the clot had not broken into my lungs and—worse—my heart, where it could have been fatal.

Four days after I returned home, April and I took a walk up the driveway with our dogs. When we reached the top I was out of breath and experiencing pain in my left shoulder and part of my chest area. "It's nothing," I said, not wanting to entertain the possibility that I would have to go back. To which April replied, "Either you are coming with me to the emergency room, or I am calling 911." I decided that it would be less embarrassing to go to the emergency room if the pain proved to be nothing. When we arrived at Los Robles they triaged me and put me at the head of the line. Shortly afterwards they wheeled me in for a CT scan, which showed that a piece of the clot had broken off and moved to my lung. I was moved from the emergency room to the hospital proper and stayed there for another five days, until the doctor felt I was stable. When I was released, the vascular surgeon put me on the table again and inserted a filter in my vena cava to prevent any more clots from gravitating to my lung.

For many days I felt terribly weak, having spent so much time immobile in hospital beds. My legs—both of them—ached when I tried to walk. I was anxious in a way I hadn't been since the angina I had six years previously, when I had a stent inserted, and for months afterwards every poke of anxiety or heart burn seemed like it might be the harbinger of a new assault. But that experience had taught me not to panic over incidents like this. Following consultations with a hematologist and pulmonary specialist, I was reassured that this too would pass, and when it did I would be all right. Gradually, I returned to my routines. My bad leg was even feeling better without the full pressure of the clot, and I began looking up and outward again. It was another lesson in the ongoing tutorial of the year: you never know what the next day will bring.

At the Edge

"Once the truck was airborne," April recalled after the accident, "I thought my life was over. And I accepted it. When I hit the bottom of the drainage pipe it was a very hard hit. The airbag didn't open, and I felt this horrible blow to my chest and passed out. I was out for a few minutes but as soon as I woke up I was screaming for help and wanting to live. I was frightened. I was in such pain, and so helpless; so alone. I could feel something was terribly wrong with my body. I saw car fumes and was seized by a panic that I might burn to death. I began to scream even louder. Then I saw two migrant workers talking just outside the cab of the truck. I screamed at them *please help me*. I knew I couldn't get out of the cab by myself. I was hanging from the seat belt. The truck had fallen to its side during the crash and I was suspended by the belt. One of the men climbed into the cab and got to the back of my seat and held me. He started talking in Spanish. I never saw what he looked like. As I passed in and out of consciousness, he continued to hold me. He reached out and took a knife from the other man and cut me loose. My body shifted and the pain caused me to black out again. When I regained consciousness I saw his leg was shaking. I begged him 'Please don't leave me.' I didn't want to die alone.

"A man was peering through the sunroof and I dreamed that he pulled me out. I felt total relief and happiness. He was smiling and his eyes were sparkling and he had such a sweet face. I started floating toward him and felt I was going to be all right. But later the rescue crew assured me I had hallucinated the man because I was pulled out of the side of the cab. When I woke up again as the paramedics were cutting my clothes off, I screamed, 'My husband is David Horowitz, please call him.' I did this over and over, and then I gave them the number of your cell. Then I passed out again. When I woke I was on a gurney being run through the emergency room. I must have screamed because one of the nurses kept repeating, 'I didn't touch you, I didn't touch you.'"

Two weeks later an officer phoned April in the intensive care unit to see how she was doing. She asked him about the Hispanic man who had climbed into the cab of the truck and held her. The officer said there were actually nine people who gathered at the site, but only this man was willing to take the risk of getting in. The officer said he was shaking and crying. April asked if she could contact him now, but the officer told her that the man was probably here illegally and would not want to be found.

Her brush with death caused a change in April in the months that followed. She had always wanted to fix up the house we lived in, and over the years we had done some work on it, putting in beautiful walnut floors and upgrading other features. However, the alterations we could make were limited by financial constraints, in particular by the desire not to dig too prodigally into my pension, which would be her only financial security when I was gone.

But now she began an ambitious construction project. It started with a gutting of our master bathroom, which hadn't been touched in thirty years. She tiled the walls in white with a crackle finish and installed a vintage bathtub with brushed nickel legs. She also showed new concern for what I ate, how much exercise I did in my crippled state, and above all my attitude—that I should never give up but fight my way to live to a hundred. The climax of all this pressure was the sweetest, most satisfying words ever to grace my ears: "Don't die, don't leave me. I love my life with you, and I don't know what I would do without you."

Of course I had the same feelings for her. And of course if one of us did die, the other would go on because we have children and grandchildren, and that would keep us going, along with our friends and life's normal distractions. But it would not be the same. If I lost her, it would be like waking up to a world where there is only night and no day, and I know she feels the same.

I Would Have Saved Her if I Could

Before the accident whose wounds made working with horses out of the question, April had been continuously involved in rescues. But not all rescues succeed, and how could they? One day each of us will face a crisis where there will be no one to save us. Since that is life's end game, it is wise to prepare oneself by keeping an eye on the rescues that fail. In medieval times it was a common practice to keep a human skull close by as *memento mori* to encourage contemplation of our common fate. Working in horse rescue is pretty close.

One of April's rescue attempts involved a paint mare. The plight of the mare came to her attention through a phone call from a Hispanic man whom I will refer to as "Hector" to protect him. Hector said he had a horse that was ill, and he wanted April to save her. In all the time April dealt with him, Hector never mentioned the name of the horse, and no one at the impoverished facility where the horse was kept would volunteer the name over the weeks that followed. So April called her Pinto, because she was a paint.

After receiving Hector's call, April phoned her vet, Dr. Smith, and they went over to have a look. The address Hector provided took them to a collection of ramshackle stalls in a dirt yard behind a railroad track. As they entered the compound, they saw Hector waiting for them. He was young and neatly dressed, and he was soon joined by his two children, who had been dropped off from school. Hector told them that Pinto was the family horse. She had belonged to his father, and he had ridden her as a child. He had seen her give birth to five foals over the course of time. He said that Pinto had been pregnant the week before but he had to pull her baby out of her because it was already dead. He also told them that the situation had gotten so bad because he had been out of town for two months; he was shocked by what he saw when he came back. April didn't trust the explanation he gave her, but she was reluctant to challenge him. She learned too late how far from the truth his story was.

When Hector took them over to Pinto's stall, the horse was standing in a pit of manure, which covered the entire floor. Every stall on the property was filthy and every animal in poor condition, but none as poor as Pinto. There was a bad odor about the horse, and every part of her skeleton, like Lazarus's, was visible through her emaciated flesh. Her hair was matted, and malnutrition was causing it to fall out. There were flies all over her. It was August, and a heat wave sent temperatures outside the stall to over one hundred degrees. Inside, it felt like an oven. April thought, "God, I hate this. How can people let this happen?"

Dr. Smith went over to the ailing mare and, after completing his examination, gave her a shot to relieve her discomfort. April said to Hector, "I can take this horse and rehabilitate her and find her a new home." But Hector did not want a new home for Pinto. He said, "No, I love this horse. I want her to stay here." Then he looked at the two of them a little nervously and said, "I don't want to get into trouble."

Sometimes people tell you things without telling you. And often you are unable to hear them. This was such an occasion. What Hector was not telling April, as she would learn later, was that he owed room and board to the owner of the property, who was also Mexican and had threatened him, warning him he had better not give the horse away. The owner wanted Hector to keep Pinto because he knew Hector loved the horse, and he was going to teach him a lesson he would never forget. He was going to starve Hector's horse to death. April never found out what the owner was holding over Hector that prevented him from seeking help. Perhaps he was an illegal immigrant, which would have been sufficient. Perhaps it was something else. It didn't really matter.

April accepted Hector's word that he wanted to help Pinto. She could see that he was a decent man and a good father. And he obviously had a deep affection for a horse that had been with his family since he could remember. He seemed like someone she could trust to help Pinto get well. She focused on Pinto's suffering and what she and Dr. Smith had to do. She had no idea what was actually going on. She thought Hector was saying to her that he was afraid of being fined or prosecuted for Pinto's abuse, although that didn't really make sense. If she had thought about it, nothing did. April tried to reassure Hector to earn his confidence. "What you are doing now is the right thing to do. You were away and had no idea what was going on for two months." But Hector did.

April told Hector she would be providing hay and supplements, so that he could bring Pinto back to health. Dr. Smith then went over the medical program he would have to follow as part of Pinto's rehabilitation. April was having a hard time concentrating. The day was hot and the manure so deep in Pinto's stall that her boots just sank into it. When Dr. Smith had finished giving Hector instructions, April whispered, "Please tell him he has to clean up this place."

Dr. Smith was already seething over the conditions they had walked into. He told Hector bluntly that he had to shovel the manure out of Pinto's stall and attend to her hooves, which were in terrible shape. They were already so overgrown they made it difficult for Pinto to move. April told Hector she would pay for a farrier. But he said, "That's great but it won't be necessary. The owner of this property is a farrier, and he will take care of it." She was shocked to hear this. If the owner was a farrier, why hadn't he taken care of Pinto before she reached this state? The whole scene disgusted her. She said, "I can come back tomorrow and help you shovel the manure. I will help you give Pinto a bath." But Hector said, "Don't worry about it. I'll get it done. You've already done so much already."

April's heart was so full at what she had seen that she didn't want to leave until she had done something to alleviate Pinto's suffering. But Dr. Smith called her over and said, "April, look around you. You are the only female here. This place can be pretty dangerous. Haven't you noticed all the beer cans and alcohol bottles lying around? I don't think it's a good idea." So they left together.

Over the next weeks, April and Dr. Smith called Hector several times. Each time he assured them that Pinto was doing great and her health was improving. "She's putting on weight. No worries." He even sent April a thank-you card. When she asked him, "Did you get Pinto's food?" He assured her, "Everything is going really well. Don't worry."

Soon after the call, April and her assistant were in the neighborhood picking up pellets and feed at the local tack store for her rescue horses. While tending to her business, she had a sinking feeling which at first she couldn't put her finger on. Then she realized what it was. She looked at her assistant and said, "We have to turn around. I have to look in on a horse named Pinto."

The heat wave had continued, and it was sweltering outside. She was hoping Hector had seen to Pinto's hooves and that she was outside in the air, where she could breathe. But she had an intuition that something was terribly wrong. When they arrived at the dilapidated stalls, her assistant was a little frightened. She had never been in such a place. April reassured her, "Don't worry, I've done things like this before. I know it looks bad, but I have to see that Pinto's okay." In her heart she just knew she wasn't.

As they approached the buildings the first thing that struck April was that the stalls were in the same filthy condition as when she had left them. Then she saw a Hispanic man standing in the yard between them and the stalls. It was the owner. He looked disturbed as their truck approached. April leaned out of the window of the cab and said to him, as firmly as she could, "Where is Hector's horse?" He didn't answer and averted her eyes. He put his head down and in a vigorous motion waved her to leave. But she was not about to go without seeing Pinto. She jumped out of the truck and walked right past the owner and over to Pinto's stall.

When she opened the door, her heart sank. It was like opening a blast furnace. The heat just came over her in waves. There was poor Pinto lying in piles of her own manure. Flies swarmed around the filth and coated her face and body. April had never seen anything like it. Pinto's tongue was hanging out and her eye that was not buried in the manure was open. Her lips were moving and April realized the horse was trying to get some kind of moisture, and she realized, too, that she had come too late.

Pinto was lost. She knew now that Hector had lied to her, and none of the many people who were around the barns had bothered to call for help. Now Pinto was beyond help. All that was left was to phone Dr. Smith and ask him to come over to ease Pinto out of this life that had been so cruel to her. All April could do was to sit with Pinto, and hose the flies off her body and brush away those that had gathered around her eyes. She got some grains and carrots and tried to feed her, and did whatever she could to comfort her.

She began talking to Pinto. She told her that she had been a good horse, which she had; she had served the family she was part of well. She didn't deserve this abuse. April told her that where she was going now it would be comfortable and clean. Where she was going the heat would be gone and the manure too. And there would be no more flies to bother her.

After a while Dr. Smith arrived and gave Pinto the shot that took her out of this world and the hell that men's cruelty had created for her. Through her tears April saw that Pinto was at peace at last.

All of us should have someone like this to help us pass over the bridge from this life and its injustices into whatever lies beyond. All of us should have someone to love us at the end.

Don't Cry for the Horses

After Pinto was put down, April tried to get the authorities to step in and do something about the hell-hole that had swallowed her. But the law moves slowly, and as she discovered, in the cases of abused horses often not at all. In the days and weeks that followed she learned how hard it was to get justice for a gentle creature like Pinto. Her abusers had won.

Almost a year later, April stopped by the place. The filthy stalls behind the railroad tracks had been shut down by the authorities for other violations. When she drove over the tracks, she saw two big signs in Spanish that read "Do Not Enter." Ignoring them, she parked her truck and walked around to the back of the property. The place was still filthy and brought back horrible memories, as she knew it would. The cars that used to be parked around the stalls were all gone. The stalls themselves were open and empty. She breathed a sigh of relief on seeing them. No more horses would be tortured here.

She went over to where she had found Pinto. The stall door was shut. The manure was still there but it had dried and looked like the detritus of a distant past. Pinto was no longer there; she was finally safe. The site of her torment was vacant and the grounds were overgrown with weeds. It was a scene of broken down, empty barns that should never have been. April looked skyward and said, "Thank you, God." She felt it was payback, however small, for the torture of Pinto and her little foal. She felt a little bit of peace come into her heart.

But she would never really be free of the memories of what happened to Pinto. Each time she pictured that place her heart was flooded with emotions and memories from her own childhood as a little girl lost and alone. She thought of the children and horses whom no one would come to save. She could not get it out of her head that she had failed Pinto. She thought of how Pinto had lain in that foul-smelling, blistering stall, swarmed by flies, helpless and alone, waiting for someone to pick her up. And how when she had come it was too late.

She could no longer do anything for Pinto, but she could try to prevent a similar fate for others. She put together a campaign to tell the people who lived on those ramshackle lots and on as many ranches as she was able to reach that when they see horses suffering, they can make a call for help and not get in trouble. My grandson Jules was working for Heart of a Horse, and April asked him to compose a brochure to inform people of the law. It was called *Keeping Horses Safe: A Guide to Identifying Horse Abuse and What to Do When You See It*. The brochure described the signs of abuse, quoted the California Cruelty to Animals Law, and urged people to phone animal control authorities and humane officers whenever they saw an animal being abused. Jules found a beautiful poem by an anonymous poet to put on the back of the brochure. It has a basic life wisdom that moves me whenever I read it.

Don't Cry for the Horses

Look up into the heaven
You'll see them above.
The horses we lost,
The horses we loved.
Manes and tails flowing.
As they gallop through time.
They were never yours.
They were never mine.
Don't cry for the horses,
They'll be back some day.
When our time is gone,
They will show us the way.
Do you hear that soft nicker?
Close to your ear?
Don't cry for the horses,
Love the ones that are here.

A Charmed Life

In my autobiography, *Radical Son*, I described my painful
discovery that the Black Panthers, who had been idolized by
the left and whom I considered my comrades, were a murder-
ous gang. They had killed not only Betty Van Patter but many

others, including those who had no one to speak up for them. I described the effect of this on me in a brief sentence: "I had come to the end of everything I had ever worked for in my life." Over the next few years, the inner turmoil triggered by this event led to the breakdown of my marriage and presented me with a daunting task: how to put my life back together without the moral compass that had guided me until then.

In the crisis that followed the divorce, it was my mother who came to my support, providing the down payment on a modest but attractive one-bedroom home in the same neighborhood where my children resided. I could not possibly have afforded this myself. I was approaching forty, had no savings, no job, and no prospect of one. I didn't know how I was going to move forward. Still, I was proud that these calamities had not crushed me, and that I was even thinking of moving forward.

At this point my parents came out to the West Coast. I described their visit in *Radical Son*: "My parents came out in the summer, as they usually did, and I showed them my new house. It was filled with a morning light, and summarized my sense that I had turned a corner. I had survived my trials and was beginning to pick myself off the floor and come back. I didn't know what I was going to do, but I knew I had to take the bad that had happened to me and make it work for good—first for myself, and then for others in danger of falling into the same black hole. When my parents and I had completed the little tour of the house, I asked my father what he thought. He paused for a moment and said: 'You lead a charmed life.'"

At the time, this struck me as a statement of my father's usual disconnect from my reality, with not a little resentment thrown in over my mother's gift. But now that many years have gone by, his words have taken on a different meaning. Did I lead a charmed life? I could have been killed by the Panthers, since killing people who got in their way was what they did. After Betty's murder and my divorce, I could have fallen into a chasm from which I might never have emerged because of the betrayals of those I had considered my friends and the collapse of my guiding faith. I could have been killed by the gangbangers I hung out with in Compton where I was doing magazine stories in the early '80s. I could have died from the blood clot following my botched operation. But I didn't.

You can look at your life and rack up the losses, or you can count your blessings. I am missing a daughter who was a beautiful soul, and I can never get her back. At age seventy-five, I have been felled by an incompetent scalpel and condemned to months of neuropathic pain and uncertainty as to when if ever I will feel whole again. My wife was nearly killed less than a year ago and is still in pain and incapacitated from the crash. Because of my writings and ideas, an army of haters is eager to distort my words and my life and do me damage whenever and wherever they can. And yet I have so many blessings to count—a loving life-mate, amazing children, animals I adore, hundreds of thousands of supporters of my work, and friends to confound the haters. I see now that my father was right. I do lead a charmed life. To appreciate this, I needed only to embrace the good and bury the bad.

An Interlude at Sinai

On a bright fall afternoon, April and I drove to the Mount Sinai Cemetery Park in Simi Valley and bought two tombs for ourselves. The cemetery is situated in a nook of the Santa Susana Mountains, a green oasis at the opposite end of the valley from its most famous institution, the Ronald Reagan Presidential Library. The tombs we selected are located in a section called the Caves of Abraham, where vaults are available with stylish granite facings in greens and reds and sandstone colors, bordered in gold. In brochures and placards, discreetly placed, the park authorities convey their intention to memorialize the Holocaust and the six million who perished, as though this were a kind of eternal destiny of the Jews. I could not help but visualize a future in which Muslim *Jihadists* came to dig up and desecrate the Hebrew dead, including April (who is not a Jew) and me.

We purchased these gravesites with no expectation of imminent demise, although in the context of this life the adjective "imminent," as we had recently learned, can be quite flexible. It had been only a year since April had come within a hair's breadth of the end of her life, and every time we stepped into a vehicle we were conscious that a split second was all that might separate us from a terminal event. On the other hand, far from being morbid, we treated our tour of the gravesites as something of a lark, with April inducing me to photograph her clowning at her tomb site so she could send the photo to family for a laugh.

The primary factor that impelled us to close an uncertainty in our future was the desire to take care of details that could be overwhelming for the survivor when the day actually arrived. April, who was the likely candidate for this role, felt she would have to do something for my many supporters who would want to attend my funeral and honor my work. It would be trying enough for her without having to locate a final resting place, particularly one such as this that came with a large chapel. Since April wanted to be near me through this journey too, she was happy with the double tombs that we found available.

But what started out as a convenience, a tying up of at least one loose end, turned out to be something else for both of us. The idea of knowing the end of our stories proved comforting. Mount Sinai was a beautiful environment with a serenity that fit its purpose. As we walked the grounds of what we knew would be our final home, we felt relief. Although we planned to live many years more, knowing where we were going was an unexpected gift that helped to put us at peace.

The Time Is Now

For many years of our marriage one of my concerns was how to provide for April's future when I was gone. It principally grew out of the gap in our ages. Although I have a pension, which has accumulated capital over the years, there will not be enough in it to provide her with an income that would allow her to keep the ranch for the years she can expect ahead of her. I can't envision a future for her that would not force her to live in reduced circumstances. So I assumed the role of gatekeeper for our savings and tried to protect this capital any time she had a project that required us to draw on it.

I was unsuccessful in holding the line when Jon and Kathleen got married and April decided that we should hold the wedding on our lawn. In her mind, this required a substantial landscaping process that included terracing the lawn and taming its wilder aspects, building a gazebo where the ceremony could take place, and paths that the bridal entourage and guests could navigate with ease. How could I oppose a mother's plans for the young man I looked on as a son? In the event, the wedding was one that everyone would remember. But it was also costly.

I had to admit that the benefits of her investment extended well beyond the wedding. The terraced lawn she created with the plot of roses at the break and the little wooden bridge to cross over affords me one of my great pleasures whenever I sit nestled on the rim of it in one of the rockers on our porch. Maybe it is just age, but taking in the ordinary glories of gardens and trees and the green of lawns is something I look forward to every day.

Nonetheless the ambitious project did reduce our savings and was a blow to my plans for her future. Moreover, it was only the beginning, as she moved on to remodeling the master bathroom. When the work on this project was completed, at just about the time my unfortunate encounter with the surgeon took place, April began to move into high gear in her internal beautification plans. She bought a saltwater tank with a magical coral reef to place in the sitting room, put elaborate cabinets in the guest room, shuttered the windows and painted the room white. Then she transformed the little office at the end of the hall with cabinetry and a desk, so for the first time I had a space for the household business that was organized and accessible. Then she added to the office a sewing machine and sewing desk so that she could do quilting and work alongside me. Then she redid the little bathroom just off the office, taking out the bathtub and putting in a shower with small multi-colored stones for a floor.

When we settled on the date for the party that was going to celebrate our return to life, she moved outside and put a new face on the front entrance to the house with a glass-paneled front door and a porch and pathway refinished in bronze flagstones from Canada and Arizona; she ordered new classic carriage doors for the garage and started work on cabinetry and a laundry room in the interior. She re-landscaped the front yard, planting statues of children and horses and cutting away trees to open up the space. She hired a crew to construct a "rock garden," which looked more like an open air temple, with the same beautiful flagstones and boulders, a water fountain, and a place to sit shaded from the sun. From this perch you could look out on the house and horse arena and take in the towering trees on our property and the mountains beyond. Then she put in a fire pit and barbecue and acquired a classy set of patio furniture on which we could dine in the country evenings. And not least or last, she had a garden designer plant hundreds of succulents and flowers and two flaming red crepe myrtles, re-composing the face of our house and its environs. And all this was only a preface to the remodel—really the reconstruction—of the half of the house where the kitchen and dining room were located, removing walls, raising ceilings, and installing fine cabinetry to create an elegant new home for us.

All this capital-intensive activity was contrary to the long-held concerns she had expressed about her financial security. It was not so much the amount of money we had to take out of our savings to finance the projects, although that was considerable. It was the principle, the discipline we had agreed on which she was now throwing to the winds. Although I expressed concern, I didn't put up any real opposition to the new projects. I hesitated at first because she was still so ill and in so much pain from the accident. But when each new tile and fixture and plot of greenery produced such looks of happiness, I could hardly say no.

It was only over time, as each transformation of our environment took place, that I began to see what she was doing and began to connect it to the accident and the new attitude that had emerged from it. She had apparently thought about those last things she always dreaded and refused to face but had come to an entirely different conclusion. Even as I was mulling these thoughts in my head, she embarked on yet another new project. Because my gate-keeping job was almost a reflex, despite what I knew, and all the other projects I had let pass, I tried to rein her in and get her to reconsider the course she was taking. She was using up the seed corn on which her future without me depended.

I will never forget the moment I said this, or the reaction that followed. We were standing in the hallway just outside our bedroom door. She took a step toward me and placed her arm on mine. Then she looked at me intently and said: "You think you're going to live forever, but a day will come when death puts its arms around you, and grabs you, and *bam* you're gone. You're going to be dead one day. I'm going to be dead. So let's enjoy it while we're here. Let's be happy."

At first I wondered if this wasn't a euphoria born of despair. Perhaps she had come to the conclusion that she was going to die or that she would want to die if I did. But then I reflected on the way she had justified these expenditures as investments in the value of the house, as though she were enhancing its sale price. I had dismissed these arguments out of hand because the housing market had been down for years and our house was well under water. From an investment standpoint her optimism didn't make sense. But then I received a call from a mortgage banker who wanted me to refinance the house because he thought it was ready to bring its original price. I had not paid much attention to the market recently because it had not changed significantly for so long. But this news put a new face on the matter. If the housing market was coming back we would still not profit from the investment we were making in the house but might have a chance to recoup some of it, and if we were really lucky call it a wash.

But there was also the possibility that the market would not come back, that it would crash as many were warning, and where would we be then? There was no way to know the future and where it would go. What I did know was that our home was looking dramatically different, more beautiful and inviting than ever. And it was *this*, not the monetary calculations that lay behind it all. It was April's determination that we should make the years still ours as joyful as we could.

Life is a gamble, a series of plays; you win some and you lose others, and there are no guarantees of which way it will go. I liked what my wife had said, and all she had done to back it up. I liked her readiness to take a chance—a big chance—and to go with her dreams. Any way you looked at it, the time we were going to have together was diminishing. We were very much in love, and making the most of what we had left was a good gamble. *Carpe diem.* It was a play I could certainly get behind, and I was grateful to April for the courage she showed in making it.

A Walk in the Sun

A walk is a basic human activity, an assertion of self. It is a matter of putting one foot in front of the other (if you are able) to say: this piece of the earth is mine, at least for the moment; mine to survey, to do my strut, to take my stand.

Seven months have passed since I lost the use of my left foot and was confined to bed and wheelchair. The slow mending of the nerves has reached a point where I am walking with confidence and a positive attitude. The pain along the sciatic ridge of my foot is mainly gone, though each step carries some pain when I stretch the still frozen muscles in my ankle and calf. I test myself to see how long I can walk without tiring or without my foot swelling to where the pressure becomes severe. I try to do a little more each day and can walk reasonable distances in the face of reasonable difficulties. For exercise I go up the driveway, which is a 20 percent incline about the length of a football field, with a row of shimmering olive trees, which April planted, on one side, and towering palms on the other, until I reach the white mailbox and turn around.

I am still walking with a cane but see it now as adding style to my gait. I have exchanged the one I originally picked up in a medical supply store for a wooden one with a fancy crook. I have already danced on my beleaguered foot and will do so again at every chance that presents itself. As long as I have breath, nothing is going to stop me from being in the world and making the most of it.

Sometimes I will take the Chihuahuas with me. With only one free hand, I don't put them on leashes. But they are pretty obedient, for which I am grateful since I cannot chase after them. The auburn Lucy is the most headstrong of the three. Ignoring my commands, she runs off into the neighbor's yard. Lucky, the little white one with the missing front leg, hippity-hops beside me and is the most responsive of the lot, perking his head up when I call him, then bounding toward my outstretched arm. The black and white spot, Jake, and the deer Chihuahua, Abby, run on ahead but do so respectfully, allowing me to retrieve them at the top and turn them around. Then we all go down the driveway to catch up with Lucy near the bottom.

Often April and I take these walks together, bringing the boxer Merry along with us. These walks are pure happiness for me, and they encourage the thought that the more I push myself and the further I go the sooner I will be back to health. In seven months I have advanced from immobility to mobility and re-entered the world from which I was removed. As we walk, I take in the mountains around the house, and as we go higher the panoramic views of the valley below. I breathe the sea air that floats in from the Pacific and lift my face to the western sun. This is the pleasure of life, and I am part of it again.

Sometimes I grow misty in my walks when I think back over the years and remember the people I loved and the times I failed them. No regret is greater than these memories, salted by the wisdom of hindsight. I should have been a better husband and father and friend. I want to believe that the man I am now would have done better. But while my thoughts can travel back in time, I cannot. Consequently, there is little I can do with these regrets other than use them as an inspiration to be kinder and more understanding toward those I love in the days that remain.

All our journeys lead to diminishing returns, and there is no way to make it different. My desire now is that April and I will still have many years to enjoy the home she is re-making.

If I should go before her, I hope its value will rise to the point where it becomes the nest egg I failed to produce for her. The lesson I draw from all this is captured in a simple homily my daughter-in-law Felicia passed on to me: "The tragedy is not that we die. The tragedy is that we take so long to live."

I often wish I had April's readiness to relish the life in front of her. Yet with her example as inspiration, there is a sense in which I do. However skeptical I may be at first, I am drawn by her passions until, before I know it, I am in the moment and enjoying it to the full. Once I have nestled into the luxurious leather chair or taken a spin on the get-along scooter I am ready to go, grateful to have had someone to push me over the edge.

When I look at the life receding behind me, I feel gratified to have composed a body of work reflecting what I have witnessed and learned; I take pride in the belief that it is good work and may be of some use to others. I am surrounded now by family and friends, and blessed in both. I have not forgotten those last thoughts that were the focus of my dour reflections at the start of this memoir. I accept that all I have loved and worked for may indeed vanish forever. But I am at a point in my passage where it no longer matters. What matters to me is this: I have lived as fully as I was able, I have produced wonderful children and am married to a woman with a zest for living and the heart of an angel, and I am looking forward to my next walk.

Acknowledgments

An early version of this text was read by four friends, Peter Collier, Stanley Fish, Norman Podhoretz, and Walter Isaacson. Each responded with challenging questions, which I attempted to answer, and critical observations, which I attempted to address. Whether I was successful in their eyes or not, their prodding enriched the resulting text, and for that I am deeply grateful. My editor Tom Spence read the manuscript carefully and with a literary eye that measurably improved it. My publisher Marji Ross gave me all the support that an author could want.

I want to thank my children and their mother, Elissa, for allowing me to invade their privacy and write about them, and also my sister Ruth. And of course my wife April who has provided me with a happiness in age that we all wish for but don't always get.

PIPER PERISH

KAYLA CAGAN

CHRONICLE BOOKS
SAN FRANCISCO

Library of Congress Cataloging-in-Publication Data
Names: Cagan, Kayla, author.
Title: Piper Perish / by Kayla Cagan.
Description: San Francisco : Chronicle Books, [2017] | Summary: Piper Perish and her two friends, Kit and Enzo, have long planned on getting out of Houston and going to art school in New York City together, but halfway through their senior year Enzo breaks up with her at a dance in the most public, spectacular, and embarrassing manner possible—and suddenly Piper is faced with a series of life and relationship changing events that threaten her dream. Identifiers: LCCN 2016026546 | ISBN 9781452155838 (alk. paper) Subjects: LCSH: Art students—Juvenile fiction. | High school seniors—Juvenile fiction. | Dating (Social customs)—Juvenile fiction. | Best friends—Juvenile fiction. | Families—Texas— Houston—Juvenile fiction. | Houston (Tex.)—Juvenile fiction. | CYAC: Artists—Fiction. | High schools—Fiction. | Schools—Fiction. | Dating (social customs)—Fiction. | Best friends—Fiction. | Friendship—Fiction. | Family life—Texas—Houston—Fiction. | Houston (Tex.)—Fiction. Classification: LCC PZ7.1.C26 Pi 2017 | DDC 813.6 [Fic] —dc23 LC record available at https://lccn.loc.gov/2016026546

Manufactured in China.

Hand lettering by Luke Choice.
Illustrations by Maria Ines Gul.
Design by Amelia Mack.
Typeset in Prensa.

10 9 8 7 6 5 4 3 2 1

Chronicle Books LLC
680 Second Street
San Francisco, California 94107
www.chroniclebooks.com

For my mother, who gave me a watch

and

For Josh, who gave me time

JANUARY

It was official: I was blind.

At least that's what I thought until Kit rolled over and helped me pluck my puffy eyes apart. "I told you not to wear false eyelashes in bed," she said.

I started crying all over again and pouted at her.

"Just help me unstick my whole face. My eyeballs hurt!"

"It's not your fault," she said. "It's freaking Enzo." (That's why she remains my best friend and I will love her forever and ever because she always knows just what to say and also she saw the whole freaking thing happen.)

"I have eyelash glue on my eyeballs."

"That's impossible, and even if you did it would be dry by now, not wet. Does it feel like glitter?"

I nod.

"Your eyes are all big and gluey and have gold glitter stickered on 'em because New Year's Eve sucked, except for I finally made out with French Marcel, until we like, almost passed out. But," she added, "that was before I saw the very worst breakup of all times."

I couldn't even begin to talk about it because my eyes hurt and my heart hurt and I refused for it to be true. Because this is not how my senior year will end. I'm not going through spring semester or the rest of my life without Enzo. Did he completely forget about New York? Is he really assuming Kit and I will go without him?

Andy Warhol said, "Everyone winds up kissing the wrong person goodnight."

Once again, he knows everything. I have to wonder: What would Andy do right now? How would he deal? Would he paint? Because that's all I want to do right now. That, and throw up.

1/2 9:41 pm

Having life explained to me at the 610 Diner rivaled every-thing, especially by someone as incompetent as Marli. Kit took me for Diet Coke and mashed potatoes and gravy. She ordered her regular tater tots and ranch dressing. We expected Nadia to come back with our order and surprise, there was Marli. I thought she'd be with STD Ronnie today, thought it was her day off, but of course, I am most definitely not my sister's keeper

2

and I don't even have an idea of when she goes back to college. Her winter break is like 6 months long, which is so stupid considering it never snows in Texas, everyone knows that.

"Well, if it isn't Angsty Warhol and Etsy Betsy," Marli said as she flung our food at us. "Hi, poseurs. Nadia didn't tell me <u>you</u> were sitting in my section."

"We thought it was HERS," Kit said and Marli said, "Shut up, KATRINA."

Kit asked her if she'd picked up any new STDs since she's been home and I coughed into my drink.

"You look like shit, Piper. What's the matter? Disappointed with another one of your arts and crafts projects? D-I-Y turn a little D-I-E?"

I looked up at her, wishing my sister would just be cool for once.

"Enzo broke up with her," Kit said.

Marli stepped back.

"Pipsqueak."

Marli had not called me that since I was 7.

"Pip, that sucks."

My eyes started watering, maybe from the leftover eyelash glue, maybe from Marli, and I turned my head to look out the window so she couldn't see my face. It was confusing whenever Marli was nice to me. A trick. In the parking lot, a family wearing cowboy hats was squeezing out of the cab of a truck, waddling toward the front door.

"Pip."

"She heard you," Kit interrupted.

"What happened? Maybe I can help," Marli said.

"You thought Ronnie contracted crabs in Galveston . . . from the beach," Kit said. "You. Definitely. Can't. Help." I almost choked on my straw, snorting.

"So much for New Year's resolutions," Marli said. "I was trying to be nice, you little shits."

Nadia called Marli over before we could say anything, which was a relief. I could eat my mashed potatoes in gloomy peace. I guess it's cool Marli has a job to come back to during winter break so she can have drinking money for next semester, but I wish she would leave for good. She always has just the right amount of miserable in her to make me feel miserable, too. So when she's nice, I can never really trust her. It is trick or treat all year round with her.

"Is it my hair?" I asked Kit, checking my reflection in the restaurant window. I leaned my head against the back of the booth seat and sucked in my cheeks. I used to have long dark brown hair like everyone in my family. Now it is short, like Andy's. And silver platinum-blond, like Andy's. And it looks better with black T-shirts, like Andy's. Even writing in my journal feels freer, being more like Andy's. When I go to NYC with Enzo and Kit, I will make art, as important as Andy's. And I will finally be away from Marli and be happy.

"It's definitely not your hair," Kit said. "It's his eyes. He's short-sighted. He can't see the future."

Marli delivered a Diet Coke refill to the table and said, "It's not his eyes, Stupid. It's his peen."

Kit and I both gave her death glares. I didn't want to discuss the insides of Enzo's pants with anyone, especially Marli, over a plate of mashed potatoes.

"That's what I've heard from the whole baseball team," Marli said. "And the football team, too."

"Still hanging out in the high school locker rooms?" I said. "I guess some habits don't change." I was being nasty but who cared. "And even though it's none of your beeswax, for your information, Enzo is not gay. When are you ever going to understand the difference between homosexual and creative?"

"When will YOU, Pipsqueak?" Marli asked, and walked to another table.

"A gay guy wouldn't break up on New Year's," Kit said. "And besides, Enzo's Italian. He's got too much . . . style . . . class . . . for that."

"His parents are Italian," I reminded her. "He's just a Texan like the rest of us."

I felt my throat get all lumpy, the reminder of how much I hate living here. I mean, I don't hate Houston. It's just wrong. Everything is wrong when you're in the wrong place, the wrong time, the wrong decade.

"We won't be Texans for too much longer. We'll be New Yorkers before the end of the year!"

My head was throbbing. I could feel the beats in it. "So like, are we all supposed to just be friends now? It has to be the three of us, but . . . he's just royally screwing this up! We've been planning this since freshman year. What does this breakup even mean?"

"It means we'll figure it out."

"Are you sure?"

"All for one and one for all," she said, clinking her coffee against my Diet Coke. Then she sat up and threw her shoulders back and adjusted her black horn-rimmed glasses and dougied her soft, springy spirals, which made me smile even though I didn't feel like it.

"C'mon, dance a little."

"I don't wanna," I said. The music was bad.

"Then I'll have to bust it for two." She jumped from our booth and moonwalked in front of the table over to the pie counter. She propped a "Soda Jerk" cap onto her head, pulling it over her eyes, Michael Jackson–style.

"What are youuuuuuu looking at?" Kit said, dancing and pointing at the diners who were checking her out.

"Not much," mumbled an old dude at the counter. "Just a fool."

That made Kit freestyle back into her dougie, dance harder, like she was actually going to win him over. This is why I love her.

I left $20 on a $15.43 check on the table.

At least Marli can't say I don't tip.

1/4 1:45 pm

I called him this morning. I don't know what I was thinking. Here's the stupid message I left for him:

"Enzo, it's me. We need to talk. Whatever I did, I'm sorry. And I know you didn't mean what you said. I love you. You know that, right? We're still meant to be together. You and me and Kit and New York. We can't mess up THE PLAN. Call me."

Ugh.

I went with Mom to the grocery store because I couldn't sit around just waiting for him to call.

"We're not drinking soy milk anymore," Mom announced. "The clinic's now saying there's not enough calcium in soy milk to help with bone strength. With all of the fractures during football season, I think there's something to it. Do you know how many of your classmates I've already seen? Besides, dairy milk isn't going to hurt you. Maybe it will even help you put a few pounds on, which would be good. You're looking a little too skinny these days. Also, soy is too damn expensive right now." She finally paused.

"Why are you so quiet?"

I shrugged.

"Uh-oh," she said. "What's wrong? You love soy milk. Talk to me."

"Wrong," I said. "I don't love soy milk. Soy milk is just a thing. I love people."

"Oh, no. Here we go. Have a fight with the boy?" Mom asked, picking up the soy milk and rereading the carton.

"I guess." I shuffled sideways to the cart and leaned down on the handle. She patted my back.

"My girls always have the worst breakups."

I didn't look at her.

"C'mon, you. Let's shop this out. Spill the beans."

"I can't," I said.

"Lorenzo's always been . . . self-centered, you know," she said.

I lifted my head to see she'd loaded the cart with chocolate soy milk.

"This isn't a week to give up the hard stuff." She winked at me.

Then I told her everything.

1/4 7:27 pm . . . .

Wasn't hungry for dinner so I just had PB&J. Mom and Dad are at a movie now. OK, so back to today, breaking it down for Mom.

"When you left the house, everything seemed fine," Mom said, unloading the groceries. "Even though the two of you were dressed like vampires going to a funeral in all that black, you still looked pretty cute. Though, coral really is your color."

I had to remind Mom that wasn't the point.

"It was just a little excessive," Mom said. "You two were dressed to the nines!"

Kit and I worshipped the seniors who started the NYE Dance tradition when we were freshmen. They were total geniuses. Extra dances? Extra outfits!

Enzo had picked me up that night and brought me a silver-sprayed corsage. We respected the New Year's Eve party theme, Everything Silver Must Turn Bold. We had painted our nails silver and I added silver streaks to my already silver-white-gray hair and he was wearing the Gaultier knockoff.

"We had to look good, Mom."

Enzo, Kit, and I had talked about how the dance committee was going to deliver us a version of Andy Warhol's first Factory, which was called the Silver Factory.

"Hello! We were basically in New York in the 1960s!"

"That's a bit of a stretch. Besides, didn't Andy Warhol and his friends do a bunch of drugs? I don't think he's such a great role model for you guys." She brushed her fingers through my hair. We were sitting on the porch at this point. Mom had insisted sweet tea would make the whole thing seem less bad, which I didn't want to admit was true, but was.

"The theme was BOLD," I said. "Why not think bolder and bigger? It wasn't a school dance. It was like . . . the beginning of our lives."

She smirked at me.

"Anyway, on our way over to the dance I thought everything was fine, but now I realize he was in a totally pissy mood. When I asked him what was wrong, he said we were a bunch of conformists and then I asked, 'Don't you remember why we're going?. . . for like, seeing what the Factory might have been like?'"

"I call bullsoup, honey. You just wanted to go to the dance," Mom said.

I couldn't explain to Mom that Enzo and I weren't just going as seniors, but for artistic exploration as well. She wasn't getting it. I stuck to the basics.

When we got there, Kit was totally holding court with the little freshmen who love her. Kit calls them her Little Fresh Fishies, which is kind of adorbs. I went to say hi to her. Enzo went to pee.

"What's up?" Kit asked, covered in metallic polka dots. We kissed each other on the cheeks, two times, the French way. Kit's girls watched us carefully.

"What's up, Piper?" one of the freshies asked.

"Checking out the scene."

"Your feathery eyelashes are wicked. How'd you . . . ?"

"Kit made 'em," I said.

"Aaaaaaauuuuhhh, ooooooh," they exhaled.

Kit twisted her arm into mine and leaned her head into my shoulder and said, "Take a picture" and we posed like we were the freaking cutest. The girls whipped out their phones to catch us, no filters required.

"One day," I told them, "those photos will be worth a lot. Andy would have silkscreened us." Then we were off to the table where the dance committee was handing out silver glow sticks.

Kit asked, "What did Enzo decide to wear tonight?"

"He's calling it Trips, Tops, and Tails but I'm calling it 15 Minutes of Fabulous and it's amazing as usual." I reminded Mom of the details. Silver chain mail fitted top, black cropped trench coat over it, skinny black jeans, black hair spiked up and through a silver top hat, a reverse skunk he calls it, silver Docs with black laces. He'd sprinkled silver powder over the both of us after we got out of his car, and told me, "No matter where we stand the light will reflect off us, like we're stars fallen to the ground."

We pulled up next to him and I went to kiss him and caught his cheek.

"You look good in silver," he said. First compliment he had given me all night.

"Wait a minute," Mom said to me now. "He didn't compliment you until then?"

"We're post-compliment," I said to her.

She shriveled her nose at me.

"Bullsoup again. You're 18 years old. You are not over compliments."

"Kind of," I said. "So, DJ Anonymous—that's DJA, Ms. Adams's son—was spinning and everyone started to move and Kit was already in the middle of the dance floor, her minions around her, shooting looks at French Marcel."

"The exchange student?" Mom asked.

"Yeah, she's all into him." Kit was dancing exactly like her idol, Janelle Monáe (she learned all her moves), except somehow even cooler. It's her weird superpower that even when's she being silly-stupid-funny, Kit's kind of incredibly hot. She's like the girl who should be head cheerleader, but chose the life of HEAD EVERY-FREAKING-THING ELSE instead. She's a crockpot of crazy, as Mom would say, but in a good way.

"Anyway, Kit was dancing and I was about to go over to her, but then Enzo put his hand on my waist so I turned and kissed him and was like, 'Let's dance! Let's dance in the new year!'"

There were 7 minutes to go according to his spiked silver watch. I wriggled my eyebrows at him the way he liked and he said no. He stood still and his eyes were watery and red and I said, "We can be pretentious asses later but let's dance now! Look at Kit!"

"I can't dance," he said.

"Since when?"

"No, I can't dance with YOU," he said, louder than me. The way he said it . . . it was so mean. I hated telling Mom this part.

"But my outfit. It twirls like Saturn's rings!"

"I know," he said. "I'm the one who designed it!"

"Hey." I was trying to be nice. "Have you gone catatonic? Can you just talk to me?"

"NO!" He was practically shouting over the music. And then. . . .

"What?" Mom asked.

"It's so bad," I said.

"What?"

"It's so embarrassing."

"It couldn't be worse than his outfit," Mom said.

"Mom! God!"

"I'm sorry," she said. "Go on."

"He said it was about to be a new year . . . that he has to finally be him, the 'real him' . . . that he can't be who the world wants him to be."

"Uh-huh," Mom said, sipping on her tea.

"So I told him I loved him no matter what."

"Piper!" Mom said.

"Mom, but then, he started . . . he started doing this whacked-out, really crazy, dance . . . like first, he pulled out these gauzy scarves from the pockets he'd sewn into his trench coat, and he was holding them up over his eyes, like some kind of belly dancer or something, and the more he whipped them around, the more I like . . . could not stop watching. He kept dancing around the other seniors with the scarves, waving them like flags over their heads, and even though Kit was dancing with Marcel, she was trying to catch one of the scarves while it was midair, thinking he was just trying to create some trippy effect against the strobe lights and the disco ball. And of course, what Kit did, all of her little fresh fish did, too. One of them said, 'Tragic cool!' like she knew anything about being tragic or cool and held one of the scarves up to her face, smelling it! Then they all tried to catch one, waiting to see what he would do next. He had everyone's attention . . . and that's when he slowed down and grabbed one of the scarves he had dropped and looped it around his top. . . ."

"The metal one?" Mom interrupted.

"The chain mail, yeah, and he started lifting up his own shirt. It looked like he was putting on a show. I thought he was doing some kind of performance, a surprise! I thought he was doing something . . . important, maybe, like for me. People were kind of clapping . . . and whistling. But then he danced out of his pants, on purpose. Like, his pants were on the floor. He did, like, a striptease, for me and everyone else in the gym. We could all see him."

"Wait," Mom said. "Am I understanding you correctly? Did Enzo . . . did he get naked, Piper? Like streaking?"

I covered my eyes. Total embarrassment and humiliation and sadness hitting me all at once.

I'm crying again now. I need a break. More in a few. Going to take a shower.

1/4 11:34 pm

Just made some coffee. Have to get this out or I'm not going to be able to sleep tonight. OK. So obvi, Mom was freaked.

"Naked? You let him get naked in the gym?" Mom was kind of laughing and holding her cheeks at the same time. She reminded me of the person in that painting The Scream, only if it was set in our kitchen.

"Naked," I finally said. "And I didn't let him. I didn't know what to do! I thought it was a dance!"

"A dance?" Mom said, shaking her head. "That kid is nuts! I knew he was off!"

He wanted everyone to quote-unquote know the real him, he said when he was standing there . . . naked (I could hardly even think about it). And he said that I'd dragged him to the dance, he didn't want to be there in the first place, and he decided he was going to express himself. He had to be true to THE REAL ENZO, which also meant breaking up with me. But I didn't tell Mom any of that part.

14

"He's on drugs," Mom said, part question—part statement.

"Maybe," I said. "I know he's done some acid before. But not like Andy's friends. They did speed. And like, all the time."

"Piper! What the hell are you doing hanging around with him? And why do you know about what drugs Andy Warhol's friends did? Jesus!" She was both laughing and yelling at me. "Wait till I share this with Dad."

"He's not going to get it."

"He's not the only one. Do YOU get it? And you know way too much about the drug scene, kiddo!"

"Mom, everybody knows about drugs. DUH! And it's not called 'the drug scene,' there is no drug scene. Just drugs. And this whole thing is not Enzo's fault," I said. "I should have known he didn't really want to go to the dance."

"Oh, honey. None of this is your fault. What . . . how . . . did your evening end?"

"They took Enzo out of the gym, right at the stroke of midnight, the school security guards. They threw his trench coat over his . . . body. I was like, 'You never loved me,' but more like a question, and he said, 'I'm sorry, Piper, we're over,' so then I was crying, it was getting all over my gold and silver feather eye lashes and Kit came running across the dance floor screaming, 'MOTHER F'ER!'"

"Oh please, don't watch your language now," Mom said. She took one of her pills for headaches, washing it down with her sweet tea. Looked like the drug scene was right there on our porch.

"Kit pushed Enzo in the chest," I continued. "Security tried to hold her back. She tried to punch him in the face but missed his eyes and nose because he's so tall and she's so short and that's why her fingers are bandaged, were bandaged. She hit his chin."

"Oh," Mom said, "I thought that was one of Kit's new looks."

"No." I laid my head on the kitchen table.

"What a crazy."

"He's not crazy. He's just misunderstood."

Mom leaned down to my ear and pulled my chin up so she could see my face.

"New Year," she said. "New start. Let's make a No Crazies promise. No crazies?"

"No crazies," I said, hooking my pinkie with hers.

I wanted to tell her it was impossible to keep a No Crazies promise when I felt crazy myself, but promises don't seem to mean anything anymore anyway.

Going to bed now. Done.

1/6 10:33 pm

Andy said, "The idea of waiting for something makes it more exciting." It isn't exciting though. I hate waiting and I hate that I hate waiting. I've called Enzo's voice mail over and over again. It's been a Sunday of this:

"Hi it's Enzo. Leave me a <u>massage</u> and I'll get back to you. Ciao."

"Hi it's Enzo. Leave me a <u>massage</u> and I'll get back to you. Ciao."

"Hi it's Enzo. Leave me a <u>massage</u> and I'll get back to you. Ciao."

Substituting massage for message isn't funny after you hear it 36x in one day. He still hasn't called and Dad almost busted me getting a Shiner out of the fridge earlier. I told him I was bringing it to Marli because she was in her bedroom with cramps and he waved me off and said, "Good luck with that" and then I went back to my room, lay down, and waited. The <u>idea</u> of waiting may be exciting but actually waiting sucks.

In my last message to him, I said, "You may not want to talk to me about our breakup but we have to talk about New York. Don't be stupid, Enzo."

I hope he listened to it.

Looking at my palette of colors, my Pantones of pain. I can't write anymore. Time to paint.

1/7 11:14 am

Just got out of third period. He's not by his locker. He wasn't there before school started either. He can't just avoid me. The worst was that after Adams asked everyone how their holiday break was, did we do anything creative with our time/selves, which I guess is a required question by an art teacher, everybody answered the same old shit, and when class ended she asked me to stay after, because I was quiet and didn't answer her. She said—oh my freaking god I can't believe she said this—

"I heard about what happened. Are you and Lorenzo okay?"

17

"Um, how did you hear?"

She reminded me that DJ Anonymous is her son, which does defeat the purpose of being anonymous.

"So what happened?" she asked. "Are you back together now?"

"No. He won't return my calls or texts. I thought I'd see him here today, but like, he's avoiding everything. Me. Kit. School."

"He knows winter break ended, right?"

I nodded.

"Well then," she said, "he can't stay away forever. I'll let you know if he comes to 5th period. He won't miss my class."

"How can you be so sure?"

"You've never missed my class," she said. "The talent never misses."

I think she felt really good about saying that.

"Where are you supposed to be?"

"Lunch."

She gave me a gentle push into the hallway and told me to go eat.

I'm writing instead. I have zero appetite.

1/7 8:45 pm

"People should fall in love with their eyes closed" —Andy Warhol

18

Totes. Then you wouldn't have to see the one who destroyed your life over and over again.

1/8 6 am!!!

Way too early for Marli's shit. She decided that she had to drive back super early to school so she could avoid rush hour on the freeway in time for her first class, Anthropology for Amateurs (no kidding). She barged into my room at 5:30 am, WTF, because she wanted her blue T-shirt back that she swore I had and I swore I didn't and I heard her yelling all the way to the laundry room until she marched back into my room and flipped on my closet light which, HELLO, blinded me, and started rummaging through all my shit. I morning-mumbled at her to get out and she said not without my shirt, like she was some kind of war hero, and I dragged myself out of bed to where she was standing in a huge pile of my stuff, picking through it, when she pulled one of Enzo's black leather coats that I had been painting on.

"What is this?" she asked.

"Art," I said.

"This isn't yours," she said and I said, "Yeah, the jacket's Enzo's, but the paint on it is mine."

"What'd he say?"

I looked into my pillow.

"Tell me you talked to that queer duck, Pipsqueak."

"Stop sounding ignorant and no I didn't. I haven't seen him."

19

Her eyes flashed hot, like the way they used to right before she'd chase me.

"You want me to send Ronnie to talk to him?"

"Good god, no. They don't . . . speak the same language." I shivered at the thought of it. Ronnie? Enzo? World War III much?

"Oh, I think Enzo'd understand Ronnie just fine," Marli said, sneering. She plucked her T-shirt from the bottom of my floordrobe and smelled it.

"Mom must have folded it in with the rest of my laundry." I'd never wear that shirt because it has no, and I mean no, personality.

"I'll send Ronnie over," Marli said into the armpit of the shirt. "Nobody's allowed to make an ass out of you, you know?" She gave me one of her devil smiles that worked on everyone but me.

I turned in bed and tried to ignore her. Who was she to tell me that nobody was allowed to make an ass out of me? She'd made an ass out of me—all of our family really—forever. Watching her trying to be nice to me was too much work. It was too early and too late for me to try and give her a chance. I had at least 27 more minutes until my alarm was going to ring.

Now it's beeped and this is me, not asleep.

1/9 Midnight

Told Mom I was going to study with Spanish group at the library, but accidentally landed at Enzo's instead, with Kit hiding in the bushes next to me. We could see the light on in his bedroom, two shadows pacing back and forth. I could tell one was his and one looked like his dad. Definitely not his mom, since she's so short and her shadow would have been tiny in comparison. We rang the doorbell twice, but nobody came to the door, even though the shadows froze. Kit wanted to knock on his window but I held her back. We watched their silhouettes until Kit whispered, Cops! and we both ducked behind the brick wall of their house. We weren't exactly doing anything wrong. I mean, if anyone did something wrong, it was him.

I'm just going crazy because you don't love someone since middle school and then get dropped because they had like, a moment of weirdo-freakiness. Love is weird and people are weirder. Andy loved a million weirdos. He loved Edie. He loved Nico. He loved Ultra Violet. Maybe not in the same way I loved Enzo, but maybe. Kind of.

I didn't think our love was supposed to be this confusing, this kind of confusing. My heart felt like when Enzo accidentally pricked me last year, that time he was draping canary-yellow polyester for my junior prom dress. Except this isn't an accident. And it keeps stinging.

Kit reminded me of our plan: We'll graduate, this will all be over soon. We'll still go to NYSCFA in the fall. We'll both meet awesome new guys and change the art world.

I don't want to say this out loud but I do, I can't stop myself:

"I don't want to meet new guys. I want Enzo there with us. He's the reason I even decided to apply there and not the New School. And we don't even know if we're in yet. We could all be stuck here forever."

"Well, you have good backup schools," Kit said, and I told her I didn't apply anywhere else because second options are dead options and she asked Did Andy say that and I answered, No, I did.

"Besides," I added, "the deal is that we all go to New York, right? If any of us went to backup schools, they would still have to be in New York."

Kit nodded.

The cops kept cruising down Enzo's street and Kit and I ran home.

Time for Spanish homework for real.

1/11 Study Hall 2:51 pm

Kit just passed me a note that says there's a party at Jen's house tonight. Enzo is going, Jen told her. We're going. I have to wear something mind-blowing. And I can't look bloated. Periods suck.

I passed back: "What costumes shall the poor girl wear/to all tomorrow's parties. . . ."

Kit nodded at me, knew it was the Velvets, of course.

We're shopping after school.

1/12 11 am

Kit is still passed out on my floor. Her jeans are unbuttoned, and the cashmere sweater vest she bought yesterday is covered in toothpaste. Mom has knocked twice to see if we want hot chocolate but I know she's secretly just checking in on us. Both of us are wrecked and Mom probably thinks we're drug addicts now. And I know that even when Kit wakes up she isn't going to be interested in talking with me. Last night at Jen's, I kind of made up with Enzo.

I'm not totally sure where we're at but like he definitely still has feelings for me, even though he thinks we need to see other people. I know he loves me and I know he thinks he wants to see other people, but once it's just us, he'll be happy again. I think. I hope. When he's talking to me, I don't understand how he could want to be with someone else. Why would he want to hang out with me if I'm so awful?

The night started off like this. A bunch of us (Amy, Niki, Rooftop Bryan, me) were doing Jell-O shots on Jen's mom's new kitchen island. Then Enzo appeared and pulled me over by the fridge and said, "I didn't know you were going to be here."

"Of course I'm going to be here, it's JEN'S PARTY. Who doesn't come to JEN'S PARTY, right?"

"Well, I just thought after New Year's Eve you wouldn't make it," he said.

"Why not? Jen's like one of my best friends." What I wanted to say, of course, was that Jen was my friend first and hell if I'm not going to her parties, you can NOT MAKE IT to her parties, but also I wanted to see you, you haven't returned my calls, why would you break up with me like that, I'm in love with you, jerk, and you aren't allowed to break my heart like that. YOU, my best friend. YOU, my supposed soul mate.

But instead I slammed a yellow lemonade-tasting Jell-O shot and tossed the little plastic cup into the sink from where I stood. Rooftop Bryan cheered, "SCORE!" and tried to high-five me from behind the island but fell over instead. Island of Idiots.

I turned back to Enzo.

"I'm surprised YOU'RE here, frankly," I said, "I thought you were dead of something."

"What? Why?"

"You didn't answer any of my calls or my emails or anything. It's been 13 days. 13 days since you . . ."

I didn't even know what to call it. My voice was trembling, which I hated, because I knew I was going to cry when I should have been giving him the worst, meanest, most awful treatment ever. I should have slapped him in front of everyone or thrown a drink in his face like in the movies but all I could do was want him to confess it was all a mistake and notice that I had a new outfit on, a bright green angora sweater dress that looks like it was made for me even though I got it for $4.99 at Another Man's Treasure.

"Look," he said, "I listened to your messages. I still want to go to New York. And I still want to be there with you and Kit."

Everyone moved to the living room to dance and I slid closer to Enzo.

"You do?" I asked him.

Somebody in the living room yelled TURN IT UP and the music started thumping. We were alone on our own island, even if it was a kitchen island.

"You really still want to come to New York?"

He nodded.

"So what was that all about then?"

Enzo shrugged and touched my hair and told me it was the truth, partially, he thinks. He was confused, still confused.

"Me too," I said. "Really confused."

Then we both started laughing (that way that we do) and he handed me another Jell-O shot and we tapped the little plastic cups against each other and threw back our shots and he looked at me and said "If anybody gets me you do" and I said "I do, I do get you" and then he said "I'm sorry" and before he could say more I leaned in and kissed him, shutting him up for a couple of seconds at least.

We were kissing and the music pounded and Kit stumbled through the swinging kitchen door with Jen and Perry and Rooftop and they were all talking about getting more drinks and Kit saw me and I saw her and I saw her see Enzo and her mouth dropped open like she was trying to catch her breath, hand on her chest and everything.

Enzo didn't see her. I tried to shoo her away, like Stop! Don't come over here!

"You've got to be kidding me," she said.

Enzo stopped kissing me.

"Hey," Enzo said.

Kit bolted out of the kitchen. I chased after her into Jen's backyard.

"Hey!" I said, "Don't be mad at him! We're okay now!"

"You're okay now? You're OKAY? He was a total dick, Piper."

"No, we're good," I said. "And besides, you know him. He just got confused!"

25

Kit grabbed her hair like she wanted to pull it out.

"Enzo's on my shit list because he broke up with you in front of everyone and he didn't care about your feelings! And now you're kissing him because you're 'okay now'? What the hell?"

"Is this about Jack?" I accidentally said out loud and realized at that moment I am the dumbest jerk ever.

"No," Kit said calmly, "BUT THANKS FOR BRINGING HIM UP!"

She stormed away and I went back to Enzo, who was chowing down on sour cream and onion dip.

"I pissed her off," I said to him.

"Yeah, I heard."

"Well, actually, you pissed her off," I said. "You know that, right?"

I didn't want to be mad at him now that we were making up, but I couldn't help myself. He nodded and continued to eat chips and dance at the same time.

"So, we're just cool now?" I asked. "Back together?"

"Yeah. We're cool."

"Back-together-cool?"

"We're post-back-together cool. We're just us."

We moved into the living room and started dancing but didn't kiss anymore because he smelled like onions and sour cream. Nobody said anything to us about NYE, the last time we'd danced together in front of people, but everyone was also pretty wasted by that point. I felt weird, but I also felt calm. I understood Enzo; sometimes he just had to disrupt everything, including us. We were post-back-together cool, whatever that meant. I think I get it. I hope I get it.

Pretty soon the cops showed up because of a neighbor's noise complaint, and I went to find Kit, who was trying to start her car. I took the keys out of her hand.

"C'mon," I said, "you can crash at my house."

"I'm fine."

"Don't be an asshole," I said. "Leave your car here and we'll get it in the morning."

She fell out of her driver's seat and I locked the door behind her.

"You're messed up, bestie," I said.

"Look who's talking," she slurred.

So we stumbled the five blocks back to my house, instead of driving all the way to Kit's in River Oaks. We kept tripping over each other the whole time. I was kind of glad Kit was so drunk because I hated when she was mad at me. She pointed at the sky and said, "Look, it's STARRY NIGHT, GET IT. Except the stars keep moving." Then she burped and tried to cover her mouth before she threw up in the street. We stopped by the park and went to our bench so she could clean up and wipe off her mouth, just in case Mom was still awake.

"Let's just stay here. Let's just stay out all night. This is perfect," Kit said, leaning her head against my shoulder.

"My mom would kill me, you know that."

"Just text her, that's what I'd do."

"I know."

Kit's mom and my mom are totally different.

I wrapped my arm around her waist and walked us the rest of the way. Mom and Dad were asleep when we got here and we raided the kitchen. Now I'm awake and Kit's asleep and there are cookies and chips and candy wrappers all over the room. It looks like a piñata broke over my bed.

I want to sleep but I keep thinking about Enzo. If I wanted us to get back together so much, why do I feel so weird about this whole back-together-cool thing? The ceiling is spinning and so is my head and all I'm imagining is The Starry Night whirling round and round, fuzzy spiraling stars never-ending.

1/13 3:07 pm

I've called Enzo all day. I thought we were cool. He said we were cool, back-together-cool, us. We kissed. My mind keeps translating all of this to Spanish as I write it, I guess because I'm avoiding español homework. SOMOS FRESCOS. NOS BESAMOS. Everything is sadder in Spanish.

I called Kit.

"What'd you expect?"

"I expected everything to go back to normal."

"Well, it is back to Enzo's version of normal."

I said that's not cool and she said, It's the truth. Deal.

"Do you really think it's over between us?"

"You have to do what I did with Jack. Let him go and just focus on New York. Because in 8 months, we'll be there and they won't."

"Enzo still wants to go," I said.

Kit sighed.

I told her I had to go study and she said, "Don't be mad at me."

"I'M NOT!" I said.

But I was. Am.

1/15 8:57 am

What I'm wearing today:

- Mom's denim romper from her high school graduation
- The chunky turquoise Bakelite necklace Aunt Jane gave me— but as a belt!
- Pink Chuck Taylors
- 1000 bracelets that keep tink-tink-tinking
- New blue stripe in my hair, done with mascara wand. Started off as accident, totally love it.

1/16 11:08 pm

I met Enzo at the park. He said he wanted to talk to me but I told him he couldn't come over. When he asked why, I said Mom and Dad are having a fight, which is a straight-out lie because they're playing Scrabble on the porch.

So I told Mom I was going to Kit's to hang and study for a bit and she said be back by 10, so I raced to meet him and also had to race back, which didn't give me much time.

29

"Hey," he said as I came up.

His face looked pale. He was wearing the deconstructed flannel scarf I made for him out of Dad's old sleeping bag, even though it was like 70 degrees out. He looked sad to me. Wounded. Like something really bad had happened. I was scared.

"Sup?"

He patted our bench and I sat down next to him.

"It's okay," I said, "I love you, too. You don't have to apologize."

He blinked hard.

"Love means making mistakes and getting over them," I said, and took his hand. I can't believe I actually said that. I don't even know where I got it.

"Yeah, well," he said, "maybe."

"Maybe?"

"Piper," he said, "I think we can really only be friends from here on out."

I got a sharp bad feeling but tried not to let it touch me. Really, why would he ask me to meet him if he didn't want things to work out, if he didn't want me to try and fight for him?

He must have seen my face change because then he said, "I'm not for you," and leaned closer to me and repeated, "I'm not for you."

"You're wrong," I said. "We're exactly alike."

I was trying super hard not to cry at that point. Enzo dropped my hand and started pacing by the swings, pushing them as he talked.

"Piper," Enzo said, "I'm not going to New York."

"Of course you are! You'll get in. You're like the next Prada. You'll be bigger than Prada one day!"

"No, I won't. I'm not. I'm staying here. I pulled my application from NYSCFA." He pushed a swing that had come flying back hard.

"No, you didn't."

"I did."

"Is it because of me? Are you so scared to be with me that you would give up New York? Our New York?"

"No. Of course not. And I'm not scared of you."

"Then why?"

"Because."

"Because . . . ?" I wanted to push him down on the playground. I was furious.

"I just don't want to go."

"I don't believe you."

He wouldn't say anything. He was just standing there, both swings swinging at his sides.

"Where are you even going to go then?" I was so loud I scared the crickets into silence for a few seconds. I sounded like Mom and Marli getting into one of their out-of-control fights.

"I'm hoping to get into Rice," he said. So cold.

"Why the hell would you stay in Houston?" I asked. "All we ever wanted was to get out of here."

31

Again, silence.

"What about our pact? You, Kit, and me? Together Forever, The NYC 3? Remember? How long have we been saying that? Was it all just bullshit? You want to have a fashion line, or do I need to remind you of that, too? You can't do that here. We have to be in New York. Kit and I are going to be in New York!"

"You have to be in New York," he said, catching and holding a swing. "New York is about you, Piper. And Kit. Not me."

His eyeliner was making a little track down his face, like a temporary tattoo.

"Since when? Why?" I was seriously freaking out. "There's something you're not telling me." I knew it all of a sudden, he was keeping some secret.

And then he turned away from me, but I could hear him whisper.

"Philip Schultz," he said. "Philip Schultz."

"What are you saying? Philip? You?"

And Enzo said, "I've just never been around the right person . . . until Philip."

"You were around ME!" I screamed. "You kissed me! We did . . . things! Why would you be with me if you were . . . are . . ."

I couldn't say what I was thinking, which was gay. How could you kiss me if you were, are . . . gay . . . and you knew it? Why would you do that to me? Why would you do that to YOU?

"Was I just your placeholder?"

"Don't say that! Of course not," he said. "You could never just be anything. . . . I'm so sorry, Piper."

"Sorry about the dance?" I said. "Or sorry you ever kissed me in the first place?"

Enzo pushed the swing hard away from his chest.

"I don't know how else to make . . . ME . . . clear to you," he said. "How can I explain me, having some feelings for you and, but . . ."

I ran home before he could say anything more.

Everyone has been saying it. How could they see it and I couldn't? How could I not know if my boyfriend was gay? Wouldn't I be the first one to know? He sure kissed me like he was straight—at least I thought he did. What if everyone was still wrong? What if he was still wrong? What if he isn't gay at all? Coach Bryan said in health class that sexual confusion is natural. Maybe Enzo is just confused. Or maybe he isn't. Maybe it really is me. Maybe he could have liked me more if I was different, if I looked more "like a girl."

I'm looking in the mirror now. My hair, even with its blue streak, still looks like Andy's. My chin is still sharp and my eyes are still alien and too big for my face. My body is thin like Andy's, too, which I can't help. I thought by now I would have had a little more up front, like Mom or Marli, but I look pretty much like Dad through and through. I've always been the tallest girl in my classes and Dad was always pissed that I never got into basketball, but running around a sweaty court is the last thing I would want to do—ever!

I've searched myself for clues all night, fixing my hair, pushing my boobs together to try and make them look bigger. I'm not even close to a B cup, even with a push-up bra. If I looked more like a girl, maybe he would think he liked girls? Maybe because I looked like a boy, he thought he liked boys?

Every time this idea popped into my head it didn't make sense. I wore plenty of dresses, when I wasn't painting. And I knew that if someone was gay, that it was okay, it was natural, it was totally normal and fine and really who even cared? But what if Enzo HAD been straight? What if my body resembled a guy's body so much, I had confused him? What if somehow I had changed him and made Enzo gay?

FML.

1/17 6:30 am

I cried all night. Fucking Philip Schultz. All I wanted to do was throw up. Kit emailed and said we should skip today but I can't, it's Painting Partner Day. I can't stop crying. Have to get ready for school.

1/17 3:45 pm

I should be happy. I love Painting Partner Day. It's one of the things that Adams does with us outside the classroom studio each month. Our last trip was to the Rothko Chapel, which was all about meditation and shape study. I loved that place. My mind felt like it shut off and woke up there.

Today we went to paint at the Museum of Fine Arts—like my favorite place in all of Houston. We were supposed to study the James Turrell stuff, all light and space. It's one of the best parts of the whole museum. I usually love zoning out, just losing all my thoughts in the electric blue hallway, but today I felt like I was in a never-ending tunnel with nowhere to hide from the walls of cool lights. When we returned to our easels, which were set up in the museum classroom, all I wanted to do was stare. Instead I painted.

We're allowed to wear headphones when we paint, if music be our muse, Adams says, and so I slipped mine on, even though I was listening to nothing. I wanted to lose myself. The rest of the class doesn't care so much about painting and "reflection time" because art is just an elective to them—but for Sam Chang and Kit and me, it's different. I always wished that Enzo was in our class, but his schedule didn't work because of all his honors classes. Today I was happy he wasn't with us.

When I was done painting, I stepped back and examined my canvas. My fingernails were splattered with violets and blues and looked like a bouquet of irises that had been run over by a car, evidence of the last few hours. I felt like I'd had nothing to do with it.

"Damn," Adams said. "Damn. Damn. Damn."

"What do you think?"

She patted herself on her heart. "Keep going," she said. "Keep going. Tap in."

I love Adams. LOVE HER.

1/18 Lunch

"Philip Schultz?"

"Yep."

"So, they're definitely having sex. Blowies at the very least. He's in college."

35

"Kit!" I yelped. "Not helpful!"

"Sorry," Kit said, taking a bite of her tuna sandwich.

"Tell me it isn't true. Tell me it wasn't that easy for Enzo to break my heart."

"You need to eat," Kit said, handing me the other half of her sandwich. "And no, it wasn't easy for him."

"Did you know about this, too?"

"No. I swear."

"Kit."

"I promise you, Piper. You know me better than that. I would never keep a secret like that from you."

"But HE did! I thought friends, real friends, told each other the truth," I said.

"Well, he did," Kit said. "He just had really shitty timing."

1/19 10 am

Last night, Marli drove back from school to have Mom do her laundry and make French toast for her this weekend. I was supposed to hang with Kit but Mom declared it Unofficial Friday Night Family Night and so plans had to be dropped and instead I got to hear about how hard Marli's classes are—she almost puked in her anatomy class it was so gross!—how hard it is living in the dorm—the rooms are so tiny everyone is on top of everyone else!—how hard it is sharing a bathroom— with a total stranger who could be like a serial killer for all she knows!—how hard it is having a meal plan—it's prison food!,

36

and how she just wished she had her own apartment and that would make everything better, because she really just needs a safe place to study and chill. And if she had just a little more money, she could probably get her own apartment. Barf. She said this with her over-the-top sweet smile, like she couldn't believe she had just revealed all of that at once. I'm sure Mom and Dad will find a way to make her happy. God forbid Marli be unhappy.

When she finally asked me how things were between Enzo and me, Mom answered.

"They are broken up for good, thank god."

Rude much?

Then Dad said, "Now if we could only get you to break up with that Ronnie. . . ."

Mom and Dad both laughed, even though Mom said, "Not nice, Hank, you're so bad blah blah blah."

Marli smiled at Dad. Her eyes flickered at him, like her brain had just been turned on by her ears. I sat back in my seat and felt my stomach drop. Moments like this I was never wrong because my Spidey sense worked overtime around her.

"Daddy," she said. "You don't mean that."

"Well, Ronnie's fine for now." He smiled back at her. "I just want my daughters to have the best."

"The best what?"

The air shifted. I could feel it. I'll never understand how they couldn't, or wouldn't, feel it, see it, smell it like I do.

"The best lives possible," Dad said. "You know that's what we want for you."

"And you don't think I'll get that with Ronnie?" She was seriously baring her teeth. "You don't think that he loves me just for being me? We're in love with each other. He gets me. He doesn't treat me like I'm crazy. HE doesn't think I make awful decisions."

"Nobody treats you like you are crazy, babe," Dad said. "College has been good for you so far. You seem less . . . agitated. You look good." He patted her hand. Miracle. Dad's lion-taming skills had worked this time. She picked up her fork and I was relieved.

But why does Dad suddenly think college made Marli less crazy? She only appears less crazy because she isn't here all the time. Maybe he was just trying to be nice. He knows you can't tell a crazy person she's crazy or else it all just gets worse.

1/20 4 pm

Mom treated Marli and me to manicures and pedicures for "bonding time." In her words, we could all use some of her favorite TLC—Texas Lady Comforts.

Mom picked Coral by the Sea (of course, Mom's OCD, Obsessive Coral Disorder), Marli got some god-awful yellow called General Mustard's Last Stand, and I picked steel gray, Heavy Metal.

"Of course you'd pick that color," Marli said to me, twirling around the salon.

"What do you mean?"

"You're always looking at the dark side of life."

"I am not," I said.

Andrea, the manicurist, pulled down her mouth mask
and said, "Uh-huh."

"I'm not dark," I said. "I'm just me."

And Marli said, "Oh, did I say dark? I meant DORK."

She died laughing.

I shut my eyes and pretended she wasn't my sister.

"You do get a bit dramatic sometimes," Mom said from her spa
pedicure chair.

"I do not," I said. "I mean, I'm not Mary Freaking Sunshine,
but I'm not like, a rain cloud."

"Well, you're creative," Mom said. "Sensitive. It's the artistic
side of you. It's not bad, sweetie. It's okay."

"Good lord," I said. "Just because I'm not . . ."

Mom looked over her magazine at me and shot me her look that
meant <u>don't ruin this day.</u>

"Fine," I said. I went back to the rows of nail polish. I put the
Heavy Metal back in its place and picked up a bottle called
Shout at the Devil. I handed it to Andrea.

"Very dark," she said.

New York. New York. New York.

Enzo called me 3x and I didn't answer. I don't know what to say to him. I don't care if he's upset. I want him to be as upset as me. CIAO, ENZO!

Okay. So weird. So weird! So weird but good weird but still weird!!!

We were having independent drawing in Art. Adams stood behind me, watching me work, and then said she wanted to see me after class.

"What's up?" I asked after the bell rang.

"I want you to know how good you are." She took a deep breath. "And I want you to know that NYSCFA called me to discuss your recommendation."

"They called?" I asked.

"They are seriously interested in having you as an incoming student."

I jumped up and down, I didn't care how uncool I looked, and then I asked if they wanted to talk about Kit too, because I knew Adams had written her a recommendation, also.

Adams leaned forward in her chair, watching the next class come in, and said, "No. Not yet, Piper."

"But they will," I said.

"Acceptance letters arrive in March. We'll find out."

"Kit has to get in!" I said. "She'll get in!"

She didn't say anything else and then the bell rang again and I had to run so I wouldn't be extra tardy here to Study Hall.

1/24 8:30 pm

HOLY SHIT.

Mom and Dad told me big news over dinner.

Marli is pregnant.

Marli will most likely be moving home.

Marli will most likely not finish her freshman year this year.

I asked what about Ronnie, and Mom said he doesn't know yet, and took a huge bite out of her pepperoni slice that she'd covered in red pepper. She dabbed at her eyes with her napkin. She was crying. She blamed the pepper, as usual. Her trick she thought I never noticed.

"I can't believe he didn't use protection," Mom said.

"But," I tried.

"Not now, Piper." Dad cut me off quick.

That was so Mom to think Marli had no choice in the matter, like she couldn't help control the situation. Once again, nothing was ever Marli's fault.

I ate the rest of my pizza watching them not talk to each other. Fun times.

I found Enzo at the salad station and asked him if he'd talk to me. He said I didn't return his calls so why should he talk to me now and I said, It's not like that, it's not about us, I'm totally freaked out about something else.

He looked at me with his big Enzo Owl Eyes, the way that usually makes me melt, but now just made me want to hide inside his cardigan.

"It's about Marli," I whispered.

"What?" He bit down on a carrot.

"She might be moving back in with us."

"She's dropping out?" he said. "That was fast!"

"Something worse."

"What's worse than that?"

"I can't tell you," I said.

"Oh, c'mon."

"My mom will kill me if I say anything yet." Mom had said about a billion times last night, FAMILY ONLY. But how could he not figure it out? How many reasons could there be for dropping out of school?

"You can tell me anything. You know that." He raised his eyebrows and when I didn't answer him, he wrapped his arms around me. Whatever, I let him. His shirt smelled like cloves and sweat and the blankets on his bed.

"She just can't move back in again. My parents said I could make her room my studio!"

Kit and Jen and Sammy pushed open the cafeteria doors and headed for the lunch line.

I pulled away from E. I know I'm not supposed to still love him, but I do. His fingers were locked with mine.

"When would she . . . ?"

I shrugged. "Within 9 months."

He didn't catch on at all. Totally clueless.

1/26 Morning sometime

Andy said, "The best love is not-to-think-about-it love."

I'm not going to think of Enzo. I'm going to paint all day. This Saturday is mine. Mom and Dad are leaving me alone and having serious, quiet discussions, obviously about Marli. Kit is with her parents all weekend because they are not on call at the hospital.

Did Andy really know how not to think of his love, his best love? To just leave love alone? I love love and I love thinking about love. And the only way I know how not to think about it 100% of the time is by doing something besides thinking.

I'm painting. I'm going to paint. Now. I'm leaving the garage door open so I can get enough sunlight before it starts raining.

Coffee first. No thinking.

Adams said in class last semester, "Art is about getting to know one's self."

Looked at what I painted yesterday. I had no idea how much time I spent on Enzo. He's in all of my work. All of it. I wasn't even building a face for fuck's sake, I was trying to capture yesterday's thunderclouds. But when I see the canvas, I see his profile, his ears, his eyelashes. Need new medium because ENZO = OILS, PAINTS!!!! Must at least try something else, even though it's hard to ignore paint, borderline painful. Maybe freaking watercolors, painting but lighter.

Told Mom I needed new pencils, so she drove me to Texas Art Supply, the good one on Montrose.

On the way there, she asked if there was anything I wanted to talk about and I told her what Adams had said about NYSCFA calling.

"I meant about Marli," Mom said.

I didn't say anything, just let her hear how that had just gone down.

"Well, Piper, remember that call doesn't necessarily mean anything," she said. "I mean, it's good. I'm happy for you, but I don't want you to get your hopes up. Just . . . stay grounded."

"Sure." So much for being excited.

"God knows your sister could have used that advice."

"Right." Of course. Always, always about Marli. Who cares if I might get into my dream school?

Kill me.

Not sleeping. Not sleeping. Not sleeping. My heart feels like it's speed-beating 100 beats a second. Marli is definitely moving back. There is going to be a baby here, too. Her baby. I should be happy to be an aunt. But I'm too young to be an aunt. Nobody's an aunt yet. And should she even be having the baby? Am I allowed to ask that? Oh my gawd, what if it's not Ronnie's baby? Or what if the baby has an STD? What if the baby is born with Ronnie's disgusting wet little mustache? Maybe she won't have the baby. Maybe she'll give it up. Can't be two Marlis in the house and I don't care how awful a sister I am for thinking that. I can't stand her or any of this.

1/29 3:40 pm

"A picture means I know where
    I was every minute.
That's why I take pictures.
    It's a visual diary."
                —Andy W.

Work in progress, Adams's class: This is my Painting Partner piece I started at the museum. I should work on it, but I feel stuck and don't want to screw it up.

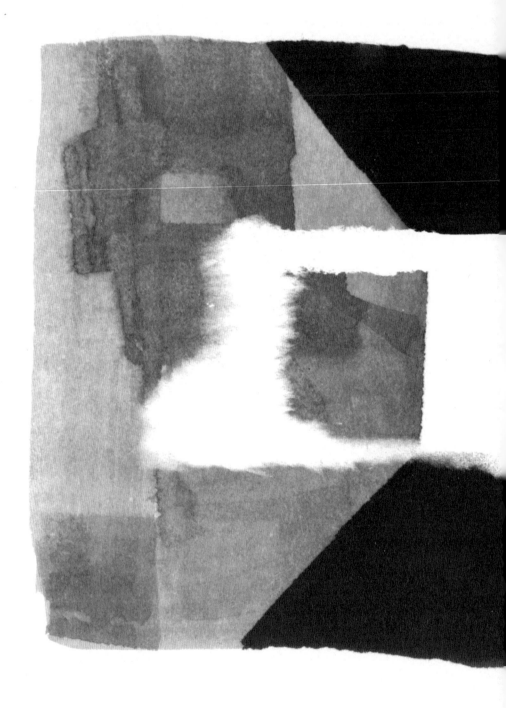

Just watched Sam Chang and Ricky Davis from Drama act in a scene from Sam Shepard's <u>True West</u> as a Drama and Art class collaboration project. Sammy's a better actor than I would have figured. I like the two brothers in the play fighting it out. It felt right. True. It made me feel like screaming too, standing on top of my chair in the auditorium and shouting "That's the way it really is! One of them always gets away with everything!"

But I didn't. I am going to check out the play from Ms. Howland's drama library though, even though I'm not a drama kid. I told her the play made me want to paint and she said that was a very good thing.

1/31 After school

I went over to Enzo's. It's the 1-month anniversary of our breakup. He still had some of my paintbrushes and I wanted them back. He cracked open the door when I got there so I had to ask him if I could come in.

"My parents aren't here."

"Since when do you care about that?"

"It's different now."

"How?"

"It's not a good time," he stuttered, and then said something about working.

I started tingling, knowing he was lying. If he had been working, he would never have opened the door.

48

I heard Tina, his mom, call out, "Who is it, Lorenzo?"

She opened the door wide and I said, "Hi, I thought you weren't home."

"Here I am!" She gave me a funny look. "Benvenuto, sweetie!"

Enzo tried to block me.

"Stop being rude, Lorenzo," Tina said. "You can fit three on that couch."

"Who else is here?" I asked.

"Philip," she said. "He's been telling Lorenzo all about his classes at the university. Now they're watching that movie. What are you watching? The funny one?"

"Yeah, it's funny."

"What is it?" I asked, and he mumbled, "DevilWearsPrada."

"You and Philip are just sitting around watching The Devil Wears Prada?"

"It's a good one," Tina added, wiping her hands on her apron. "I have to go check my tomatoes. Those babies are roasting!"

"Philip's here?" I whispered/asked. "Does your Mom know-know?"

"Please don't say anything."

"Of course not!" I said, rubbing at my tears.

Philip showed up behind Enzo with a smile. So smug.

"Hi."

"Hi," he said loudly.

He's as tall and muscle-y as I remember him being when he went to our school last year, maybe taller. Why couldn't Philip find

49

some other college freshman to fall in love with? Why did Philip have to come back for Enzo?

"Can I have my paintbrushes?" I asked, staring at Enzo, trying as hard as possible to avoid Philip.

"Hold on," he said, and then disappeared, leaving Philip and me standing there, face to face.

"Oh come on, you're gorgeous," he said. "You'll be fine, y'know."

"You took my boyfriend," I said to him.

Enzo reappeared with my basket full of brushes.

"Here," he said, handing it to me. "These are all yours."

I dragged all the way home, knowing nobody could possibly understand an inch of my pain. Nobody. I no longer belonged to Enzo. He no longer belonged to me. And something about dating me had made him choose a boy. It didn't matter if I was pretty or talented or that we had been friends forever. We were ruined. We couldn't even be real friends anymore, which killed the most. He'd lied to me about Philip being at his house. He'd lied to me about being . . . himself. How much more lying was I supposed to take? Real friends were supposed to be honest.

So, my "New Year" looks like this:

- Enzo breaking up with me? CHECK.

- Marli (and baby!) moving back in with us? CHECK.

- Feeling 100% freaked out that my life is falling apart, that my heart is broken and I will never, ever be rid of Marli, that she will always come back to ruin my life? CHECK FREAKING PLUS.

THIS IS NOT THE NEW YEAR I WAS PICTURING.

January, you can piss right off.

Kit just found out Jen is having another party—her parents
are gambling in Louisiana at L'Auberge, THEIR PLACE as
they call it. Kit's going to spend the night here afterward,
then we're going to paint and craft all day tomorrow. I sent
Enzo an email saying please don't go to Jen's and please don't
bring Philip and he promised he wouldn't. He said he had
other plans and that made me cry. I'm glad he couldn't see me
over email.

Jen's cousin, Barlow, was in town and at the party last
night. He's fly.

51

Jen's aunt and uncle who are kind of hippie-dippies moved him out to Marfa to give him a "quiet life." Said he's always bored. I told him he needs to move to New York with Kit and me so he could do whatever he wants to do and he told me he likes to build miniatures, like dollhouses, and he's always making mini versions of things and I asked what better place to study small things than New York because everything I've read about New York apartments is that they are really small.

The next thing I knew I was running my fingers through his wavy brown hair and we were kissing each other all over the mouth and face, and his hands are so strong—NOT LIKE ENZO'S—but I didn't mind that they were different. I tried hard not to think of Enzo, tried not to think how I felt awkward about my boyish body, wishing Enzo would drop by and see us together making out all over the kitchen counter crowded with red plastic cups and Dixie cup–sized Jell-O shots and potato chips, just like Enzo and I did when we were "post-back-together cool." Barlow and I landed on a bag of Zapp's and it popped because we pushed the air right out of it. Haha.

Jen danced into the kitchen and then backed out through the swinging door. I said into Barlow's kissing mouth, "Jen just saw us" and he said, "I don't care" and took a sip out of one of the cups.

"I like you. You should come visit me in Marfa."

"What would we do?"

"Whatever we want. We could have serious fun." He pulled me toward him again and said, "The last time I saw you we were both in 8th grade. Why haven't we seen each other until now?"

His eyes looked me up and down and I instantly understood every possible meaning behind HORNY. I blushed, just thinking of the word. He leaned in, making sure our jeans were touching. I could feel how hard he was, or at least I think that's what that was.

"Are you nervous, little chickie?" Kind of sweet and really sexy.

I wasn't nervous. We made out some more and he unbuttoned his pants, right there in the kitchen.

"Let's go to the back porch," he said.

I followed him but then we bumped into Kit in the hallway.

"I'm going to be sick," she announced into my hair, grabbing my hand. She pulled me away from Barlow, into the bathroom, where I proceeded to rub her back while she puked chunks. The absolute opposite of horny. Jen's parties always made her puke.

"I'm sorry," she said, pointing toward me but kind of everywhere at the same time. "You were with Barlow."

"It's okay. He'll wait."

And then we spent until 3 am this morning in the bathroom. When we came out, he was gone. FTW.

2/3 Noon

I called Jen and invited her to come over to watch the Super Bowl and bring her cousin, too, if she wanted. Mom was making dips and most of the neighbors were either here or coming over soon. Kit was still here, staying over the whole weekend. Jen said she'd talk to Barlow, then kind of grunt-giggled. I ask her what was so funny and she said, "It figures you two weirdos would hook up," and I could feel my cheeks getting hot and I asked, "Why'd you say that?"

"Because, you guys are all artists and shit. All fucked up and feeling stuff."

"I'm not fucked up," I said.

"Oh please," Jen said. "Well, you always look the part."

I checked myself out in our hallway mirror: plaid skirt, black tights, black T-shirt. I didn't think I looked fucked up. I thought I looked cool and kind of cute. My skirt was girly. I licked my thumb and smudged my eyeliner a little more toward my eyebrows so my look would be more cat-eye and less smoky Sunday morning.

"You should know he's a player, dude. Whatever you do, be careful with Barlow."

I told Jen I had to go. I didn't really want to know that last part.

Went to help Mom, who was stirring three different pots of chili at once.

"I invited Jen and her cousin," I told Mom and she said, "The more the merrier." She licked a spoon with spinach dip on it, then began to cut up cilantro.

"By the way," she said, "We still haven't exactly told anyone Marli's moving back home. So . . ."

"So, I still can't mention anything."

"Not yet," Mom said. "No reason to get everyone talking."

"They're gonna know eventually, right?" I asked.

"Sure will. But not today. Today's about football. Your dad and I just want to watch the game."

Maybe they actually thought Marli didn't need to be the center of attention every damn day, which was a surprising relief.

She leaned across the counter for the pill bottle she kept above the sink. She grabbed her glass that was filled to the top with ice and Diet Coke and took a big swig, throwing her head back dramatically and aaahing afterward.

"Headache?"

"Not too bad," she said. She smiled with her lips together which meant she was done discussing it.

Now I have to change outfits so I'll look like I woke up just naturally looking cool if Barlow does come over. My hair already looks awesome. It's the best when I sleep on it just the right way and it's extra flat and silky looking.

2/4 9 pm

Barlow didn't come. The Ravens won. And I have a project due tomorrow that I haven't started yet.

Barlow's parents drove him back this morning. Why would anyone live in Marfa? Jen says it has one traffic light. That's like no civilization. That's like before time.

I wonder how many traffic lights are in New York. I wonder if Barlow is as bummed out as I am. Marfa sounds like a total jerk-off town.

Okay okay okay. Going to draw. Working with pencils is weird, but trying to stay away from paints. For now. But I want to paint. I just want to paint without my brain drifting toward Enzo. So, pencils.

Senior Project Notes 🦋 from Adams's lecture

- Divide your personal geography.

- Doesn't have to be whole thing at a time, can create little sketches, piece together for one large sketch possibly.

- "Obsession & bane of existence will be hardest."

I asked if I could start with whatever comes before obsession and bane of existence, and Adams fiddled her turquoise skull earring at me.

"The hardest will be the most emotional. Go there."

"But what's the easiest?" I asked her, half-joking.

"Living your life without art," she answered. "Is that easy enough for you?"

Then Sam Chang snapped his fingers and said BOOM and Adams curtsied to the classroom.

She reminded us that most college acceptance letters arrive in about a month, that we should use the time we have now to focus and create and make, before we all get distracted about where we are or are not accepted, and prom, and graduation etc. . . .

I have plenty of time. Too much time. I'm not worried.

I asked her after class if she'd heard from NYSCFA again, maybe about Kit this time, and she told me to just concern myself with my own acceptance.

I hate all this waiting.

Personal Geography Senior Project
Brainstorm / Ideas / Sketch

2/7 After school

Kit came home with me. We're going to work on our personal geographies together. When we went into the kitchen to grab chips, Marli was sitting at the table, red-faced and blowing her nose. Wadded-up Kleenexes were everywhere.

"What's up?" Kit asked her.

Marli dabbed her eyes and let out a hiccup-yelp and then smiled at us like nothing in the world was wrong.

"Ronnie break up with you?"

Marli looked at me and tilted her head toward Kit.

"She know?"

"Know what?" Kit asked.

"Mom told me not to say anything to anyone," I said. I didn't add that I'd tried to tell Enzo. He didn't get it anyway.

"Did you drop out or something?" Kit asked and kind of looked pissed at me for not giving her a heads-up.

Marli covered her mouth and big tears fell down her face.

"She's pregnant," I blurted out. I didn't mean to.

"Piper!" Marli said. "I didn't want anyone to know yet!"

"I kept the secret until right now! Kit would have guessed eventually."

I stepped closer to Kit, who was clearly shocked. We knew girls at school who had gotten pregnant, but none of them were our close friends.

Marli hid her head in her hands and Kit and I knew we should leave then. When Marli grew quiet was when she went from bad to worse.

Kit followed me to my room and said, "That shit is bananas."

"Yeah."

"What is she going to do?" she whispered, in case Marli was outside my door.

"She's moving back in. She can't live at the dorm with a baby, right?"

Kit handed me the bag of chips and just stared at me.

"Shit," she said. "There goes your art studio."

"Super weird, right?" Kit freaking out only reminded me how much there was to freak out about.

"You can move in with me at least until we're up at NYSCFA."

When she said this, I thought of Adams. What if Kit doesn't get in? Adams said the school hadn't called again. We both have to get accepted. I know we will. Just because they didn't call about her yet doesn't mean anything. I pulled out our supplies, turned on Arcade Fire, and then we sketched.

I peeked over at her graph paper. It looked like a blueprint, like a grid.

"What are you mapping?" I asked. I tilted my head to look at it from a different angle. It kind of looked like a mash-up of a sketch of a room in a house and a flowchart.

"I'm building a wireframe," she said. "I'm going to make a website for my project. And what could be more personal than starting one from scratch, instead of a dumb, overdone template? Fuck a Tumblr." She tapped her head. "But I need to see it here first."

"Since when do you know how to BUILD a website?"

"Piece of cake. I'll figure it out. And all of my little freshies? They know how to code already. They'll teach me for free." She thought for a second. "They would probably pay ME just to get to teach me."

She was right, no doubt. "What kind of site?"

"Fashion and art, natch. Totally curated by moi. Thinking Fashion+Art, maybe?"

"No! People will call it FArt!"

She elbowed me. I can always make her snort at least. Then we started drawing again. She's 1000000x better than me, as usual.

2/8 5 pm

Sketching in the backyard when Enzo texted me: *What are you doing?*

I called him back and told him I was sketching. He said he was thinking and I could hear "Pictures of You" by the Cure playing in the background. He told me he missed me, he's sorry the way everything went down, and he wants to be real friends.

Before I could say anything, he asked me if I wanted to go to the Valentine's Day dance with him because his mom asked if he was going. He wasn't going to even consider it but his mom wanted to know if he was taking me.

"Maybe," I said. "Do you really want to go with me or are you just using me as a pretend girlfriend?"

"We would go as friends."

I told him I had to think about it.

"Why? Do you have another date?"

"Maybe," I lied. "And you know, the last dance we were at together is where you broke up with me . . . in front of everyone.

60

Do you remember that?"

"Yes, of course. It was a shit move. I know that. But we'd go to the V-Day dance as friends. Nothing more. And I wouldn't be an asshole, I promise."

"No shit, Sherlock."

"Go with me," he insisted. "Nobody dances like you." (WHICH IS TRUE.)

And then I told him I had to go sketch.

"Working on Adams's project?" he asked and I answered, "Like a boss."

"Me too," he said. "Capsule Collection, thinking of calling it the Naturals. Using every shade of nudes in all my designs. Like literally baring it all for an entire fashion line. What do you think?"

"It sounds very . . . you," I said. I felt tired, sad. I should be happy for him, but how could his line not remind me of his striptease and my total humiliation?

When we got off the phone, I was super low. I looked back at my sketches and ripped them up. I was trying too hard. I had to stop thinking about it.

"Obsessions will be hardest.
Banes of existence will be hardest."

True.

All of my work sucks. And I can feel it, my heart pounding HARDER HARDER HARDER. Love Harder, Create Harder, Fix it all!!! I feel like I'm being squeezed by the pressure of him and whatever this new friendship is supposed to be, of love and art.

It is too much.

What would Andy do? He would start over. Start again. I have to start the sketches again.

2/9 11 am

Dad is trying to lose weight so he asked me to jog with him after breakfast. He's way faster than I am. My favorite part was ice cream afterward. I don't think that's part of the weight-loss plan, but I didn't bring it up. Dad takes up new sports or exercises when he's stressed, I shouldn't be surprised. He did a lot of yoga during my SATs. He swam during Mom's back surgery. And now I guess he's running because of Marli. Or from her. If we run in the morning we miss hearing her throw up.

2/10 3 am

Just woke up/
dreaming of Andy/
talking to me/
telling me to remember it's all funny/
when I ask him what is/
he says All of it./
Then he winks at me and tells me nice hair./

Drawing the dream tomorrow, I mean today.
When I wake up.

ZZZZZzzzzzz. ⋀⋀⋀⋀⋀⋀⋀

"It's all funny. All of it."

2/11 First period

I was smudging my eyeliner, looking into the mirror hanging on my locker door, when E came up and asked if I'm going to the dance with him. I asked him if he should consider telling his mom the truth. As soon as I said it, I could see his face wince in the mirror. When I turned to apologize, he was already down the hall.

Why do I feel horrible? He's the one who hurt me. Happy f'in Monday to me.

2/12 610 Diner

Kit and I headed here after school. We both needed coffee and to sketch and be away from home. Marli's throwing up all over ours and Kit's mom accidentally took Kit's keys with her to the hospital so she's locked out until her mom gets back. Her dad's on call, and she never knows when he'll get home. I asked her if she's going to the dance and she said hell no and I asked her if she wants to go and she asked me why and I told her about Enzo. She said OK, she'll go and she'll put our two outfits together—she loves pretending she's on Project Runway with crazy challenges and deadlines. Enzo usually likes to design all of our going-out outfits, but Kit's inspired and said she's making something JUST FOR HER AND ME. Enzo can go and be at the dance on his own. I asked her what she's thinking and she began sketching on a new sheet of paper. From the looks of it, we're going as Daft Punk.

2/13 8 pm

At dinner, Marli asked me if anyone at 610 asked about her.

She was flipping her fork in her hand, subtly, like a magician practicing sleight of hand.

I told her no, I didn't see anyone on shift that she knew.

Her face started turning red, like when she was about to cry. The fork stopped in rotation, flat against her left palm.

"Nobody cares," she said quietly. "Nobody cares about me at all. I called for my job back, to be full-time again since I won't be at school, and nobody has even called me back."

Her lips fell to a perfect horizon, the way they rested before she lost control.

"Oh."

"They didn't say anything about me? Not a single word?"

"I don't even think our waiter knew I was your sister, Marli," I said. I could tell at this point nothing was going to get through enough to keep from ruining her dinner. (Whenever I hear that phrase walking on eggshells, I think about Marli, except in our case, it's really more like walking on land mines.)

Dad put on his running shoes and announced he was going to stretch before his run if anyone wanted to join him. Mom was already at book club, so she got to miss tonight's episode of the Marli Show.

I kept eating my turkey burger and then Marli put her dirty-ass plate right in front of mine.

"I'm not doing yours."

"Of course you wouldn't," she said. "Nobody cares about me." Revving up.

"You've got Ronnie," I said, biting into my burger.

She chucked her glass into the sink and we both heard it break.

"What the fuck, Marli!"

"YES?" She turned fast toward me, like the first spark of a campfire, all yellow and snap, flash and pop.

"Never mind," I said quietly.

She shoulder-shoved past me as she left the kitchen and her bedroom door slammed closed.

On our run, Dad told me I have to find a way to be nicer.

"I thought I WAS being nice," I said between huffing and puffing. "I cleaned up her broken glass!"

"You could have washed your sister's plate. You didn't have to upset her in the first place."

In my head, I thought What the Serious Fuck Are You Talking About but what I said was, "Seriously? Since when can't she do her own dishes?"

"It's the little things," he said. "Your sister is pregnant."

I bolted to the end of the street and waited for him to catch up.

2/14 After school

Kit declared today GALentine's Day, and I helped her work on our outfits for tomorrow night. There's a lot of sequins involved. If Enzo was making our looks, they would already be finished. He is so fast. Kit always needs more time for her visions.

I texted Enzo that he's on his own, and sent an email to Barlow, asking him what he's doing for Valentine's Day in Marfa. Haven't heard back yet. We are going to look like the shit tomorrow night.

2/15 7 pm About to leave for Galentine's dance!

"The best thing about a picture is that it never changes, even when the people in it do." —Andy W.

OUR AWESOMENESS, WHICH WILL NEVER EVER CHANGE:

2/16 9 am

Last night turned out to be the best. Kit and me, in our matching silver jumpsuits, covered with tiny white LED lights around the hoodies, danced for like 5 hours without any Enzo drama. Enzo did show up, wearing red plaid pants, combat boots, and his Union Jack T-shirt. He hung out with Sammy C. and Rooftop and Jen. I knew where he was all night so I could make sure we didn't bump into each other, or dance next to each other. Two of Kit's fresh fishies asked if Enzo and I were going to get together again, if he was going to do his "Crazy Scarf Dance" and Kit scooted them as far away from us as possible. Near the end of the night, Enzo asked me if we could talk, and I said no, not here not now, we're dancing. He asked soon? And I said soon, sure. I wasn't trying to be a bitch but I also wasn't trying not to be a bitch.

Dad thinks I'm going to run in 2 hours. Hell, no. My feet hurt from dancing in space boots. DJ Anonymous was spinning, so that was like, exercise. Awesome, awesome exercise.

2/17 Noon

Ronnie is in the kitchen! I'm trying to hear everything but all I can make out is Dad's voice. The four of them are being very quiet, except Marli's occasional threat and Mom's frequent Mom-angry-voice thing. I guess I'm not supposed to hear any of this but hello, now I'm an aunt. I'm just doing my job.

2/18 Art class notes

"How is your personal geography project coming along?" Adams asked me.

"Slow."

I told her Andy said it does not matter how slowly you go so long as you do not stop.

"That's fine, as long as you're attacking it. It's your senior project, after all. Now is the time for fearlessness," she said. "Go after it. Get it. Chase it down."

"Go after what?" I asked.

"All of it. I want to know who you are right now, in 10 years, 20 years, 30 years. I want you to recognize yourself when you're 90. And I don't want you to rely so much on Andy. You still have to do the work. You are your own treasure map."

Typical Adams.

She stepped over to Sam Chang. Did she tell him the same thing?

We are our own treasure maps. Hmm.

2/19 First period

Enzo was crying at his locker this morning. He says he wasn't, but his cheeks were puffy and his eyes were swollen.

"What's wrong?" I asked.

"Nothing. You won't understand."

"Try me."

Then Jen passed us and E whispered not now, in total Bro Code.

I'm seeing E after school today.

❀ FOLLOW-UP ❧

OMG PHILIP CHEATED ON ENZO!!!!!!!

69

I can't stop thinking about Enzo and Philip. Andy said, "Fantasy love is much better than reality love." I wonder what Andy knew about that, since he made his own life seem so fantasy-like. I wonder if he made it all fantasy because he had real love and it almost destroyed him. So he had to turn it into something else. Something more.

It's not that I want Enzo to be heartbroken, but I wonder if this is karma. I wonder if he understands what he did to me now. I wonder if this makes me matter more to him. I wonder if he puts this all together like I do:

✦ Me and Enzo.

✦ Enzo and Philip.

✷ Barlow? (whatever the hell that whole thing was)

✷ Ronnie and Marli.

Maybe nobody can really explain love.

Kit always says to love what you do not who you're with, and maybe she's on to something. Ever since Jack, she won't date just one guy and she's been so much happier.

And I do love what I do. I love painting. I love drawing. I'm never let down, even when the picture isn't exactly what I want. I can keep working at it. Paintings speak back. They argue. But it's just because they still want attention. They aren't done yet. They want to keep the relationship alive. And when they break your heart, it's only because they're that good, not because they're that bad. Bad art can be fixed or transformed. But bad people? Bad choices?

I think they're with us forever.

Supposed to be doing homework, which is hard, considering what happened at dinner tonight.

It was Mom, Dad, Marli, and me. Mom made an almond-tuna casserole from some recipe she got from a patient's mom at the clinic and STD Ronnie—though I guess I shouldn't call him that anymore—was invited over and it was super awkward. AWKWARD.

Dad could barely look him in the face and (STD) Ronnie's tiny mustache kept sweating which was so gross.

"Since we're all family now, I'd like us to start acting that way," Mom said.

Then—THEN!

Then (THE STD IS SILENT) Ronnie said, "Nothing's exactly been decided."

Then Marli said, "Not right now."

She started twisting her fork around—the bad sign—and inched it toward his hand, smiling like she was being coy, but she wasn't.

She said, "I'm keeping our baby."

"You could put it up for adoption, that girl Nicole in school did it," I said and Mom said quickly, "Nobody is giving the baby up!"

71

Dad pushed back from the table and pointed at me and said, "You're going running with me," even though I was starving and dinner actually smelled really good.

When we were outside, Dad said to me, "Kiddo, you've got to learn to keep your mouth shut sometimes."

"But I'm not wrong!"

"All of this is wrong," Dad said.

"Then how come you don't do anything about it? Why do you let her get away with . . . being Marli?"

"I don't let her get away with everything. And there's nothing I can do about Marli's baby. It's not up to me to make decisions about her body!"

"Well, Mom gives in to Marli! As soon as Marli talks back to her, Mom backs down."

"Not always."

"A lot!"

"Your mother"—Dad sighed—"both of us struggle with Marli. And having a baby? Well, that's a very delicate situation, Piper. But that doesn't mean we let her get away with everything. We choose our battles. The same with you, kiddo. That's why you don't get away with everything either. You'll understand when you're older," he said. "When you have your own kids."

"OK, talk to you in 20 years."

"Look," he started, "Your sister isn't always easy. Sometimes she's a real challenge. We know that. She can sweep in and tear us apart. She doesn't mean to do it, but that's what she does. We still love her. It's her nature. And you know what I always say about nature. It has a path of its own."

I could feel a hurricane metaphor coming on, ar
Dad always relied on work talk when he was up

"If the Galveston hurricane of 1900 occurred t
result in $40 billion in insured losses," Dad s
nature does, what it can cost."

"And what does Marli cost us?" It seemed like Dad was kind of
losing track of the point.

"She's our first daughter, Piper. Believe it or not, she's worth
every penny."

Dad bent down to tie his shoelace.

"I'll race you to the park," I said.

And we took off.

Mom and Dad being confused over Marli is like the most
annoying, irritating, awful thing in the world. I should be used
to it by now, but I'm not. I might never be.

Even though I ran faster than ever, he beat me by half a mile at
least. When I reached the park I asked him, leaning over and
out of breath, if everything was going to be okay. He nodded,
stretching his hand out to me.

"Help me out," he said.

"Sure."

"Promise me you won't have sex until you're married."

"OH. MY. GOD."

I hate having these kinds of conversations. And I hate lying.

"I'll do my best," I said. Not mentioning that I had already done it
with Enzo, and lost my virginity to Jeffrey Marcus in 10th grade.

st don't," he said.

"Okay."

We raced home. I was so glad I didn't have to look him in the face anymore because even if he did suspect I had already done it, I didn't want to have to promise him how I wouldn't do it anymore.

Back in the kitchen, Ronnie was hugging Marli and Mom was moving her casserole back into the oven. It looked like a photograph I've seen before, like some soldier home from the war hugging his wife—but it wasn't. It was just Pawn Shop Ronnie (that's nicer and true, since his family owns a chain of them) and my sister.

I called Kit, but she's out with Marcel—"practicing French."

I called Enzo, and he texted me back that he and Philip were working things out.

Maybe I really don't mean anything to Enzo, even as a friend. Maybe this whole relationship, and friendship, has been nothing but one weird joke and I've been a punch line all this time. I'm tired of being sad because of the people I love. I feel used up.

Andy once said, "A friend of mine always says, 'Women love me for the man I'm not.'" Well, maybe a certain friend of mine would say that's what I've been doing about him this whole time. Loving him for the man he's not . . . not for the Enzo he is.

I wish Andy could come back. I wish his Factory was still running. I wish I could pack a bag and leave tonight. I'd hide out with him and paint and dance and make films and stay awake as long as I could. I'd escape.

2/24 7 am TFE (TOO FUCKING EARLY!!!!) IT'S SUNDAY!

Dad and Marli are arguing downstairs. Dad's trying to go on his run but Marli asked him to go to church. Marli has never gone to church once in her whole life by choice.

I. Am. So. Confused.

Maybe I'm dreaming all this. I hear her say it's important to Ronnie's parents and now Mom is padding down the stairs to see what's going on. Even if there was no baby, this is how it always is—Marli and her dramas and everyone running after her and nobody ever trying to stop them. Whether it's one of her low, dark-purple dramas or when she explodes, all flashing and yellow, she knows how to control Mom and Dad. Always has. She could commit murder and Mom would still call her sensitive/special/different. Dad would of course back Mom up, though I know he loses patience with Marli more than Mom does. That's why sometimes I know he gets it, like me. That's why I can talk to him about it a little more. He doesn't completely fucking shut down.

Marli is not special. She's weird. Twisted. She fights for what she wants until the end, she can never be wrong, and then when she's outside of the house, when she's around other people, she acts so sweet. Kit and Enzo know the truth. Jen, too. I've had to spend way too many nights at Kit's and Jen's when Marli was out of control. When she starts throwing and breaking stuff, when she starts yelling and ranting, it feels like walls of our house will crack and fall down. On the day Kit and I learned

75

about sociopaths in psychology class last year, she passed me a note:

Are you thinking about who I'm thinking about?

And I wrote back,

Finally, there's a name for it.
For her.

And Kit went with me when I tried to talk to Mom about it after school. I was so excited we went straight to the clinic and sat in Mom's cubicle, waiting for her to finish with a client who was rehabbing a broken ankle, so that I could tell her the good news—my discovery! Mom listened and sat very still and said that while she appreciated Kit and me paying so much attention in class, perhaps we shouldn't act like junk psychologists, that maybe we shouldn't try to diagnose other people since we weren't in any way qualified.

"But Mom," I said, "everything matches up with her. You should read the chapter in my psych book."

And Mom said, "Piper, that's the last thing I have time to do. I have a headache and another client in 2 minutes and paperwork to fill out. And besides, I think it takes more than reading a chapter to diagnose someone of a medical disease. Kit, can you please talk her out of this nonsense?"

She walked to the clinic communal kitchen that was across from her desk and took a pill, washing it down with water she cupped in her hand from the sink.

Kit and I looked at each other.

"Denial much?" Kit said.

So yeah. Any time I've ever tried to call Mom or Dad out on how they cater to her, Mom's said she just has two "spirited daughters." And then she tells me I'm lucky I found a place I could channel all of my energy (art). But Marli? She never found her people, her place. Our home is the closest thing she has to stability. That's what Mom says anyway. Sometimes Dad agrees, sometimes he just stares at something far-off and distant, like he's looking through the walls of our house, even though I know he hears me. I know he agrees with me. But he won't say it out loud. Marli gets to be Marli, and fuck the rest of us.

Dad and Marli are still arguing over church. Great. Putting on my headphones to drown them out. Listening to Blondie and dreaming of a New York where I'm not in this shitty-ass backward house anymore.

9:30 am

Marli and Dad are back. They left church early. She hated it. So there goes any hope of her getting saved or me getting any more sleep.

2/25 Lunch

Aaaaahhh! I think Enzo has herpes. He has a cold sore. Kit told me. He's never had one before! Do I have herpes now? Kit keeps giggling but it's not funny. It's not! Karma for calling Ronnie "STD Ronnie"???

Found out Enzo DOES NOT have herpes and it's not a cold sore, it's a poorly placed zit. Should have known except his face is so perfect.

"You're being a stereotyping homophobe," he said.

"Not at all," I said. "Ronnie gets STDs all the time! And he's straight! Do you really think that of me?"

He covered his face like he was a monster and I thought he was playing and then I realized he wasn't. He was crying all over his hands.

"Do you have any idea how hard all of this is?"

I pulled him out of the hallway to save face (oooh, funny!) and into a stall in the third-floor bathroom.

"Piper, believe it or not, I know I hurt you. I really love you, just not like . . ." He dabbed the crunchy toilet paper against his nose and carefully touched his mouth. "I'm sorry, okay?" He cried hard into my shoulder. "You don't know how hard this has been. Is."

"Breaking up with me?" I couldn't help it, I was flattered.

"NO." He gritted his perfect teeth. "Being with Philip. Being . . ."

"Being you?" I asked.

We both knew what the other three-letter word was.

Then I told him and I 100% meant it, "Enzo Romero, I love you just the way you are. You."

I saw, for real, what everyone had been trying to tell me. I had been blind. I didn't want to see it, or accept it. Even when Kit suggested that maybe Enzo and I should only be friends, I didn't want to hear her. But now, it clicked. He loved me the way he could. I loved him the way I could. That meant our love had limits. But that was OK. My heart buzzed, electric currents pulsing back and forth, anger at myself-love, anger at him-love, anger at love-love. I felt electrified and relieved all at once.

He tugged softly on my hair. "Friends?"

I nodded and shrugged at the same time. It's what I could give him and it wasn't an outward no or yes. I didn't know what we were, but we weren't NOT friends and we weren't friends. Something in between? Something more? Something deeper? Because we had shared more than friends.

"Good," he said. "Then we have to talk about Barlow."

"What about him? ME-OW."

Enzo shook his head. "That boy is trouble. T-R-O-U-"

"Please don't spell," I said.

"B-L-E," he rushed out. "And you have to stay away."

"Don't worry about him. He never texts back. And I'm kind of done with guys dropping me if you know what I mean. Anyway, what about Philip? HE's trouble. He cheated on Y-O-U!"

"It was a misunderstanding," Enzo said.

"How?"

"He was breaking up with his boyfriend. When I saw them kissing, he was kissing him goodbye for the last time."

"Really?" I asked.

"I think so," he said. "At least that's what he said."

I have a bad feeling about Philip. And not because I'm jealous. I swear.

2/27 Right before Art

Jen came up to me—cornered me—in the hallway. "Barlow says hi," she said.

"So funny. I was just talking about him and guess what?" I wiped my hands against each other, like I was wiping them off. "DONE."

"I thought you would be happy!"

"He doesn't text back. He doesn't email. He ghosted me, Jen. Enzo told me I had to watch out for him even though I told him I'm not even interested anyway." I was still kind of hoping Jen would tell me he had been talking about me.

"Enzo doesn't need to gossip," Jen snapped. "There's plenty people can say about HIM."

"Don't dog on Enzo," I said.

"Fine," she said. "But Barlow isn't that bad. He just has, um, like, a bad temper and stuff. More like your sister. You should just try dating a normal guy for once, Piper. At least TRY it. Charlie may seem boring to other people, but he's sweet to me. You always go for the art weirdos and like, are you ever happy?"

"Yes, I am happy," I said. "I'm happy a lot of the time. Just because I don't want to date the same boring guys in our

boring-ass high school doesn't mean I only go
That's so suburbs of you, Jen."

"Dude, we live in the suburbs," Jen said. She poii
classroom. "Get back to art class, Picasso."

Holy hell, I don't want to date someone like Mar⎸
want to date someone boring either! Maybe I'm d   ⎸ ⎸ ⎸ the
whole dating thing. Doesn't matter right now, class is starting.

The quote on the blackboard is actually from Picasso:

*"Art washes away from the soul
the dust of everyday life."*

It's a sign.

2/27 2:55 pm

Now sitting in Spanish class, or should I say, sentado en clase
española, waiting for Señor Gonzales to pass back our homework and thinking about Adams's lesson in shading today. How
shading changes the way we look at things, depicting depth, and
then subconsciously, warmth and layer. We talked about cross-
hatching, where lines are drawn in a grid. The closer the lines
are together, the darker they appear. The farther apart, the
lighter the area appears.

My mind keeps floating over to Marli. I wonder if when I go to
New York, I'll like her more. I wonder if we just shouldn't live
in the same house. Maybe we're two lines that are too close
to each other. Maybe we bring out the darkness in each other.
Maybe when we're farther apart we'll despise each other less.
It'll be lighter between us. We'll actually be able to breathe, not
suffocate each other.

81

does that mean it's partly my fault, the darkness? I know I'm not as mean as her. At least, I don't think so. I'm like Andy, taking what's already there and making it bolder, more in your face. But Marli? Marli is like the Escher poster hanging in Adams's classroom, staircases leading everywhere and nowhere at the same time. No matter which way you walk, you can't get out. You can't ever leave.

MARCH

Any news yet?

I had to wipe my eyes to read the text that woke me again. I blinked, trying to figure out what Enzo meant.

Right! Of course! It's March! I checked my email to see if there was anything from the school. They send an email and snail mail when you get accepted, and the acceptances should start coming in March, they said.

None yet, I typed.

What are you doing today?

Sleeping.

Let's go shopping instead. Be over in 30.

So, now? About to shop. And though Enzo thinks he might go to Rice, I need to see if he's seriously not going to New York with Kit and me, regardless of whether he's my boyfriend or not. The deal was that three of us went together. There's part of me that still really wants him to go, but there's this other part, the pit in my stomach, that says maybe, no. Maybe he shouldn't go now. And that feels so absolutely sick to me. We were supposed to be the NYC 3. I feel weird when I think about him not being there with us—because without him, who will Kit and I be? I wouldn't know how to be me, to be us. I think? The three of us are more than friends, we're limbs. But maybe two out of three of us would be okay. Maybe Kit and I representing would be enough. Maybe we could still kill it.

3/3 After dinner

My List of Awesome That I Bought Yesterday at Another Man's:

❋ a brown fedora with a silk green band and a feather sticking out (so 1970s!): $1.49

❋ bowling shoes (HELLOOOO! MY INCREDIBLY LARGE FEET SIZE!): $5

❋ an old Madonna concert T-shirt that says LIKE A VIRGIN (which I now regret and will probably give to Enzo because I realized I totally can't wear that around my parents right now): $7

❋ a fitted purple prom dress like Courtney Love used to wear— (Enzo thinks we can make this into my prom dress this year, like an updated CL look): 50 cents—WUT!?!?!?

✿ two black vests—one short, one long, total: $15 (They are going to be part of what Enzo is calling my New York Look Book. He's shooting photos of my whole wardrobe and doing a layout of what I should wear to do different things: Class look! Date look! Serious coffee look!)

✿ a little gold picture frame with a photo of two cocker spaniels kissing and the words Friends Forever written on the back. (I gave it to Enzo and he held it to his heart.): $2

✿ We also bought two strawberry milk shakes at Becks Prime. Shopping with Enzo always requires a ton o' calories.

Thanks to the bad rain overnight, the study hall room flooded and we got to meet in the computer lab, which is perfect. Just went on Etsy to look at Kit's new pieces and she hasn't uploaded anything yet, which is crazy, because they are ready to go. I love Kit but she always holds off on showing her stuff. She could totally sell our Valentine's looks and matching accessories in like a day, if she posted them. She always thinks her looks aren't ready, not perfect enough, but when she posts her stuff, people buy her jewelry and outfits so fast. Fashion+Art could be the ultimate place to get her stuff. I still don't think the name is right. Too general. I told her she needs to use her name in it somehow.

K can be so insecure sometimes, but that will change when we go to NYC and all the other artists tell her how good she is. She'll have to believe them even if she doesn't believe me. Nobody here knows how to talk about what we do, except Enzo and Adams and the other art kids. THIS IS WHY WE HAVE TO VAMOOSE!

My bowling shoes need some pop. Time for the highlighter.

3/5 After school

In the art classroom studio after school, waiting for Adams to come around and check my canvas before I have to head out. She's been helping Sam Chang with his paper cuts. Now DJ Anonymous is here, leaning on her desk and waving. It's weird to see him in his ordinary clothes, not in his helmet that he always wears at gigs and parties.

PAUSE. He's coming over!

I'm back! This just happened:

DJA: Hey. What's up, Piper?

Me: Working on my project.

DJA: Extra credit?

Me: Nope.

DJA: Mom says you're going to New York.

Me: That's the plan. (I crossed my fingers.)

DJA: That's a big city, man.

Me: Anything's bigger than here.

DJA: How's Kit?

I tucked the long piece of my silver hair behind
my ear and wiggled my eyebrows at him.

Me: Why ya asking about Kit?

DJA: You guys are always together.

Me: Do you like her?

THEN HE DIDN'T SAY ANYTHING. OH MY GOD,
DJA likes KB.

She's been crushing on DJA for-EVER, even though he
has a super huge nose to hold his super huge nose ring.
She's going to flip out.

Whoever made up the term "Hump Day" should be shot because I just overheard Marli and Ronnie making "Hump Day" jokes—as they were doing it—in her bedroom!!!! I don't think you are even supposed to do it when you're pregnant! Isn't that like the baby doing it? If Ronnie and Marli have to do it, they need to get a house and go do it in their own place, not ours!

I'm in the kitchen now so I don't have to hear everything. How can Mom and Dad not hear them? How can Marli and Ronnie not care that Mom and Dad are practically right there? I know Mom and Dad ignore everything weird Marli does, but this is super gross. They compliment the hell out of her if she does one good thing, but totally disrupt the house? No word. I know they have to hear them, if I do. They should be freaking out because I AM FREAKING OUT. Nobody wants to hear Marli having sex!!!! Whether she's moaning because she's barfing or moaning because she's doing it, Marli moaning is just gross.

3/7 After school, after mailbox

Marli called to me from the porch, watching me at the mailbox.

"What do you want?" I yelled.

"The mail. I'm too tired to get it and it's hot. I don't want my thighs sticking together."

Her face looked kind of rounder and sweatier, but she didn't really look super preggers.

"Hurry up."

I wanted to throw the mail at her for making me overhear her morning-sex grossness with Ronnie.

"Here," I said, and gave her the stack of bills and coupons.

She pulled out a magazine called Trimesters and dropped the rest on the porch.

"Get that, won't ya? Thanks."

I picked up the fanned-out flyers and mail. Why does everything have to be a power play? Fuck. Her.

NYSCFA said letters would be mailed the first week of March. Technically, I could get an acceptance letter tomorrow, but I was hoping they sent them earlier and it would be in my mailbox today. But it wasn't. Bad sign, right?

I can't stay here, in our house, with sex-crazy pregnant Marli, anymore. It will kill me. Or she will kill me. Mom and Dad and Ronnie will just have to deal with Marli on their own when I go to school. But what if I don't get accepted? What if I am doomed to stay in Texas all of my life? No no no.

3/8 Beginning of English class

Just told Kit we have to go dancing and she was like of course but she has no idea that DJ Anonymous is into her and tonight she's going to find out!!! Enzo's going to meet us there, which is so whatever.

I cannot sleep because I drank all of the coffee in the world before we hit the dance floor at Numbers and now Enzo and I are crashed out on Kit's bedroom floor wrapped up in a mess of sleeping bags and blankets from the guest room and I don't want to stand up and wake them but I really have to pee. Kit passed out in her bed after making out with DJA after his set, which is the good part. I basically shoved their faces together until those shy boots had to kiss—DJA had to take off his helmet, Kit had to pull back her Breakfast at Tiffany's–inspired tiara—and then they were all over each other. Kit's crushed on him way longer than any of the boys (and girls) that always fall for her. She's always made me kind of jealous that everything comes so easy for her—everything she designs looks like she didn't even try (tonight: red velvet catsuit, tiara, black leather moto jacket, blood-red lips to match, natch) and anyone she encounters becomes her biggest fan. That's probably how it's going to be in NY, too. I can almost never paint a painting the way I see it and obviously, I can't get a single guy—a normal, basic guy ACCORDING TO JEN—but who really wants that?—to like me for like a serious thing and she can always just get . . . everything. Now she's sleeping in the silky turquoise robe her parents brought her from Japan with a huge red lippy-stained smile on her face. If she wasn't my best friend I would totally hate her. Oh my god, I just looked over at Enzo curled around Kit's body pillow on the floor. He has the biggest boner. I. Can't. Stop. Looking. I shouldn't take a picture, right? AAAAAAahhhhh! I have to pee my leggings. Too funny. Gotta go!

90

When I got home yesterday, Mom told me I needed to take a shower because I smelled like I had been dancing all night and my hair was greasy-looking and like I knew it, but thanks, didn't need that first thing when I opened the door.

From the couch, Marli added, "She might have been dancing so much because of doing all of the drugs. All her friends are druggies."

Mom asked, "You weren't doing all the drugs last night, right? The drug scene wasn't happening, right?"

"No, Mom," I said. "The drug scene wasn't happening. By the way, remember how I told you nobody called doing drugs 'the drug scene'? I drank coffee and burned like a bazillion calories dancing."

"Hit the showers," Mom said, "and ditch the sarcasm."

I'm so super tired and wired from yesterday and when I stepped out of the shower Marli was standing in the bathroom and telling me that she needed to use it and I said use the living room one and she said Dad is in it and that she needed to go right now because OH MY GOD SHE'S PREGNANT like none of us knew that and so I had to dry myself off through the hallway and into my bedroom and when I got in here, Mom was sitting on my bed.

"We need to talk about drugs."

I started laughing, because I'm 18 and we've never talked about drugs this much in my whole life.

"Mom," I said, "get real. You know I don't do drugs."

"I know you don't. But then Marli got me thinking. I can't help it. Don't give me that look."

"What look?"

"That one," she said, and lifted her chin like I guess I was doing. I lowered my chin right away.

"Mom, you take Klonopin. That's a drug, right?"

"Klonopin is a pharmaceutical, yes, but it's a prescription from my doctor. You can't mess around with drugs, Piper. You don't know what I've seen in the clinic due to abuse."

"Mom, I'm not 'messing around' with drugs."

"Marli thinks some of the kids, even Enzo, who let's face it, doesn't have the greatest reputation in this house right now, does drugs and influences you. And you said yourself he did acid."

"Mom," I sighed, "I've been around drugs. I've tried a few. I have no interest. I just drank too much coffee."

"I know. You had coffee breath when you came home."

"So can you leave me alone? I want to get dressed."

I wrapped the towel tighter around my body.

"You're getting too thin," she said.

"Thanks!"

"That's not funny."

She gave me a really good Mom hug, the kind I liked best that sometimes I pulled away from but still really loved.

"Are you really okay?" I asked her as she walked to the hall.

She waved her hand like it wasn't a big thang. Then she was weird all day.

I went jogging with Dad later on and he told me Mom feels like she failed with Marli, wasn't proactive enough about drug and sex talks and stuff.

"Mrs. Napolitano says proactive isn't a real word."

"Who's she?"

"English teacher."

"Well, you know what I mean."

"Is that why she tried to give me a drug talk this morning?" I asked as we leaned against the park fence post, trying to catch our breath.

He nodded yes.

"I'm not Marli, y'know. I don't even like Marli."

"We know you're not Marli," he said. I could tell he was trying to be careful with me, trying to keep me on his side. "That doesn't mean you don't still need us being PROACTIVE. And you don't have to like her," he said, "but you do have to love her. She's your big sister."

"Do you ever feel like that?" I asked. "Do you ever love her but not like her?"

"I like your sister AND I love your sister, Piper. I don't always understand her, but she probably doesn't always understand me either."

"You're sooooo fair," I said to him.

"Is that an accusation?"

I shrugged. "It's a drag."

"Everyone deserves a break, kid."

"She gets a lot of breaks," I said.

"You know the one thing more uncontrollable than nature?" Dad asked.

I shook my head.

"Human nature."

MY EYES ROLLING SO HARD.

But the whole time we ran home I thought about it: Why do we have to love the people we happen to live with? And what happens when we don't live with them? I love Dad and Mom and always have, but what if I don't actually love Marli and never did? Would distance change that? Could it make me love Marli, or at least like her more? What if when I move to New York, away from her, I can love her easier . . . or more . . . or differently? Or what if I just don't have enough love in me to love Marli, from ANYWHERE? What, then? Maybe my own human nature is junky and broken.

3/11 10:31 am

We brought quotes about art to class today.

Mine was from Andy, of course: "Art is what you can get away with."

Then we discussed everyone's quotes and when it came to mine, we talked about why anybody would want to get away with making art, not just create something beautiful or tragic or

mind-blowing. Why would you spend your time creating something and trying to con someone into thinking it is art . . . when
it isn't?

And then Adams said, "Unless that's the point. Unless the point
is to play with the boundaries one can get away with. Maybe the
art's the manipulation of the boundaries and not the actual art
itself? And in Andy's case, don't forget, he was a businessman.
He was the great advertiser. I'm sure you know that Warhol also
said, 'Making money is art and working is art and good business
is the best art.' Maybe Mr. Warhol was making a statement about
the artists of his day, a judgment? Context is everything. Isn't it?"

And then art class basically turned into debate with all of us
trying to figure out if that quote is actually like true or real—
and none of us could settle on a definite yes or no, which Adams
said was good. We should think more on it, listen to our gut
reactions. Figure out our POV.

But weirdly my POV on this one makes me super frustrated
with Andy. There are so many ways to read that quote, now that
I think about it more, and I want to know what he thought he got
away with and what he knew he couldn't. What did he hide from
his art and what did he use? And how did he know how to draw
a boundary?

One other quote I really liked was the one Sam Chang brought
to class:

*"Art is the only way to run away without
leaving home." —Twyla Tharp*

I get this one deep down. Every time I paint, I feel like I'm not just
leaving home, I'm moving closer to something bigger and better

than my life. I'm dissolving into a part of the world. I know
Sammy feels that way with his creations, too.

3/12 4:30 pm

Went into the kitchen. Marli's feet were propped on top of
the dinner table right where I usually throw my backpack and
Ronnie was rubbing her toes. They were saying names at each
other—just throwing them out:

Robert E. Lee Haysmith

Madeline Mackenzie Haysmith

April Rains Haysmith

Stormy Nights Haysmith

Sunshine Reyes Haysmith

(What's with the weather names? Tribute to Dad?)

"What would you name our baby," Ronnie asked me. "You're all
clever and shit."

"She gets no say in the matter," Marli said quickly.

"I was just curious. Maybe Piper'd come up with something
artistic and such."

"No, it will be some freak name, like . . . Galveston Van Gogh."

"That's not so bad," he said.

"I would never name a baby Galveston," I said. "Maybe Austin,
but not Galveston."

"I like Austin." Ronnie sat up. I smiled at him before I could
stop myself.

"OW! You're rubbing too hard. What are you trying to do, break off my big toe?" Marli said, snapping one of the table napkins at him. "Don't be such a dick."

I came to my room before I had to see her meltdown.

I can hear them from here.

Ronnie just said, "I was only tryin' to be nice. Family an' such."

I wish he would tell her she's the one being the dick.

3/13 English class

Sunlight streaming into Napolitano's class-room fades from hot, melty yellow to cool white on the floor. Spreads. Light is wider on the floor than outside the window. Does this make sense? Explore yellow & whites. Talk to Adams in art tomorrow.

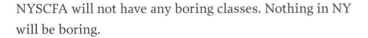

And now back to talking about "THE BRITISH NOVEL." Snore fest.

NYSCFA will not have any boring classes. Nothing in NY will be boring.

3/14 After dinner

Enzo and Kit came over after school and helped me trim the ends of my hair, which were growing out weird. E asked me who's going to do this for you when you aren't here anymore and I said I'll get a glamorous new hair stylist in New York and he said they are like a million dollars and you'll miss me.

"Well, you could still come with us," I said. "It's not too late. Right?"

He didn't answer and Kit said, "You know you're still gonna come, you wouldn't really desert us."

He waved his hand and said, "I'm not talking about it." Then he started draping fabrics (peaches, ivories, browns, golds, blacks) across my bed, showing us ideas he had for his capsule collection. GORGEOUS. I want to wear all those fleshy tones, even though I usually prefer pop colors.

Kit was stringing together some of my broken earrings and making them into a necklace. She was working with the tiniest pliers I've ever seen. Her mom is getting her into a stone-setting class, even though she doesn't want to work with real gems, she said. (She thinks it's another way her parents are trying to make up for the fact that they are never around. Stick her in a class and then they will feel less guilty.)

Kit says she wants to work with naturals like rocks and pebbles and granite, said she's going to make necklaces that look like they've been popped up and flung off the highway—she wants to work with rubber, like blown-out tires, too. I know I'll end up wearing one of those and then everyone will ask me where I got it and I'll tell them my BFF, she's amazing.

3/15 4:45 pm

Back at 610 Diner. Kit's sketching and still working on her wire-frame. Pencil lead has rubbed off on her hands and her silver fingertips keep making smudges every time she taps her graph pad and she keeps getting frustrated because it's not clean. She's so far along on her project and I need to like, really start mine, not just think about it. Ideas just come faster at the end, when I'm not thinking through each step, just doing. Kit has to see it though, forecast it. It drives her crazy that I can work so fast. I'm just jealous that she can focus for so long. She's a marathoner; I'm a sprinter.

I'm waiting for another cup of coffee, which I've been doing for like 5 hours. We ordered the Ides of Mashed Potatoes and Julius Caesar salad to share because when else are we going to do it, right?

"Here, bitches."

It was Marli, pouring coffee into my mug.

"You're working?" I said. "I didn't realize you were back. That's good, right?"

"Yeah, pregnant and waiting tables. What a dream come true."

I looked at Marli's stomach as she took another table's order. I wondered if her ankles were going to swell now that she's waitressing again. That would involve me witnessing more public foot rubs.

"Do you think she spit in your coffee?" Kit asked under her breath. She was outlining her fork on a stack of paper napkins with her pencil.

"What do you think?" I pushed my mug away. "If I'd known she was going to be here, we could have gone to my house."

"She's always gonna be there," Kit sighed. "Always has been, always will be."

"Can you imagine living with your parents, like, forever?" I asked.

"Only if I could change the furniture," Kit said. "Not like they'd notice." Kit picked up the napkin she had drawn the fork on and pretended to shovel the napkin-fork into the mashed potatoes. She acted like she took a big bite out of them, fake-rubbed her stomach and said, "MMMMmmm, so good."

"Homemade?" I asked.

"You have to try them!" She handed me her napkin-fork and I pretended to take a big helping.

"Let's eat here forever!"

Then we did our thing—ate, drank, and drew until the dinner crowd showed up and we got kicked out of our booth.

3/16 11 am

Don't even know how to write this. Kit just found out she didn't get in. There has to be a mistake. Going over to her house now.

3/17 3:15 am

If there is any justice in the world, and I'm beginning to think there isn't, Kit would be going to school with me. Kit would be my dorm roommate. Kit would be moving to New York with me. And Enzo, too. I don't understand how all of this is falling apart.

But Kit is definitely not going. She got rejected on email and by regular mail. I held the letter in my hands while she sat on her bed (where she's now asleep) and stared out her window. She hasn't told her parents—because they aren't here, of course. Enzo came over right away and when I saw him, my heart hummingbirded a little. Not because he came here for me in particular and not because it was love at first sight again or anything like that, but because I knew he wouldn't let Kit go through this by herself. Because deep down, Enzo was our friend, whether I wanted him to be more or not. Because Enzo made me feel safe.

"You can still go to Rice or U of H or even take a year off," he said. "Maybe you could go to France and hook up with even more French dudes." He was trying everything.

And it was like she didn't hear any of it. She just sat there, the light from her half-closed closet door dividing her face, twisting up her comforter in her hand, her knuckles white from her grip.

She made me check my email in front of her 3 times to see if I got anything. I held my breath each time because. Because because because.

Because now if I don't get in, I'm stuck here.

With Marli.

With Marli's baby.

Without New York.

But with Kit and Enzo?

I don't know.

I'm confused.

Could I do it for another year?

No no no.

Marli against me for another year? I just can't. I promised myself I'd leave.

If I don't leave?

I won't live.

And if I do get in, I go. Without Kit. Without Enzo. Like moving without my arms and legs. No, worse. Like going without my heart and eyes.

It's no good if I open my email and it's no good if I avoid it. And I've been checking it nonstop ever since Kit passed out. Enzo had been working on some kind of limoncello drink, which is like lemon alcohol something, his mom's recipe, and he brought it over and Kit drank it like it was lemonade. It was good, but really strong. I wish I had gone home tonight. I shouldn't have slept over. But her dad's not getting off his shift until 5, and Enzo and I didn't want to leave her alone. He's passed out next to me, holding my hand.

Before he fell asleep, he whisper-mumbled to me, You're gonna be okay.

"What do you mean, I'm going to be okay? What about Kit?"

"All of us. We're all going to be okay." He was already dozing off.

I would do anything for a little sleep right now. But my heart is racing. I'm trapped.

I wish I was running with Dad.

3/17 Morning

I lied to Kit and Enzo and told them I promised Dad I would take a morning run with him. Now I get to be home listening to Marli bitching into her phone about morning sickness to one of her friends, probably Beth Ann, after not sleeping all night.

I just didn't know what to say to Kit. We ranted about how unfair it was, what a mistake it was, how it couldn't possibly be right. She just kept staring out her window.

"You're just not mainstream enough, that's probably it," E said.

"Does that mean I'm mainstream if I get accepted?"

"Why does it always have to be about you?" Kit snapped.

"It's not always about me," I said.

"Sorry," E mouthed at me.

"Don't say you're sorry, if that's what you really think."

"I don't know what to think!" he said. "I'm just pissed for Kit!"

"SHUT UP!" Kit finally screamed. "I swear, you two would have been perfect together if Enzo wasn't . . ."

She didn't finish. Enzo wouldn't look at her and I was pissed off. Blasting at Enzo like that when he was just trying to help, even if he messed up, was no reason to get rude. It's not like gay's a bad word, but the way she was going to sling it against him, us, was way not cool.

"What am I going to do?" Kit whispered.

We hugged each other because our words sucked. All of them.

I really hope I see Adams at school before I see Kit. I want to know what I'm supposed to say. One of those quotes she's always putting on the blackboard—which one would work now? Because I need words, the right ones, and all I want to do is get away from everything and paint. Everything sucks too much.

Kit wasn't in school today after all. I texted her and she said she wasn't feeling well and also had a bad hair-dye accident. I'm going over there as soon as I'm done with studio time. Adams told me to listen, not talk too much, and just be a good friend.

Then she asked me if I had gotten a letter yet and I said no. She crinkled her nose and adjusted her turquoise eyeglasses chain.

"Huh."

"Is that good?" I asked. "Or bad? Because now I can't tell how I should feel."

"Just sit with it. Be with it," Adams said.

"What?"

"Your confusion. Kit's confusion. School. It will work itself out. But don't rush it."

"What if I don't get in?"

Ms. Adams's relaxed smile stretched across her face. Sometimes she looked like a lazy cat to me. "Remember when we did the Polaroid transfers in class and everyone had to wait to see how the photographs would process through the day lab? How we weren't sure what images would develop? It's the same thing, Piper. You have to wait."

"I hate waiting," I said to her. "I'm not good at it."

"Well, that's very self-aware, Piper. Now stop grumbling and go be a good friend."

Can't help but think that Adams knows something I don't know. Can't help but think this means I got in. I get tingly-dizzy just thinking about it. I want to go to New York more than anything I've ever wanted in the whole world.

Just back from Kit's and the hair-dye sitch. Her hair was greenish and spotty in a bad way and we tried to fix it. She told me to just shave it all off, so we did.

"I can't have it just short like yours. If it's going to be short, it has to be gone, all gone. Just hack it off. I don't want anyone thinking I'm trying to copy YOU," she said. She looked phenom, but she was so pissed she couldn't see it.

"Of course nobody would think that. I would be lucky if anyone thought I looked like you."

Nobody would ever mistake Kit and me for each other; I was as pale as she was dark. She was as curvy as I was straight. She was circles and arcs, I was a line. Her hair, gloriously curly, could be bouncy or cropped into a cute Afro. And now she would be bald and beautiful, total boss style. My thin hair could be long and stringy or short and stringy. Without a ton of hair-spray, it did nothing. I guess my hair could take color better than Kit's but that was about it.

"Well, nobody ever would want to look like me or be like me because I'm such a loser that even NYSCFA could tell without even meeting me. They could tell how awful I am just by my application." I had never heard Kit put herself down like that, even on a bad hair day. She looked tight and springy, like a puma ready to pounce.

"That's not true," I said. "They obviously made a mistake! You can apply again."

"Oh really? Are YOU going to apply again when you get a rejection?"

I couldn't tell her that Adams really makes it sound like I'm getting in. Kit not getting accepted sucks, but she's not stuck with a Marli like I am if I don't get in.

Everything in my life depends on me getting out of here and Kit knows that better than anyone else and that's why it hurt so much when she said that to me. Kit can work anywhere she wants in her ginormous house. Her mom has set up a jewelry shop just for K in their library. And nobody is ever in her house to bother her, which sucks for her, but still. She doesn't know how lucky that is. Not to mention Kit is 10x the artist I am and makes stuff people actually want to look at/have/wear, too—her stuff sells out online and the site she is making for her senior project looks cool and is so HER.

If NYSCFA didn't pick her, why in the hell would it want me? But, Adams makes my chance sound so real. But #2, I am convincing myself into a total mess. If I'm wrong about what Adams keeps hinting at I am going to be destroyed.

I don't know if I have heartburn or what—is this what Dad always gets?—but I feel like my whole chest is on fire, maybe because we finished the rest of Enzo's horrible lemon drink. Does alcohol go bad or something? I think I'm going to puke and I can't even go into the bathroom because Marli's taking one of her crying showers.

Spray-painting a canvas in the backyard when Marli practically flattened the screen door.

"WHAT IN THE HIGH HELL ARE YOU DOING? Trying to kill my baby?"

"What?" I jumped back. "What are you talking about?"

"There are warning labels all over this thing! God, you're so SELFISH!" She pointed to the back of the can, where there's a warning label for pregnant women and people with lung problems.

"I didn't know. I thought it was okay if you were inside—you weren't out here! I really wasn't trying to hurt the baby." I was freaking out, scared. I really didn't mean anything by it.

"Yeah, right."

I couldn't resist telling her that I wouldn't have to spray in the backyard if I had my studio.

"It was never your studio, you little thief, it was—AND IS— my bedroom. It was always my bedroom, even when I left for college. Stop trying to make everything in my life yours— including Ronnie. And stop trying to make everything my fault."

"Marli, I really am sorry," I said again. All I could think was . . . Ronnie? She thinks I want Ronnie? No thanks! And he didn't want me either. Bleck!

"Stop sighing at me," she said in her really scary quiet voice, slowly rubbing her stomach. I held my breath. "I will NOT accept a guilt trip from you. I've had to share or give up every single thing ever since you were born, Piper. So just Watch. Your. Step."

"I'm sorry," I said again.

"Get away from me."

I felt sick and paralyzed. There was nothing I could say back to her without causing her to explode. Her tipping point was between us, invisible but so heavy. Maybe I should have said something more but I didn't want to take her wrath. I didn't want to be in her path.

I hate constantly saying I'm sorry. I hate apologizing to her over and over.

So now I'm in my room hiding.

Again.

I don't want to sit with it or be with it. I'm wishing I was anywhere else.

Holding my breath.

Trying to disappear.

3/21 11 pm

After dinner, I went with Mom to pick up her cowboy boots that she had re-soled. It is like her 5th time getting them redone.

"Why don't you just buy a new pair?" I asked her.

"Too expensive. Besides, these took forever for me to break in. Too bad you never wanted a pair."

"I like them, but they don't go with anything I have."

"Piper, you are so perfectly you. You've always had your own style." And just like that her bottom lip was trembling. She put her hand on top of mine on my leg and kept the other one on the wheel.

"What's wrong?"

"You're growing up too fast, kid."

We were quiet until we pulled into the parking lot of Cavender's Boots.

"I'll get some boots if you really want, Mom. I can make them cool." I was trying to make her laugh.

"You aren't boots, Piper."

"Well, what am I then?"

She smiled and pointed to my paint-splattered wingtips that Enzo and I picked up last year on our road trip back from Austin.

"I'm sorry I got in a fight with Marli yesterday," I said. I was sure that was what she was thinking about, why she had insisted I drive with her when she knew I had a mountain of homework to do.

"You're starting to sound like me," she said. "We both have to stop apologizing." She looked at the rearview mirror and dabbed her eyes. "God knows Marli isn't a goddamn angel."

"Right?" I said and tried to high-five Mom. "THANK YOU!" FINALLY.

"Forget it," Mom said. "I should keep my mouth closed. I'm a horrible mother."

"You're not horrible," I said. "You're the World's Most Okay Mom!" which got her to smile for half a second.

"Marli's okay, too," Mom tried. "She's just . . ."

"She's just always going to hate me," I said.

We got out of the car.

"She doesn't hate you. You know that."

I absolutely did not because she absolutely did. But that was not going to fly with Mom.

"But why don't you and Dad do something about her? Just kick her out or something?"

"The hard ones are the ones that need the most love, Piper. You know who needs the most attention in physical therapy at the clinic? It's not the grandmothers with the hip replacements. It's the football players with the dislocated shoulders, the big tough ones, the ones you'd think could handle the pain. Their stubbornness and pride get in the way of their healing, but they need the most tenderness and compassion and of course, actual therapy and help. Marli is like a quarterback."

"Sooo, Marli definitely needs help like them, too, Mom, don't you think?" I looked at her. "Some kind of therapy."

But Mom did what she always does. When the Marli Talk got to be too much, she avoided my eyes and focused on what was in front of her, anything that wasn't me. Just strolled to the customer-service counter like she hadn't just been about to waterfall tears.

It wasn't till we were back in the car that she got real again.

"Your dad and I, maybe we didn't do right by Marli. Maybe we made some mistakes."

"What kinds of mistakes?" I asked.

"Sometimes, it's not always a good thing to say yes. To be indulgent. You might not understand that now, but you will eventually."

"No, I do understand," I said. When had Marli EVER not gotten her way? "But, you don't say yes too much to me."

"You don't need it, not like Marli. When you hear no, you just figure out another way, your own way." And Marli, what? Just, when she heard no, exploded?

I looked out the window at the Sonic and the Whataburger and the tire place and the mall.

"What if I don't get in?" I asked.

"Get in?"

"New York." What in the serious hell else would I be talking about?

"That would be okay. Your father . . . and I . . . think you should consider other choices anyway . . . either way."

"What do you mean?"

"I mean other places. Other schools. It's a little scary for us that you've only applied to one. A tough one. A conservatory!"

"There are no other choices for me, Mom. It's either there or nowhere. I just know that's my place. You don't think I'm going to get in?"

"I didn't say that."

"You didn't <u>say</u> it, but . . . ?"

"Piper, you're really good. Dad and I believe in you, but we're not dummies. There are a LOT of talented young people in the world, and Dad thinks you're really taking a risk counting on one place. You know him. He likes predictability. There's a reason he's a forecaster."

Did Mom think she could distract me from what she was saying? That they, or he, didn't think I could get in?

"So, this is coming from Dad?" I was really hoping she was just getting easily convinced, that at least one of them was on my side.

"He doesn't want you to be hurt. And it's expensive, honey. And between you and me, I just don't think your father wants you traipsing around Manhattan. You've never been there before. You've only seen it in the movies and on TV. It looks glamorous, but there's more to it. It's a tough city and you're just a girl. And the world is just so crazy right now."

"Just a girl? Is that all?"

"Our girl. You're used to being a big fish. You and Kit and Enzo have your own special thing. But you're going to be starting over, Piper. Your success doesn't carry over, y'know. I don't know if you've thought about what that's going to be like, being a small fish. Nobody in New York knows who you are or how talented you are. Why should they think you're so special?"

WTF Mom?!?!? Jeez.

"New York is the only REAL city. And anyway, wouldn't I be starting over anywhere I go to school, Mom? Or am I just supposed to not go to college. Like Marli." I couldn't help it. Mom wanted me to give up, like I could just quit being an artist.

As if I could just drop the one thing I live for, like it was some elective class and not my life.

"Hey." She snapped her fingers at me. "Don't be a smartass. Your dad and I . . . just think it's good to have options."

"Fuck options!" I said, kicking at the car mat.

"HEY!" she said. "Unacceptable, Piper! And straighten that out!"

I said sorry and fixed the mat.

"We know you, Piper. We just know you can make any city a REAL city, whether you're in New York or elsewhere."

"It will be New York," I said. "You don't have to say elsewhere, Mom!"

She pulled into our driveway and parked.

As we walked into the house, I felt shaky, like I had goose bumps, even though it was still hot as hell outside. Mom kissed Dad on the cheek and winked at him, and I don't think I was supposed to see it, but I did. Were they like, conspiring? What the hell was that?

They want me to fail. They don't want me to think about New York OR elsewhere, they want me to stay here, not even try to travel and create and live somewhere new with new people and new ways to look at things. They want me contained. New York? Dad's never gone, Mom's never gone. I'll be the first one. And they don't know what to expect. And maybe I don't either, but at least I'm not terrified of the big bad world! At least I'm willing to try something that freaks me out and might be the best thing ever! And they just can't deal. It pisses me off. I'm tired of living this way. Don't they ever get tired of just being scared of the world all the time?

And now I'm supposed to do my damn homework.

"As soon as you stop wanting something, you get it." —Andy Warhol

That's the quote on Adams's chalkboard in the art studio today.

"Whatever," I said.

"I always write that one on the board this time of year. It's a good reminder for all the seniors. I thought you'd like it."

"I haven't heard anything yet," I told her. I was really not feeling it.

"That's great. That means you haven't been rejected. And besides, you need to focus on more pressing matters, like your personal geography project, remember that? Any progress yet? I haven't seen you working on it."

I shrugged and told her I was. "Too much time is bad. It kind of has to feel like a rush, y'know?"

She frowned and made a tsk-tsk sound, which I hated to hear. She usually used it on other students, not me. "Artists have to concern themselves with time management, too," she said. "Don't use your creative process as an excuse."

The truth is I have no clue. Have to come up with something great. Something fantastic. Something that will prove to Mom and Dad I'm better than they think and make them believe in ME.

3/22 5:30 pm

Oh my god. I did it.

3/23 12:45am

I knew it I knew it I knew it. I knew I could get in and I did it!!!!
HAPPINESS EXPLOSION!!!! I got home from school yesterday.
Mom was back from work earlier than usual because she had
two cancellations at the clinic. She asked to see me in the
kitchen. I thought she was going to have another Marli conversation with me, but then I could see she was trying to hide a
smile. She clicked open Skype on her laptop, and Dad was on
the other side. Then I thought WOW it was going to be some
kind of extra-weird Marli intervention, but Mom looked too
excited, like she was going to jump out of her skin. For a second,
I kind of thought she and Dad were going to say they were
pregnant, too. Hello, stomach drop.

But then Mom pulled the thin white NYSCFA envelope from
behind her back.

"We don't want you to open this alone."

"And kiddo, no matter what happens, we love you. You don't
have to be in New York. You don't have to prove anything to
anyone," Dad said.

"But if you are in New York, we're just as happy for you," Mom
said, shooting him a weird look.

I DID NOT WANT TO OPEN THE ENVELOPE IN FRONT OF
THEM. OH MY GOD. THE WORST.

But I did. Opened it right there. Read and reread the opening paragraph over and over again and again and again:

Dear Ms. Perish,

Congratulations! We are pleased to offer you admission to the New York School of Contemporary Fine Arts. You have been accepted to the Visual and Critical Studies program in the Fine Arts wing. An invitation to NYSCFA is quite an accomplishment. Should you choose to accept the challenge, there's no doubt your time at the conservatory will have a lasting and positive impact on your life.

"POSITIVE IMPACT!" Mom screamed. Dad looked like his face had lost all of its shape. He had tears stuck in his eyes and cleared his throat before he said, "This is just great, kid. Just great! You did it! We knew you could do it!" (Even as I was exploding I was thinking inside that I couldn't believe he was saying that.)

I kept reading the letter to them and Mom and Dad kept looking at each other, Mom with her hand on her heart, Dad leaning in on his office desk, looking into his computer, like he could read the letter with me.

Mom messed up my hair and squeezed my shoulder, hugged me tight to her. I couldn't stop reading it over and over.

"What's going on?" Marli strolled into the kitchen.

"Marli, I got in. I'm going to New York!"

I don't know what I was expecting. A high five? A fist pump? Marli jumping up and down?

She nodded her head a little bit.

"Tell your sister you're happy for her," Dad said from the laptop.

She walked over and gave me a hug. I could feel both of us hold on and pull away at the same time, like we didn't know how to do it, like we had never even held hands as little kids. As she left, she grabbed the jar of peanut butter from the counter.

Mom winked at me and said, "Go ahead, Piper. Read it again. Read it to both of us again."

And I did.

And then I totally, 100%, freaked the fuck out.

3/23 11 am

Usually I would be sleeping in on a Saturday morning but hello I didn't sleep all night and Enzo is taking me New York shopping! When I texted him last night, he wrote back, *FUCK YOU, YOU AMAZING ARTIST. COFFEE, KOLACHES, SHOPPING OUR BALLS OFF ALL DAY TOMORROW NO EXCUSES.* And he added like 100 emoji shopping bags.

And then he called me and we talked for 2 hours on the phone and I told him no matter what he wasn't allowed to tell Kit, or slip up, or accidentally spill it.

Now he's picking me up in 10 minutes. We decided we're going to strategize together about how I tell Kit because I'm scared. I'm so excited to see Enzo and celebrate and I have to remember not to try and hug or kiss him or anything. I know things aren't how they were. I'm just still figuring out what that means. But at least it's not January, where we could barely talk or text each other. That was so awful, pit-of-my-stomach-aching awful. I never want that feeling again.

We are the new and improved Piper and Enzo now. We're friends and most of the rest of it is behind us, maybe. I can't help but still get nervous-excited when he wants to hang with me, but maybe that's my, our, new normal.

7:30 pm UPDATE: PURCHASES

- cheetah-print skinny capris
- red and black paisley dress (to go over cheetahs, totally works)
- perfect-condition black loafers—and from the men's section, but Enzo found them for me and they are my size and they were $8 WHAT!?!!?
- silver money clip I'm going to give to Kit to use for a necklace or something awesome

Ugh. It hurts just thinking about Kit. Enzo and I decided I should talk to Adams first.

3/25 1:15 pm

In English class. Barely made it on time, after spending my lunch period with Adams. When I ran into the studio, Adams said, "Let me guess."

I started giggling. I couldn't help it.

"You did it!"

She leaned back on her desk and folded her arms across her chest.

"Of all my kids this year, I knew it would be you. You must be thrilled. Your parents must be tickled."

I sat down on one of the stools by the hand figures.

"I'm so excited! I couldn't have done it without you," I said.

"Sure you could."

"No seriously, without you, I never would have figured out even the simplest stuff."

She was just shaking her head, smiling.

I told her I still needed her help, with something big, bigger than me getting into school.

"What could be bigger than getting into your dream school?"

"Kit's and my friendship."

She told me she understood, there was a lot of competition and jealousy in the art world and the world in general, but that didn't mean we couldn't be supportive of each other.

"Let me confirm something for you," Adams said. "Kit has her own path. She's very, very good at what she does."

"I know!" I practically yelled. "That's why I can't understand how she didn't get in and I did. How can she not go to New York? How can I go to New York without her?"

"Survivor's guilt," Adams said under her breath.

"What?"

"It means you made it out. You have a chance."

"And Kit?"

Adams was quiet for a second and twirled her fingers around the tan, split fringe falling from her poncho.

"Kit's going to be fine wherever she is. Kit doesn't need New York."

I thought for a second—did I need New York or did I just want it? And what was the difference? And how would I know? Did it matter? I wanted to see the world outside of home, outside of a squeezed section of our garage as my studio. I wanted to go to the places where great artists, like Andy, had gone and changed the world because of the things they made. New York would be my artistic pilgrimage!

But I also needed relief—is that the right word?—from Marli. I needed to know what a life, my life, was without her. I needed to feel that, even if it was just for college. Kit had no Marli. Kit had a big home. Kit had Kit's brain. I didn't have any of those things. It was true. I would never feel like my life was complete if I didn't see what it was like to be with no Marli. By myself. In New York.

I knew then that I did, I needed it.

"How do I tell her?" I asked. "Please tell me. Because I'm . . . I just feel awful and weird and all tangled up about it. And Enzo and I tried to brainstorm talking to her about it, but we didn't come up with anything that would make it easier."

"Well, it's not going to be easy. You have to approach Kit calmly, openly. Give her a chance to take it in. Give her . . . the space of a Mondrian."

"Mondrians are all locked up," I told her. "There is no space in them."

"There's space in the block of colors. May seem crowded, but that's just because the color blocks are limited. They have boundaries, their exterior lines. But inside those boundaries, anything can happen. Do you understand?" She took a breath. "You're giving Kit a new boundary. You need to give her room to feel all of everything that she's feeling within it."

"I don't think I can give her Mondrian space, not when I feel like a Pollock."

"Pollock used what he had. And you have to do that too, Piper."

And then she sent me off to class, where I am now, and I'm supposed to be part of a group discussion on Henry V and I'm just not.

3/26 7 am

Marli is moaning in the bathroom again. Some things never change.

Kit called me last night and I didn't pick up the phone. And then I didn't text her back either. I tried on outfits and pretended I didn't see my phone blinking.

And then just now, I couldn't hold it in anymore. I texted Kit and she's going to meet me after school. Every day I don't tell her I feel sick. All I want to do is paint, hide in our garage and paint. But I can't paint until I tell Kit. But I hate thinking about telling Kit so I'm just thinking about painting. I know Adams would call this procrastination but whatever.

Andy said, "During the 1960s, I think, people forgot what emotions were supposed to be."

I wish that's how it was now. I wish I felt nothing, or better, that Kit had just fucking gotten into the school.

This whole day is going to be insane.

PS I just heard Marli throw up and miss the toilet. UGH.

3/27 12 am

There should be some kind of life rule that you never have to tell your best friend bad news.

Kit came over after school yesterday. We headed to the kitchen and she told me You seem weird and I said What's new and she said Not good weird, WEIRD weird and I told her, "I got you something."

I ran to my room and got the money clip for her and put it in her hands and said, "I'm sorry I didn't wrap it in something awesome but I just got too excited and knew you could do something with it, some kind of cool pin or like a necklace or something." She turned it over and held it up and said, "Initials—cool! KRS. Who do you think KRS is?"

I shrugged. "It has a K in it so I thought you would like it. Maybe it means KIT RULES SOMUCH."

She looked at me sideways and said, "You're being really nice. You don't have to buy me stuff just because I didn't get in."

Hearing that made me feel like all of the air was caught in my throat, like I was stuck somewhere between a swallow and an exhale, and I reached around her and grabbed a handful of grapes. She picked one up and studied it like a gemstone, the way I've seen her do when she's using her jeweler's loupe, and she popped it in her mouth, all funny like, and made a fish face at me. All good so far.

Then she went to the fridge to pull out the lemonade and that's when she saw it. My acceptance letter.

Mom or Dad—most likely Mom—had taken it from my bedroom and posted it on the fridge. What didn't they understand about my fucking privacy? How could they do this, just post my stuff without permission? What if Marli decided to destroy it? What if someone got a stain on it from something in the kitchen?

"Is this what I think it is?"

I stepped in front of the fridge door, folded the paper, and stuck it in my back pocket.

"At least let me see it. At least let me see what an acceptance letter looks like."

"You're going to know what one looks like. It's dumb. It's so formula."

She stood perfectly still, stared at our kitchen tile.

"I was going to tell you," I said, as if that would help.

"When?" she asked. "WHEN?"

"I just wanted you to be happy for me," I said.

"I AM HAPPY. DON'T I LOOK FUCKING HAPPY?"

"Pissed."

"You lied to me," she said. "You probably got it before I got mine."

I shook my head NO. She put her hands over her ears, the metal cuffs on her wrists making her look like she was chained to herself.

"Let me see the date on it."

"Why?"

"I want to see it."

And I didn't even consider that that meant anything. So I unfolded the letter and we looked at it together. It was dated March 10.

"You've known since March 10th?"

"No, I swear. I just found out on Friday."

"You waited a whole weekend?"

"My parents wanted to celebrate," I lied.

She stared at me. "I wasn't sure it was real," I tried again.

Her eyes laser-focused on the letter.

"I didn't know how to tell you. I'm sorry."

"Don't be sorry for getting in," she said. "But you didn't have to lie."

"I tell you everything," I said. "You know that!"

I started crying and hating that I was starting to cry. I wish I could just be like Dad and make an argument all the way through without mascara streaking my face like a fucked-up zebra.

"By not telling me, you just . . . lied, Piper. You knew you got in, but you acted like you didn't."

"I knew it was going to suck when I told you," I said. "What was I supposed to do? Tell you at school?"

"Is that why you didn't want to hang out all weekend?"

"I was just busy."

"Doing what?"

"Family stuff. You know. I went shopping with Enzo. That's where I got you that!"

I pointed to the money clip that was now sitting on the kitchen counter.

"Did you tell him yet?"

I kind of nodded my head, more like drawing a figure 8 with it.

"Yes or no, Piper?"

"He knows." I had to whisper it.

"So, you both were lying?"

"He's the one choosing to stay here. I knew HE wasn't going to be upset."

"Don't turn this around on me," she said. "This isn't my fault."

"What's not your fault? Did you do something to my little sister, Katrina Bash?"

Kit and I both whipped around to see Marli standing in the kitchen doorway, with a hand towel in front of her not exactly covering all of her very naked parts. Her wet brown curls were stuck on her shoulders like one of Mom's weird hanging house-plants and there was a small puddle forming by her feet.

"Get out!" I said.

"Excuse moi," she said. I was immediately on edge. "But since Piper couldn't be bothered to fold and put up the clean towels like she's supposed to, she made me go through the whole house to get to the laundry room. If only there were fresh towels in the bathroom . . ."

"I'll get you one!" I snapped.

"Don't worry about it. Looks like you're busy breaking up." She smirked, dripping wet through the kitchen into the laundry room. Her body was rounder and smoother, and more hulking, too. The hard edges of her cheekbones and collarbones seemed to have filled out and her hips shimmied when she moved. There was so much more to Marli than I realized. All her corners were disappearing, her own flesh just taking over her body. I didn't want to look but I couldn't look away. She was fascinating.

"Just get out!" I yelled again. "I'm sorry," I said to Kit. "Let's go somewhere else."

Marli was opening and slamming the dryer door shut.

"THESE TOWELS ARE FRIGGIN' WET!" she yelled. The dryer went back on.

"We can't do this here," I said to Kit. "Let's go in the backyard. Or to the park. Or to your house."

"What am I supposed to dry off with now?" Marli asked. "God, Piper, so selfish once again. Isn't she selfish, Kit? Is that why you did something to her?"

"Here," I said, handing Marli the roll of paper towels that hung near the sink, "just use these."

"Gross," she said in this simpery Valley Girl voice. "FAR too harsh for my skin. I have veeeeery sensitive skin, you know. Especially with the baby!"

"MARLI! COME ON!" I screamed. "JUST LEAVE ALREADY!"

Marli raised her hands up, barely holding on to her hand towel, and started to back into the dining room. Kit winced and I felt like gagging.

"Just trying to help, little sis," she said, and she waved a wet white paper towel like a flag of surrender, which just pissed me off more.

When she was finally in the living room, I asked Kit if she would come back to my room.

"Give me the chance to explain," I said. "I just needed some time."

Kit looked down at our kitchen tiles and traced her foot alongside the cabinet. "Don't worry about it, Piper. I get it. I'll call you later."

I tried to follow her out the kitchen door into the backyard, but she broke into a jagged kind of run and I could see her wiping her eyes with the back of her hand.

"I'm sorry," I called out.

I came back into the kitchen to find the money clip sitting on the counter, and Marli holding my acceptance letter.

"Give that to me," I said.

"This?" She fanned herself with it.

"Don't play games, not now," I said, totally crying.

"Isn't it funny?"

"What, Marli?"

"You just always hurt people, Piper. Poor, poor Kit. Poor, poor Ronnie. Poor big sister Marli. Tsk-tsk. You're not the only one who lives here and you're not the only one who has feelings in the world. Think about it."

She stuck my acceptance letter inside the money clip and then thrust the whole thing flat against my heart.

"Hope it's worth it," she said, and flashed a totally awful beauty pageant grin. Then she left me crying and I didn't care because I hated her and worse, hated that she'd seen Kit and me fighting.

3/28 Lunch

I had weird dreams all night, they all seemed to be tinted in blue lights, kind of strobe-y and trippy. Like the Turrell hallway at the museum had gotten into my head. Most of the dreams were about Kit and me playing some kind of hide-and-seek tag in a bunch of buildings, and everything was foggy. We were like Spider-Man or Superman and we had superpowers and could jump between buildings. But every time I was about to catch her, she would leap to another building. She was chasing me, too. But we could never just land in the same spot together. And it wasn't fun. It wasn't like when we go dancing. It was like we couldn't stop and it was panicky and rushed. It was like drinking a million cups of coffee, and not being able to sleep, except I was asleep. I woke up with my legs kicking and clutching the sides of my sheets. My pillow was on the floor. I have this weird feeling I was not sleepwalking, but sleeprunning. Is that a thing?

Didn't eat this morning and I can't eat lunch. I left a card in Kit's locker and I think she got it, but we haven't met up in the hallway or anything all day. I asked Enzo if he had seen Kit and he said to maybe give her a day or two.

"That feels impossible," I said.

"She's bummed out. Wouldn't you feel the same way?"

"Yes, but . . ."

"But what?"

"I don't know. I feel like you're taking her side."

"It's not about sides," Enzo said. "When I have to pick a team, I pick Team Friendship and you're both on that team. When we went over there when she didn't get in, that was for you too, not just her. I knew you would need my help dealing with Kit not getting in more than she would. Didn't you know that?"

I shook my head.

"Well, it's true," he said. "Why do you think I was holding your hand and not hers?"

I shrugged.

"We'll get through this," he reassured me, and left for calc.

Adams said I could work in the studio during lunch, so that's where I am. Picking up all of her half-used cans of blues, the colors I can dive into. What did Adams say—"let the color inherit our stories"? That's what I need to do, inherit my reality, my dreams, all of it. Try to find the dream shades, the motion. Try to get that blue dream fog on paper. Make it move. Need momentum. Need escape.

3/29 7 am

Mom said after I get home from school we have to call the financial aid contact at NYSCFA, Helen Mundy. We get to confirm my attendance today! I can't wait to talk to Helen Mundy and ask her everything! Mom said I should make a list of questions.

Mom will be home by 4 pm so that we can call her at 5 pm. (They are an hour ahead of us! Eastern Time instead of Central Time!)

After yesterday's suckfest, kind of happy to just not be crying this morning. Sculpting hair into fauxhawk! Off to school.

3/29 5:47 pm (CENTRAL TIME!)

Mom and I just got off the phone with Helen Mundy. Helen Mundy, who told us to call her Helen and not Ms. Mundy like Mom told me to do, is so smart, I can tell. She sounded calm and smooth and nice. She didn't sound like anyone from around here, but also didn't sound very "New Yorky" either, or at least the way I thought she would sound.

Helen told Mom and me about a bunch of packages for scholarship money and financial aid, and something called Pell Grants. I thought she said Bell Grants, but it's Pell because a U.S. senator named Claiborne Pell made it happen, but it was originally known as the Basic Educational Opportunity Grant for low-income families.

I asked Mom if we were low-income, and Mom said, "Low enough." She pulled a head of lettuce out of the fridge.

"So low I can't go?"

"One step at a time. Let's figure out dinner first."

"Mom," I said, "can you just give me a straight answer?"

"No." She handed me the napkins to set the table. "I really can't."

"Why not?"

"Because your dad and I need to sit down and crunch numbers. Because going to a conservatory out of state isn't cheap, Piper." She took her pill from its case on the windowsill and swallowed it.

"I know," I said quietly. "But with all of the loans . . ."

"You have to pay those back, Piper. That's not free money."

"What about the scholarships?"

"We'll see. We're going to do the best we can do. Believe me?"

And I nodded. Because I did, and do, believe her. I don't think she really wants me to be stuck here forever either. She can't, not if she loves me.

She poured herself a glass of wine. I asked her if I could celebrate too, and have some of the old champagne in the fridge.

"Oh, what the hell. A sip can't hurt, you or me."

She finished her glass of wine quickly, grabbed the champagne left over from their New Year's Eve party out of the fridge, and popped it open. Fizz waterfalled to the floor and Mom said, "Don't slip. You're the last kid I want to see at work!"

"Cheers," I said, sipping the little bit she poured me. The cold felt good on my tongue, but the taste kind of made me feel sneezy, like I could feel the bubbles scratching the inside of my nose. I like shots more, they go down faster.

"Cheers," she said, as she used her bare foot to swipe a paper towel over the floor.

"This is good, right? A good thing?"

She nodded, picked up the soaked paper towel, and threw it in the trash can.

"It IS good. And you asked very good questions. Let's look at the notes you took."

❀ MY NOTES ❀

1st Conversation with Helen Mundy from NYSCFA:

How many classes do I get to take? How do I get to pick them?

Do I have to take science (chemistry/biology)?

All of this is answered at orientation. No chem or bio, this is a conservatory program. Yes! Conservatory! This is the best!

When do classes start?

Orientation = last week in July or first week in August! I didn't even know there was an orientation. WHAT DO I WEAR? Any footwear that is comfortable for getting around the city. THE CI T Y!!!! Need new shoes pronto!

Do I get to take the subway to class?

Depends on where I live or if I stay in dorms.

How many are in my class?

20-40.

What art supplies do I need?

_____

Depends on schedule and classes each semester.

Will I get to meet any current students at orientation?

_____

Yes, but new students also get a student-mentor buddy who we can email and ask questions directly. I'll get my assigned buddy shortly!

EXTRA

Mom and Helen stuff: Talking about $ and faxing back my acceptance form. I have to accept THEM now! SO WEIRD!!!!!

3/30 11:30 am

Dad asked me to go for a run this morning and I said I would, but I just texted Kit again, hoping she would text me back. I asked her if she would go to 610 Diner with me—my treat, breakfast root beer floats—and if she said yes, I totally would have dropped Dad. But, no.

Anyway, Dad and I were supposed to leave an hour or so ago, but he and Marli and Ronnie are having some serious talk at the kitchen table. I don't know how long it's been going on. I just went and hid in the hallway and tried to make it out—they were whisper-arguing, some of it really loud and then some of it muffled. It was insurance, then Ronnie's job not having bene-fits and the costs of the baby and Marli staying on Mom and Dad's insurance but then some premiums go up and who covers the baby and child care and what kind of man is Ronnie, Dad wanted to know.

Marli said this wouldn't be a problem if Piper didn't think she had to go to school in New York, that it's really because of me, and Dad actually stuck up for me.

"That's not fair. Piper has a right to go to college just like you did."

"Yeah, but I didn't pick one that's totally artsy-fartsy elitist bullshit. If she knew her place," Marli said, "Piper would have never put you guys in this situation. I respect you more than she does. It's just like Piper to put herself first, like she always does, and like you guys do with her—put her first."

And then Dad said something about not putting him and Mom first by getting knocked up and then I heard the word talent and some kind of hand slam on the table. Dad's or Ronnie's? Maybe Marli's?

Then the words "grandchild, not mistake." Then the words "of course, love."

Then the screen door from the kitchen to the backyard popped open and I had to run back to my window to see Marli and Ronnie screaming at each other in the backyard. They looked like a bad episode of Cops.

By going to New York, will I really be hurting Mom and Dad that much? I know we're not super rich, or rich-rich, or medium-rich. We're like, medium-medium, although according to Mom we might be low-income, too. I never thought of us that way. I guess we are?

I WILL get a scholarship. I WILL get a job as soon as I graduate. I'll show her. I'll show Marli how incredibly wrong she is about me. When I'm gone, she won't be able to blame me for anything anymore.

I'll be gone soon.

I'll be gone soon.

I'll be gone soon.

Trying not to cry.

Dad is knocking at my bedroom door now.

"Ready?"

I just told him 1 minute. Can't let him see I've been crying. Will put on amazing running outfit, something blinding.

3/31 3:30 pm

Dad and I finally went for our run—all the way to the donut shop, which is like 3 miles from our house—and he barely talked to me the whole way there, except for the occasional 'atta girl.

We saw Enzo and Philip at the shop and they were holding hands and then stopped. Dad saw them but was cool. We sat outside the shop, ate our donuts and drank our chocolate milk sweating on the curb.

"He wasn't right for you, never was," Dad said. "You'll find someone . . . more right."

"Did you know Enzo was gay?"

"Kiddo, that's like asking if I knew a donut had holes." He dunked part of his cake donut into his milk carton and winked.

I just rolled my eyes. "I thought you wanted to go running earlier this morning before it got so hot." We were both sweating more than usual.

"I had to take care of some things with Marli first."

I wondered if he would admit that their fight was partially about me.

"I didn't think you would mind sleeping in a little anyway. And besides, apparently you needed extra time with your getup." Then he gave me a funny eye and looked my outfit up and down.

"Hot pink makes me run faster," I told him. "And besides, that way cars can see me and we won't get run over."

"No doubt," Dad said. "You look like one of those Barbie town houses you and your sister shared. I'm glad I wore my sunglasses today."

"You need new ones, by the way," I said. "Wraparounds are old."

"I thought old was good. You're always wearing old stuff."

"But your shades are like OLD old, not GOLD old."

"Not vintage?" He struck a pose with his hand in his hair, pretending he was a model.

I raised my eyebrows at him and shook my head NO. What a nerd.

"So . . . is everything okay with Marli?" I tried.

He shook his head a little, and muttered, "As usual."

"If I go to New York, am I causing more problems?" I wanted to hear the truth from him.

"With or without Marli, you deserve to go to college, Piper," Dad said.

"I know it's expensive."

"Quite."

And, he added, New York was dangerous. And I was still his little girl. And I didn't know how to defend myself. And who would take care of me? And did I know what I was asking of him and Mom, just letting me go like that? Subways and snowstorms and rainstorms and blackouts and all that came with that?

"I'll be fine," I told him. "I can take care of myself. I've stood up against Marli plenty of times, and if I can do that, I can do anything."

"Marli's nothing compared to the real world. I don't want to see you hurt by bigger things, worse things. You're thin-skinned. And you've never even lived through a real snowstorm, kiddo, which, trust me. I got stuck in a whiteout in Boston once. They're bad. It's scary to be stuck."

"Tell me about it," I said.

"You don't really feel stuck here, do you?"

"Not stuck," I said, "but not moving, either. Do you know what I mean?"

"Like running in place?"

"Like running in place. Exactly."

I took a sip of water before I asked the question that had been scaring me most.

"But you believe in me, right, Dad?"

"Well." Dad wiped his forehead with the bottom of his T-shirt. "I just don't see why in the hell your art has to be made in New York. Art can be made anywhere, can't it?"

This didn't exactly answer me.

"Dad, I need to learn from the best. I need to study where all of the greats studied. And I could always come back here, if I wanted. Marli came home, after all."

"Once you go, Piper, it's going to be different. You're not going to come back, not for good."

And I said, "How do you know?"

And he said, "Because if I was you, I wouldn't come back either."

I felt pinched in the stomach, like a cramp.

Dad asked if now that we were filled with sugar we were ready to run home and I nodded, but just because I didn't want to talk anymore. I didn't want him to see me cry. I didn't want him to think I was thin-skinned, that I couldn't be tough. It was kind of weird/scary/sad to hear Dad say that about me never coming back. I knew I'd always come back, to see him and Mom. But I guess I hadn't really thought about what that would be like. That going to New York really would change everything, change me. It seemed like maybe part of the reason he didn't want me to go was because he liked having me around. And that made me feel sad/confused/heartsick for wanting to get away so badly.

Kit and I met at 610 tonight. She said she could tell by my texts yesterday and this morning I was freaking. I told her everything, though I left out a lot of the details about Mom and me talking to Helen. It felt like I would be rubbing it in too much.

Kit told me my dad was really smart. She swirled the half-and-half into her coffee, enough to make it sandy white, and said, "He knows things are going to be different. We all do."

"But I'll always come back to see them, always. And you, if you're still here. And Enzo." My stomach got that same guilt/dread/pang of truth feeling I'd had with Dad earlier. Some 1950s song came on over the speaker, something about a high school dance. "Are you still mad at me?" I asked her. "Be honest."

I wanted to assume that since we were sitting there, drinking coffee, everything was fine. That we'd both pull out our sketchbooks and our homework and projects like usual.

"I'm trying not to be," she said. "It's just new. You going. Me staying. And I guess I'm kind of—"

"But you still met me here," I interrupted her. "Our place."

"Well, I thought maybe you were losing it. You texted me like a million times. And after all, you're thin-skinned."

"Jerk," I said, and we both laughed.

"It's my duty to be your best jerk," she said.

"Can we just sketch?"

139

"I thought you'd never ask."

We pulled out our notebooks and stopped talking.

And that's been the best part of my whole weekend, except for talking to Helen Mundy.

This morning Adams announced she was being reassigned to cover math for Mr. Lopez for the rest of the semester and I just about died.

Everyone in class asked who was going to replace her and what about our senior projects and gallery showcase and did she even know how to teach math and why her?

And she said, "April Fool's, you fools!"

I could not even imagine getting through the rest of the school year without her. And it hit me right then: I wouldn't have Adams in New York.

"And now that I have your undivided attention, it's come to <u>my</u> attention that many of you have been falling behind on your pieces. You may call it senioritis, but I call it laziness and procras-tination, a.k.a. the tools of artistic creation prevention. Don't think I won't fail you, even if you're my favorites. From now on, I want you to show me what you are working on DAILY. It's too easy to stop, to get caught up in the distractions of our lives."

Sam Chang said, "It's easy to stop and hard to start."

Adams said, "Good point, Sam. 'For every action there is an equal and opposite reaction.' Sound familiar, anyone? So let's keep our creations in motion. It's basic physics."

We all said, "Yeah" and Rooftop Bryan said, "I see what you're doing there."

Then she wrote on the board,

"Great things are done by a series of small things brought together." —Vincent Van Gogh

I looked down at my sketchbook and thought about how far I had to go on my project.

Sammy looked too and pointed to a bunch of faces I had penciled.

"What is it? Who are they?"

"Unfinished," I said.

"Distorted. You going to paint them?"

"Probably," I said. "Maybe."

I don't know if I'm going to paint them. They seem bigger. Looming. I wanted to do something other than paint. But the watercolors and the pencil stuff . . . aren't big enough, strong enough. They just aren't right. So . . . what? Scary. I don't know.

142

Mom and Dad and I took a family walk (without Marli) after dinner to discuss college and money. The honeysuckle in the neighborhood smelled heavy, and it was extra-muggy-humid out. All of us were sweating immediately, like summer was already here and blasting us in the face. I won't miss that shit at all. The thought that I could see actual snow for the first time in New York gives me hope, even if it's a scary whiteout like Dad talked about on our run. I like that word: whiteout. Like a blank canvas. A whiteout seems like a place where anything can happen.

I told them that I would do everything possible to go, that I would make money—somehow?!?!—to go this year, that I can't defer until next year, that it would kill me. The thought of waiting would be way too much for me. Andy didn't wait to start his Factory, his life. He made it happen when he could.

Dad told me not to be dramatic.

Mom said she has to express herself.

Dad said she's doing just fine.

"Please don't fight, please just help me do this. I won't let you down. I promise," I said.

Dad said you don't understand my concerns.

Mom said there's no way she can understand your concerns, not until she's there.

Dad said you want her to learn by starving and sacrifice, trial by fire?

Mom said we did it, we survived.

Dad said yeah, but not in New York, not in a place so big nobody knows your name.

And I said, "Maybe that's what I want. A place nobody knows my name."

And Dad said, "Why would you say that, what's wrong with your name, with our name? There's nothing wrong with our name!"

I shrugged. "Maybe I just need to be ME, alone. In a different city. A new city."

"I know, I know," Dad said. "Without us."

"It's not YOU GUYS," I said. "It's not you!"

Her name hung in the air, even though none of us had said it.

When we reached the cul-de-sac, Mr. Mendez was in his pajamas, dragging his recycling bin to the curb.

"How we doin' tonight?" he called to us.

"Just fine," Dad said. "How are ya tonight, Joe?"

"Vertical and ventilating," Mr. Mendez said, smiling and wiping his forehead with his robe sleeve. "By the way, Sylvia and I saw Marlene the other day at the gas station, with that Ronald Haysmith boy. They still an item?" he asked.

"They are indeed," Mom answered.

"Like Sonny and Cher," Mr. Mendez said. "He's so short and she's such a big girl but they're good together somehow. I guess they just fit. Every pot has its lid!"

Dad and Mom agreed and then Mr. Mendez said, "Well, y'all have a good one," before he waved and followed the brick path back to his house.

And then as we went home, I said I was going no matter what.

Mom touched my lower back. Dad took my hand and gripped it, maybe a little harder than usual. Not mean, just tight.

They didn't say no.

4/3 2:53 pm

I went to the principal's office so Ms. Gilmour could help me fax back my acceptance letter. It's official. I'm going.

4/4 (Look! 4/4/4!) 4 pm

Sent a text to Kit last night: *I said yes.*

Got one back this morning: *Of course you did.* Then she added an emoji with hands clapping, like applause.

Sometimes we communicate better when we don't use words.

4/5 11 am

In art. Adams discussing senior projects and gallery showcase.

I keep having this weird thought that my project won't be paint, but sculpture, or a mix of sculpture and paint, which is 100% weird because I don't sculpt. Kit sculpts, like on a micro level, with her jewelry. And Enzo kind of sculpts, like with fabric, like

145

draping. But I don't build things with dimension like that. I can layer with paint. Maybe it kind of works the same way. Kind of the way Play-Doh worked?

Keep thinking about the faces. I think they're in my project. I think they'll be in my showcase. Need to talk to Adams one-on-one.

"Your project is your artistic mission statement," Adams just said. "A mission statement, in this case, is the articulation of your purpose of existence."

When nobody said anything, she said, "NO PRESSURE."

What the hell is my purpose of existence?

Sam Chang just nodded at Adams, like yeah, he toooootally gets it, but there's no way Sam Chang totally gets it.

Adams announced that she is going to keep the classroom studio open late on Thursday nights in May so that we can focus more on our work right before showcase.

That's good, because I'm going to need all the time I can get.

4/6 Just now

Marli caught me looking at her during breakfast.

"WHAT?"

"You—" I tried to be nice. "You look different."

"How different?"

"Softer."

"FATTER you mean!"

"No, not that. I mean, kind of, yeah but not in a bad way." Even though she is eating everything in the damn house. She leaves her banana peels everywhere.

"And you're perfect?"

"No, I didn't say that."

"Your hair looks like shit. You look like a little boy. No wonder Enzo liked you."

"Hey!" Mom said. "Don't start!"

I picked up my pad and pencil and Marli grabbed my wrist.

"What the hell were you drawing, anyway?"

She twisted me around so she could see my notebook.

"Is that supposed to be me?"

"No," I lied.

"Yeah it is," she said.

I should have just said yes you're right calm down and she could have ripped it up and then I would have started all over on something else and she wouldn't have had to freak out.

"Y'know, Ronnie always says you're lookin' at me. Watchin' me. He thinks I'm your fucking inspiration. How uh-bout that?"

"I'm not watching you," I said, quietly.

"The hell you aren't."

Mom told Marli to excuse herself, no daughter of hers was going to talk like that at her breakfast table anymore.

"Well, you can't talk like THAT to me anymore. I'm not just your daughter now. I'm a parent, too."

"Then start acting like one," Mom said. She picked up Marli's plate of half-eaten toast and threw it into the sink.

I crept out.

I can still hear them in the kitchen.

I. Hate. This.

Texting Enzo and Kit now, have to get out of here.

4/7 4:24 pm

Kit, Enzo, and I went to 610 for breakfast this morning. We ran into Jen and her family as we were sitting down. Her mom told us that Jen got into UT before Jen could tell us, and Jen was pissed at her mom for telling us, but was also really happy that she got in. She wants to live in Austin and be a songwriter and study medicine.

Kit told Jen's mom that I'm going to New York.

"Your parents must be so proud."

"They are," I said.

"And what about you two?" she asked Kit and Enzo. "Are you also going to New York? You've always been such a little trio!"

"I'm going to Rice," Enzo said. He stood tall, striking a fierce supermodel pose.

"You got in?" me and Kit said at the exact same time.

"Was just about to tell you guys."

I had hoped that it wasn't official that he was staying here, but the way he said it, I knew he wasn't leaving Houston.

"That's so cool," I said. I smiled at him, even though my organs felt like they were grinding together inside of me.

"That's wonderful, what a fantastic school, and so close to home," Jen's mom said. "What about you, Kit?"

"Figuring it out," Kit said. "I have a few options."

"Oh, I bet!" she said. "You deserve the best. I can't believe you all were just babies a few years ago."

Jen rolled her eyes and said, "Okay Mom, enough with the Cheez Whiz. Can we get out of here?"

"There's nothing cheesy about wishing good friends good luck," Jen's mom said as they walked to the cashier. "I'm proud of you all!"

I turned toward Kit.

"You have options?" I asked her.

"Yeah," she said. "Kind of."

"What, are you going to Rice, too?"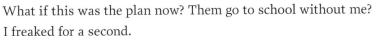

What if this was the plan now? Them go to school without me? I freaked for a second.

Nadia brought over three mugs and filled coffee up to the brim.

"No way," Enzo said. "She's doing something cooler. Tell her."

"I'm not going to school."

"What?"

I shook my head like I had water in my ears. Enzo knew this before I did? I guess I did the same thing to Kit. But . . . still. It was different.

"I'm not going to school."

"What do you mean you're not going to school? You have to go to school! People who don't go to school end up like . . . like Ronnie and Marli!"

"Well, actually," Kit said, "She did go to school. And see what happened to her!"

I took a sip of coffee just to avoid looking at her. Would I have done the same thing if I didn't get into NYSCFA? Just not gone? This was never supposed to be part of our plan, one of us going and one of us staying and one not doing school at all.

"So, does that mean that you're just like, giving up? Aren't your parents freaking out?"

"I'm not giving up anything," she said. "I have an awesome plan. I'll SHOW you. Tomorrow after school."

"Just tell me," I said.

"You have to wait." And then she smiled her straight-on boss smile at me.

4/8 8 pm

Wanted to skip dinner to write all of this down, but Mom was insisting we sit like a family, that I would miss these homemade dinners when I was in New York. (Ha. Ha.)

Anyway, Kit and Enzo came over after school to tell me KIT'S BIG PLAN and then something totally amazing happened! And I have to write about both!!!

KIT'S BIG PLAN: Kit hadn't really been keeping up with her website and Etsy store. She pulled them up on my laptop to show me what was happening, how much traffic she was getting— and had tons of emails from people who wanted to buy her stuff, even though on her Etsy page she had written SOLD OUT because she wasn't making more to sell yet. She was just making stuff for her, for us, whatev. . . . So last week she figured out if she accepted each order, plus the other stuff she was selling on Etsy and through her website, she could make like serious, serious money. She talked to her folks, which is like a huge deal that they even gave her 5 freaking minutes, and they agreed to let her defer college for a year to intern as an entrepreneur for herself! Kit is using her senior project as the launch of her actual business! She's going to run it from their house. And her mom said she could take over their library full time for her office for the year. (Kind of like how I was supposed to have Marli's room for my studio but obviously that didn't turn out.) Anyway, she's going to sell a few of Enzo's pin-drape T-shirts, too. She's going to call it Bash Lab—her last name plus a laboratory for artistic experimentation and exploration. In my head I was still kind of scared for her—what if it didn't work? But I told her I thought she was genius and amazing, which I did and do.

"You're going to be a millionaire by the time you're 21," I said.

"She already is," Enzo said.

"But it will be my own money," Kit said.

"You're going to be the boss of all of us one day," Enzo said. "ART BOSS!"

"That's the plan," Kit said.

As she pulled out her sketchpad, Enzo pointed to my email and said, "INCOMING."

"Get your nose out of my laptop, nosy," I said, pulling it to me.

And that's when the next amazing thing happened!!!

From: JSilas888@NYSCFA.EDU

Subject: Hi. I'm Your Mentor.

"Hellooo," Enzo said, plopping down next to Kit against my bed. I could barely hear him my heart was beating so hard, just looking at that email in my inbox. They were flipping through Kit's pages of sketches.

"We're over here," he kept going. "Email is for like, checking later, loserbell. You are missing the chance to witness the birth of the first really great jewelry, fashion, and art website in all of history. All of it," he repeated, "including Cleopatra's time."

"I wasn't aware that Cleopatra had a website," I said, bad joke but I was totally not there right then. I wanted to read the email so badly. I looked at Kit, who was pretending not to look up at me. I scooted on the floor next to them and sat on Kit's other side.

"What are these," I asked, trying to remain focused on her.

"Logos," she said. "I have to get my brand just right."

She pulled out her pencil and erased a few hard lines around the letter B.

"Do you care if I just . . . ," I started to ask, and she was already waving her hand at my computer. "It will only take a second, I promise."

I memorized the email. I've read it about 100 times since they left.

This is what J. Silas wrote:

Hi Piper.

I'm your student mentor. I'm supposed to reach out and ask you if you have any questions. This is kind of awkward, right? Asking you if you need to ask me anything? We could forever be on an endless loop of asking each other if we need to ask anything of each other, which is kind of weird.

I'll be a sophomore in the fall. I'm studying photography with a focus on 3-D printing and photorealism.

What do you do? Is Piper Perish your real name?

Was I supposed to tell you about the subway and stuff? The student affairs office doesn't exactly tell us what we are supposed to say in these emails. If you need to know about the subways, let me know. They aren't that hard.

Jamie Silas (everyone calls me Silas)

———————————

Here's what I wrote back:

Hi Silas!

Thanks for emailing me!

I can't wait to move to New York. Do you live in the dorms? Where are your favorite places to hang out and shop?

I've read about a lot of thrift stores in the East Village, and they don't look far from school. I plan on going to the East Village like pronto. Want to go shopping with me when I get there?

I've been reading the website obsessively—especially about the instructors—and can't wait to take a class with Robbins McCoy. He knew Andy Warhol, right? I've seen some of his pieces and really dig his crazy broad strokes. They remind me of power pop.

Piper is my real name. I was going to be Penny, but my parents chose Piper at the last minute. My best friends here are Kit and Enzo, also artists. I work mostly in paint for now but definitely want to try other mediums. So, thanks for writing me. Email back soon?

—Piper

PS Do you know if it's hard to get financial aid?

PPS Is there anywhere online I can see your work?

4/10 6 pm

Silas hasn't written me back yet. I wonder if I sounded like a complete hick. I couldn't find him online either. I did find a Facebook account, so I know he's a guy Jamie not a girl Jamie, but his profile pic is an eyeball and his photos are of different body parts (elbows, knees, an ear) and sculptures. Kit said she would help me try to find more photos of Silas, but so far there's nothing. If he's on Twitter, he's not going by his name. WEIRD. His Instagram account has just a few photos, the same ones as on Facebook. Hhhmmm.

I told Mom my student mentor had emailed me.

"Look at that, you're already making friends," she said.

Marli exhaled loudly from the recliner. I turned my back to her and tried to keep talking to Mom, but she wasn't done.

"Are Mom and Dad seriously paying all that money so you can have A MENTOR who's my age? Shouldn't your mentor be someone who has actually done something? Your school doesn't just sound pretentious, it sounds lazy. I probably know more than some dumb mentor."

Mom handed me napkins to set for dinner and mouthed, Ignore her. Marli lifted herself from the recliner. There's so much more of her now, as if there wasn't already enough. She's taking up more space.

4/11 Art

When I got to class today, Sam Chang was talking to Adams about how he felt like he was blocked with his senior project and she was nodding her head a bunch, her chin moving in and out of her palm, and then turned to me.

"How's your project coming?"

"Kind of still on hold," I said. "Kind of hard to concentrate and make stuff when I've been dealing with other stuff, like getting into school. And I still don't even know what those faces mean that I've been drawing. Like they may or may not be a part of it. I don't know. I'll know when I start."

"What's your plan then, Piper?"

"I'll get to it."

"When are you going to start?"

155

"I'll have it in by the due date, don't worry."

"That isn't specific enough. Just because you've been bitten by the senioritis bug, doesn't mean you can let this class fall off. You're not done yet, y'know."

"You wouldn't fail us," Sam said, kind of a statement and kind of a question.

SO STUPID.

"Oh, you're wrong, Sam. I'm a big fan of failing. Failing can be the best thing that happens to an artist," Adams said, turning to the class, "but the failure has to be from the trying, the creating, the process, the product. Failing from not trying, from not creating, isn't just passive and annoying, it's sad. It's destruction. It's not using your life. Failing from TRYING, though, can be so much more interesting than success. Don't you think? Failure is where we learn. What would we learn if everybody got everything right the first time?"

Sam said we would be a lot happier. LIKE A DUMMY. The class laughed even though it was obvious Adams was starting to get pissed.

And then she asked me, "What are your thoughts on failure, Piper?"

"I'm not sure," I said. "I don't know. I don't want to fail. At anything. Ever."

"And you figure, if you never start, you never put your art out there, you never have to risk, which means you never ever have to fail?"

That nailed me hard. It felt mean, even if it was the truth, a truth I hadn't realized before.

"Get to work," she said. "And remember, don't let the perfect be the enemy of the good. You have a lot more failing to do before you succeed. Samuel Beckett said, 'Try again. Fail again. Fail better.'"

Sam asked, "Who's Samuel Beckett?" and Adams said, "A dead Irish playwright."

Worst. Pep. Talk. Ever.

4/12 After school

Told Kit about what Adams said.

"I have an idea," Kit said. Of course she did. "You know how I'm going to sell some of Enzo's stuff on my site? Maybe we can feature something of yours, too. Something that can't be reproduced. Like, one-of-a-kind."

I could not have a better best friend. I asked her when she needed it by and she said as soon as possible. I wonder if anyone would actually ever buy anything I created. That's so weird to think about. Like somebody would hang one of my paintings in their house? Besides Mom and Dad, I mean. . . .

"Let's look at the stuff you have." She slid a couple of canvases out from under my bed. "Why is this one warped?" she asked.

"Marli," I said.

She nodded. "You need to keep these somewhere else."

"Obviously. But I don't have any other space except the garage, and it's always damp in there. I mean, I was going to keep them in my studio, but then Marli came back from school. So, you know. At least they aren't in direct sunlight."

"But you have me," Kit said. "I'm running my business, remember? I can keep whatever I want in my office."

I looked at Kit and wondered if she shouldn't be president of the entire world. She's so together, and I can't even focus on my senior project.

She was supposed to stay longer and help me track down more about Silas online, but she had to eat dinner with her dad tonight. "Oh, and I'm meeting up with DJA afterward."

"WHAT?"

"It's nothing," she said, but her smile took up her whole face. "It's not a big deal. He's going to help me with music ideas for the website."

"Yeah," I said. "Whatever you say."

"We're—" She corrected herself. "It's not a big deal."

Oh my god, Kit is in so much love.

4/13 Noon

Went to get breakfast and Mom and Dad were already at the table with forms spread out in front of them. Dad was pouring coffee. I grabbed a bagel to toast.

"Hi?" I said.

"Hmm," they both answered, looking down at the forms.

"What are you doing?"

"Mom and I are going over the budget."

"Oh," I said.

Out on the back porch, Marli and Ronnie were drinking coffee. Marli was eating a bagel. I put mine down.

"Are we going for our run today, Dad?" I asked.

"Don't think so, kid. It's gonna rain. Besides, your mom and I have a lot of work to do and this morning's the only day we can sit down together."

"Budget's hard?"

"Stretched," Mom said. "We're looking at second mortgages. Refinancing."

Refinancing sounded important. Hard. Not good.

"Anything I can do?" I asked.

Dad started to say something and Mom put her hand on his and I could see her barely shake her head at him.

"Mom?"

Mom patted my chair and told me to sit down.

"Between your sister and you, our expenses are shaking out differently than we expected. You know that. We haven't exactly sugarcoated that this year is going to be financially . . . challenging." She paused. "Well, every year is financially challenging, but this one is providing us with extra concerns. However, there are solutions to everything. And one of the things that's going to help, we hope, is you having a summer job. It would be great if you could start looking into that. Maybe if there was even something part-time you could start before school ended? The sooner the better."

"Okay," I said. "I can try. It's kind of hard without a car."

"You never have a problem finding a ride when you want to go downtown," Dad said, straightening his papers hard against the table.

"That would be great," Mom said, cutting Dad off. "Ronnie's trying to pick up more work, too, and Marli's picking up a few more shifts. Everybody's helping out."

"Oh, and Kit's going to try and sell some of my paintings online!" I said, thinking they would like that.

"That's great, kid," Dad said, but he didn't look like he actually meant it. His face creased up and he looked like Grandpa Perish.

"I promise I'll do something," I said. "How much money do we actually need?"

Mom sighed and Dad coughed into his mug.

"As much as possible, kid," he said. "As much as possible."

I brought my bagel back to bed, where I am now. I'm scared. All I want to do is hide in my room. I wish I was Kit: more money and more brains. I texted Enzo, but he just wrote: *NOT A GOOD TIME*. Then I texted *what's up?* and haven't heard back from him. What's his deal?

4/14 11:50 pm

Kit and I spent today doing homework, redesigning her website layout, thinking of part-time jobs for me that wouldn't cut into my art time and that I could get to without a car.

Here's our list so far:

- Lifeguard at the park pool when it opens in May? But I'm not a strong swimmer.

- Neighborhood babysitting if anyone doesn't have a sitter already? A backup babysitter?

- Is art tutoring a thing? Selling my art on Kit's website?

- Working at the Galleria or one of the thrift stores on Westheimer or in the Heights, but then not shopping there with my paycheck—yikes!?!? I could probably do that and not spend all my $$$. I'll see if anyone is hiring. I should get started.

Kit also tried to help me dig online for anything more about Silas. BTW, as of now, still no email back yet! What is up with that? I've reread my email a bunch and I don't think it sounded dumb, but obviously he didn't like it.

We went further back on Silas's Facebook page, but still no photos of his face. I wonder if there is something wrong with him. He doesn't post there a lot. The few pictures that are up are really trippy . . . super blown-out, overly filtered body angles and corners—elbows, creases between fingers (we think!), and ears. One eyeball, for sure.

We also worked on our senior projects for Adams. I really feel lost with my weird faces, which I thought might be good jumping off points, but I still feel jammed. Kit talked to Adams, and confirmed that her building of her website—NOW COMPANY— is her senior project! So long as Kit turns in Creative Director reports weekly as part of her project, explaining how she is bringing her vision and project to life, she can do it. Her reports can be written or creative demonstrations. WTF.

"You make me feel like the laziest person on Earth," I told Kit.

"I've been trying to tell you that all along!"

I could kill her except I love her too damn much.

Kit ordered pizza online and we texted Enzo to come over and eat with us. It was taking forever to get here, until we realized we could smell it. It was already downstairs. Marli was eating it.

"You don't mind me having a piece or two," she said.

Half the pizza was gone.

"That was for us," I said. "Kit paid for it!"

"I know," Marli said, "but I gave the tip."

"That's not the point," I said. "It's not yours! You owe Kit $10 and now there's not going to be enough because Enzo's coming over, too."

Marli nodded, biting into her piece, which killed me because I was basically starving already.

"MOM!" I screamed.

"They're still out," Marli said through cheese and sauce, which I could see. GROSS. "Won't be home for another hour or so."

"You're such a jerk! We would have shared it if you had just asked first!"

"It's not me," she said, swerving her head like Beyoncé. "It's the baby." She licked her fingers at us.

"Sorry," I said to Kit.

"C'mon," Kit said, picking up the box. "Let's motor."

She texted Enzo to just meet us at the park.

"I'm not even hungry now!" I shouted at Kit.

"You're HANGRY," Kit said. "So am I. HUNGRY-ANGRY. HANGRY. WE ARE HANGRY HANGRY HIPPOS."

"I hate her," I said. "And her baby is going to be fat."

"I think that's supposed to be a good thing," Kit said. "It's not the baby's fault. And don't be a fat hater. Not cool, Piper, not cool."

"I'm not a fat hater," I said. "I'm a Marli Madeline Perish hater."

"Well, that's understandable," she said. "Marli Madeline Perish is a crazy bitch. Always has been, always will be, even if she takes Ronnie's last name. Marli Madeline Haysmith will be just as crazy as Marli Madeline Perish."

"Why would she do that?" I asked. "It's not like he's going to marry her."

"Even though they're having a baby together?" Kit raised an eyebrow at me. "They'll get married sometime and like, move into their own house and whatever, right?"

"Really?"

"Right, well, maybe not," she said. "Here. Eat this."

We sat down on the park's curbside, diving into our pieces of the pizza like vultures on roadkill. When we looked up, Enzo was standing over us, red and wet and blotchy.

"You look like shit," Kit said, holding up a slice to him.

"My mom knows everything," Enzo said. "She knows I'm gay."

And then he lay down in front of us, crying and giggling and breaking in half, right on top of the street's sewer cover.

"You're going to get run over," Kit said, pulling him up between us.

"It doesn't matter," he said. "I don't matter."

"Enzo!" I said. "Yes, you do. You are everything to us. We're not us without YOU."

He sat, crumpled, against both of us.

"What have you been drinking?" I asked.

"Everything. Anything," he said.

Kit held the slice up again and he took a bite, crying onto the pepperoni.

"Can we not talk?" he asked with his mouth full.

So we didn't. We just sat there together and waited until the pizza was gone and then got Enzo home.

And now I feel heartbroken all over again. Not for me. Not for us. For him.

4/15 11 am (ART)

Quotes on the board:

"Only put off until tomorrow what you are willing to die having left undone." —Pablo Picasso

"Stop procrastinating, PROCRASTINATORS." —Your Teacher, the Estimable Ms. Adams

Sam Chang and I have been sharing a worktable. Sammy just told me my sketches look derivative of Mount Rushmore. I told him his yarn looks like a bunch of limp stick people.

Piper. call Helen someone in NY. About $.

This is the message that's scribbled and left to me on the kitchen table, tucked underneath Marli's mug, which is pasty with her morning's residual Metamucil.

No phone number. Great. And it's night there. I wish I would have seen this sooner.

Found Helen Mundy's number and left a message on her voice mail yesterday, but haven't heard back from her today.

The good thing is that I did hear back from SOMEONE in NY!

Hi Piper.

You'll like McCoy. He's got a reputation, but I find him very honest. You kind of just have to get over the fact that he's set in his ways. He's been doing his thing forever.

I don't send pictures over email. I promise I'll show you my work when you're here, but I don't want my pieces seen by anyone before they are ready.

My roommate digs the East Village for shopping. She'll be able to tell you where to find the goods. My friends play in bars there, so I'm always over there anyway. You mentioned power pop. Who are you listening to these days?

Ciao,
Silas

"So, that's why Silas is virtually offline?" Kit asked. "He doesn't show his work before it's ready? Hmmph."

Kit cracked her neck and pulled up his Facebook page again.

"Remember what Andy said? 'The best thing about a picture is that it never changes, even when the people in it do.'"

"Yeah," said Kit.

"So maybe he doesn't want his art to be seen, or he doesn't want to be seen, because it's still in motion? Still evolving?"

"Yeah, but he could at least update his profile pic," she said. "Like, he doesn't have to be all mysterious, y'know."

She stood and looked at the face sketches I had clipped to my canvas. I've been putting off painting them, still not sure about the paint. But putting them at least near my canvas had felt like a start.

Kit traced the chin on one face and said, "Even if you didn't know this face, you would know she is crazy by this line. Look how it goes from strong to thin to strong again. She's inconsistent. A dotted map of crazy."

"I didn't know I did that," I said.

"Of course you didn't," Kit said.

"A dotted map of crazy?" I asked.

Kit nodded.

"Kit," I said, "you are a freaking genius."

"Why this time?" she asked.

"Because," I said, "because you just saved my ass. . . . I just figured out what I'm doing for my senior project."

4/19 Art with Adams

Senior Project.

Personal Geography.

Dotted Map.

It all makes sense.

Making a map out of the faces.

The entire country.

Their faces.

"Except for in one part of the country," Adams added. "Leave one part of the country without them. Just a suggestion."

I knew which part she meant.

I knew where I could leave open.

My brain started flickering, the world's fastest flip book: heads, bodies, arms, mountains, rivers, states.

Borders and boundaries, boundaries and borders.

4/20 Afternoon

In the backyard. Brought a bunch of poster boards and laid them on the back porch, like a huge checkerboard. Penciling out and diagramming a blueprint of my project in the hammock now. Spent all last night talking scale with Kit and also how we could help Enzo, who hasn't called or texted us back since the park, which has me really freaked out. He's been avoiding school, too.

"You need to pick up all of your mess," Marli said from the porch. "You can't just leave it out here. Why are you always so messy?"

"I'm working."

"It's about to pour, Einstein. Have you looked up once today?"

The sky weighed a ton, about to downpour.

"Thanks."

"I swear if you had another brain, it'd be lonely," she said, shaking her head like she pitied me. Then she clucked her tongue like a chicken and went back in the house. I could feel her staring at me from the kitchen window. Even when she was watching out for me, or thought she was, it was always tinted with her Marli-darkness. If she had two hearts, I think she'd still be a heart short.

I don't want to go inside. How am I supposed to be in there when I can't spread my work out and Ronnie is screaming at the Rangers game on TV?

There is just no freaking space here.

4/21 6 pm

Rained all day, night, and this morning. Spent the rest of yesterday sketching and today with Enzo at his house. His mom was out shopping with his aunt, so it was safe to real-talk.

"So, your mom is just planning on ignoring you for the rest of her life?"

"Basically. Until I go to confession and 'get this gay out of me.'"

"That works, right?"

He rolled his eyes at me. "If it did, maybe I would have tried a long time ago. Maybe not. I don't know anymore, Pipes. She's so upset with me."

"What does your dad think?" I asked.

"He wasn't there when it all happened. Mom was the one who saw us. And we were only kissing, thank god. I didn't even hear her. Philip saw her first."

"So she's not going to tell him?"

"I think she's waiting for me to be saved. And no. Telling someone else, even Dad, would make it too real for her."

We both sat quietly for a minute and he was breathing hard.

"It was hard for me, too," I said.

"Piper."

"I'm just saying I kind of get feeling a little . . . shocked, that's all. I mean, we did a lot of stuff together. Stuff-stuff. You know?"

Enzo's shoulders started to shake and I put my arm around him. I wasn't trying to make him feel worse. But he started to cry full out, leaning into me, and even though he's only a few inches taller than me, it felt like I could barely hold him. There was way too much of him.

"What can I do to help?" I asked.

He took a breath and shook his body away from me.

"Um," he said, wiping his nose and eyes with his wrist, "I was working on sketching your prom dress before all of this—" He waved his hand. "Can I show you what I've been working on?"

He showed me his pad, then pulled out a starry fabric he had already bought and draped it on me. Told me that he had a plan for the purple dress we had bought, something fantabulous, sticking with metallics, combining this new fabric and the purple one.

"Notice how the stars match your hair. . . . Now watch. . . ." He turned out the lights and it was all gray outside and then I looked down at the fabric, and I was glowing, stars and constellations all over me. He twirled me around, wrapped his hands around my waist, and whispered "Galaxy Girl" into my ear. I could feel my body warming up against his again, his bony arms and my arms wrapped into each other like knots again, and I said, "Whoa" and he said, "Yeah, whoa, you look so good in this dress, so perfect, it's you." I pulled away from him and he said he was sorry.

Being that close to him, it just felt so . . . us. But for the first time it didn't feel . . . right.

4/22 1st period

Shouldn't be writing. My hand hurts, wrist hurts. Think I slept on it weird, though I didn't sleep much because I was thinking about Enzo all night. Of course when I saw him in the hallway he acted like everything was the same as it ever was.

4/23 Art

Hand hurting again. "I haven't been holding my pencils too tightly either," I told Adams, "just sketching and drawing a lot in the last few days."

"Well, that's a relief," she said. "But, talk to your mom about it. Just to make sure it's not tendonitis."

Great. Right when I'm finally cracking it!

Adams told me to draw with my left hand, see what happens. UM, shit is going to happen, that's what's going to happen. Left hand = no bueno.

Going to rest wrist now even though I don't want to. And not telling Mom or Dad.

171

4/24 After school

Sketch by left hand with feelings
of helplessness and despair and Kit
laughing at me right now:

4/25 Adams/Art

Just showed Adams what I sketched yesterday, proof I was
useless with my left hand. She said the Irish say that the left
hand of a dead man dipped in a milk pail causes cream.

NOT HELPFUL.

4/26 After school!

My hand feels better! My fingers aren't tingly or tight.
Everything felt normal and the same today. That means I can
draw now! Marli's out at a doctor's appointment. Have whole
house to myself with Kit and Enzo. First we eat, then we draw,
then we go to K's house for scary movie night. Jen is coming
over, too. Kit mentioned that DJA might be stopping by and E
and I teased her and she told us to shut up.

4/27 1 pm Park

I should have just stayed at Kit's the whole weekend. Came
home a couple of hours ago to Marli being a witch. She said I
woke her up when I opened the door, that of course when she
was finally able to sleep in, once again, I was inconsiderate and
rude. I said to her what about you throwing up every morning,

no wait, all the time, I always have to hear that and I think that's inconsiderate and rude and am I not even allowed to enter my own home and she said I'm too dumb, too small and ignorant to really understand anything, she's busy creating LIFE. Then she said, "Ooh yeah, that woman Helen called back yesterday and I told her you were out for the rest of the day and night and that you would call her next week."

"Why didn't you text me?" I said, freaking out. "Helen is super important! It takes 2 seconds to text me!"

"Just because you deign something, or someone, as super important doesn't mean they are. Besides, I didn't have my phone with me. So sue me." She shrugged.

"Mom!" I yelled.

Mom came in already looking pissed.

"Mom, Marli didn't give me a message that Helen called!"

Mom rubbed her temples. "Marli, when anyone from Piper's college calls, it's imperative you tell Dad or me or Piper."

Then Marli really lost it.

"Always to the fucking rescue for Little Piper Perish! God forbid, Little Piper Perish have one thing in her life not go right for her! But who cares about when things go fucking haywire for me? You know who? Nobody! Not in this family! Piper misses a phone call and it's the end of the fucking world! Call Mom, call Dad, call the wah-wah-wahmbulance! Just make sure Marli looks like the bad guy, that's all that matters so Mom can take your side!"

"Marli!" Mom said, obviously trying to use her quiet voice instead of her angry voice. "You didn't give a phone message. You don't have to overreact, honey. Just do the right thing next time."

Marli was crying all over the place.

"Your hormones are really doing a doozy on you," Mom said. "Let's try and get you calm, okay? We don't want to upset the baby."

Mom tried to sit Marli down in her chair, and Marli wasn't having it, slipping out of her arms like a hooked fish hell-bent on staying alive.

"It's just hormones," Mom tried again. It seemed like she was trying to convince herself and me too. "It's okay. Shhh, shhh, you're okay." And I thought we were done, but then Marli kept muttering loudly, and then she pointed at me and said, "Everything gets worse when she's here."

And then it was my turn to lose it.

"WHY THE FUCK DID I EVEN COME HOME?" I screamed at her. Dad charged in from the kitchen and told me to go outside and not come back until I cooled off.

"Why don't you just tell her the truth?" Marli asked. "Tell her!"

I looked at Mom and Dad. What truth?

"Go ahead," Marli said. "Tell Precious Piper." You could actually see the spit coming out of her mouth when she said the Ps.

"What truth?" I asked. My vocal cords were so tight they felt like they would tear in half. I didn't know if I was just falling for another nutty Marli-ism or if there was something they were really keeping from me. Did they know something I didn't want to know? Were they not going to let me go to NY?

"I don't know what you're talking about, sweetie," Mom said to Marli.

"Sure ya don't."

"Marli, pipe down," Dad said.

She smiled at them, glowing like a candlestick that had just been lit.

"WELL?" I yelled.

"I've waited this long," Marli said. "You can wait a little longer, too."

Obviously, I HATE WAITING, so I vibrated there for the next 30 seconds, that's all I could take, before I bolted here and just cried, harder than I've cried in a long time. Loud. Embarrassing. If the neighbors were home, they definitely heard me.

I can't hold it in anymore. I can't pretend everything is normal at our house. Or if this is normal, then we are just really screwed. Mom always says that she hears all kinds of stories about troubled families at the clinic, that we should be lucky for the family we have. But not every family is like this, I know. Not all of them are this fucked-up because of one person. Jen's isn't. Kit's isn't. Enzo's isn't.

Why can't Mom and Dad just accept that she controls our family? That she's a liar and a controller? That's all there is to it.

I'm sitting here messy with tears now. Waiting for Kit and Jen to come get me, even though I just left Kit's.

4/28 11 am Kit's kitchen

Totally got busted by Dr. Bash as he was leaving for work a few minutes ago. He asked if that was me vomiting in the bathroom in the wee hours and I said I'm sorry and he wanted to know if there was anything unusual on the pizzas we ordered.

175

I hesitated.

He said, "Whenever I used to get hangovers in med school, my roommates and I went for french fries." And then he winked at me. GROSS. Totally embarrassing. Of all people, I don't want Kit's dad thinking I'm some kind of alcoholic or something.

Before he left, he asked me if I had also been crying, it sounded like I was crying, and I just stirred the coffee Kit had made and mumbled that I'd gotten into a fight with my sister and he said that's what sisters are for. To everyone on the outside we looked like normal sisters with normal fights. Normal. Ha! I had to hold back from asking, What sisters fight THIS way? Not just regular fights, but yell the walls down kind of fights! Dangerous fights! Dirty fights! Do you know many sisters who do that?

"How is Marli feeling? I saw her at work the other day."

I told him, "Fine, I guess." I didn't know how much he knew.

"You know, Piper, you are always welcome here anytime. Door is always open. You're like Kit's sister from another mister. That's what the kids say, right?"

I smiled. He was so goofy. And he had been saying that to me for years.

"She knows, Dad," Kit said, coming in.

"Looks like somebody got up on the wrong side of the bottles this morning." He pulled out the brown trash bag we had hidden behind the regular trash can and said, "Take these to recycling before your mother sees them. And ladies, you wouldn't feel as bad in the morning if you drank better beer at night." Then he winked again—at both of us that time—and left. DOUBLE GROSS.

I asked Kit if I was really that loud when I was sick and she said well yeah, kinda, but he was also probably just awake getting home from his previous shift.

Now Kit is sitting across from me at their long glass table with website layout options in front of her and Jen is picking at a breakfast bar and her trig homework and I'm supposed to be drawing. Starting as soon as I finish my coffee.

4/29 6 am

Last night was a mother-effing train wreck and I haven't slept. You can't make this shit up.

Finally left Kit's, though I was tempted to spend the night again. But Mom called and said I was needed at home, so Jen drove me back. Before I even got inside, I could hear Mom and Marli and Dad screaming at each other, with Ronnie throwing in his much-needed wisdom (not!) every few seconds.

It was this:

Marli: Look, the princess has arrived.

Me: (sighing)

Marli: Don't breathe on me!

Then Mom tells us to both calm down, it is Sunday night, and she would like to have a family dinner where we can sit down and discuss things like a normal family. There's a lot that has happened this weekend, things that need some clarification.

Marli propped her feet up on my chair and rubbed her ankles, giving me her Fuck You look. Ronnie, Dad, and Mom all sat down and I was just standing there. "I guess I'll go get a chair from the garage," I said, making a point, and Dad asked, "Ronnie, why not be a gentleman and pick up a chair for Piper?" and Ronnie said, "Piper's a strong girl, like a horse, she can go get one."

"A HORSE?"

"You got them big teeth," he said. "All bright white."

"I had braces! My teeth are normal-sized!"

"They're big."

Then Marli covers her mouth and nose, like she's trying to cover a cough, but it's obvious she thinks he's hilarious and that they've discussed my big teeth before, which by the way they aren't, they're normal. (I think?!)

"You're rude," I told him, leaning against the counter.

"Well, I think you're rude. The way you treat your sister! The way you treat your family. Our daughter, no way she's gonna slam her way out of the house, talkin' about why did she even ever come home? You're straight-up rude, baby girl."

And then I got real quiet. Because all I could think was that they were having a girl. Those two freaks were going to have a baby girl and I'm going to be an aunt to a baby girl. Suddenly their baby became real. I saw swirls in my head, like seashells, like sea horses, like curls and paisleys. All of this happened in like 2 seconds. And then as soon as I felt something, something good, for the possibility of that tiny baby even though it's Marli's baby, Marli said, "Thanks a lot, Ronnie. Now the whole world knows."

And I realized they hadn't told Mom and Dad.

"This is wonderful news!" Dad said.

"You should have told me!" Mom said. "Us. You should have told us."

And Marli said flatly, "I didn't think you'd care. It's not about her"—she threw her thumb in my direction—"so why would you? It ain't news if it ain't Piper news."

All I had done that night was come in the door. That's all it takes to make her cast me as her villain.

"That's not true and you know it," Mom said.

"Well," Marli said, "the other day I asked you to come with me to look for nursery furniture. But you said you had to talk to that woman at Piper's school. Helen."

"I had a limited amount of time to call her back," Mom said. "I told you I would go with you after the call."

"But then you never did! Because you had a headache, you said. Like always. You always have a way of getting out of doing anything for me. So I went by myself."

"Why didn't you call Beth Ann? Or Ronnie?" Mom asked.

"She was busy! He was at work! Don't you pick on him!"

"I'm not," Mom sighed. "I'm not, Ronnie."

"Anyway, NO ONE WAS AVAILABLE FOR ME AND OUR BABY! So I just assumed you guys wouldn't even care that it was a grand-daughter, because you barely have time for your first daughter."

"How could you think that, Marli? Of course we care!" Dad said.

"Could have fooled me."

"That's enough," he said. "You need to give your mom a break."

179

"Of course, defend her, do what you do," Marli said. "Right, Piper?"

"I don't know," I said. I didn't even understand what she was trying to drag me into at this point. All I kept thinking about was that I was going to have a niece.

"Tell them, Ronnie."

"Well, Mr. Perish." I could tell Ronnie didn't want to get dragged in either, but it was more dangerous not to. "It does seem that way sometimes. You do favor these ladies more."

Dad flipped. "YOU KNOW WHAT? MAYBE IT IS TRUE! MAYBE YOU HAVE FIGURED OUT THE BIG BAD SECRET ABOUT US, THAT WE LOVE PIPER MORE!"

And just like that Dad and Ronnie were pinning each other against the wall, yelling in each other's red faces, about to hit each other. Mom was crying. Marli hopped up to protect Ronnie at the same time I ran between the middle of him and Dad. Dad pushed both of us out of the way (so we wouldn't get hurt) but I caught my temple on the corner of the table, which explains why I look like I have a black eye today. Marli started to fall but caught herself on the table and Mom rushed her into the living room.

"Ronnie's gonna hurt Daddy!" Marli cried to Mom. "Don't you hurt him, Ronnie! You leave Daddy alone!"

"I got this, baby," Ronnie called back.

It was the first time I had heard Marli call Dad Daddy in a long time, and even longer since I had seen real fear in her face. She was crying hard and ugly, totally losing control. I think she was surprised at herself. Marli and I were both out of breath and looked at each other like, what the fuck just happened? For a split second, I think we were both about to charge the kitchen to save Dad.

Neither one of them actually hurt each other, thank god. Dad pulled a big steak out of the freezer and put it against my face. Ronnie slammed the back door open and paced around the backyard, cussing to himself and cooling off. From the living room floor, Marli said the raw meat was going to make her barf and barely made it to the bathroom. I just sat on the floor with the steak on my face, crying. Mom kept asking me to talk to her and I wouldn't give her, or them, anything. I was done.

When Ronnie came back to the kitchen, he extended his hand toward me, offered to help me up. I turned away from him and Ronnie said peace offering in a really nice voice, one that didn't sound like usual Ronnie bullshit, but I just kept my back turned. I was too scared to take his hand. And mad. And freaked out.

Dad wouldn't stop saying sorry. Marli stayed in the bathroom for the next 3 hours, sobbing and puking.

4/30 7 pm

Sitting in the kitchen, looking at my portfolio, which has all the stuff from my junior year in it. It's what I submitted to get into school, but I guess it's not enough. Mom and I finally spoke to Helen Mundy again a couple of hours ago, and what I've made isn't going to get me any scholarships. It's loans for sure now, which totally freaked out Mom. She's been talking nonstop about responsibility, about debt, about starting off buried before I've had a chance. I'm staring at my work. I thought I was good. The school accepted me. Mom touched my forehead, her fingertips on my temple, asked me how my head felt, and I told her—honestly—it hurts.

Just checked my email in the library. Silas wrote me.

Dear Piper,

Happy May Day. May the May Day Be With You.

Do you graduate this month?

Silas

And I typed him back:

I graduate in early June. I can't wait to get out of here. You have no idea. Tell me about New York. If I can really ask you anything about school or whatever, just please, tell me more about New York. The galleries. The museums. Your classes. Anything! And tell me it's not that expensive.

Thanks, Piper

~~~~~~~

5/2 5 pm ART STUDIO!

At the end of class, Adams called me to her desk. She reminded me that the studio was now going to be open until 8 pm on Thursdays, and I could work on my project tonight if I wanted. I told her I had to check with my parents. She wrote my name down on the sign-up list, right after Sam Chang, and then said, almost whispering, "I think we should talk."

"What happened?" she asked, tapping her temple and pointing to my face.

"Oh!" I said. "That was a mistake. Everything is fine."

She wrote down on a piece of paper, ENZO? and I shook my head no. (Ha!!)

SOMEONE ELSE? she wrote down.

"You're not hurting yourself, are you?"

And I twisted my neck a little, shrugged. How was I supposed to tell her about my dad and Ronnie and for it all to make sense before I had to get to my next class? It wasn't even all clear to me; it happened so fast and so slow at the same time.

Adams changed the quote she posted from today's class for studio time. Now it says:

"When it is working, you completely go into another place, you're tapping into things that are totally universal, completely beyond your ego and your own self. That's what it's all about."
—Keith Haring

She knows I'm ready to go into another place. Time to disappear, to draw.

5/3 Another CrAzY Friday night at Kit's crib

At Kit's again. Mom wanted me home tonight, but she can deal. I'm not ready to be home yet. I don't know what to say to Dad and I don't want to see Ronnie. So I told Mom we were working on Kit's website after school. Kit designed a bunch of options for banners and I helped her choose the perfect one: royal blue and hot pink with the flashing lightbulb logo embedded in it. It looks like a vintage marquee. We referenced off a photo we found of Times Square in the 1970s for an old strip club! We also made our prom corsages and limeade Jell-O shots.

Jen, Kyle Crosby (Jen's newest normal dude), DJA, and Enzo are over here too. Enzo is Philip-less because they had some argument, which I think they do a lot, and he keeps trying to hug me and I'm letting him and I don't care how much he wants to touch me—or whatever—tonight. I'm going to let him. It feels good. He's probably reading this over my shoulder. YOU SHOULD STOP, ENZO! YOU'RE NOT MY BOYFRIEND, REMEMBER?

Good night!

The worst: Going on a jog with Dad this morning to get donuts while hungover. (I still am.)

I messed around with Enzo last night. Total mistake. Just causing more confusion in my life and his life, too. We started kissing and were mostly hugging, and then he started to put his hand up my shirt and I pushed it away.

"What?" he asked. Total innocence.

"Whatever the hell we are doing needs to stop."

"Why?" he said. "I still like you."

"But you can't like me like that anymore. And I can't like you like this either. Okay? Besides, what would your mom say?"

"It doesn't matter," he said. "She's barely talking to me anyway. She hates me."

"She doesn't hate you," I said. "And I'm not a way for you to win her back."

He turned away from me and I kind of spooned him for a while before I got up and splashed water on my face. It's so easy to be with him but it's so wrong. I believe—even if he doesn't really want to acknowledge it—what everyone has been telling me. He's not really interested in me as like a boyfriend/girlfriend thing. He wants love and I'll love him as a friend, but that's all it can be. When he's not fighting with Philip, he'll be back with him.
I know that now even if he doubts it.

All I want to do is lie on this bed right now.

Dad still feels bad about the bruise on my face, now yellowing, and the fact that I don't want to talk to him about anything that happened.

Our conversation over donuts:

"Honey, we need to talk about what happened."

"Not at the donut place, Dad. God."

"Well then, where? You name the place."

"We don't have to talk about it."

"Yes, we do. You need to tell me if you're depressed or sad. Or you're angry. Or all of it. You need to be honest with me. I'll be honest with you first. You look like hell."

"I just ran, Dad!"

"Your face is puffy."

(I couldn't tell him I was hungover.)

"My face is puffy from running. And these!" (I waved a donut at him.)

"Just talk to me. I feel awful."

"Don't. I'm not angry at you."

"But you're mad?"

I got up from the table and asked, "Let's just run, okay?"

"Running away never solved anything."

I looked down at his running shoes.

Right in the middle of the donut store he hugged me and kissed my forehead and I said, "I'll race you," and then we ran home.

I smell like sweat and donut and Enzo. Shower and nap.

186

Sketched all morning, did homework all day, avoiding family and staying in my room until dinner. Mom keeps passing my door. I think she thinks I'm depressed. But I'm not. Reading about Andy again. How can he be so fine with just, like, everything? Doesn't anything make him lose his cool? Doesn't he ever get so pissed he can't see straight? I keep reading things like:

"I think everybody should like everybody."

Nope.

"Isn't life a series of images that change as they repeat themselves?"

Great. So Marli is always going to be in my life in different images and forms. Just be cool with it! Well, I'm not cool with it because she's no kind of art.

"Sometimes people let the same problem make them miserable for years when they could just say, So what. That's one of my favorite things to say. So what."

How am I just supposed to say SO WHAT to my WHOLE life, to Marli, to NYC? He makes it sound so easy but it's not. How could you say SO WHAT if you actually care about the things?

Some people are just assholes. That's what I would like to tell him. Did he know that some people were assholes and still say SO WHAT about them? How did that work out for him?

Well, probably just fine.

Bleck.

Also: Silas wrote me. He is my total escape from everything right now. I keep rereading his email.

Piper,

You are really ready to get out of Texas! Is it really that bad? How can it be awful anywhere people are wearing cowboy hats 24/7? You guys do that, don't you?

I hope you have a cowboy hat you will wear up here.

So, New York. I grew up here. I don't think it's expensive, but I've heard kids new to the city, new to school, talk about it like it really is. You just need to know where to go. Some parts are real drags. Like you have to watch for puddles, because there's always piss on the ground, animal and human. And it's crowded, not like Paris or Tokyo crowded, but kind of like Milan without the smoke. Sometimes I think it would be great to live somewhere like Texas or Wyoming, but who am I kidding? I will never leave here. Why? Because though my city smells like piss, it also smells like hot dogs and wet paint and thunderstorms and saltwater and pickles. It smells like hot bagels, which I have to have every single morning or I don't even know what I would do. It smells like late-night cloves and spilled beers and breakup tears. It sounds like car horns and trumpets and subway-car screeches (you might not like that part) and every crazy-beautiful language you can imagine, like a symphony for your brain, and vibrations, vibrations everywhere. And it feels like strangers' warm wool coats pressing up against you when you're packed into a train, or bumpy and bucking when you're in a cab, or pure-on adrenaline when you're in the class studios, surrounded by all of the paints calling to you, Hey you, figure me out. It just feels like home. The city does. My family home doesn't feel like home. But now that I live with my roommates, it's better.

188

Now tell me why you want to get out of Texas so badly. Tell me what I'm missing. Because I think it would be just great riding a horse named Hawkeye to class. Yee-haw?

Happy trails to you, Silas

How do I explain Texas to someone who has been to Tokyo and Milan? How do I explain what he's missing when he isn't missing anything at all?

5/6 9 pm

All day I've been thinking about how to write Silas back.

I can't.

5/7 Art

"Have you ever been to Milan or Paris?" I ask Adams.

"Both," she answered. "After I finished art school, I took a year off and traveled Europe."

"How did you afford it?"

"Hostels and . . . other ways," she said. She turned toward the window like she could see Europe in front of her.

I asked her how she ended up in Texas and she looked back at me like I'd woken her up, and she said, "Mr. Adams, of course."

"You're married?! You never talk—"

"I was. My son can tell you all about his father sometime if you are interested. Now stop stalling and get back to work."

Adams, married! And divorced! So weird. Have to tell Kit and E.

5/8 6 am

Just heard Marli complaining to Mom in the hallway about not being able to sleep comfortably. Now I can't sleep. I was having such a good dream, too.

Andy and I were sitting in a cafe in New York and I asked him for advice about my senior project and he said, "I'm afraid that if you look at a thing long enough, it loses all of its meaning. Pop it out."

Then I said no.

(Who was I to say NO to Andy Warhol? But I was me, saying NO to Andy Warhol!)

And then he told me to stop looking and start doing and reached over and touched my hair.

"That's mine, silly girl."

"I love you," I said.

"So what?" He kind of chanted it. "It's still mine."

I think I might dye my hair back.

I just don't want to get out of bed yet. Cozy, even with the sounds of the complaining cow in the hallway.

Zzzzz.

Kit came over and is helping me finish map out my senior project. The Bash Lab site looks really good and I'm not jealous or anything, but like, it's really, really good. There's no way she's not going to get an A.

Adams gave me one of the rolls of art paper (36" x 1000') that was donated to the class. Me and Kit broke down some cardboard we found in the garage, laid it on the patio, then stretched two queen-sized bedsheets over the board. Then we laid the art paper (rough side up of course) on top of it. We put rocks from Mom's garden on the four corners to keep the paper flat while I created the graph. Kit had a brilliant idea and let me borrow her snapline, the little lifesaver with the red-chalked string that helps make a straight line, instead of trying to draw a bunch of connected straight lines with my dinky plastic ruler. When she first suggested red chalk, I asked why red, and she was like, It's just a mock, Pipes, and if you use blue, there's a chance it can smudge into the pencil work too easily. Just easier if you make the borders work for you.

She's so smart.

Just ate lunch with Enzo. This happened:

Me: Your egg salad sandwich smells horrible.

Him: Then I guess there's no chance of you kissing me.

Me: Can you stop already?

Him: It was just a joke.

Me: I don't think you're so funny anymore about that stuff.

Him: What stuff?

Me: Us. We, like, we, the couple, it's not funny anymore. Let's just be friends, okay? Stop with all the funny stuff.

"Sure," he said. "If that's what you want."

WHAT. THE. HELL.

5/11 4 pm

Slept in, drank coffee in bed, thought I was going to sketch on project today.

Dad came into my bedroom and asked me how I was feeling. He's still kind of on eggshells around me (HOW IRONIC), looking at my eye and forehead now, constantly checking for a bump or something.

"I'm good, Dad," I said.

"Your eye feeling okay? No blurry vision?"

"I'm okay, I promise."

"And everything else?"

"Okay."

I knew he was looking for a way to talk about the fight still, but I just really didn't want to go there. I don't know why I wanted to hold it in. Maybe I didn't want to discuss every single feeling I was ever having with him, especially when I didn't even know how I felt about everything except that it was horrible and I wish it had never happened.

"Okay." He looked awkward, scratched his head. "Well. Tomorrow is Mother's Day. I'd love if you would come with me to the mall to pick out a gift for Mom, one from me and one from all of us."

I asked if Marli was going and he said no, then added that he thought it would be a nice token if we got her something, too. "She is a mother now, after all."

"Are you okay?" I asked him and he said, "Sure."

So I told him I would be ready in 30 minutes and then he kind of smiled at me and said, "We'll have a fun day, Piper."

Dad hates the mall but we spent all day there and looked in every single store. Finally we bought a blender and a new rain-coat that was on sale for Mom, and I picked out a new curling iron for her too, and then some baby books for Marli. We ate popcorn shrimp in the food court and Dad also got a big pretzel and we saw Jen there, arguing with her mom outside the JCP entrance. I didn't say anything to them because they looked totally stressed out and Jen was practically crying.

When Dad was driving home, I said I was surprised he'd want to go to the mall on a Saturday and he said sometimes you have to go somewhere generic and I asked what he meant and he said like hospitals or airports or malls, someplace you're just a part of it and I asked a part of what and he said the big nothing.

I asked him if he was okay again and he squeezed my hand and told me he loved me and said, I'm just fine, just old, just tired.

"You're not THAT old."

"I'm a dinosaur."

"No, you're just Dad. You're a Dadosaur."

He laughed, finally. "Perfect, kiddo." He wrapped his arm around me and rubbed my shoulder. "Promise me you'll be nice to your sister tomorrow."

I was about to try and be funny again but he looked so sad I just said yes.

5/12 3 pm Mother's Day

Dad had the idea to make a pancake brunch for Mom and Marli. I wanted us to go out to 610 Diner because they have awesome pancakes and I knew they would have theme pancakes today, but Dad said it would be nicer to stay home and also it saved money, since we blew through too much at the mall yesterday. While Mom stayed in bed and Marli and Ronnie slept in her room, Dad flipped the cakes and I decorated the table. I took photos that I had of them and put them in oval picture frames I found in the garage and then hot-glued pearls and cut-up doilies around them to look like old-fashioned cameos.

"Wow," Dad said. "You have such an eye. Good job. They're going to love them."

"Um, okay."

"Sweetie, I could never do that. I'm no artist!"

"Yes, you could."

I love how if I make something that takes 5 minutes, Dad thinks it's genius, but if I create something I really care about, he doesn't even know how to think about it. I shouldn't be pissy

194

with him, but sometimes I have to wonder how he can be so . . . simple about it. How does he not see the difference between real art and some crafty shit I just threw together?

Mom and Marli came downstairs at noon. Mom had on her pink robe and her hair in a ponytail and Marli was dressed in (MY) oversized overalls and one of Ronnie's denim work shirts. TOO MUCH DENIM.

Kit showed up at 12 too because her mom had to work at the hospital. Kit brought Mom really pretty bluebonnets (Mom's fave) and a box of chocolates.

"Thank you, honey," Mom said.

"Well, you're like my other mom," Kit said, hugging her.

It was weird. We were all there: Mom, Marli, Ronnie, and Kit were sitting around the kitchen table, Dad was putting the platter of pancakes out, I was serving coffee.

"This is nice, real nice, isn't it?" Ronnie said, rubbing Marli's back. Which I guess wasn't a bad thing to say. But, still. I was on guard for the slightest thing to turn this table into Fight Club like the last time we were all eating together. When I poured the coffee, I turned my back toward him a bit so that we didn't have to make eye contact. Mom said she was so happy the whole family was together, and held up her frame with her photo in it, the one of her holding Marli's and my hands while we were standing outside on my first day of first grade.

"Look at my babies," Mom said, kind of sad-sounding. "Now you're all grown up and serving me breakfast, and how did that happen? Aren't our picture frames just the cutest thing, Marli?"

195

I checked Marli out of the corner of my eye. I thought maybe she wasn't talking because her mouth was full, but she was just staring at the table. My whole back got tight.

"I didn't make or buy you anything but a dumb card. I messed up."

"You did nothing messed up at all. I love the card you gave me," Mom said, running her hand through Marli's hair. "It means more to me than anything in the world, Marli, because it's from you. You don't have to do anything but be YOU. PLUS, you are making something extra-special for me: a granddaughter."

"You're just saying that because you have to," she said, "because you feel bad for me. Everyone always feels bad for me."

"Not at all, sweetheart," Mom said. Mom seemed extra blissed-out and lovey-dovey, like she didn't have a care in the world.

Kit rolled her eyes at me and unfortunately Marli saw.

"Are you judging me?" Marli asked. "Ronnie, is she judging me? Because you don't even really belong here. You know that, right? You're not even family. Piper just lets you hang out here because she takes in all of the weirdo strays, you and that little gayball freak Enzo."

Kit turned toward her, immediately pissed off.

"Marli, your mom just said something nice about you and you didn't even hear it. You just never—"

"Well maybe you should go listen to <u>your</u> mom," Marli interrupted her. "Oh wait, that's right. She's at WORK. Isn't it funny how you have two WORKAHOLICS for parents? What do you think that's about?" She sipped her OJ. "Could it be that they are both trying to avoid their precious little Katrina?"

196

Then I said, "JESUS, MARLI! Rude much!?!?"

Dad said, "Hey hey hey, we're having a nice Mother's Day here. Let's all just enjoy these pancakes while they're still hot."

Marli pushed back from the table. "I can't eat while everyone is judging me. Sorry I didn't make you a gift, Mom."

She pounded off to her room. Ronnie, for the first time, didn't defend her or run up after her. He just kind of moved his fork around the pool of maple syrup on his plate and said, "I think she's just real sensitive because she's feeling bloated. She's been feeling real big and uncomfortable in the mornings. I don't think she's bloated, but . . . I mean I wouldn't care even if she was. . . ."

I looked over. Mom's eyes were turning pink, Dad was holding her hand under the table. "I don't want this today," Mom tried to say but her throat was tight. "I don't want this day to be like this. I want this day to be nice. For me, for Marli, for my future granddaughter."

She made a little squeak, like whatever crying was about to start was pulled back inside her.

"I'm sorry," Kit said. "I didn't mean to start anything. I know I shouldn't get her riled up. I'll leave."

"It's not you, Kit. You know that," Dad said.

Then Ronnie excused himself to check on Marli and Mom pushed her plate out of the way, turned her head to the side and laid it on the table. Her back and shoulders were shaking.

"Maybe you guys should take your pancakes to the backyard," Dad suggested.

We did.

And now we've been listening to Marli sobbing and Mom and Dad whispering for the last 2 hours. What a great fucking Mother's Day for Mom.

5/13 After lunch

Only a month until we graduate.

I have no idea what I'm going to wear under my cap and gown, wasn't even thinking about it until Enzo mentioned it while we were putting away our trays.

Enzo: I'm about to kill it with graduation, once I'm done with your prom look.

Me: You don't have to do a grad look for me too. The Galaxy Girl already killed it.

Enzo: No girl of mine is going to look Plain Jane.

Me: Cut that shit out.

Enzo: Whoa! You know what I mean. Muse. You're my muse.

And for some reason, today, that just really pissed me off.

Me: No, I'm not. I'm not your muse. I'm not anyone's muse. I'm the ARTIST. ARTIST! GET IT? I've been telling you for weeks now that we aren't a thing. I'm not your girlfriend. You aren't my boyfriend. And then we messed around and things got all confused again and I can't keep doing this, okay? I just can't!

Enzo: Jeez, sorry.

Me: Just stop it, stop all of it.

Enzo: Touchy today?

Me: Yeah, touchy as fuck.

He slammed his lunch tray into the rack and I slammed off.

I don't know what's wrong with me. I'm just sick of him. Sick of home. Sick of everything. I am tired of caring about everything and everyone and I don't really care if I hurt his feelings or anyone else's. I don't belong here anymore. Never fucking did in the first place. So what if I have to take out loans to go to school? I just will! I know the idea of me having loans kills Mom, but I don't care how many loans I have to take out to transport me away from this place. I'm going to start applying for all of them, like today. There's got to be a scholarship out there for me. I am the guaranteed winner of the Scholarship for Artists Who Are Sick of Living with the People Who Drive Them Crazy. Marli is making home miserable, I don't want to see Enzo anymore. I can't even wrap my head around what I am actually making for my senior project. I'm probably never going to finish it and it's probably going to suck anyway. Maybe I'm PMSing, maybe I'm just pissed. I just feel so fucking done.

5/14 Study Hall

Was using the library computer to print out maps for my project for reference and check my email, when: (!)

Hey Piper. Did I scare you off New York? It isn't that bad, I swear. Not everything smells like piss. And I was just joking about hats and horses.

Anyway, write me back if you want.

Silas

P.S. Have you seen Chuck Close's photography? Lots of shrunken images creating one huge, solid impression. Or Cindy Sherman's portraits? She was kind of the first one to do artful selfies, in my opinion. Chuck has always reminded me of New York and Cindy is kind of all the people in this city, in one person. And you should check out Keith Haring, too, though you probably know his stuff because everyone does. If you mash all of them up, it might get you in kind of the New York state of mind. I guess I would call that my artist playlist for the city.

Silas

5/15 Art class

Our library had nothing on any of the artists in Silas's email. (No surprise there.) So I asked Adams about them and she said she would bring some of Chuck Close's work to the studio tomorrow afternoon. She has 2 books on him. I told her my college mentor recommended I check them out and she said sounds like you have a very intuitive mentor! Then:

"By the way, Piper, I'm really looking forward to your senior project. It WILL be ready for showcase, right?"

Ugh, I'm running out of time. And finals are coming. Crap. How can I think about finals when I have to think about my project and Chuck Close?

5/16 Home, after art studio

Kit worked in the art studio with me today after school. She had her headphones on and was typing away on her website, accidentally singing out loud a couple of times. She was killing me because she loves Guns N' Roses and I could see her pushing into the floor trying to bust out some crazy dance moves in her metallic loafers.

Enzo texted to see if I could come over, but I told him I was focusing on my project today. I think he thinks I'm still mad at him. I'm not. But I don't feel like hanging and I NEED to WORK.

Sam Chang was in the studio too, dipping about a million strands of twine in white glue and wearing a mask over his mouth so he wouldn't breathe it in. I don't think that does anything, I think it's just all affect. Elementary school kids use buckets of glue so it can't be that bad.

Adams saw that I was starting to paint on some of my graphed-out lines. She kind of stared at it and tucked her head into her right shoulder, wincing, like she was trying to see something that wasn't there. She stepped back and said, "Do you need a ruler to help you keep your lines straight?"

"No. I tried the snapline but I didn't like it."

"You sure?"

"Yeah." I was nodding. "I'm going in another direction."

"Why?"

"It doesn't feel right. The lines don't have to be as straight as I thought. The boundaries aren't rigid."

"You sure," she said again. Now she was nodding.

"Yes."

"Good."

"What?" I was worried she kept asking so much.

She shook her head. "No, I'm just glad to hear you're trusting your instincts. So many artists stop trusting theirs, letting too much outside information in. Decide once to use a snapline and never think twice. You need the impulse, the gut, the heart, the meaning. You're using your spark, you're thinking about it. It's good."

Then she reached into her big Indian-print hobo bag and pulled out two thin Chuck Close museum catalogs. She put them on my backpack and said, "They're here when you need them."

5/17 11 pm Friday night

I'm at home. Nothing going on tonight.

Kit's out with both her parents for once and I can't deal with Enzo and Jen is on a date with Kyle and keeps texting me that she's going to break up with him any minute. So, I'm rewriting my emails to Silas instead of working on my project.

Hi Silas.

Silas!

Hey Silas—what's up?

Dear Silas,

Arg.

Why am I suddenly tongue-tied? Type-tied? Is that a thing?

Rather look at the Chuck Close books anyway. His work is like the opposite of Andy's. Andy was about taking one image and making it bigger, exploding with color, popping it. Chuck is all about taking images, shrinking and reducing them, little dots and pixels, and connecting them to make one huge impression.

Chuck's faces feel thicker, like they could jump and live off the page. Andy's portraits look kind of trapped. Not in a sad way, in a frozen way.

I feel like I'm cheating on Andy somehow. Not that he would know. But I can like both, right? Chuck's just feel more . . . real . . . right now. Andy's portraits are still my happy place, but they feel too safe to me right now. Does this make sense? I don't know. Two ways to think about size and color and my brain stretching and snapping like a rubber band.

5/18 11:32 am

Just went to the kitchen to get coffee. Marli was eating bananas like a crazy woman. There were three peels on the counter and she was peeling another one.

"Don't judge me, stop judging me," she muttered through her banana mouth.

Her eyes were watery and her cheeks were blotchy, her neck too, and she was wiping her nose with the back of her hand. Her stomach was pushing against Mom's pink robe that she was "borrowing."

"I know you're judging me," she said again.

I poured myself a cup of coffee.

"SAY SOMETHING."

"Good morning?" I said all sarcastic-like.

"I DON'T NEED THIS."

And I just said okay because she looked so bad.

I couldn't fight a sad monkey first thing in the morning.

5/19 4 pm

Kit and I worked on her website most of the day—it's almost ready!!! When she had to tune out and do her own thing, I was working on this:

Dear Silas,

I'm sorry it's taken me a while to write you back.

My horse ran away and I've been searching for Old Peanut across the plains of West Texas. Hate to disappoint you, but I own no horse, no ten-gallon hat, no boots—well, boots, but cute ones. My mom has all of that stuff though (no horse now, but did growing up) and the rest of my family uses a bull to get around town, our Ford Taurus. I think I'd prefer the noise of the screeching subways to our screeching brakes.

Your New York sounds soooo . . . cool. It sounds just like the way I imagine it to be, maybe even better. Texas isn't what you think it is—maybe some parts are but I just don't know them. Texas is like being stuck around people who don't mind being stuck. It's like driving 30 miles an hour and never ever wanting to go faster, even if you can (though in Houston you can't because of traffic usually). Texas is walking in place because it's too lazy to do anything else. Texas is a lot of people who think they are cowboys and cowgirls, which pisses off the real cowboys and cowgirls who are still here—usually old, usually grumpy, usually not in the city. If I didn't have my art class and Kit and Enzo, I would go crazy, though Enzo does kind of piss me off anyway. Enzo can be very irritating actually. We used to date, and now we don't and sometimes it's hard to figure out how we're supposed to be friends. Do you have an ex-girlfriend like that by chance? One minute he's all I have to have sex and the next minute he forgets he is into me in whatever weird way he is.

I'm just really ready to leave. Really just get out. My sister, who isn't worth getting into here, is a big—the biggest—the reason. She drives me crazy and it's getting worse. I wish I was an only child.

I promise I will bring you a cowboy hat when I finally get up there in August, which seems so far away right now. What is your favorite color? And your hat size?

Piper

PS I am devouring the Chuck Close stuff. How did I not know about him for so long? Have you seen his work in real life? I really want to see some of it when I get there.

PPS Thank you for telling me so much about your New York. Your city, and your emails, give me hope.

5/20 6:30 am

I was brushing my teeth when Marli pushed past me and barfed in the toilet. I kept my toothbrush in my mouth and even though she smelled horrible, like she hadn't taken a shower in a few days, I just leaned over and lifted up her hair while she barfed. Then she wiped her mouth and took my glass of water and rinsed with it.

I spit my toothpaste in the sink and cupped my hand under the faucet, gulped some water.

"It sucks waking up this early," she said. "All I want to do is sleep, but I have an early shift at 610 this morning. I barely slept all night."

"I thought you weren't working any more morning shifts."

I remembered the pile of loan applications sitting on my desk that I had stopped filling out when the forms needed bank account and parent salary information that I didn't have and didn't want to ask Mom about at the time. I need to work on them soon so I can get out of here this fall. And so Dad won't be mad at me.

"I need the money, Ronnie's job cut his hours. It wasn't his fault, if that's what you're wondering."

I put gel in my hands and pulled some hair from behind my ears to create girl sideburns. Kind of rocking a 1920s jazzy flapper thing.

"Are you letting it grow out?"

"Yeah."

"It's about time you look like a girl again. You look better with longer hair. More like me."

When she left the bathroom, I waited for a second to see if she was going to come charging back in, but she didn't. I guess she was too tired to fight, which was so much relief that I didn't really trust it. I pulled out Mom's tiny scissors, the ones for hangnails, and held them up to my bangs. I cut but the blades weren't sharp enough and only a couple of strands fell out. Not enough to make a difference.

Chuck Close had this totally crazy thing happen to him where he had chest pains and then within a few days he was a quadriplegic. It was a spinal artery collapse and he called it The Event.

I don't even understand how that works. How can you be perfectly fine one day and then the next day . . . you aren't you? How do you become someone else when you're still you but without all of the pieces working? How do you work when you're broken?

Chuck Close said, "Inspiration is for amateurs."

I texted E: *Do you know Chuck Close?*

And E texted back: *New exchange student?* (After that he put three flame emojis and another question mark.)

I sent him a link. Sometimes, I am such a good friend.

Dad walked in and I asked if he'd ever heard of CC and I told him about what happened to him.

Dad: That's one tough son of a bitch.

Me: Yeah. Artists are pretty tough sometimes.

He leaned over and kissed my forehead.

"Yes they are, sweetheart, yes they are, which brings up something we need to discuss."

"Okay," I said. "Shoot."

"It's about a job, Piper. I know we've discussed it briefly, but you need a job . . . now. You needed one yesterday. And as far as I know, you haven't even been looking. If you're going to New

York, we need to get on the ball here. And if you wait until summer to try to get a job, well then, it's going to be too late. So I was thinking you should ask Marli if you could get a job at the diner, with her. Then you could share a car to get there and it would save on gas, too. I've checked in at the station, but the internships aren't paying and they won't give you a receptionist job without any training, plus Brenda is still full-time for now. So, these are some options I'm thinking about for you. But I need you to be thinking too. And more than thinking. You need to be doing, at this point."

"I was thinking that, too, just yesterday, I swear! I promise I'll get one," I said, "but I can't work with Marli. I'd rather kill myself."

"Well, don't do that."

"Give me a couple of more weeks. I'll figure something out."

"Piper," he sighed, "you don't have a couple of more weeks to think about working or figuring something out. A lot of people don't hire artists, Piper."

"But they'll hire me," I said. "And I am going to New York, Dad. And I'll be ready."

And he said okay.

I hate when he looks scared.

Must find job right away.

5/22 With Adams in art

Right before class started, I asked Adams if she knew of anyone hiring for the summer, or if she needed like an assistant or anything—cleaning out the classroom or art supplies or something—and she said she was going to Paris for the summer.

Me: You're going to France? That's cool! I've always wanted to go there!

Adams: Yes and no! Paris, Texas—not Paris, France. France is out of the budget. I'm going to clear my head. Think. Just work for a while.

Me: But you work here!

Adams: No, not work-teach. Work-paint.

Me: (trying desperately) Any chance you need an assistant in Paris?

Adams shook her head no and pointed to my desk. "Your work is right over there. Now get to it."

Been trying for last 30 minutes to mix paint for exact right shade of nighttime dream blue. Nothing's close to it yet.

5/23 After school in the art studio

Kit's working on her site. Jen just drove me around so I could drop off applications at Starbucks and Jamba Juice and some places at the Galleria, and now I'm back here and doing homework and peeling oranges for us even though I'm supposed to be working on my project. Adams is in the corner helping Sam Chang scrape edges of dried glue off his twine mess.

Kit tells me that she's going to sell my geography project when it's done and that will be my job.

"How do you know it will be worth anything?" I asked.

"Leave it to me."

I wish I could leave everything to her and trust her 100%, but she didn't see my dad's face the other night.

"If I don't make enough money," I said, "I don't think I can go."

"Bullshit." Kit snapped her fingers at me. "Don't talk that way. One of us has to get out of here and you've got the better outfits. And if you don't figure out how to get a job and make some money, we're not hanging out next year. Either we're long-distance besties or I'm ghosting you."

"That's rude."

"Well, you know what you have to do. And I'm not just talking about the J-O-B. I'm talking about N-Y-C."

She turned back to her computer.

Her site already looks so good, it's like she's out of here anyway. Nobody is going to believe she's running it out of her house. It's so pro. Kit's going to blow their minds. All of her tabs are color-coded like a Pantone chart and my name—my tab that she's making for me so that my stuff can have its own page—has this silver blue font that pops against a really light lilac box that is outlined in black. When I pointed to the box, I said that's so me at the same time she said that's so you.

"It looks like my hair!"

"It's like Andy's hair," she said. "And his Factory! That's the point! It will coordinate with your artist headshot, which we have to set up like, soon." She wrote PIPER—HEAD down in her notebook. "You don't mind that Philip is going to shoot it, do you?"

"Philip? Enzo's Philip?" I asked. "I thought they were still fighting. And I don't think that's such a good idea. Enzo's been pissing me off."

"I know," Kit said. "He told me. He knows he's a hot mess."

"That doesn't help me."

"Well, Philip won't charge anything and he has a good camera and you're broke and he owes you. Just trust. I'll handle all of this."

"He's going to make me look horrible," I said.

"No he's not."

"Yes, he is because he's . . . his . . ."

"You're not competition for him. And if he's fighting with Enzo, that's their business."

"Well, I'm growing my hair out," I said. "So he can have fun with my split ends."

She sighed at me. "You do whatever you want after the shoot, but for now keep your hair game tight for me. I need YOU to look as glam as usual."

"Well, I have to approve the photo," I said. "I can take really good selfies, you know."

"I know. But you don't get to art-direct this, Pipes. You only get to be the subject."

Arrrrrg.

I'm back on my geography project now. Wearing my headphones and ignoring everyone for the next 2 hours. Time to fucking paint.

Waiting for Kit and Jen to pick me up. I pulled an all-nighter painting, slept through half of my classes today. We are supposed to go dancing, DJ Anonymous spinning tonight. I don't even feel like going for once, especially after getting this:

Dear Piper Perish:

My favorite color is deep midnight blue-black.

(What the hell? The color that's been haunting me!)

My hat size is probably XL.

I definitely want a cowboy hat, so if there's one thing you pack, it's that, right?

Ha ha.

That sucks about your sister. She sounds like a tool. At least you have your friends, right? And are you and Enzo still a thing? Or does he just like you? Guys CAN be annoying. I mean, I'm not, but other guys are. :) I have a brother named Dean and he can be an ass, but he leaves me alone. He's 7 years older than me. I was a "surprise child." We both had the same nanny, Nags, but sometimes it feels like that's all we have in common.

Whatever's up with your sister, I'm relieved for you that you'll be away from her soon. That said, there are definitely still annoying people in this city. Like Joe Gillman, who thinks he's god's gift to the art world. He gets a ton of press and shit because he's supposed to be this young hotshot upstart, but his work is crap. Everyone in school knows it, and he's constantly coming after me even though we do different things. But he can't touch my stuff anyway.

Anyway, hope things chill out for you and Sister Perish. At least you'll be here soon and she'll still be there, right? And I'm glad we, New York and me, give you hope. That's what we're here for, yo.

Cowboy Hatless for Now,

Silas

P.S. Enjoy this!

The hard lines are—perfect. Somehow the buildings look full, not empty of life, of what could be in them. It's in those lines . . . they're energized. It's magic . . . magnetic.

How can I go out when I'm just going to be imagining New York the whole time? All I want to do is hide under the covers and imagine Silas and me strolling around the city together, our New York, whatever that is. He just gets me.

5/26 5 pm

When I finally woke up yesterday, Mom or Dad—had to be one of them—had placed the Chronicle on my bedside table. The newspaper was open to the classifieds, and had some job listings circled in red on it. I'm not sure what they expected me to do with it. Who puts jobs in a newspaper? Besides, I've already started filling out applications.

Kit and Jen, also hungover, picked me up for cheeseburgers. When I got in the car, Jen said, "By the way, Pipes, there are going to be surprise special guests . . . Enzo and Philip."

WHAT! "I look like crap, that's not fair." I shouldn't see Philip like this. "If he's supposed to take my photo he's not going to want to because hello, bags." I pointed to my eyes.

"It's the only day he could meet with us because of his class schedule. You two just need to get over the initial . . . freakiness."

"I'm gonna be the buffer," Jen said, "and I'm so goddamn thirsty." She bent her head against the backseat like it was about to become disconnected from her neck.

So, lunch.

We went to Becks Prime. Kit claimed it was a work expense, so she paid for everybody. Jen got two strawberry milk shakes and then spent most of the time in the bathroom.

Sitting and ordering, I got more and more nervous waiting for Philip and Enzo to arrive.

214

But only Philip showed up.

"Enzo had to bail," he said first thing.

"Why?" I asked.

He shrugged his shoulders at me.

"We're kind of in this fight-thingy again. No big whoop. He doesn't want Tina to think we're together and I'm like you need to own your truth, it's only our lives here! Anyway, we only need the three of us for this meeting."

He paused and looked at me. "You look a little . . . tired."

"I know," I said. "We were out dancing all night. I told Kit this was a bad idea."

"No, Piper P, it's a great idea. Because I get to see the real you. I get to see the girl who was out dancing all night and then creating all day."

"But I wasn't creating, I was sleeping."

"When we do your photo shoot, nobody will ever know that," he said.

"Nobody shoot anybody, everybody calm down," Jen said, sliding back into the booth, and laid her head down on the table.

Kit and I finished our burgers, but the whole time Philip and I were just eyeing each other.

We finally went back to Kit's, where she and Philip made me look like a better version of myself and dressed me in almost complete Andy wear—black denim jacket, black and white striped shirt, black jeans and no shoes, and I looked like me, looking like him. Philip shot me during "the magic hour"— when the sun made my skin look golden and sunny and not just pasty-pale. Everything I could have imagined and more. And better.

I guess I don't hate him.

5/27 3 pm

We just got back from the cemetery.

We go there on Memorial Day because one of Dad's friends is buried there. Dad always pours out a beer for him near his headstone and then he and Mom split one.

Today he gave Marli a hug and said, But life continues.

And she smiled and I almost said something, but then Mom shot me her <u>Not now</u> look, so you know, just shutting up as usual.

5/28 Art class

Quote on the board:

"A picture is a secret about a secret.
The more it tells you the less you know."
—Diane Arbus

5/29 Lunch with Kit

Kit and I dropped off more applications all morning. I could waitress, I guess, like Dad said. How hard can it be if Marli does it? But I want to work with clothing or shoes more than with food. Kit also thinks it will be better for New York if I have fashion experience over food experience. I would have applied at Another Man's, but they aren't hiring and barely pay minimum. Stores in the Galleria will definitely pay more. Okay, Kit is back with pretzels and froyo. Time to eat.

5/30 Back from studio. 11:30 pm!!!!

Got so much done on my project tonight. I had to leave my canvas there, because it's too big and too wet, but I wish I could sleep with it tonight.

Kit came over once and nodded. I just kept going. Felt like I was drunk, my head opened up in the best way. When I'm in my zone, the colors and my body become one big electric pulse, like they are moving through me and I'm moving through the color, moving light-years faster than my everyday life, but they're moving me along too, like I have no control over them or me, like I can't stop until I crash right through the canvas. Like running as fast as I can, like I'm the lightning. I'm so hyped. Don't feel like I can sleep tonight. Wish I didn't have to leave the studio.

5/31 After school

Sitting in the bleachers, waiting for cap and gown try-ons. All the seniors (702 of us) are in the gym, where PROM is also happening tomorrow night! Didn't think I was excited, but now that we're here and seeing the decorations, I think it has like an 80% chance of maybe being fun. Haven't been to a school dance since Galentine's Day with Kit.

Enzo is supposed to come over tonight with my dress for a fitting. I wonder if he and Philip have made up. If they haven't, is he going to try and get with me again? Because NO. Kit and Jen will both be with me because I don't think he and I should be alone when I twirl around in it again. I'm gonna get all Alamo with him and stand my ground.

6/1 10 am

Have no time to write, hello, it's PROM DAY!!!

6/2 1 pm

Just got home. Haven't slept in like—days. Prom turned out even better than I expected!

❋ THE BASICS ❋

◗ Theme: Casino Nights: Winner Takes All!

◗ Dance: Viva Las Vegas by Elvis

◗ Queen: Abby Grace (duh)

- King: Ryan Elliot (double duh)

- Senior Breakfast: Blackjack Flapjacks & Casino Coffee Milk shakes

❄ BEST PARTS ❄

- My outfit—all of my stars glowed, as Enzo promised, and none of them fell off my dress—plus the lilac color was prettier last night than my first fitting.

- The magician who made Mr. Lopez disappear.

- Dancing to DJA—he refused to play crappy requests the whole time and he was like so obviously into Kit! She was dressed like the Queen of Hearts and he kept playing songs with the word "heart" in them and by the end of the night they were seriously making out!

- Somebody spiked the drinks and we called it the Royal Flush because it was so ROYALLY bad it should have been FLUSHED! Get it!

- Jen and Kyle got busted underneath the bleachers.

- Sam Chang, of all people, won a trip to Cancun from the senior raffle and he's obviously going to take Boring Janice. That should be fun!!! Ha ha ha!

❄ WEIRDEST PART ❄

- Enzo and I danced but he left me alone for the most part, which made me sad, too. It was okay, because everybody was dancing together anyway, but when it was time for the last dance, we kissed again, by accident, and I didn't want it to end and it was so obvious that it was the end. I told him I was sorry and he said that's one for the road and I asked what's that mean and he said last kiss before New York.

"We have the whole summer together," I said. "Well, not together-together, but you know what I mean."

He tilted his head at me, kind of like a puppy.

Kit pulled me away to sneak shots in the bathroom and tell me about frenching DJA.

It has been the longest, funniest, weirdest 24 hours. Need to sleep for like 10.

6/3 Homeroom

It's weird to come back to school after prom. Nobody wants to be here and everyone is half asleep this morning. Prom should be our real graduation. This is finals week, which nobody cares about because everyone either is going to the school they wanted or didn't get in so what's the point of final-finals. Saturday is our gallery showcase and I am freaking. This is my last week to work like crazy and finish it. Hello, all-nighters. Also, I think I have to fill out more forms for my dorm room for New York, which is the fun stuff.

And also because oh right, sometime I'm supposed to get a job before I graduate, which I haven't done yet, which means I have like 5 days, which is totally freaking me out. Why haven't any of the stores called me in for an interview yet? I called two of them this week and they said they weren't hiring until mid-June, so crossing fingers for Sanrio and/or Aldo. I feel like Mom and Dad are thinking: Why is she just chillin'? I swear, I'm not.

We get yearbooks this week!

6/4 After school, art studio

Adams is keeping the studio open after school every day this week so that we can have as much time as we want to work on our projects. So relieved, because I can't work at home right now. Marli and Ronnie have been raging at each other nonstop about money and moving out of our house—which is apparently on super hold—and trying to work there would just result in misery. Oh my gosh, DJA just "dropped by" to hang with Kit while she works. Total love affair. I wonder if Adams knows.

6/5 At home, after school

Things are super freaky. Marli called the cops on Ronnie last night. They were having another fight—Ronnie threw a beer can in the front yard and Marli said it was aimed at her. I was in my bedroom, thinking about my project, and I could hear them yelling, but I didn't even want to get up and watch anymore, so I didn't see what happened and Mom and Dad weren't here. They said they needed a DATE NIGHT, but I think that just meant they were going for a long walk to get away from home.

Anyway, after Marli got really high-pitched, squealing almost, I turned on music to block her out because she sounded insane. In between songs, I heard Ronnie saying I didn't mean to and you know I wouldn't do that and c'mon now, you're exaggerating.

I figured it was the usual until the red and blue lights were flashing outside and Marli was holding her stomach and the police were asking her if she wanted to press charges. I was watching from the open window and one of the cops pointed to me and said, Please come outside. Scary. So I did.

When they asked me what I'd heard, I told them the truth. I looked over at Ronnie and he looked real sad, giving Marli and me the hound-dog eyes and everything, and I just knew he didn't do it. But Marli couldn't be stopped. She cried about getting a kitchen knife—her? Him? I wasn't sure. "You don't understand," she said to one of the cops, "my whole family is out to get me. They think they know better than me, but they don't."

"And why are they out to get you." The cop sounded like he thought she was full of shit.

"Because I'm smarter than all of them. I know things they don't want me to know. All my life, I've been able to know things they've tried to keep from me. I know about her. I know why Piper was born."

The cop looked over his shoulder at me.

"Are you Piper?"

I nodded. Totally surreal.

"Your sister here says that your family is out to get her."

I didn't know what else to say. I watched enough Law & Order reruns with Enzo to know you're not supposed to say anything if you don't have a lawyer and you're a kid, but nobody was going to appear out of thin air to be my lawyer. Also, what the hell did she mean she knew about why I was born? That was weird and gross! I was born because Mom and Dad had sex, that's why I was born.

"Is someone in your family trying to hurt her?" the cop asked me. "You can trust us." He leaned in so I could read his badge. "I'm

Officer Ramos. We're all just here to help and try to figure out what's happening."

I shook my head.

"Where are your parents?"

"Date night," I told him. "I dunno where exactly."

"Want to call them?" he asked me.

"I don't need them," Marli said. "I'm an adult. I'm over 18."

The cop gave a soft, reassuring smile to me and said in a really nice voice, "Why don't you give them a call, Piper?"

As I started to hit favorites on my phone, Mom and Dad showed up. Perfect timing. Mom almost fell over when she saw the cops in our yard.

After the police left and Ronnie had told Marli he was going to sleep at his brother Darryl's house for the night and Marli had talk-cried herself to sleep, I overheard Mom say to Dad, We're not that kind of people, we're not the type of people who have the cops make a house call, we're not the kind of people with that kind of kid, she's just pregnant, it's just hormones.

Then it was really quiet and I turned on my music because I just couldn't stand to hear Mom do that anymore. It was always not Marli's fault. It was always a condition that was happening to Marli. Nobody in my family is ever going to admit that maybe Marli didn't just have problems, she IS the problem.

My heart is beating fast just thinking about it. I could seriously throw myself against the walls and scream at the top of my lungs and nobody would ever hear me trying to tell the truth about her.

Marli is a fucking hurricane. And what the hell was she going on about? Was that just rambling? Was she just trying to freak me out? I knew I shouldn't take anything she said seriously, but I couldn't drop it.

She's an earthquake, a tornado, a destroyer.

I know this. I shouldn't let her get to me. I should grow the fuck up.

I was so glad that I didn't have my project with me last night, because all I wanted to do was smash things.

6/6 Art studio after school—11 pm

Just spent the last 7 hours finishing my project. Not even tired, just psyched. Kit is finished too, although she also said a website is never finished, it's always just starting. And Sam Chang's crazy-ass yarn hammock is actually stunning. He said it's a tribute to his mom, who always talks about wanting a vacation. When he asked about mine, I told him it's about being trapped. My voice cracked for some reason, maybe I was just tired, and Sammy said, "I'm going to miss you when you're in New York" and I said, "Yeah, right." Then he elbowed me and then we just were there working together in silence and I realized I'm actually going to miss him too.

Enzo dropped in, DJA stopped in to see Kit, of course (I think they're actually a thing though she keeps saying he's just fun), and Adams bought pizza for everyone. I wish this was my real life. I wish every day I worked in a studio with people who make awesome things. I wish I didn't have to go home. I wish that this feeling would last forever.

Kit's going live at midnight. Enzo has been obsessing about whether his garments "shine" enough on the site, whether they need more spotlighting. I took one more look at the photos she added of my personal geography project that I JUST FINISHED AN HOUR AGO and though I'm not sure my project is even any good, I do think it's finished. If something is finished, that doesn't mean it has to be good, right? Just the best it can be? Maybe nobody should be seeing it yet. What if people hate it?

Adams has been congratulating us all night, telling us we're going to have a terrific show this weekend. Maybe I'll just think of Kit's website as like a pre-show, a sneak preview. Sneak previews aren't bad. They're just previews. And changes can be made.

Gaaaaaah! I'm nervous nervous nervous.

6/7 2:22 am

Dear Silas,

I can't sleep. I was in the studio all day after school finishing my senior project. My friend Kit took some pictures of it, and I know this sounds corny, but it would mean a lot to me if you would look at the photos. I'm no Chuck Close, I'm not even close—ha ha—but I can't sleep and for some reason it would just help me to know if it wasn't totally crap from someone outside of my school, friends, art teacher. My parents are going to see it on Saturday night at our showcase and I know they're going to like it because they're my parents and they have to say they like it, but they aren't artists, they aren't you. And besides, they've been seeing me work on parts of it, so they won't have fresh eyes.

I hope this doesn't make me sound desperate. I've just had a lot of coffee and I've been thinking about this project and working on this project since January and now I don't even know if it's any good. It probably isn't.

Okay, I'm going to try and sleep now. If you can't look at the photos, it's okay. But if you can, it would mean a lot to me. You are supposed to be my mentor, right? :)

—Piper

6/8 10 am

Didn't sleep. Showcase night is finally here! Kit is coming over. She's freaked out because it's only been 10 hours and her website is blowing up. Enzo is coming over to dress all of us for tonight. Silas hasn't emailed me back probably because he knows I'm awful now and everybody is going to see that tonight. Unless people love it. I feel like I need to be drunk tonight. I hope Mom and Dad don't hate my project. I hope they don't think it means I hate them. Maybe they won't recognize their faces in it, which would be good, but also would mean I'm actually really bad.

Now Dad wants to go for a run and I'm so wired I might, before everyone comes over. I'm electric.

6/9 4 am

Not sleeping, too freaked out about entire night. Kit just fell asleep. I keep replaying it all in my head.

227

We left at 7 pm. Kit drove us in her car. I was wearing a Chinese robe-like blue dress with red silk-screen ferns and a red rope belt around it that Enzo got thrifting. It was the perfect match for the colors in my piece. He'd found this little hat that looked like the pillbox style that women wore in the 60s and dyed it blood red, and he did all my makeup. Starry, powdery light-blue shadow around my eyes, heavy black mascara, little eyeliner-drawn stars on part of my neck. I loved it. When he was finished, he called me his modern-day Edie Sedgwick.

I asked, "Not Andy?"

"Actually, you look like YOU tonight."

I checked myself out in the mirror. I didn't look like Andy at all, but I think he would have approved. I looked like a cooler paper-doll version of me. Or maybe just me, actually. The real me.

Enzo dressed Kit exactly like Prince in the 80s. An oversized purple jacket, brooches, long black leggings, and heavy dark eyes. She would have looked cartoony if she didn't wear a blazer like a badass. She tried on a curly wig to look more like Prince, but decided to rock her royal baldness instead.

Enzo wore a full peach-colored suit. He said he preferred to be as close to naked as possible last night so he could be vulnerable, and let his fashion line, the Naturals, really shine. And it 100% does. The fabrics look so rich and lush, so expensive. And he made all of it on a super tight budget. He could win Project Runway in 5 minutes flat, no doubt.

Before we left, Mom and Dad took pictures of us like we were going to the prom—in fact they took more pictures of us last night than when we actually did go to the prom!—and we were downtown by 8.

228

By the gallery's door, adults were lingering around, talking to Adams—not other teachers or parents, people we didn't know, and when we got inside, everything looked SO REAL. There was a sign-in desk, and DJA was spinning in the corner, and there was a bartender serving sparkly grape juice and a cheese and crackers table. There was plenty of space for our pieces, which Adams had curated, and there was REAL lighting—lighting that didn't cast shadows or spotlight only a small part of a canvas. Sam Chang's hammock was right in the middle. Some of the other kids in class whose work I hadn't been paying attention to for most of the semester were there too, and all of a sudden their stuff looked really good. Adams had made everything look so real. I could tell Kit and Enzo thought that too, because Enzo said, "This is like Adams's art project, right? Build an actual show for us?" And Kit and I nodded, taking it all in.

We found three of Enzo's mannequins draped in his collection, and they seemed to respond to us, like they saw us too and were like, Yeah, we're finally here. Enzo looked like he was about to leap out of his creepers when Philip showed up next to him and kissed him on the ear and said, "Congratulations, Enzy."

"You came," Enzo said.

"You didn't think I'd miss your first show, did you?"

So Enzo was a pile of mush after that.

I felt a tiny lurch in my heart, an extra beat. Kit whispered in my ear to breathe, and I did, and I actually felt better now that Philip was there. It meant there would be no chance or space or time for Enzo to be weird toward me. And Philip had actually been so decent during our photo shoot that I didn't hate him. Maybe I even liked having him around.

Adams had set up Kit's own corner: a clean white laptop on a clean white table with a BASH LABS sign, which was stunning. Kit stared at it for a second before she clicked through to check if there had been any more hits. There were tons of them and she exhaled with a little hum.

"It looks good, right?" she asked me quietly.

Enzo and Philip appeared beside us.

Enzo said, "You're a genius, it's gorgeous."

"I could have made it better."

"Well, I don't know how," Enzo said. "It's perfect."

She tapped her fingers on the table. "Let's find Piper's piece."

We moved through a wide hallway around a bright white wall that looked like it had been erected just for tonight and then we saw it: my piece, by itself, on a wall. It was big. Bigger than I think I realized. Huge. And I stepped back from it, we all did, to take in the size. And maybe I'm bragging or it's the feeling artists are supposed to get when we see something we made that we love, but I buzzed, electric pricks stinging my skin, like my entire body was being tattooed by tiny lightning bolts. My eyes unfocused and my ears flooded with white noise.

I thought I had built a country for my personal geography project, but it was something else.

I had created an oversized heart. The borders were veins. The rivers were arteries. The states as faces? They were chambers. Somehow my brain had mixed up biology and geography and art.

"Cartography," Adams said from behind us.

"More like HEARTography," Enzo said.

"Do you like it?" I asked Adams.

"I think you have something really special here," she said.

"I thought it was going to be something different. Is an oversized heart too . . . too . . . boring? Predictable?"

"Hearts keep us alive." She put her hand on my shoulder and squeezed it. "You're going to be fine. It's a lot to see, it's a lot to hold, it's a lot to own. But that's what you have to do. Own it, Piper, just own it."

I nodded and tried to make sense of everything, which was impossible.

"It's pulsing, pushing right off the canvas. You made it 3-D," Kit said.

"Did you know it was a heart?" I asked her.

"Did you not?"

"Is that her mom?" Philip asked Enzo. "And oh shit, is that your mom, too?"

I looked to where he was pointing.

Mom and Dad and MARLI AND RONNIE were at the check-in desk. Tina was standing behind them. Enzo shot Philip a pleading look and Philip moved across the gallery, away from him, looking pissed-off but understanding.

Why the hell would Mom and Dad bring Marli and Ronnie? I thought. And what the hell is Enzo going to do about Tina?

Kit asked us if we wanted to take a back exit so we could avoid them and I said no. I didn't want to leave my project, and if that meant seeing them see it for the first time, fine. Maybe they would actually get it. Even if they didn't. . . . Either way, I needed to be here. Kit and Enzo kept talking, I could tell he was nervous to talk to Tina, and the next thing I knew we were hidden behind DJA so we could just watch them looking at everything.

Mom was talking to Sam Chang and his dad, and even over DJA's speakers I could hear her go on about what a nice young man Sam had become, how she remembered him since kindergarten blah blah blah, and I watched Dad wandering around, making small talk with Tina, looking a little bit lost and confused, asking the junior serving grape juice if there was any real wine in the gallery. Marli and Ronnie walked right past us, his hand on her lower back, her yawning, and I watched them see my piece hanging on the wall. I couldn't hear everything she was saying, she was covering her mouth, but Ronnie took a few steps back from it and took off his trucker cap and scratched his head. He didn't look confused, but more . . . surprised. Marli stepped back next to him. I could hear enough to read her lips.

"What do you think?" she asked.

"The girl's good," he said.

"Don't tell her that, it will just go to her head."

"You should be proud of her," he said. "This is fancy."

"It's not like she saved the world or anything. Arts and crafts don't mean a damn thing in real life."

Ronnie patted her lower back again and then Mom and Dad were there and all four of them stared at my work, my heart, their faces in each of the chambers, and I wish I had taken a picture of that moment, because seeing them there, like that, made me so happy-sad sad-happy, I didn't know if I would ever feel anything so big again in my life. Even if they hated it, they were seeing me, and whether they knew it or not, they were seeing them, too.

I couldn't contain myself and went over.

"Hi guys," I said.

Dad pulled me over to him and pointed toward my heart and said, "Okay, talk me through this" and Mom said, "Yes, tell us all about it, we're very proud of you Piper, it's so beautiful."

She must have been able to tell from my look that I thought she was laying it on a little thick but I tried not to be an a-hole and said, "Well, it's my senior project—the personal geography one— and I thought it was going to be shaped more like America, actually, but the shape kept changing, evolving, and then it became bigger and smaller at the same time."

"Now in English," Marli said, "for us common folk."

She actually gave me a real, genuine smile. She might have been joking, but for a second, she just looked really nice. Even if she didn't like me, maybe she actually liked what I made. That was something. To just get a compliment from her without it feeling like I was stepping into one of her traps made me feel so surprised and happy. So many times I would have killed for a sister like Jen's—nice, smart, actually cool—and for a split second, I felt like Marli gave that to me. Got me right in the throat.

"The colors are real strikin'," Ronnie said. "It makes me feel somethin'."

I smiled at him and thought maybe he and Marli weren't so bad together, even with all of the fights. Maybe it really was her being pregnant that made them argue more.

"Thanks," I said. "I thought I was building a country and it turned out I was creating an organ, a heart."

"So you don't know everything," Marli said.

All of us were quiet. Nobody wanted to throw us off-balance. I could tell.

Then Kit finally asked, awkwardly, "Do you like it, Marli?"

Marli paused, like she was trying to figure out how to answer as a human being and said, "If I'm being 100% honest, it's alright, but I wouldn't want it hanging up in our bedroom."

So I tried to be nice back.

"Well, it won't be there," I said, "lucky thing for all of us." Everyone laughed a little uncomfortably, because that's how it always is.

She looked away, pulling Ronnie toward Enzo's mannequins, and then we were through it. I heard her say, "Hers is a heart and these have no eyes. What is this, some kind of creepy body parts museum?" Kit and Enzo followed them, leaving me alone with Mom and Dad. Tina was rubbing Enzo's soft fabrics between her fingers, and when he came up she squeezed him so hard.

"We won't keep her here long," Mom said, glancing at Marli. "She wanted to come. She wanted to be supportive. She's trying."

I could tell Mom wanted to say a lot more, probably lecture me about how to respect Marli TRYING to be nice, but she clicked her cowboy heels together and turned back. "I really love this, Piper. You're just so good. How did you learn how to do this stuff?"

"Sure didn't get it from me," Dad said. "It looks so professional in here. The gallery makes your stuff look real, Piper. GRADE: A!"

Then Adams, circling with the group of adults from outside, came up right behind Mom and Dad. Dr. Bash, Kit's mom, was standing with the group like she was a stranger. None of us had even seen her come in. I waved to her and she gave me a quick smile. She was always all business and tonight was no different.

"This is the work of one of our star students, Piper Perish. That's P-I-P-E-R P-E-R-I-S-H."

A bunch of them wrote it down! "Piper will be going to art school in New York, at the New York School of Contemporary Fine Arts, in August, and we feel confident she will be representing us well. In the past 3 years, she's mostly worked in oils, but this piece marks her first foray into dimensional canvas work, her own unique take on floor-to-wall sculpture. We're so excited to see what this young artist keeps making, and how New York will influence her."

A guy—a redhead, preppy—with a notebook said, "There's a lot of passion here, I can feel it."

And Adams was nodding.

"It feels tense, like her anger is in this," he said.

I could feel Adams watching me though she was also staring at my heart. "Well, Piper is an artist capable of conveying many emotions, I think there's no doubt about that." The group nodded and whispered to each other. Man, I wanted to peek at what they were writing down. The redheaded guy bit down on his pen, and then wrote another thing in his notebook. He

saw me looking at him. Did he know that was my work? Did he know I was Piper?

As the group moved past me toward Sam Chang's hammock, Adams adjusted her glasses and winked.

"Should you have introduced me?" I asked her.

"I'm creating a little mystery," she said. "The world can't have your full story yet."

"What story?" I asked, but Adams was off, joining the group, who was now taking pictures of the hammock and talking to Sam and his dad.

"Is that what this piece is about, Pipes? Are you tense and angry?" Dad asked. He seemed like he was trying to be light-hearted but I could tell what that guy had seen in my piece had worried him.

I'd never thought about what the piece was ABOUT really. I didn't think I was tense and angry, not all the time, no matter what my piece looked like to that guy. Just because I didn't walk around whistling all day didn't mean I was tragic. I didn't think my piece looked angry, but . . . energized. Passionate, like the guy said. I shook my head at my dad, confused, because I don't know, maybe I was, maybe I wasn't, maybe it depended on the very minute, whether it was a Marli minute or an inspired minute or a hungry minute or a sad minute, and obviously I'd spent a lot of minutes on my piece.

"That guy was just seeing what HE saw in my piece, Dad. He's just being a critic. I'm only tense and angry like, a normal amount."

Dad awkwardly hugged my shoulders and kissed the top of my head and said, "Okay, kiddo" into my hair.

Tina came over to say goodbye to my parents and remind them that we were invited over for the usual July 4th party. She gave Enzo a tight hug and said, "Ti amo," and touched his mannequins once more on the way out. Then she blew him a kiss before leaving the gallery.

Philip and Kit found us immediately, and Enzo and Philip just as immediately grabbed hands.

"Did you see your mom?" I asked Kit.

"She came?" Kit said. "She said she and Dad had to be at the hospital all night."

"She was with the group." I pointed to where Adams was mingling with a few of the remaining people, but Dr. Bash wasn't over there.

"I guess she had to go back," Kit said, looking at her laptop, alone in the corner.

Mom put her hand on Kit's shoulder and said, "She was very proud of you, sweetie, I'm sure. We all are, Kit."

"Why didn't she find me?" Kit asked. "The gallery isn't THAT big!"

"You know how it is when you're on a tight schedule," Dad said. "Your mom probably was on a quick break. Besides, it kind of looked like you guys were busy, um, hiding Enzo's, um, friend, there."

"Sure," Kit said.

"Well, I know she loved it," Mom said to her. "How could she not? If we weren't saving our pennies these days, we'd buy up the whole site!"

237

Kit smiled, knowing Mom was pushing it. I think Kit sensed she was bringing people down (not on purpose obviously), because she suddenly announced that we needed to go out and celebrate! Dad said he was a little too old but thanks for the offer, which made Kit roll her eyes, and Mom pulled on his sleeve and said let's gather the kids and head out, it looks like Piper has a big night ahead of her. She kissed me on the forehead in front of everyone and said, "Don't you ever forget how proud we are of you, my little Picasso" and Dad shagged my hair and said, "How about a picture of the artist and her work!"

I moved closer to my heart, to the side of it, and Dad took a picture. And then all of them started pulling out their phones, snapping away. I felt weird and shy and excited all at the same time and then I stepped away. "Just do some without me in them now, okay? I want those." Enzo and Kit kept shooting, determined to get some without our shadows for her website.

"All right," Mom said. "Time to VAN GOGH." She waved her hand over Dad's phone to get him to stop taking pictures and said, "C'mon, Piper needs to be with the gang now," and waved to Marli and Ronnie to bring them over.

"FINALLY," Marli said.

"Before we go, one picture of the girls in front of it," Ronnie said. "I feel like this is a real special moment."

"That's okay," Marli said.

"Yeah, it's okay," I said.

"I think it is a good idea," Dad said and nodded at Ronnie, some kind of weird guy-acknowledgment thing like yeah buddy you're right, and then we both stood in front of my heart again, getting our picture taken. Mom suggested putting our arms around each other, maybe a hug, and that made it more

238

awkward because neither of us even tried. We just stood there, our arms kind of bump-swinging into each other, and I said I think this is fine, but it wasn't. We were like broken magnets.

They finally took off.

"If you're going to be out past midnight, text me," Dad said.

"I'll see you around 2," I told him.

I could tell he didn't like that but he slipped me an extra $20 and told me to have fun and be careful.

As soon as they were gone, Enzo was at my side.

"How are we?" he asked.

"A lot better now." I breathed a sigh filled with so much breath I didn't even know I had held in.

"I can't believe she didn't have a hissy fit."

"I'm sure there will be one later."

Enzo slipped a little red ticket into my hand and said, "Compliments of DJA. When the gallery closes, we're all going dancing at the Greyhound." (The old bus station on Main.)

"How are we getting in? Isn't it 21 and over?"

"Not tonight. DJA is spinning and we're all going."

I gave him the biggest hug because he read my mind, just knew exactly what I needed.

Before we left, Adams told us again how proud she was of each and every one of us, how no matter what we did in life or didn't do in life, we would always have this, this magical night. When she pulled back from hugging me, she said, "High school, this day, your graduation—it's all important. But I don't want you to think of this as the end, Piper. This is truly just the beginning for you. Some students see high school as the finish line. When times get tough, it may seem easy to think that, too. But don't. Stay open and brave to the big world. Grow. Move. Expand. Always create. Always be the present you, not the past you. Be now. Then be now. Be now, now, now." She nodded her head on every NOW. "Do you understand?"

"I think so," I said. "I'll try. I really will." I gave her one more big hug before I left. I was torn between wanting to sit and talk with her for the rest of the night and dancing with my crew. But I knew they were waiting for me.

We all piled into Kit's car. Enzo asked, "Was Adams drunk or something?"

"Yep, grape juice gets her wasted." Kit snorted.

They heard the whole thing. Whatever. They could make fun of her being extra syrupy if they wanted, but I was still really feeling every word of it. She had meant it just for me. Sometimes it was like she understood where I was coming from—and going—more than Kit or E did. I wondered what Adams was like when she was High School Adams, College Adams, before she was Now Adams. I bet she dressed the same, maybe even funkier. I guess she wasn't even Adams then. I wondered if she's doing now what she thought she would be doing then.

We got to the Greyhound and didn't even have to wait in line. The red tickets got us right into the club and Kit and I went straight to the bathroom to fix our looks.

"You look bummed out," I said to her.

"No, I'm good."

"Are you pissed at your mom?" I asked.

She shook her head.

My hair was at a stage where it was short enough to be Andy but long enough to be sexier-Andy. Tonight, I didn't want anyone to think of Andy when they looked at me though. I wanted to hook up with someone. I felt like making out. I felt good.

In the mirror, Kit was patting her eyes with a paper towel.

"Seriously, what's up?" I said to her.

"Can we just dance already?" She handed me her flask and I took a swig of tequila and she took one after me and then she pushed me out the door and onto the dance floor.

The music was THUMPING THUMPING THUMPING. It felt good, like it was bouncing deep inside my veins. I pulled Kit right into the middle of the floor, underneath the rainbow lights. She was stiff at first, like she always is, but soon she was popping her neck and dropping low and I knew she was getting into it. Enzo Tiggered his way over to us, popping up and down like the music was his trampoline, and then Philip was there, too. I was feeling it all, feeling unstoppable and hot and fun as hell, feeling free, and as I spun around, there were all my beautiful friends.

I wonder if life could get better than that, really? Because all of the people I love were right there in front of me. Maybe New York won't be better than that. I won't have my people with me in New York. What if I want to go dancing and nobody will go dancing with me? What if I'm alone, all alone, and everything that was supposed to matter doesn't, just spirals down to the ground like a hot comet. Will Silas do any of this with me?

I grabbed the flask from Kit's pocket and threw back another drink and I heard Enzo say whoa. I swung the flask back at Kit who grabbed it, and then I felt a hand on my hand, a hand I didn't recognize, and I turned toward the body connected to it and I looked up at this guy, kind of tall, sort of familiar.

He twirled me around and I looked back at him and asked, Who are you and he shouted over the music, I was just at the gallery, I saw your show. He had red hair and blue eyes and freckles and wore the best tortoiseshell glasses and he looked like a jock who had stumbled into a thrift store. He was the black notebook guy!

"Did you follow us here?" I shouted over the music.

"No, maybe," he said.

"Who are you again?"

"I'm C.J.," he said, loud. He got really close to me and shout-whispered into my ear, "I'm writing a review for the paper."

"What paper?" I asked.

"The (something)."

"What?"

"The Thresher, at Rice," he yelled.

I pointed at Philip and said, "Hey, that guy goes to Rice." Philip and C.J. looked at each other and kind of waved hi.

"Aren't there like a million clubs near campus?" I shouted over the thump-thump-thumping.

He nodded and smiled at me and holy hell it was the best smile ever. It was like everything in my body caught on fire at once, maybe it was the tequila but I'm pretty sure it was him.

"So you're gonna dance with us?" I asked.

"I'm gonna dance with you!"

Then we were like, grinding, in seconds. (MOM AND DAD if you should ever read this—and you shouldn't because hello, privacy—it was just dancing not sex or anything like that.)

The next thing I know we're kissing right there on the dance floor. He tasted like cigarettes and something kind of funny too, like the hard butterscotch candies Nana used to have on her dresser.

I shout-sang to the music, "I LIKE THIS."

"I LIKE YOU," he said.

"Do you always dance with artists you're reviewing?"

"You're the first!"

Then we were totally making out again. His hands were on my hips, then my lower back, holding onto me so I could dip and roll back. My eyes were shut and I started losing my balance when I felt someone's hands on me from behind, familiar hands, and I turned my head and there he was, Enzo.

I gave him a look like no way, even though Enzo looked super hot tonight, too, and he yelled, "I wanted to make sure you didn't fall."

"What," I shouted, and lost my balance leaning into him.

C.J. was holding my hands and Enzo had his hands on my shoulder blades and my upper back. I could feel his fingers spidering out over my spine.

"I got you," Enzo said.

He was jealous!

I turned toward him and that's when he put both hands on my neck and kind of lifted me up to him and kissed me right there, RIGHT AFTER I HAD JUST KISSED C.J.!!! I couldn't stop laughing, not because it was funny but because I had no idea what to do. I wanted to turn back to C.J. and apologize and I wanted to keep kissing Enzo and I felt like the world's biggest slut and the world's coolest chick all at the same time. I had never kissed two guys in the same day, let alone in the same 2 minutes. This was so Studio 54! This kind of stuff happened to Andy's friends all of the time and now it was happening to me. And it was funnier and scarier than I had imagined. In all of those black and white photos of the Factory and Studio 54 everyone looked so sexy-tired-glamorous-over-it, but I was freaked out. How did they not freak out?

I tried to find Kit out of the corner of my eyes, hoping she would share the look of Holy fuck what was all that with me, but she was dancing over by DJA and now Jen was over there too, dancing with some random cute guy. I was surprised Jen's outfit was so on point—amazing red wedges BTW. Need to ask her about those.

Anyway, I was looking at them, hoping Kit had seen what had just gone down, and then I felt C.J.'s tap on my shoulder.

"So you have a boyfriend?"

"Ex-boyfriend! He gets a little overly kissy. But he likes Philip."

I threw my thumb in Philip's direction. He was dancing in little gothy circles, spinning himself into a tinier and slower version of himself.

"You just let him kiss you when he wants?"

"He made a mistake," I tell him. "We're just friends."

"Well, what are we?" C.J. asked.

If I believed in the devil I would say it was C.J., right there in front of me with his frosted white-blue eyes, except he didn't scare me at all. He made me want to melt my skin right into his. I danced up closer to him and turned my back to his chest, the tops of my shoulders rubbed up against the bottom of his, my hands on his hips and his on mine, and he was kissing my neck, breathing on my hair, whispering in my ear, "Piper Piper I'll follow you anywhere."

That's it, I thought. I'm officially in love. There's no other word for it. I could make babies with him right now. I didn't doubt that I was 100% girl right at this moment. This guy liked every part of me and I liked every part of me, too.

Enzo slipped over to Philip. C.J. asked if I wanted a drink and we danced to the bar to get bottles of water.

"I guess you can't drink yet," he said.

"Can you?"

"One more year. Besides," he said, "I can't do anything to mess up my scholarship."

"What are you studying?"

C.J., holding his water bottle against his sweaty neck, answered, "Right now? You."

I burst out laughing.

"I know, I know," he said. "Dumb."

"Kind of," I said. "But also funny."

He smiled at me. "I'm dumb, I'm funny, and I'm into you."

"I might be into you, too." (The might wasn't even close—I was so into him.)

"Can I kiss you again?" he asked.

And then we were making out right at the bar, like really making out. I felt his stomach through his shirt, and it felt tight, rippled, like the kind you would see advertised as "after" on TV commercials. All I wanted to do was slip my hand underneath his shirt and feel his skin, but I was too busy kissing him and also, that would be weird to feel a guy up, right? I wonder if that's even a thing.

Anyway we were making out, taking only a few breaks, I didn't even care that people I knew might be watching us, and then suddenly he pulled back from me and took a huge inhale.

"What?" I asked.

"You!" he shouted. "Maybe we should take a second."

"You okay?" I asked. I got nervous suddenly that he was second-guessing himself.

"More than okay." He smiled again. His lips curved into perfect 45-degree angles. He adjusted his jeans and moved a tiny notebook from his front pocket to his back pocket. I couldn't help glancing down and seeing that his jeans fit him very, very well. It made me want to stick my hand not just up his shirt, but other places, too. There was just something about him . . . so different from Enzo. It's like his body slipped my body a love potion. It's like we were supposed to be mashed together.

"Can we dance, please, or something?" I asked. I couldn't just stand there anymore unless we were going to kiss. Just staring at him was beginning to make me feel like a weirdo, and we could barely hear each other over DJA's tunes.

So then we did, we danced until 2 am, when the club became a total buzzkill and turned on the overhead lights. Then the club just felt like our school gym. Everyone looked like turtles, ducking their heads and shielding their eyes from each other and the god-awful brightness, except for C.J. and me. We were staring right at each other. He looked even better in the horrible lights. He didn't look like a dude from high school. He just looked older and better in every possible way.

"Can I call you?"

I answered yes so fast I was embarrassed. We traded numbers and emails and I said, Text me, and he said, I will. He kissed me again under those dumb bright lights and then Kit and Enzo and Philip and Jen were there next to us.

"Hi," I said to them, covering up my mouth a little bit. "This is C.J."

They all said hi. I could hear Enzo puff, like he was tired out by the whole thing, even though he was right next to Philip!

"Hey," C.J. said, extending his hand to the guys. "I'm Chris Jones."

"Hey Chris Jones," Philip said. "Don't I know you?"

"Maybe," C.J. said. "You go to Rice, right?"

Philip nodded. "English comp maybe?"

"Took that last semester," C.J. said. "I'm a journalism major."

"Biology," Philip said. They shook hands quickly, dude-style.

"How do YOU guys know each other?" Enzo asked, in kind of a fussy-grandma style.

"Just met," I said.

"Total fluke. I was covering the gallery for the Thresher Art Review," C.J. said, "and I came here afterward. Happened to see you guys and y'know."

"Well, I hope you write something good about us too," Enzo said. "I'm the creator behind the Naturals fashion line. And hot-tip alert, our friend Kit designed the baddest new website for art curation and artist discovery, Bash Labs. I'm sure you saw it." He threw his arm around me and Kit's shoulders.

I smiled and shrugged Enzo's arm off, gave him the what-the-fuck eyes. Then the Greyhound bouncers told us, You don't have to go home but you can't stay here; if you love us so much, come back next week, and so we were off.

Kit and I got back home about an hour ago. Dad had left a light on with a note that said: When you get home, turn off this light. If you don't turn off the light, I'll know to call the police in the morning. Hello, Kit.

And then he drew a smiley face.

I was just about to fall dead in bed when I double-checked my phone to see if C.J. had texted me. There wasn't anything from him.

But there was an email from Silas.

I held the phone to my heart.

If he hated my work, I didn't want to read that right now, not after such an awesome night.

If he liked it though . . . then what? If Silas liked my work it would be better than all the rest of tonight combined.

I couldn't not know.

I read it.

Piper,

If the photos of your work are half as good as your work in real life, you have to leave Texas now. Come here. Your piece makes me want to meet you, Piper Perish. I want to know everything about you.

Silas

My heart is racing. Not about C.J.

6/10 First period

This is what I was writing before Marli barged into my room this morning and pushed me off my computer, because her computer died and IT LIKE COMPLETELY FUCKED HER WORLD.

(Luckily, I sent my email before she saw it.)

Dear Silas,

I want to meet you, too. I really hoped you would like my work— more than just like it, actually. I can't explain it, but I just really wanted YOU to feel it. Do you think it looks good, like you know, serious? How does it compare to the real stuff? Do you think I will fit in with the NYSCFA scene? Will you send me photos of your work now? I can't wait to get to New York and meet you in person. I wish you could have been here this weekend. It was incredible. I hope I have more weekends like this one up in New York.

Piper P.

6/11 8 pm Day from hell

Dad picked me up after school today. He got off work early. He looked so serious I thought he was going to tell me he was going to die or something, but it was almost worse. Over coffee and donuts, he laid it on me.

"Piper, your mother and I were so proud of you Saturday night. You really did something great." (Stuff stuff and more stuff.) "But if you don't get a job, and soon, I really don't see how we're going to make New York work for you. You have to start bringing in some money. We spoke with Helen Mundy—"

"You did?" I interrupted.

"Yes, Mom and I talked to her to find out all the options for you. They're slim, kid."

"People go to college all of the time!" I said.

"Yes, but not in New York, Piper. Not in one of the most expensive cities in the world, not to a private school."

"So what do I do?" I said.

"We're all going to have to sacrifice. Limited shopping for you. Limit the art-supply trips."

"Dad!"

"You haven't put any job applications in anywhere, have you?"

"I have!" I said. "I haven't heard back from any of them but I swear, Kit helped me apply to a bunch of places in the Galleria. Two of them begin hiring in June, they said."

"Look, Piper," Dad sighed. "I've done something you might be unhappy about, but your mom and I agreed it was for the best. We know the job market out there is tough and you're a hard worker, when it comes to what you care about . . . but we need you to connect the dots. Mom and I found a job for you, something that would be easy for you to get to and from, something that we know you could make work. We discussed this before."

My stomach was dropping so fast it was like I was on the Texas SkyScreamer at Six Flags.

"It's at the diner. With your sister. You start this weekend."

"WITH MARLI? Are you kidding? I graduate this weekend! I can't work with her! She will kill me!"

"You can start on Sunday. She said you can train during brunch."

"WHO said that?"

"Marli's boss, Nadia. I guess she's now your boss, too. Mom ran into her at the store and told her about our situation." Dad raised his eyebrows at me.

"Why would you possibly think this is a good idea?"

"Because," he said, putting his coffee down, "I want you to go to New York, too, but you aren't doing anything about it. You don't understand the severity of the issue."

"You're forcing Marli on me. You need to realize that."

"You need to work, Piper, and YOU need to realize THAT. Your mom and I are busting our asses to figure out how to make all of this work and frankly, you're coming off as a real snot, kid. We love you and we support you and we want you to see your dreams come true, but we can't just bankroll you and pretend we're not stretched beyond our means. As much as I hate to admit it, we're bone-thin. You think this is easy for me? For your mother? It's not. None of it is. It's downright embarrassing. So." He took a breath. "If you are serious about making your dream come true, as serious as your mother and I are, you will get your ass in gear and you will say, 'Yes, Dad, I'll take the job at the diner. Yes, Dad, thank you for getting it for me, and helping me afford my dreams.' This job is the easiest, quickest way. You don't even have to interview or wait around. You know the menu. In 2 months, you'll be in New York. And I KNOW you can endure anything if it gets you to New York. So you can take Marli for 2 more months."

I'm stopping writing now. Crying.

6/12 5 pm

More time with Marli scares the fuck out of me.

Still hearing Dad calling me a snot.

Feeling like one too.

Too tired to write.

This is me:

It's pouring outside. POUR-ING. Dad's at work because the flash-flooding is getting worse and there might be a hurricane on the way if Tropical Storm Tiffany outside of Mexico keeps its momentum. Hurricane season only started 2 weeks ago.

Enzo just left our place, dancing down the street in the rain like a perfect weirdo.

We were going through my closet, deciding what I would wear for graduation in 2 days. HOLY CRAP. No more high school. It's about time!

Enzo wanted to shop today but I told him I have to save what allowance I have left.

"Buuuuuuut it's graduation," he whined. "Since when do you not care about dressing up?"

"It's not about not caring," I said. "It's about my dad killing me if I spend any more money before going to NY."

"He wants you to look good though."

"Yeah, probably not as much as you do. Dad doesn't notice if I'm wearing something for the bazillionth time."

"That's a shame," Enzo said. Then he started throwing clothes on my bed, layering them on top of each other, rearranging them, pulling out my shoes and purses and all my necklaces. Watching him go through my clothes, I realized how over him I was as boyfriend material. Plus, I couldn't stop thinking about kissing C.J. the other night, and then all my mixed-up intense feelings about Silas hovered over everything I did.

It looked like a thrift store had exploded by the time he was done. But we came up with:

- 1950s flirty skirt dress with black patent-leather gloves
- black pillbox hat that I'll strap over the graduation cap
- red disks Bakelite necklace
- silver oversized portfolio clutch

Enzo calls our creation GRAD-FACTORY-MOD.

I think we're going to re-dye my hair tomorrow too, because it's grown out so much and the silver-gray is just clinging onto the ends. I'm thinking hot pink or red, but I want it to match my clutch.

Enzo's going to wear coordinating colors and try to get Kit to also. I asked her to come over but she said she was busy—doing what, hello, we don't have any homework left—and Enzo said he thought she was hanging with DJA, but I don't think so. Ever since Sat. night she's been weird to me. I asked Enzo if he thought she was being weird to me and he shrugged.

"I can't remember that much about Saturday night—oh, except for you and that guy. . . . What's up with that guy, anyway?"

"His name is C.J. And nothing is up with that guy, right now. . . ."

"Somebody was having fun."

"Yeah," I said. Still no text from him.

"Wow, you're like INTO him," Enzo said.

"Maybe." (I wasn't going to be into him if he wasn't into me, or at least texting me.)

"You're SOOOO into him," Enzo said.

"Why do you care?"

"Because," Enzo said, "You are my best friend. And I don't want to see you hurt."

"Enzo," I said, ready to clock him one, "YOU totally hurt me!"

"I didn't mean to," he said, his voice soft. "You know that."

"Well, you did though."

"I don't want to fight. Not now."

"We're not fighting," I said. "But you should go."

"Don't be mad," he tried one more time.

"I'm not. But I just don't think YOU should be talking about who I'm dating."

Enzo threw his hands in the air like he was giving up. "You're the boss."

"Yeah," I said. "I am. Now get out!"

I planted a big fat kiss on his cheek and sent him out into the rain. He reminded me of the wet cat in Breakfast at Tiffany's. I couldn't help but think about what Andy said: "They always say time changes things, but you actually have to change them yourself."

So freaking true.

6/14 LAST DAY of HIGH SCHOOL. FOREVER.

Today was a blur. Everyone signing yearbooks. Everybody crying. Voice Box, our a capella group, was singing Fun's "We Are Young," like over and over, in the courtyard.

Enzo, Kit, Jen, and I stood under our tree watching everyone freak out.

"This is it, you guys," Jen said.

"For them," Enzo said.

"We have all summer together," Jen said.

"We have all of our lives together," I said. I bumped into Kit's side and smiled at her and she stepped away from me.

"What is up with you?" I whispered.

"Nothing. C'mon."

"You're being weird to me."

"Piper, it's like our last day, everyone's weird."

I rolled my eyes at her and looked over at Enzo who was singing along, loudly and out of tune, with Voice Box.

Adams crossed the courtyard to us, her nest of jangling necklaces bouncing up and down on her chest. Sam Chang trotted right behind her.

"Look at all of my ducklings in a row!" she said. "I'm going to miss you all so much."

We group-hugged her, Enzo crying and singing to and on her. She was wiping his face off even though she was crying herself. Her mascara was everywhere.

"You all must be so proud of your review!" she said. "Your first!"

"What review?" I asked.

"I didn't see a review," Enzo said.

Sam and Kit shared a look.

"Who reviewed us?" I asked. "Like a real review?"

"It's not that big of a deal," Sam said.

Voice Box started singing "Happy" by Pharrell Williams.

"It's a very good review," Adams said. "Even your part, Kit. Just think of it as informative . . . instructional. You caused controversy!"

"My piece wasn't controversial," Kit snapped at Adams.

"Kit," Adams said. "It's not bad."

"What are you guys talking about?" I asked. I felt so out of the loop.

"Here," Sammy said. He held his phone out for me to read the review. There was a huge photo of my piece before the review even began.

The work from the Kathryn J. Whitmire High School Fine Arts Department Senior Class Artists' Exhibition at the Oilers Gallery downtown this week is exciting and accessible. Though some pieces had sentimental feelings emanating from them, some were rigorous and technological. This raises the once-again divisive argument of contemporary culture: Just because something is made by a person, a maker, doesn't mean it's art. Does it?

One of the strongest showings, *Map*, was created by Piper Perish. Perish's heavy wash of blood red on her heart map balanced darker patches of blues and purples on adjoining panels. Looking at it long enough, one could imagine that heart beating right off the wall that held it; so alive, so powerful, so relentless. One can only imagine the passion that pulses inside this vital new artist.

The exhibit included many inspired pieces, such as Louisa Spalding's *Grimace*, an irreverent take on America's obsession with fast food, and Wendy Nixon's *Houston Hands*, a tribute in plaster and ceramic to those members of the Greatest Generation who are still alive and residing in Houston. From Samuel Chang's personal story in *Hammock*, a loving tribute to his mother created entirely in yarn, to the sartorial Lorenzo Romero's *The Naturals* fashion collection, featuring mannequins dressed and draped as flesh-colored robots, making a statement about identity and individualism, these students expressed their points of view with sincerity and fearlessness.

Unfortunately, some pieces were less successful. John Hay's *Bulletproof School* and Greg Lin's *Tarmac* relied so heavily on recent events in pop culture that it was hard to find the innovation or invention in the creations themselves. Katrina "Kit" Bash's *Bash Lab* creation, an online gallery that features the works of other artists, felt slightly opportunistic and dependent. It's a perfectly admirable business, but the question must be answered: Is this art? Just because Ms. Bash has coded and designed this website, can it be considered anything but entrepreneurial, commercial, and, dare I wonder . . . parasitic? The artist statement on the wall behind her laptop read "Art for sale." One can't help but think that says it all.

On the whole, these seniors' theses promise a graduation into greater achievement and articulation. I can't wait to see what they come up with once they have experienced the world outside their high school walls.

The Kathryn J. Whitmire High School Fine Arts Department Senior Class Artists' Exhibition at the Oilers Gallery continues until Monday, June 17th.

"Oh." I couldn't think of anything more than that. I was kind of stunned.

"That's your new boyfriend writing that about me," Kit said.

"What?"

I looked at Sam's phone again. The byline was Chris Jones, Staff Writer, The Rice Thresher.

"Oh," I repeated. Of course. I forgot.

"It's actually not bad at all," Adams said. "It's asking a question. An important one. What do you want to do with your life? Where do you want to go with it? Kit, I think there's no doubt that you have talent. He didn't say anything about your talent. He asked a bigger question about art. The question came from what you created. If you hadn't created that website, he would not have asked."

"Please," Kit said.

Adams was really out-Adamsing herself, even I could see that.

Kit looked blue-gray. Deflated.

"It's all feedback," Adams said.

"No, it's not feedback. He called me a parasite." And then Kit turned to me. "Your new boyfriend thinks I'm a parasite." She said it in this gross girly voice.

"He's not my boyfriend! And you're not a parasite! I'm sorry!"

"Don't be," she said, "You got a <u>great</u> review. I wonder why." I tilted my head and raised my eyebrows at her, like UM? But she really looked like she was about to cry.

"My review was pretty great too," Sam said.

"SHUT UP, SAM," Enzo and I both yelled at him.

"Guys. This is not how our 4 years will end. We part not in competition but in cooperation; not in envy but appreciation. Now, one more hug, please?" Adams pulled us all together and when we clumsily hugged, I could feel Kit shift her body away from mine. Usually we would have giggled and been extra silly and smushy with each other, but this time, she created a space between us.

"I have to go," Kit said.

"Wait!" I grabbed her arm. "Please stay!"

"Seriously, Piper, just let go." I let her go. She huffed off.

"Give her a little time," Adams said.

I didn't really have any choice. Why couldn't C.J. have just given her a decent review? She's already been mad at me for getting into school, and now this. What was I supposed to do? I never wanted to make her feel shitty. But also, I kind of wanted her to be like, happy for me. Never in a million years did I think making stuff would come between us.

6/15 6 am

There's no school today, or ever again. Just graduation. In 4 hours, we walk in our caps and gowns, then we're officially done. I never thought I'd get to this day without Kit spending the night before, and getting ready together. After all of the texts I sent her last night, after Enzo stayed up calming me down, after sending the meanest text ever to C.J.—and not hearing back—I thought Kit and I would have talked by the time we got to the stadium today. I can't believe she's blowing me off this hard. I didn't write that review. And I love her website. This isn't fair.

6/16 9:30 pm

So tired I can't see straight.

Yesterday's graduation included:

🍁 The worst "inspirational" songs ever.

🍁 Kit avoiding me during the ceremony even though I screamed like crazy when she dominated the stage in her floral platform wedges. So major—total shoe win.

261

✤ Enzo and I giggling and teasing each other throughout Jen's valedictorian speech about how We Were . . . No . . . <u>Are</u> . . . the Future!

✤ And a text from C.J. in the middle of the ceremony, which he didn't even know I was at, asking if we could see each other and talk about the review. He was swamped with finals and that's why he hadn't texted me during the week.

Mom and Dad surprised me with a mini graduation party in the backyard. They set up the smoker and a barbecue station and the neighbors came over and Enzo and Philip were here and Jen stopped by with her parents. Adams even brought her famous vegan pineapple upside-down cake and wished me luck in NY. She was heading to Paris soon for her summer retreat, which terrified me, but she promised to have a lunch date with me at holiday break and gave me her email. Mom had DJA set up speakers in the corner of the yard and he played a lot of relaxed-adult-rock music, like stuff from the 70s that Dad really liked.

Kit was supposed to come but she told Mom she had plans with her family, which is absurd.

Marli, after eating like 5 ears of grilled corn, sat in the corner complaining about her gas while everyone else talked about the food and graduation and what was next.

Mom and Dad made a toast and Mom started crying, talking about how her last baby was flying the coop and then Marli said, It's not like there isn't going to be another baby soon, and everyone kind of nervously giggled and looked at Marli's stomach (which is pretty hard to miss) and just like that the whole conversation was back to Marli.

Which I guess was a good thing because . . . this was also a surprise baby shower! That explained why all the neighbors were there, and then suddenly, why some of Ronnie's family came out from behind the side of our house. It was a surprise-surprise party.

And for the next 3 hours, people showered Marli and Ronnie with diapers and toys and strollers and stuff—I didn't give anything because I didn't know—and me with envelopes with cash and gift cards inside.

Of course I had to share my party with her. Of course of course of freaking course.

When they saw I was on the verge of tears, Enzo and Philip snuck me away to our liquor cabinet and we did shots of Wild Turkey, which must have been created to taste like actual turkey crap. That shit is the nastiest.

I basically stopped talking except to say thank you to our neighbors. I also talked about the weather or something with Ronnie's grandpa, Big Daddy Haysmith, who smelled like a combination of the Wild Turkey I had just shot and like, old-man sweat. He was nice enough, I guess, and he told me I could also call him Big Daddy, now that we were family, but I told him, that's okay, I'd call him Mr. Haysmith. And then he said, Nothing wrong with good manners, child.

I helped Mom and Dad clean up after the party. Marli and Ronnie were busy checking out all of their new baby gear.

"We really couldn't afford two parties this summer," Mom said. "We thought it would be fun to you know, combine the two. Not tax the neighbors too much either."

"Right," I said.

"That was a good call your mom made," Dad said. "And look how much fun we all had! Jen and her folks didn't want to leave."

I nodded.

"I think Enzo and his friend enjoyed themselves?" he continued.

"They did," I agreed.

"Well, I for one missed Kit," Mom said, smiling and wiping down one of the picnic table benches. "I wish she and Roberta and Kendrick could have dropped by. I know they're always at the hospital though. Such devoted people."

I threw an armful of paper plates smeared with potato salad and BBQ sauce into the trash can.

"Ronnie's family—" Dad said, looking over at him. "Well, we could have done worse."

They kept talking, agreeing with each other and being happy. I didn't want to destroy whatever they thought they had done that was so right so I went to my room. They didn't even notice I was gone. My graduation party was lame. All of it was so lame.

So that was my yesterday and I had to work my first shift at 610 today. Which I did.

Marli wasn't there, thank god, because her gas was so strong it would have made the diners sick. Made me glad I wasn't home, almost.

I filled out paperwork and read over the menu a lot, even though I do basically have it memorized. I talked to Nadia about my hours. I "trailed" Iris, which means I watched her serve brunch to people I knew from school, most with hangovers. I got to serve one table myself.

Basically, I think I made under $15 today. And my graduation cards and gifts from yesterday totaled about 200 bucks, which is kind of a lot, but I don't see how it's enough to help with New York.

Now that school is over, there is nothing about my life that is remotely artistic anymore.

6/17 10 am

It's weird to wake up and not have school and not feel like I'm on break either. I'm doing a Monday dinner shift, which I bet is going to be like 5 tables or something.

265

I'm going to paint today. And call Kit. And hope she picks up.

6/18 2 pm

We all had to go get our pieces from the gallery today. It's the last time we're going to see Adams. She's leaving for Paris tonight.

Kit didn't show. Enzo said he'd told her he'd bring her laptop to her.

"How is she?" I asked him. "She won't return my calls or texts."

"She's just pissed. Not at you, just the situation."

"It's not my fault."

"It's not about YOU," Enzo said. "You kind of have to get that out of your head. It's not about you. It's actually about her."

"So what am I supposed to do?" I asked. "If she doesn't want my help? It's like I'm being punished for something I didn't do."

"She's not asking for your help," Enzo said, exhaling hard as he lifted one of his wrapped mannequins into the back of Adams's U-Haul. She had rented it for the day to transport our projects. "What she wants is for you to understand that she's a total freaking mess because she got a horrible review by a guy you hooked up with and you don't care because you're outta here soon."

"But I do care!"

"Don't tell me that," he said. "Tell her. Just send her an email and she'll get back to you when she's ready." I didn't tell him I've already been texting her and emailing her and she hasn't said one word.

266

Enzo and Sam and Adams helped me lift my big heaving heart off the wall and lay it on the gallery's blankets—they let us borrow them for the day—to wrap it up before we slid it in the back, barely enough room next to Sam's hammock, and pulled the truck door shut.

Before Adams climbed into the front seat, she gave us each a set of postcards, already stamped and addressed. She told us she expected us to keep in touch over the summer, even if it was just dropping one or two lines or a couple of good quotes. And if we didn't use them now, we could use them in the fall. She was going to miss the fall semester and stay in Paris, working on her stuff until December.

"What about school?" Sam asked.

"You've inspired me," she said to all of us. "I need to get out. As Anaïs Nin said, and I paraphrase here, 'When ordinary life shackles me, I escape, one way or another. No more walls.' I need a break before it's too late."

"Too late for what?" Enzo asked.

"That's a good question," she said, so mysterious, and hopped into the truck's front seat and we squeezed into the back of the cab.

I felt sad. She was driving us back to our separate houses, to drop off the pieces we had worked on all semester, and it just felt so . . . final.

We didn't talk much on the ride, just listened to Adams singing some sad French song, repeating Non, je ne regrette rien, over and over again.

As soon as I got home, I sent three emails:

Dear Kit,

I know you're mad. Please, can we talk? :) I love you.

Pipes

Dear C.J.,

Finals suck. I hope you got all As. Can we hang out soon? I want to talk to you, too, face to face.

Piper Perish

Dear Silas,

My entire life has blown up. Graduation happened, my best friend isn't speaking to me, my parents basically forced me into getting a job at the diner with my sister, my art teacher is leaving town, and . . . I just feel totally alone. My piece got a good review (I didn't know we would even get reviews), which should make me happy, but has actually caused all kinds of shit. I can't wait to be in New York, to hang out with you, and forget this place. Help?

Piper

6/19 In the backyard

Dad and I were supposed to go running once he got off work, but now he's working late. I'm sitting at the picnic table, looking at my heart, all wrapped up still, figuring out where we should put it. It's not going to work just keeping it in the backyard all summer, it's guaranteed to warp from the humidity. I would put it up in my room, but it's too big to store there. And there's no way I'm going to ask Kit to put it in her office now, not when she's not even speaking to me. Asking her to stare at something that would remind her of her review all the time would be the worst. So I guess that's where it goes, from the gallery wall to the garage floor. Depressing. If Adams was here, I bet she would have the best sad quote for me about storing beautiful art in a dirty garage. All I can come up with is that the one place my heart doesn't fit is my home. What a mean joke.

I did another training this morning with Iris and it was boring. Being a waitress at 610 is boring. Maybe that's why Marli is so mad, her life is just so boring and stuck. At least she wasn't there this morning, and I don't have to train with her at all because Nadia asked me if I wanted to train with my sister and I said no thanks.

"Your sister is tough as nails," she said. "Nails down a chalkboard."

I nodded.

And then she told me I'd do fine and handed me a bunch of silverware to roll in white paper napkins. Roll-ups.

At least Nadia is kind of watching out for me.

My share of tips for a 6-hour training today: $9.35 cash (plus I get $7.50 an hour.) How is it that I actually feel broker now than before I started working?

6/20 Midnight!

Emails from Silas AND C.J. here when I got back from hanging at Jen's house tonight!

C.J.'s said:

Hey Hottie! I want to talk to you too . . . among other things. heh heh heh

Let's hang this weekend. You free tomorrow night? Or now? ;)

I wrote him back and told him I was going to a party—I didn't want to seem too available! Plus, I don't think Mom and Dad would exactly care for me taking a booty call. (Mom and Dad, if you are reading this, DO NOT ASK ME ABOUT BOOTY CALLS.)

We're going out Friday night. I told him we should go to the Heights or Montrose for people-watching and he said he would pick me up at 8. Luckily my shift ends at 6. I hope I never get a late-night shift on a weekend—who would want to work then?

Silas's email was like, of course, so right on. Perfect. He's so smart. He sees through the bullshit.

P. Perish:

When you are here, none of it is going to matter.

Not your sister.

Not your job.

Not your best friend. (Let me guess: Did it have something to do with the good review?)

Not your art teacher. (Though that part really does suck. Can you get in a studio this summer somewhere else?)

Not even your graduation. (Congratulations! You officially get to think for yourself now!)

None of it.

And all of it.

If it all still matters when you're here, you will use it in the new stuff you make.

Everybody here uses their crap; it's like nobody can stop putting the old parts of their old selves in their new stuff, but it's cool.

Almost everyone here is from somewhere else, except me.

Everyone accepts it.

And everyone is going to accept you.

I accept you.

Just face it: you belong here.

Now send me the review.

And start making something else. You'll see my stuff when you're here.

And write me back.

—Silas

Why do I feel like Silas gets me better than anyone else? Why can't I wait for his emails?

Today, I feel adult. So weird.

First of all, it's 10 am on my summer break and I've already been up for 3 hours. Marli was slamming her bedroom door and stomping down the hallway, early, maybe around 7ish?, and she woke me up. I tried not to get up but the noises from the bathroom were so . . . pitiful . . . I thought she might really be sick. The door was open and she was slumped over the toilet.

"What's going on?" I asked her.

"Don't worry about it."

"You seem like you're not okay," I said. Kind of a question, kind of an answer.

"How can I be okay?" She wiped her hand across her wet face, and pulled her hair out of her eyes, slicking it back. I could see a little throw-up on the corner of her mouth.

"Do you want me to get Mom?"

She shook her head no and sat all the way down, patting the floor. An invitation.

(The last thing I wanted to do.)

I carefully went over to her and lowered myself. I was waiting for her to trip me or pull my hair, things she had only recently stopped doing, like in the last 5 years. But she seemed wounded, not strong.

"Are you and Ronnie . . . ?" I didn't want to say having a fight. I didn't want to say the word fight right then, give her any ideas.

"I'm scared," she whispered, kind of to me, and kind of just out in the air.

I tried to pat her shoulder but we were sitting too close together and it was awkward.

"You're going to be okay," I said.

She bit her lip and her eyes darkened.

"Do you think you're going to be okay?" I asked.

She shook her head. "I had a headache so I took a few of Mom's pills," she said. "Now I feel, I dunno. Out of it."

"I'll get someone," I said. She didn't try to stop me, so I woke up Ronnie and he went in the bathroom and I shut the door behind them. The last thing I saw was Ronnie trying to lift her up and Marli leaning on him. She was moving like she was drunk.

I climbed back into bed and tried to go back to sleep, but I couldn't. I had goose bumps. Mean Marli I could take. Melancholy Marli was scarier. Slow Marli was the scariest.

So I got up and sketched for a while. And then I ate cereal. And now I'm back in bed.

It's my last day of training with Iris. I have to be at work from noon until 6 pm. And then I'm going on a date with C.J. I need to think through what I'm going to say to C.J. about Kit.

She still hasn't emailed me back. I just want to hang out while we still can. I want everything to be normal. I want her to know I still think she's amazing, and always will, and I would (and HAVE) said I'm sorry a million times to her, even though I didn't write the dumb review. Part of the reason I'm going out with C.J. tonight is to get him to explain himself. This date isn't just for me, it's for her, too.

273

I need to be at 610 in like 3 hours, which is going to suck since I can't sleep. I'll just have to drink ALL OF THE COFFEE here and at work. Work. So weird. So not where I want to be today, especially when I'm probably going to make a whole $6 or something ridiculous. Can't exactly quit yet. I guess. Dad would kill me 100x over.

I stayed out until 2 kissing C.J. WOW WOW WOW. College guys = different. Also, the red slip dress that I wore is ruined—his beer soaked my whole front. Luckily he had a blanket in his trunk, so I could cover up with it. Our date was so different different different and awesome. We had dinner downtown instead of Montrose, which is where I had originally wanted to hang out—and then we went back to his place. YES, HIS PLACE! He doesn't live in a dorm! He lives in an apartment over a garage that he rents from some chill couple who live off of Shepherd.

I came home right after work. Iris shared her tip money with me since I trailed her on a bunch of tables and spent a lot of extra time rolling silverware for the weekend rushes, so I actually came home with almost $50 ($47.50), which was kind of exciting. Sure beat the nothing I was expecting. Anyway, I got dressed really fast—antique red slip dress with the drop waist and my flapper Mary Janes and feather earrings—a nod to the headwear without actually going there. Looking cute. Snuck into Mom's room to borrow a little of her Dior J'Adore that she never wears, then back to my room for perfect red lipstick to match the dress. Waited there until I heard C.J. pull up. Really didn't want to have to encounter anyone before I

went out, even though Mom knew I had a date. When the doorbell rang, I ran downstairs, but Mom was already opening the door.

"You must be Chris," I heard her say.

"You can call me C.J., ma'am. Everyone does."

"Well, welcome, C.J.," Mom said, her voice a little bit higher than usual.

When I came into the living room, Mom was stepping back from C.J., resting her hand against her heart. Her cheeks were pink and she seemed . . . weird.

"Hi C.J."

"Hey, girl. Don't you look like the belle of the ball."

Mom giggled and turned pinker.

"We should go," I said. I was mortified that Mom looked so interested in C.J. That was just so gross and besides, she's never that pink with Dad, HER HUSBAND.

"It's a pleasure meeting you, Mrs. Perish," C.J. said, extending his hand to shake hers.

"Likewise," she said, all dreamy-like.

"Mom!"

Mom touched her hair and then crossed her arms, standing more like Dad.

"What time do you expect to bring Piper home?"

"Would midnight be all right with you, ma'am?"

"2 works. Right, Mom? I got to stay out until 2 for graduation?"

Mom looked back and forth between us and said with a little hesitation, "2 should be fine." She leaned in to give me a hug, moving my feather earring out of the way, and whispered, "Have a good time. And if you need me to come get you, I will."

I hugged her back quick. C.J. and my mom shook hands again, and then he ran to the passenger door to get there before I did and opened the door for me. As he jogged around the front of his car, some kind of cool classic black car—maybe it was a Mustang?—I took stock of his whole outfit. Tortoiseshell glasses, a blue and white gingham button-down shirt, and really dark-wash blue jeans. His shoes were boring, just brown leather. But the way he moved, he didn't really need a "look." He could throw on anything and look good.

"You ready for our hot date, hot stuff?"

"Uh, yeah." I giggled and it sounded like Mom. Weird. "Where are we going?"

"First stop, dinner. I'm starving. I need some meat!"

We ended up eating at this steakhouse I had seen before but never been to. C.J. ordered a steak, I got a hamburger. He talked with his mouth full, which was nasty.

"So, why New York?" he asked when I told him where I was going to school.

"Ever hear of Andy Warhol? Or Chuck Close? All the greats go to New York," I said. "And besides, I don't want to live in Texas all my life." (I didn't add anything about Marli.)

"What's wrong with Texas?" he said. "My whole family's here! Never left!"

276

"And you're cool with that?" I asked. "Don't you want to see other places?"

"Texas has everything," he said. "Even you, for now." He was so cute, even with steak sauce on his lip. "I'd go somewhere if I had a free ticket," he said. "But I like being here. It's why I go to Rice."

"Is college what you thought it would be?"

"It's all right," he said. "You know, good days bad days. I have an economics professor who sucks ass."

I burst out laughing, now I'm not sure why. It wasn't that funny, I guess I just kind of Girly-Exploded for a second. My nerves were all over the place.

After that we talked a lot more about college and high school, our favorite Houston hangouts (none of them were the same, which was kind of cool), etc., and then he told me he wanted to take me on a drive. So we went to the top of the garage of the Williams/Transco Tower and parked and got out. I had never seen all of the Houston skyline at night from a high-in-the-sky perspective before. Downtown office buildings outlined in neon green piping, stadium lights creating halos over Minute Maid Stadium, and the Galleria right behind us. It was humid. I wanted to look red-hot and I was afraid I looked like a wet sponge.

"Now you see why I think this city is so darn perfect?"

"It does look pretty good from up here." I scooted closer to him, leaning in, hoping I wasn't sticky. "It's hot up here, don't you think?"

"I do." He looked me up and down real quick. "You want a beer?"

"You have one?" I asked. "I mean, you shouldn't if you're driving."

"We could split one," he said.

He pulled a beer from a cooler in his trunk (he keeps a cooler in his trunk!) and when he brought it over and opened it, that's when my dress got sprayed. He was just as surprised as I was. He ran to his car and got a blanket and now my dress was stinky and sticking to me and we were both cracking up, sharing the rest of the beer—there was maybe half the can— between us.

"Let's go back to my place," he said. "You can use an actual towel. No funny stuff, I promise." He looked me in the eye, solid, like he meant it. I thought he was going to kiss me but he didn't.

We got back to his little apt. and walked up the stairs. His staircase smelled odd—musty and musky and boy-like, foreign. Nothing like our house, or like Enzo's.

But inside was a futon, a guitar, candles, a bunch of textbooks and a computer on his kitchen table, and a couple of stacks of books and magazines, an oversized plasma TV on the wall across from the futon. It smelled . . . warm. I liked it immediately.

"So, this is it, Casa C.J.," he said. "Towels in there." He pointed to a door in the corner, the bathroom. I tried to dab my dress dry, but somehow kept making the stain spread. I was a sweaty mess.

There wasn't anything to do about it, so I came back out, feeling awkward. I didn't really know what to say now that we were alone in his apartment. He had turned some music on and I stared at his books, looking for any art collections or music biographies.

"So . . ." he said really quietly, "can I kiss you?"

And like that, it was ON.

We made out for like 4 or 5 hours, with only occasional breaks when we got too hot—his AC seemed like it was barely working—and sometimes we stopped to drink water or talk or whatever. Things could have gone all the way but every time he put his fingers near the hem of my skirt, I just couldn't not think of Marli. I wanted to be with him, like really be with him, but I just knew . . . I just knew . . . I couldn't. What if his condom broke? What if tonight was one of that .0000% chance when the pill failed? Before Marli got pregnant, I never even seriously worried about it, but now . . . I really didn't want to mess up. I didn't want to resemble her in any way, shape, or form. I couldn't imagine telling Dad, when he'd wanted me to promise him I would wait until I married. But most of all, I couldn't imagine not going to New York. I couldn't imagine being stuck here. I couldn't imagine telling Silas. So I kept pushing him away.

It didn't really matter. It was an amazing night.

And I 100% didn't want to ruin anything. I didn't want to ruin his lips that tasted like beer and meat and sweat and his hair that smelled like a campfire and his hands that were so damn strong, like marble. So it was really hard to bring up the review on the ride home. It was the last thing I wanted to do and I almost didn't.

But I had to.

"You know," I said, "you are so awesome."

"Thanks, baaaaby." He kind of said it like Elvis, with a snarl.

I laughed a little, and then when it was quiet, I said, "But you were kind of mean in that review."

"What are you talking about? I loved your piece." He kept both hands on the steering wheel. His eyes bent like they were hurt.

"You were super nice about my piece," I said. "But like, you were kind of tough on Kit."

"Kit?"

"The website?" It pissed me off that he didn't even seem to remember.

"You mean the computer? That's not exactly art. That's something anyone could do. Easy-peasy."

WTF. I dug my fingernails into my palm.

Out the car window the fig trees were wilting. The air smelled like honeysuckle and fried food. The Neighborhood Watch van was driving super slow down the opposite side of the street from us.

"That's not true," I finally said. "I couldn't do what Kit does. She's like, an actual genius."

"Do you know how many people build websites at Rice? She's not a genius, she's just another coder."

I was getting more pissed, which sucked, because I didn't want to be so mad at him and I was. I wanted to keep kissing him.

280

"I don't know anybody who <u>codes</u> like her," I said. I made sure to make it sound like I was mocking him with that word. "I couldn't do what she does. Plus, did you even really look at the site? I have NEVER seen a website that works like hers. And she built it from scratch!"

C.J. pulled up to the curb in front of my house. Mom had left the porch light on. The dashboard clock said 1:58 am.

"You can think what you want, sweetie pie, but you're wrong. It's just not a big deal that she made a website. I don't call it art. And I was the reviewer."

"Didn't you say it was your first review?" I remembered suddenly. "If a real art reviewer came out that night, I bet Kit's write-up would have been amazing."

C.J. tilted his head down and looked over his glasses at me and smiled, a smiley devil in last season J.Crew.

"It's just that Kit's my best friend."

"Course," he said. "You're loyal. You're a protector. I respect that."

"And she's good," I added.

"Whatever you say," he said. "Isn't that the great thing about art? It stirs up all this discussion!"

"I guess," I said. My nails had left marks in my palms. I stretched my fingers out.

"Maybe I'm still learning all the tricks of the trade. Funny dumb, remember? Don't be mad, baaaaaby." He smiled again. His weird Elvis vibe was starting to gross me out.

"Well, don't try to explain my best friend's art to me and then tell me to not be mad," I said.

C.J. sighed. I think he could tell I wasn't going to kiss him again till he stopped messing around about Kit's site. "I really didn't mean to hurt your feelings. Or hers. I'm sorry the review was so rough on . . . whoever's mad about it. Can't you forgive me?" He made a cute sad face at me.

All I had wanted to hear was an apology that I could believe he actually meant. Because if he didn't apologize at all, I could not keep hanging out with him. I guess this counted.

"Did you have a good time tonight?" he asked.

I nodded because I really did, except for that conversation, and put my hand on his leg before I could stop myself. I'm not sure what exactly I was reaching for, and I started giggling. Another bundle of nerves, another unintended Girly Explosion.

"I take that as a yes," he said. "That mean I can call on you again?"

"Call on me? You sound like you're from the 1950s."

"Nothin' wrong with being a gentleman. That's what my pa always says."

"I like gentlemen," I said, right before I leaned over and totally kissed him again and then we were both laugh-kissing.

"You should go in before I get skinned by your mama."

He waited until I opened the front door, and then waved to Mom, who was holding a Diet Coke and looking out the living room window, waiting for me.

"HOW WAS IT?" she practically screamed. No, she actually screamed it.

"Mom!"

"Did you have a good time? Looks like you did."

"What's that mean?" I asked.

"Your hair is out of place . . . and you have a little something right here." She pointed to her own neck.

In the hallway mirror I checked my neck. It looked like there was a small red burn on it.

OH MY GOD.

HICKEY.

MORTIFIED.

I tried to pull my feather earring forward to hide it but it wasn't long enough and besides she already saw it.

"Um," I said. I was so embarrassed I didn't know what to say.

"He reminds me of my high school boyfriend Gus."

"Gross, Mom."

"I'll show you how to cover it up in the morning," Mom said. "A little harder to do with short hair. But it sure does look like you had a fun night."

She was waiting for details, smiling at me like I had just joined some secret hickey club.

"Most moms would be mad."

"Well, I'm not most moms," she said. "And besides, I like him."

"I could tell, you weirdo," I said.

"What?" She blushed. "He's a charmer. It's not my fault."

Gross gross gross.

"I'm going to bed," she said. "I'm glad you're home. Don't stay up too late."

She went to bed, I raced to my room and stared in the mirror at my neck until like an hour ago.

I don't remember him giving me the hickey.

I just remember kissing and talking. . . .

We're different from each other.

I'm finally falling asleep.

Good.

GOOD NIGHT.

6/23 Sunday 10 am

Not working today, which kind of sucks because it's a brunch day. Yesterday I came home with 72 bucks from working the brunch and felt like the complete shit. I was so tired but like happy wired.

The GOOD THING—BETTER THING—BEST THING: Kit texted and we're going to get coffee in 5 minutes! FINALLY!!!!

Plus: Silas's email!

Piper:

Well, you can see why the other artists are pissed about the review, right? You were the star of the show. That's of no surprise to me.

Once Kit has thought about this for a while, hopefully she'll see he's not asking a bad question—it's just one that has nothing to do with her piece. Still, that sucks for her. I bet she is feeling rough.

But don't let anyone trash you or your work.

Just get up here where nobody jealous can take it away from you.

Silas

Kit isn't jealous of me, but I know what he means. Trying to stay calm on my way to see her.

6/24 Monday noon

I don't have to work today, which is good, because yesterday was crap and all I want to do today is draw and eat pizza.

In the backyard. Have been avoiding writing about this all day because I just didn't wanna. Here's what I wrote Silas:

Silas—

Are you sure we're not related and you're not really my secret twin? Because when you write to me I feel like you know me better than anyone else here; you get who I am when nobody else does. I don't know how that's possible considering we haven't met but it makes me even more excited to see you in a little over a month.

I finally met up with Kit. We went to the diner. It was the worst. Basically, she acted like nothing was wrong, tried to dodge why she hadn't returned my texts or emails or calls or anything for so long and then she finally blurted out: YOU WENT ON A DATE WITH HIM? after I told her that I went out with C.J.

KIT: Why would you go on a date with HIM? He RUINED me. And, he's a total dork.

ME: Actually, he's not. I mean, he is, in a kind of cute way, but he's also awesome.

KIT: Greaaaaat.

ME: But I wanted to tell you that I went on a date with him to talk to him about the review.

(TOTAL SILENCE. All she did was stare into her coffee cup, like I was at the bottom of it.)

KIT: And?

ME: Look, he's not an artist or an art critic or a reviewer. He's just a journalism major and this was his first live review. He didn't know what he was talking about.

KIT: Then he should choose a new major. Now it's online forever. Now people can read it whenever they want, for the rest of our lives.

(Now I was silent. I hadn't thought about that.)

KIT: Don't you see what he did? He decimated me. I hope you told him that.

ME: I told him you were a genius. (And it's true—I do think Kit is a genius.)

KIT: Oh, Piper. Get real. I'm not the genius. I'm not the genius who doesn't even realize that what she makes levels up so high the rest of us can't even reach for it.

(Then she stared at me.)

KIT: He just wants to eff you, ya know. I saw you guys making out at the club after the gallery.

ME: That's what people do—they make out. You were all over DJA too, who cares?

KIT: You were making out with the enemy.

ME: I didn't know that at the time and neither did you!

KIT: Still.

ME: Still what?

KIT: You don't even see it.

ME: I. Didn't. Write. The. Article.

KIT: But you didn't have any problems with it either, because YOU got a glowing review.

ME: So did Sam Chang! Is that my fault, too?

(Then she was quiet again.)

ME: I'm sorry, okay. Of course I didn't like the part about you in the review. I told C.J. that.

KIT: C.J.? You're on cute nicknames already?

ME: Everyone calls him that.

KIT: Gross.

ME: (I laughed.) Kind of. Yeah.

KIT: I bet he gave himself his own nickname.

ME: Maybe. (I laughed again.) I think he did.

KIT: You can't eff someone named C.J. who gave himself his own nickname and more importantly, who gave your best friend a horrible review. Not when you're leaving so soon.

(And then we were both quiet for real.)

ME: I'm sorry, K. (Though this time, I wasn't really sure what I was apologizing for.)

We paid the bill and hung around the vinyl store next door for a while and then she made up some lame excuse about having to go. When she got into her car, I asked if we could hang out the next day, and she said, "I'll text you."

Still waiting on that text. I talked to Enzo about the whole thing and he said, Hey at least you guys are talking again. It shouldn't be this hard. It feels like we're freaking dating.

So, all of that drama happens and then I get home to my sister, which I can't even get into right now.

Basically, it's what you said. I don't belong here anymore. I belong in New York, which I've known all along. I could tell you I had an awesome date and you wouldn't judge me. You could tell me whatever you want and I wouldn't judge you. But this place? This place is just full of judgment. I bet nobody judges anybody in New York. Like you said, no one could take my stuff away from me there. There I bet you can be as free as you want. That's what I want to be: free.

Okay, sorry for the longest email ever.

What's going on with you? Are you ready for summer? What are you going to do?

Can't wait for August in NYC!!!

Piper

6/25 Tuesday 7 pm

Worked lunch today—$54! Mom said I should make a plan—10% spend, 90% save—which is 100% suck to me, but I will. Now, after my shifts, she takes my "savings" and deposits it in my account at the bank the next day so I won't be tempted.

I want to go shopping so badly. I need things for NY!

6/26 Wednesday 3 pm

On 15-minute break in the back room. Working a double shift today—my first! Sketch De Afternoon Snackage:

Marli seems like she has gone from pregnant to super pregnant. Even Iris noticed it today during the lunch rush. She's slower on her shifts and takes a lot more bathroom breaks. We basically avoid each other unless there's some seating issue.

Today though, I went to the lockers in the back room to put some of my tip money in my purse, and she was sitting on the bench with her feet up. Her tummy was so big it didn't quite look attached to her, more like it was sitting on her.

"What are you looking at?"

"Nothing," I said.

"Why don't you get out of here?"

I ignored her and was twisting my lock open, rushing to put my money into my wallet. She was in no mood to play.

"We're still not through from the other night."

I looked over my shoulder at her, just to make sure she wasn't going to try and jump me. Even super pregnant, Marli could still probably take me down if she really wanted to.

"I didn't take your Diet Coke," I said to her.

"You know I count on my one hit of caffeine in the morning. And what, that means nothing to you?"

"Marli, Mom drank it." I felt like a snitch, but I had already told her that when she first flipped out.

"Mom would never do that to me."

"Well, she did. I came home from my date and she stayed up late and was drinking a can of Diet Coke. What's the big deal Marli, seriously? I already offered to buy you a whole two-liter and I still will." I knew I had better just be nice with her or it was going to get ugly—which it did anyway.

"You can't accept responsibility for anything."

"What? I am!" I said. "Even though I didn't take it!"

"NO, I AM TAKING RESPONSIBILITY," she said, and then circled her hand around her belly, as if to point out what she thought I couldn't see. "I'M DOING EVERYTHING RIGHT. OKAY. So, stop stealing from me."

"I don't steal from you. I never have."

"If there is Diet Coke in the fridge, it's mine. Don't take it."

"You don't own DIET COKE!" I screamed at her and I knew I shouldn't have. I lost it. I just felt trapped in the room and she was blocking the door to the kitchen and bar.

Marli kicked one of the lunch table chairs and it fell over. Two of the busboys, Marcos and Tommy, burst in to see what was up. Nadia was behind them.

"You two okay?" she asked.

"FINE," Marli said.

"I'm sorry," I tried.

"If there's any more disruptions between you two—especially any more disruptions that the customers can hear—you're both out of here, no notice."

"Yes, ma'am," I said.

291

Marli hugged her arms around her stomach. Tears were rimming her eyes.

"I told you you should have never given her a job," Marli muttered, NOT under her breath.

I moved over to Nadia. "I'm sorry," I apologized. "It won't happen again."

"Thank you, Piper. Now get back to your tables. I just sat all three 4-tops."

When I swung the doors open and was back on the floor, I focused on my customers. I could not think about Marli. I just turned that channel in my brain off. And I ended up making $41.75. Not bad.

At home, after both of our shifts ended, I told Mom what happened.

Mom didn't like that Marli had one of her "outbursts" at work. I asked if any of Marli's outbursts actually surprised her and she actually looked shocked, like she thought Marli only acted this way at home. After all of the times teachers had called and Marli got sent home, Mom still somehow thought she was a "good girl" outside our house. She's so delusional. She grabbed her pill bottle and unscrewed the top, gulped one down with a glass of water.

"By the way, Mom, Marli took a few of those the other day for her headache. I think they really messed with her."

Mom looked at me, confused. "What?"

"A couple of mornings ago. Marli had a bad headache and took some of your pills."

Mom balanced herself against the sink. "She's not supposed to do that! How many?"

I shrugged. "I guess her headache was really bad," I said, "but I think it made her feel worse."

Mom shoved the bottle into her purse, and then zipped it up. "Marli shouldn't be taking medication like Klonopin, nothing she doesn't know anything about during her pregnancy. Thank goodness . . ." She trailed off.

"Isn't it FOR headaches?"

"No," Mom said. "Well, yes, in a sense. But not the kind of headache Marli was having."

"Okaaaay," I said.

"Klonopin is for prescribed use only," Mom said. "Don't take my pills."

"I didn't," I said. "Don't yell at me."

"I'm not yelling at you," Mom said.

"Fine."

"Fine."

When I got back to my room, I looked up Klonopin on my phone. I thought it was just like, the brand of aspirin Mom used. But nope. Anti-anxiety pills.

Looks like I'm the LAST person in this family who needs any kind of talk about "the drug scene." They're all nuts. And nobody's ever gonna do anything about it.

Was getting ready to go for a run and maybe accidentally stop by Kit's house and get her to go out for donuts with me. But then . . .

Ronnie was out in the backyard, opening a cardboard box, wiping his sweaty forehead with his red bandana. He saw me and waved me over.

"Ever put together a crib? You're crafty."

"Not that crafty," I said.

But for the last 2 hours, I just tried to help him instead of running or going to Kit's.

We only talked about Marli once, at the end.

"You pissed your sister off something good the other day," he said.

"What else is new?"

"You need to cut that out," he said. "At least try."

"All I do is try," I said, heaving a wall of the crib up on its legs.

"Well, try harder," he said. "Not for her. Not for you. For my daughter. She shouldn't have to hear you guys crap all over each other all the time. You need to start working on being a better aunt. I'm not saying Mar's perfect, but you ain't, either. Cut her some slack. She can't always control those big emotions she has. And neither can you."

I looked over at him, sipping on his Lone Star bottle, and wanted to remind him it wasn't even lunchtime yet, even though it was hot as hell outside.

294

"I've known Mar a lot longer than you. How about you don't judge me and I won't judge you."

"You've always judged me, Fancy Pants," he said. "And that's alright. I'm used to it. People underestimate me all the time. Let 'em. I know who I am. But that has nothing to do with what we're talking about. Don't be mean to your sister, alright? You need to show her some love."

I didn't know if it was the heat or what he was saying, but I was done. I didn't wake up expecting a lecture today, especially after I spent the past couple of hours helping him instead of taking care of business with Kit.

"I gotta go," I said.

"Thanks for your help, Auntie P."

I unlatched the gate and ran.

6/29 Lunch

Enzo asked me to hang out tonight, but I'm not doing it. I'm going on another date with C.J. instead. Didn't tell Enzo I am hanging out with C.J. because I don't need his input and also don't feel like being Enzo's backup date just because Philip has a cold. I'm just so happy I don't have to be at home.

6/30 Sunday night

Long day and my feet and ankles hurt. Brunches are hard! But today and last night were filled with so much good! $102! And an email from Silas!

C.J. and I went to the movies at the River Oaks 3 last night and ended up kissing through almost all of it. As soon as the lights were out, it was like bam, all over each other. At one point he asked if I just wanted to go back to his place since the theater was so close to his apt. but I said we should stay at the movie and at least try to see some of it. I think I know what would have happened if we went back to his place!!!!

He told me I could crash on his couch if I wanted but I told him I had to work the brunch shift this morning (true) and also, um, I don't think I could really just casually tell Mom and Dad, oh yeah, I'm staying at C.J.'s tonight, although who knows, maybe I could get away with it, they are so in Marli World these days.

And Silas! FINALLY! I thought maybe I'd scared him off with my last email. So relieved—more than relieved!

Hey Piper—

1st) I don't think we're related. I know what you mean. But I hope not.

2nd) Sucks about Kit's attitude, but honestly, I think she may not want to hear about you and Chris (she's right about "C.J.," though ;)). I get it. I mean, maybe that's just rubbing salt in her wound and it isn't going to help you with your friendship in the long run. I'd say x the Chris talk with her. Besides, it's not like you're going to keep dating him forever. You can't pack him up and bring him to New York.

3rd) Speaking of. I like that you think New York isn't judgy. In some ways, you're right. It depends on what part of New York you're in. The part I grew up in? Extremely judgy. My parents are Judgy McJudgersons. If you're not chairing the Met Gala or on the board of ABT, they don't know you exist. It's part of the reason I chose roommates over living with them. I couldn't put up with that shit anymore. If you ever meet them, and I hope you don't have to, but if you ever do once you're up here, prepare yourself for their ridiculousness. It will make you miss your own parents and even probably Texas.

4th) Sorry about the sister shit. Siblings can eat it.

That's it for me.

Going to see an outdoor screening of *Jaws* tonight in DUMBO and have to leave now. Subways on a Sunday schedule = suckage.

—Silas

Had to google this stuff because I didn't want to tell him I didn't know what he meant.

DUMBO = Down Under the Manhattan Bridge Overpass.

Sunday schedules = Subways come less frequently.

Also, he's happy we're not related!

7/1 3 pm

Dad came to the diner for lunch today, ordered half a tuna sandwich, coffee, and a donut. I hung around his table because it was so slow. Mondays at the diner = death shifts. ($28.50 for 8 hours on my feet!)

He told me that tonight we need to talk and I said we could talk at the diner, there was practically no one there, and he said no, later.

I asked him if he was okay.

"Yes, I'm fine."

"You're not, like, divorcing Mom or something, right?"

"What makes you say that?" Coffee dribbled onto his chin.

"I dunno. You just seem weirded out."

"Weirder than usual?"

I nodded, keeping an eye on the hostess stand to see where Nadia was going to sit the couple who had just come in.

"Schedule me in for a jog tonight," he said. "I need to think some things through with you."

I told him okay and then reminded him to leave me a tip.

I'm sure I'm going to have to hear about some new Marli drama tonight.

7/2 10 am

Dad had to work late so we didn't jog and I went over to Enzo's instead. E and Philip were making decorations for his parents' annual big-ass 4th of July party.

"Is it okay that Philip is here?" I whispered to Enzo.

"Yeah," E said. "Mom understands that we're just friends now."

"Seriously? And this is cool with Philip, too?"

"I can hear you," Philip said. "And yes, it's fine with me. Tina can believe whatever she wants about us, even if it's not the truth."

"Chill," Enzo said.

"Whatever, you guys," I said. I didn't want to be there if any arguments broke out between them. I had enough drama at home.

Sam Chang came over because Enzo wanted to surprise his parents with a life-sized papier-mâché mannequin of Uncle Sam and our Sam was building it. Philip kept calling Sam Uncle Sam Chang which kept cracking us up, especially Sam. I asked E if I could invite Kit over and he said he already had but she said she couldn't make it. E and Philip exchanged a look.

"Was she coming over before I said I would come over?"

Enzo shrugged. "I don't exactly remember when I asked who."

"You're lying," I said.

"She's still pissed at you," Sam Chang said, painting Uncle Sam's face.

"Sammy, she's not totally pissed at me anymore. We straightened stuff out."

"About the new boyfriend, a.k.a. the reviewer?" he asked. "I don't think so."

"ENZO! Did you tell Sammy everything?"

"Yes, he did," Philip said.

"Don't be mad," Enzo said. "He already knew most of it. He read the review, remember? And it's not like Kit's exactly being quiet about how she feels."

"Well, she's telling everyone a lot more than she's telling me," I practically shouted.

"Chill," Enzo said again.

"You are kind of dating the guy who destroyed her, you know," Sam said.

"So none of you like him?"

"There's no doubt he can dance," Enzo said. Philip playfully slapped his arm. "What? It's true."

"Well, he may be hot but he's also a J-E-R-K," Philip said. "Remember how I thought I knew him when we met at the club? He has a column online and in the <u>Thresher</u> . . . and it's definitely not about art."

"Well what's it about?" I asked. So annoyed.

"Let's just say his politics aren't . . . leaning toward us," Philip said, wrapping his arm around Enzo's shoulder. Enzo shrugged it off and looked at the back door, checking to see if his mom was going to come out, I knew.

"Yeah," I said. "He's not like me, but maybe that's what I like about him. Did you guys ever think of that?"

"Not you, <u>us</u>," said Enzo. And I realized, OH. "I think you need to check yourself before you wreck yourself. You're defending some dude you just met against the girl who's been your sister, your real sister, since day one. How would you feel?"

For some reason, being lectured by Enzo felt even worse. It made me madder.

"Here's how I feel," I said. "I feel, I feel . . ." and then I swear, I couldn't get the words out. I was just pressing my teeth together and twisting my lips against each other and trying so hard to think of something straightforward that made sense but all I wanted to do was stomp my feet into the grass because it's not fair, Kit has all the money in the world and has always gotten everything she's wanted and for once in her life she didn't and now I have to pay for it!

That's what I wanted to yell.

Instead I exhaled hard.

I didn't know I was holding my breath.

Enzo's mom brought out iced tea.

"Why does it look like a bomb just went off out here?"

She was looking at the piñatas and the just-begun papier-mâché of Uncle Sam and half-soaked paintbrushes on her old magazines and newspapers, but she could have easily been looking at all of us, standing far from each other, the space between us so real and hot it felt like lightning had just touched down and scorched the grass.

"It's gonna rain, bambinos," she said. "Make sure you put this all up in the laundry room so it doesn't get ruined." She backed into the house, looking at all of us, shaking her head, repeating something I'd heard her say before, Pazzo, pazzo.

"What does pazzo mean?" Sam asked.

"It means crazy," I said. "Crazy crazy."

7/3 7 pm

Worked all day.

Left Kit a message to come by the diner, said I'd give her coffee on the house. She didn't show up.

Texted with C.J., who wants to meet up for fireworks tomorrow night.

Dad taped a note to my door:

We need to talk. You and your mother and I. Alone.

Stomach drop. Going to pretend not to see it.

Done with this place. Done with feeling like crap constantly, always making everyone upset. Going to draw.

7/4 6 am 4th of JULY!

INDEPENDENCE! WOO-HOO!
I WANT TO BE FREE TO STAY IN BED!

Working at the diner until 2 pm, then going to Enzo's to help them get ready because I promised his mom I would.

Would rather tell them the diner needed me to stay later today, but Marli knows the diner is closing at 2. Plus, Mom, Dad, Marli, and Ronnie will all be at Enzo's at 3.

Must get out of bed and get dressed to be at diner by 7. Uniform today; flag dress tonight.

7/5 Noon

So much for independence. So much for a holiday. So much for fun.

Zero fucks for this town, that's how much I give. Last night was a disaster.

Was the worst part Kit showing up with some new guy and not introducing me and basically ignoring me all night?

No, though that was awful.

Was the worst part Marli eating all of the watermelon—and I know she was doing watermelon shots, too, because I saw her and she was like, What? It's fruit!, then throwing up in the corner of the backyard behind the bounce house Enzo's parents had put up for the little kids in the neighborhood?

No, though that was embarrassing and disgusting.

Was the worst part when Enzo's grandfather told me he hoped Enzo and I would get married someday because we were "spiriti affini," two beautiful artists?

No. (That was just sweet. And sad. He will never know the truth about Enzo. Or maybe he knows knows, but isn't going to say it.)

The worst part happened with Dad.

The worst part was when Dad broke my heart.

The worst part was when Dad asked me to come talk with him out on the driveway.

The worst part was when Dad said he was sorry to do this here, he knew it made no sense, but that he'd been trying to get me alone lately and needed to talk to me sooner rather than later.

The worst part was when Dad said:

Piper, you're not going.

When Dad said Piper, I'm sorry. We can't afford it. Your mom looked into all of the loan possibilities. We missed the deadlines. We didn't save enough. We thought we did. And then Marli.

The worst part was when I asked Dad did you and Mom just not believe I was good enough to get accepted in the first place.

The worst part was when Dad said maybe not.

The worst part was Dad trying not to cry.

The worst part was that because Dad was crying I didn't get to cry.

The worst part was when fireworks were cracking over our heads, was when Mom was over there chuckling with Enzo's dad, sipping a beer and looking like she was having the time of her life, was when Enzo's mom was handing out sparklers and she gave us both our own and between the little sparks of light she saw our faces and said to Dad, "You didn't tell her now, did you?"

The worst part was when I ran away from the party, tripping in my wedges.

The worst part was when I texted C.J. and asked him to pick me up, even though he was at another party.

The worst part was when he picked me up at the park and said, Look at my sad little cat, what's happened to you, baby? Did somebody hurt you? I'll kill 'em.

The worst part was when I fell into him, pressed my head hard against his shoulder and chest, just twisted my sweaty hair and wet face against his heart so I could listen to it beat and block out the voices in my head.

The worst part was that I lied to him and said, I just really missed you, when I didn't miss him, I'd never miss C.J. I missed Silas, someone I'd never met and would never get to meet now. A ghost.

The worst part is that I've been thinking I was going to be in NY a month from now, starting my real life.

The worst part is I've been so wrong for so long. So stupid.

305

If Adams was in town, I could tell her. She's the one who would get it.

What would she say to me? What great quote would sum this horribleness up?

There is nothing. No words.

7/6

My eyes are swollen. Can't write. Going to paint and see what happens. Only place to go. Have to think.

7/7 Noon

C.J. thinks something awful happened to me at the 4th of July party and I haven't been able to tell him the truth. I told him I'd gotten in a fight with my dad, that's all, but I haven't been able to tell him about not going to NY. He's not going to see why it's so bad and I don't think I can take that. How can I explain it to him? He's not going to get it.

I spent all of last night online, trying to find any kind of last-minute scholarships or loans. One semester—not even a full year—at NYSCFA costs $32,000 before living costs. Why should I even go to work (which I'm supposed to be at now, actually)? Why did Mom and Dad think a dumb wait-ressing job would be of any help at all? I haven't even made $1000 yet.

I feel like I can't breathe, like I'm choking. I'm going to Kit's. She'll talk to me. She has to.

Spent all day and night at work so I could avoid my house. Went to Kit's. Her dad told me that she and her mom had gone to Galveston for the day, then asked me if I was getting ready for my great-big-New-York adventure. He told me about when he did his undergrad work at Columbia, how he had the time of his life, how if I made it north past 110th Street (and he smiled to himself when he said this, some kind of inside joke), that I should definitely go to Sylvia's for soul food when I got homesick.

"I don't plan on being homesick," I said. (Not because I thought I would anyway, but now how could I get homesick if I never left? Sick of home? Yes. Homesick? No.)

"I thought I wouldn't either," Dr. Bash said, "but I swear I did. No matter how many fun parties you go to, no matter how busy your schedule, you always miss home. You always miss your place, your people."

I nodded so he would believe I believed him.

"You'll miss Katrina," he said.

"Of course!" I said, when really, how could I miss Kit when I knew I was staying here? She barely wanted to hang out with me anyway. I missed her now more than I probably would if I was away. "Will you tell her I stopped by?"

"Sure," he said. "Oh, and by the way, we have something for you. A graduation gift. Since I was stuck in the ER and we didn't get to see you on the big day, Kit's mother and I have been meaning to give this to you. Hold on—"

I waited at the front door while he went rummaging around the kitchen.

"Here it is!" He came back with a purple envelope. "Hope this will come in handy up there!"

"Thanks," I said. He was making me too sad. "See ya, Dr. Bash."

"Goodbye, Piper Jane!"

On the way home, I opened the envelope and read the card:

"Congratulations, Graduate! Here's a little something to get you started!"

Inside, there were 5 clean, crisp $100 bills tucked in the card's pocket. Both Dr. Bashes wrote notes.

"We're so proud of you for making the leap to NY," Kit's mom wrote. "We know this gift will probably seem excessive, but Kit's best friend deserves the world! We're so proud of you. With love, Roberta"

And from Kit's dad, "Don't forget the little people! We know you're going to make a big splash (of paint!) in the ART world! —Kendrick"

I looked back and forth from the card to the money. $500 meant so much and so little at the same time. $500 was so much to hold in my hand, but it wouldn't make a dent in my tuition. I smelled the dollar bills like they would have some power over me. Nothing but stale paper. Totally powerless.

I texted Enzo: *Kit went all the way to Galveston to avoid me?*

He texted back: *Her mom made her. It was her day off.*

Me: *Kit hates Galveston!*

E: *But her mom doesn't!*

Me: *This is bullshit.*

Me: *What are you doing? Want to paint?*

E: *Can't. At Rice doing orientation "exercises" with parentals. BTW, student body needs total makeover. TRAGIC! Don't worry about K, she'll text/call. Chill. Ta-ta.*

When I got back home, I grabbed my paints and headed to the garage. I painted in greens and silvers and coppers. I painted all night, not knowing what was going to be the result, just something with motion and energy, not static or frozen. Part of me felt weird/scared, not knowing what I was even hoping would come out on the canvas. But mostly I felt freaking free. I was painting a pure Perish this time, I was painting life. And it was swirling and circling on itself tornado-like. My pulse took over. It took over and let me go at the same time.

I was so in the zone that when Ronnie came out and asked me if I could turn the music down because Marli was trying to sleep, I spun around and flung paint onto his shirt. I was sweaty and exhausted. The garage floor was covered in paint and Ronnie took a step back.

"I'm so sorry." I was out of breath.

"It's cool." Ronnie smiled, looking down at the green slash of paint across his stomach. "You should see you. You're a mess, girl."

"Here, blot your shirt," I said, handing him one of Dad's tool towels and my almost-empty can of turpentine. "Dab some of this on too. Then take it off and put it in the washer. Warm water. Right away."

"It's really not a big deal," Ronnie said, turning down my music. "Besides, one day this shirt might be worth something." Ronnie winked at me and then looked behind me at my canvas.

"What's that gonna be?" he asked. "It looks like some sorta monster."

"I'm not sure," I said.

"Well, something's eatin' at you, Auntie P. Keep on workin' it out, girl."

He went back to the house, quietly whistling.

I looked at my big monster piece, still wet, and pretended I wasn't scared. My head kept saying figure this out, figure this out, you can figure this out, you can still get to New York. But the rest of me was crying. When I caught a glimpse of myself in the mirror by Mom's unused treadmill, I was covered in green. Money-green. Envy-green. Monster-green.

7/9 8:45 pm

Got home from work. ($69, nothing special to report, Marli started her shift when I left.) Mom was sitting on the porch with a beer and a cigarette, holding a folded magazine, swatting away mosquitos.

"You're smoking?"

"Let's talk, baby," Mom said. "We haven't talked."

"Since when did you start smoking again? I thought with the baby on the way . . ." I stopped talking but I looked her in the eye.

"Well, she's not here right now," Mom said. "And I'm allowed a cigarette if I need one."

310

I scooted away from Mom on the porch. "So," I said. "What." I was so not in the mood to talk.

"I didn't want any of this to turn out the way it did," Mom said. "You not going to college. Marli not going to college. You two need to be the first women in our family to finish college. I didn't want you to end up like"—she waved her cigarette around to the neighborhood—"this. You need to make a plan, Piper. You're technically an adult."

"What do you mean?"

I coughed on purpose and she stubbed out her cigarette.

"You can go to U of H," she tried again. "Or HCC for a year. Then transfer. You can't just not go to college just because you aren't going to NY. College isn't negotiable."

"I can't talk about this right now," I said.

"Why?" Mom said. "We have to talk about it sometime and now's as good as any. Your dad's not home yet, Marli's gone, and you don't have anywhere to run off to."

She took a swig of her beer. Maybe she was actually drunk. That scared me. Her mouth trembled like Marli's. Unpredictable. She and Marli looked a lot alike when Mom was tense.

"I'm a lousy mother," she said. "I never protected you."

"Mom!" So unfair. I was allowed to be mad at her, I didn't want to have to be nice to her but she was kind of forcing me.

"And now you think I've failed you, not being able to get you to college in New York. And you're right. We tried, Piper, but we just didn't try early enough, hard enough. Maybe secretly we didn't think you were going to get in. That it wouldn't be a problem."

"Excuse me?" (Insult to freaking injury.)

"Not because you're not good enough—but it's a competitive program. Conservatories don't accept thousands of candidates, y'know."

"You didn't think I might be one of the ones they did want?"

She ignored that. "We could have found a way if that's all we had to focus on," she said. "But this whole thing with Marli . . . it's really thrown us for a loop, baby." She pulled me to her. "You have every right to be mad as hell. You don't deserve to stay in this shithole."

"It's not a shithole," I said, surprised and laughing nervously. I looked out at our neighborhood. It wasn't fancy, but I never thought of it as a shithole. And now I was feeling guilty. Did she think I was a snob about our neighborhood? Did she think that's why I wanted to leave? I was never mad about our neighborhood. I was mad that I'd actually thought I could go to art school in New York, when I was so, so dumb to ever believe that was actually possible. I was mad that Marli was part of the reason I would end up not going and staying here. I was mad at Mom and Dad for not helping me get there, but now I was feeling guilty about being mad, too, and mad that I had to feel guilty. And then guilty again and sad over it all. So much so fast. FUCK.

Her eyes were serious through the puffiness, but trying not to smile, too.

"Okay, it's not a total shithole. Darn it, kiddo, why are you so good to me? You shouldn't take shit from anyone, not me, not your sister, not anyone. You shouldn't be okay with staying here."

"I'm not," I said. "I'll figure something out."

"I'm counting on that," she said. "Now, I'm gonna go get dinner ready."

She stood up, pocketed her cigarettes, and walked to the kitchen.

Was it true? That they just didn't think I would get in? That's why they didn't save enough money? They thought I was Houston–good, Texas–good, but not New York–good, not NYSCFA–good. I was good enough, for being their daughter. But the real world?

Dad always talked about being prepared for everything, for anything. He could predict hurricanes, but he couldn't help his daughters? Well, the one thing Dad couldn't predict was that people might actually take me seriously. And Mom, with her physical therapy clinic, helped everyone get better but us? And she thinks she can just fix this by sending me to community college?

I'm not okay with staying here or going to some school that isn't right for me just to make her happy.

So beyond frustrated. Beyond beyond.

7/10 8 pm

I skipped work today. Called in sick.

Painted all day, except when Enzo brought me lunch. I told him everything Mom said about them not thinking I would get in, but didn't tell him about not going to NY yet. I wasn't ready to admit it. I wondered if his mom had told him, since she obviously knew what was up from what she said on the 4th.

He said my mom probably didn't mean it, it just came out wrong, maybe because she was drinking.

"Are you depressed?"

I shrugged.

"I'm calling Kit," he said.

"Like she'll respond."

He put his phone down and hugged me until I cried, stopped, cried again, and finally stopped enough to keep painting. He sat in the garage while I worked, listening to music and texting, not talking until he had to go home for dinner. When he left, he hugged me again.

"You know I love you," he said.

(I knew what kind of love he meant.)

"I love you, too," I said.

"And I believe in you."

I started to tear up just a little. I nodded so he would leave quickly without me having to say anything else. It was so sweet of him to say he believed in me, even if I already knew he did. I just wished it was Mom and Dad saying it, and believing it, too.

7/11 11:50 pm

Well, Marli told Nadia I wasn't sick, I was painting, and Nadia told me she would appreciate it greatly if I didn't feel the need to lie to my boss (her). I apologized. What else could I do? She just shook her head and told me to get back to work, she didn't have time for any more nonsense from THE DRAMATIC

PERISH SISTERS today. Great. Marli brings everyone connected with her down to her level.

I made $122! Nadia gave me two 20-tops, I think as punishment, but feeding 40 people who were there after some kind of church fellowship didn't seem too hard to me. All they wanted were sundaes, which made my wrist hurt due to ladling sauces and scooping ice cream, but they didn't really require much. I over-heard them include me in a prayer before they ate, "God bless our waitress, working so hard on her feet, may she too be under your watchful guidance," and for a split second I wished I was sitting with them. It would be good to know someone, anyone had my back. But I would just be praying to get to New York, to school, and that probably wasn't what you were supposed to ask for when praying to god or whoever.

C.J. came in while I was on my shift and sat in my section and ordered coffee. He introduced me to one of his friends, Rick. Rick had a dumb mustache, but is hot underneath, you can tell.

"She does look like a model," Rick said to C.J., right in front of me, which was both kind of gross and flattering. It wasn't like I was dressed particularly cute; I was in my uniform. But my makeup looked good (daytime cat-eyes).

"I'm sorry, baby, I know you said I shouldn't come here while you're working," C.J. said. "But I couldn't stay away."

"I just can't sit, is all," I said. I looked back at my 20-tops, who were busy diving into their hot fudges of happinesses.

"What time do you get off?" C.J. asked.

"I'm here late. Probably past 11."

"Come over?" he asked, sparks in his eyes.

"Ooh, you know I want to," I said. I didn't really. "But I don't know about tonight."

"Well, I'll leave the door unlocked if you wanna stop by later. If things are . . . weird . . . at home."

He kept acting so pleased as punch that he'd BEEN THERE for me on the 4th of July and he kept bringing it up, like it was some medal he'd won for Doing a Good Thing. I was still avoiding it . . . just letting him think I'd had a fight with my folks.

"Yeah, well, okay," I said. "I'll text you."

One of the big, older men from the 20-top was waving me over.

"I have to go," I said.

C.J. grabbed my hand and wrist, gently tugged me back. "Quick kiss?"

I looked around to make sure Nadia wasn't looking and barely kissed him. I knew I could get fired for that, which would really screw me. I needed to keep making money, even if it was just so I could pretend to myself that I would actually make it to NY one day.

7/12 4:25 am

"A little early for a Walk of Shame, isn't it?"

I flipped on the kitchen light.

Marli rubbed her tummy at me, sipping on a glass of milk.

"Why are you awake?" I asked. I had hoped I wouldn't have to explain why I was coming in past curfew.

"I needed to cool off. Too hot in here and Dad doesn't want to run the AC. Usual cheap-ass. It's like he forgot I'm lugging an extra 50 pounds around with me or just doesn't care."

I nodded. The way she talks about Dad is the worst. He's not a cheap-ass, I wanted to say, he just wasn't planning on SUPPORTING YOU AND A BABY.

"I covered for you tonight, by the way. I told Mom and Dad you were so tired from working a double today that you went straight to bed when you got home at 11."

"Thanks?" I said.

"You owe me."

"Okay." I really didn't want to deal with Marli's weirdness. I wanted to think about what had just happened with C.J., just be lost in that a little while longer. Real life wasn't appealing.

"I hope you didn't do anything I would do tonight," she said.

"Um, I didn't," I said. UGH, GROSS. My whole body tightened.

"You sure?" Her smile was smug.

"C.J.'s not like that." (Why did I owe her an explanation?)

"Trust me, little sis, they're all like that."

"Okay," I said, moving to leave. But she kept talking.

"You know I'm always covering your ass for you. You know that, right?"

"Sure," I said. "Except like 2 days ago when you told Nadia I wasn't sick."

"How did I know you were lying to her?"

"You knew I called out sick."

"I for-got," she said. "Pregnancy brain." She slapped her head gently and stared at me. "And you never even say thanks. It's a wonder why I do it."

"I do, too," I said. "I just did."

"No. You said, Thanks?" She mimicked me in this really smarmy way. "Not, 'Thank you, Marli.' Not, 'Thank you for saving my ass.' Not, 'Thank you for helping me not get busted so I could go off with my pretentious, Ivy League—wannabe boyfriend.'"

"Okay, Marli," I said. "I'm sorry." I was trying to play her game. Keep her calm. I hated it. I hate this. My skin was growing icy, even though it was still humid outside and the heat was now sitting in our house.

"I'm going to bed," I told her.

"Piper."

"Yeah?"

"You're only going to New York because of me, you know."

I was stunned. She thought I was still going to New York. She didn't know. They didn't tell her? I had a flash of STUPID, INTENSE HOPE Mom and Dad were planning some kind of wacko surprise for me. Maybe I was actually still going. Maybe this was all just a big surprise from Dad. But he wouldn't go this far. Would he? No. And Mom wouldn't be a part of something that mean/weird/cruel. My heart felt clamped again, that now-familiar tight ache.

"I know why you're leaving. You can't stand that I'm the center of attention and that you don't have a job to do, to be the Perfect Child, our little savior."

"None of that is true, Marli."

"Just admit it."

"Admit what?"

"That you're jealous I'm having a baby. You won't be the special one anymore."

"I'm really tired, Marli. I'm going to go to bed."

I tried to head toward the door again, but she blocked me.

"NO," she said. "You go to bed in a minute. You . . . are . . . jealous."

She was now so quiet, I was scared. Same way the sky is right before a hurricane.

"Fine," I lied. "Sure. I'm . . . jealous. Can I go to bed now, please?"

(I felt sick to my stomach.)

"Do whatever you want," she said. Her face went so soft, no edges, no lines. When she's angry, her face goes tight. But when she's most dangerous, her face, smooth and slack, is almost putty.

"Nobody's keeping you hostage." She smiled and it looked like oil spreading in a puddle.

I bolted through the kitchen door. My whole night/morning was/is almost ruined.

Now I can't sleep but I don't want to leave my room because of her. I feel trapped. I want to tear the sheets off my bed and scream. I wish I had just stayed at C.J.'s and fuck the consequences.

Postcard from Adams was sitting on the kitchen table for me!
On the back of it said "Greetings from Paris, TX" and it had a
tiny Eiffel Tower on it. In Adams's handwriting, it read:

> Hello Piper,
>
> I write this to you from my beloved Gonzales Paris
> Bakery, where I come every morning and drink my
> coffee and eat fresh baked bread before I start the day.
> The people who run it have become charming friends.
> Paris was just what I needed; a break from all the distrac-
> tions of "real life." I'm painting like a madwoman and
> have started weaving baskets, too. Can you believe it?
>
> I can't wait to hear about your days in New York.
> When do you set off?
>
> Yours,
>
> Alice Adams
>
> P.S. "The real voyage of discovery consists not in seeking
> new landscapes but in having new eyes." —Marcel Proust

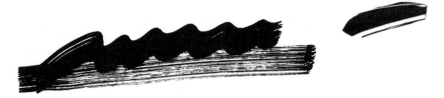

Seeing her handwriting felt like medicine. I've been rereading
the card. I wish I had her cell number. I wish I could talk to her,
just hear her voice.

She doesn't know I'm not going to New York. Marli doesn't know I'm not going to New York. I have to tell someone else. I'm going to explode. I have to talk about it with someone not them. Texting Kit. Maybe she's awake.

7/14 6 am

It's cruel to be up this early on a Sunday morning but I have to work the brunch shift and wanted to write before I left. Had the weirdest, not-good night ever.

Went over to C.J.'s last night. We ate pizza and drank a few beers that were kind of gross and then kissed forever on his couch. He wanted to take me to a Dark Side of the Moon laser show at midnight at the Museum of National Science. I told him I had to be up early for work, and if the show wasn't over until 1 or 2, it would suck for me in the morning, so we agreed to just hang out at his place until curfew.

"What if I told you I might not be going to New York?" I said. I had kind of been dreading asking the question, since none of the answers seemed like they would be good, but I sort of couldn't not ask once I thought of it. It was on repeat in my head.

"What do you mean?" He shifted back on the couch, putting his glasses back on and straightening out his shirt.

(He looked so much cuter with his glasses.)

"I mean, what if I decided I was going to stay here in the fall? Not go to New York . . . yet."

"Why would you do that?" he asked. "That's all you talk about. That's all you want to do."

"I thought you didn't want me to go to New York," I said. "You talk about how great it is here."

"Well, for me," he said.

"Would you be happy if I was here longer?"

"Well, sure." (He didn't seem sure.) "But you want to go. I don't want to hold you back."

"Do you want to ask me why I won't be going?"

"If you want to tell me, honey, I'm sure you will."

He was being weird and pissing me off. Cagey. I could tell he didn't want to say anything more about it, and didn't want me to discuss it anymore either.

"Are you happy for me?" I tried one last time.

"Well now, that's a trick question. If I say I'm happy for you, that means I'm happy you're not going to New York, which is what you've been saying you want to do. If I say I'm not happy for you, it sounds like I'm . . . not supportive."

Why had he picked now to show off his stupid "nice guy" skills? My eyes started watering. Fuck fuck fuck I didn't want that to happen. I started crying. I don't know what I was expecting from him, but I guess a lot more questioning and concern, some kind of surprise, maybe happiness, some one good thing about staying.

"You don't care at all!" I said, standing and grabbing my bag. "It's like I just told you . . . the weather report!"

"Piper!"

"I'm outta here," I said. I slammed his door and ran downstairs. He called from his window, "Piper! Piper, how are you going to get home?"

"You don't have to worry about me now," I yelled back. "I'll be fine."

I ran from his place to the diner. Nadia was just getting off her shift and I was going to ask her for a ride home, but I called Enzo instead. I still hadn't heard from Kit. I'd talked to my best friend's dad more recently than I'd talked to my best friend.

E and Philip drove me home, telling me I was ruining a perfectly good Saturday night, that we should all be out dancing. I could tell they were worried about me. They kept trying to be too nice.

"Fight with Marli?" Enzo asked.

I shook my head.

"Was it C.J.?" Philip asked.

"Kind of," I said. "Kind of me, too, I guess."

"I'm telling you, he's no good. You're too good for him. And too pretty, too."

"You don't have to be so nice," I said to both of them.

"If you saw you, you'd be nice, too," Enzo said. In his rearview mirror I saw midnight-blue mascara smeared around my eyes.

I jumped out of his backseat when we arrived in front of my house and leaned into the driver's-side front window.

"Let's hang out soon, okay?" I said. "I need to talk to you about some stuff."

"You can hang with us tonight if you want," Philip said. His eyes were sweet and sad.

"Tomorrow," I said. I wanted to talk to Enzo alone.

E touched my face and looked serious.

"You sure you're okay?"

I gave him the so-so hand gesture. Any more words would have made me start crying again.

7/15 10 am

Just sent this text to Kit: *HAPPY MONDAY. Can we please hang out today? I really need to see you.*

Short. Sweet. To the point. If she ignores me, she can fuck off.

Going to lock myself in the garage and paint until I hear from her. I don't have to work today and I want the rest of the world to leave me alone. I'm finally feeling as pissed off as Mom and everyone always thinks I am. Everyone is right. They win. This is the Piper they want, this is the Piper they get.

7/16 7 pm

Got this:

Piper.

Haven't heard from you in a while. Everything okay? Hope last email I sent you didn't piss you off in any way. Anyway, hope your summer is going well and can't wait to see you next month.

324

Maybe I could meet you at the airport, if you want. Let me know. Also, I'm taking a French cinema seminar until August 1 where we get to watch all of the classics and it's great but I'm busy from noon to three every day. So hope I haven't seemed like I'm ignoring you. You can still ask me questions about school and stuff.

Peace out, Silas.

Why does everything have to be so complicated? How can I tell my first real friend in NY that I can't actually meet him because I won't be there? I feel such a strong connection with him. How is this life even possible right now?

7/17 9 am

Kit texted. Said she'd been in New Orleans, after Galveston, with her folks for a few days for her belated graduation gift and a family vacation and forgot her phone (which is something she's never done in her life) and didn't get my messages until now. She asked if I could come over now. I told her I'm at 610 all day. I don't believe for a second she forgot her phone. Bullshit.

But I want to see her. Marli was completely raging last night and threw Ronnie out of the house, or attempted to. She made him sleep in a tent in the backyard, which was the dumbest thing in the world. Mom brought him out a baloney sandwich and a Shiner Bock and sat with him. He picked at the grass and shook his head, wiping his forehead with the rim of his hat. Mom kept patting his knee. I opened my window and heard her say, That's how it is when you're pregnant, it's the hormones and Ronnie kept shaking his head, saying, I'm trying, I'm trying.

Then I missed out on the rest of what they said since the soundtrack of our house basically became Marli screaming down the hallway, Marli screaming at Dad to get out of her way, Marli slamming her fists against my door, Marli trying to break into my bedroom for no apparent reason. I locked the door and pushed my dresser in front of it. I heard Marli screech that nobody respected her and then a loud smack. I wasn't sure if it was her slapping something, or her slapping Dad, but it got really, really scary quiet. I was glad my door was blocked. I blasted the Clash and made a killer playlist to drown out the noises of my family for the rest of the night.

7/18 10 pm

E took me thrifting tonight. At Another Man's, he snuck into the dressing room with me while I was trying stuff on so he could adjust my outfits. (I know I'm not supposed to spend money, but kind of who cares now and there was a green beret with the tiniest gold pin in it for $7 that was absolutely perfect.)

As E zipped me up, he asked: Pipes, did C.J. hit you? Or hurt you?

Me: No! What makes you think that?!?

E: Because I've never seen you like that.

Me: Like what?

E: That upset on Saturday night. You can tell me. But if he hurt you, we're going to kick his ass.

(I could feel myself smirk. There's no way Enzo and Philip combined could have kicked C.J.'s ass. He's way too strong.)

Me: He definitely didn't hurt me, or my body at least. He hurt my feelings, but not on purpose. It was my own fault.

326

E: Piper? Don't say shit like that. You don't deserve to be hurt, no matter what. Or how.

Then E and I caught eyes in the dressing room mirror. We both heard that word again, hurt. I knew what he had done to me on New Year's Eve was really, truly over. And in a flash between us, I forgave him, really forgave him with a clear heart, right then and there. He and I should just have never dated in the first place.

Me: C.J. basically didn't listen to me. I had something I wanted to talk to him about and he didn't really say what I thought he was going to say.

E: You didn't tell him you love him, did you?

Me: NO! No of course not!

E: Then?

Me: I told him, I asked him . . . (I couldn't get it out.)

E: That you didn't want to have sex with him? I kind of figured you guys already did.

Me: NO!

I was laughing because he was so far off.

Me: We didn't, and we haven't, not that he doesn't want to, but no, that's not it. I told him, asked him what he would think if I didn't go to New York yet . . . if I waited around a year.

Enzo dropped the belt he was holding and turned me toward him.

E: Why would you ask that?

I got really scared really fast.

E: Why would you possibly ask that, Piper? Not for him, right? Not because you want to bone some Rice dude? You can bone anyone in New York!

Me: It's not about him.

E: Then? What?

I looked down at his patent-leather Converse and told him the secret I had been holding in for 2 weeks. We couldn't afford New York. I wasn't going.

7/19 Have no idea what time it is.

Worked all day. Made $68.75, not that it matters anymore . . . but including Dr. and Dr. Bash's cash, I have almost $1500. That's more than I have ever had.

Sending Adams a postcard. I painted the back of an index card with watercolors for her yesterday, a blurry image of Enzo, Sam, Kit, and me. I think she'll get it. Trying to write Silas, though I don't know how to send an email without telling him I'm not coming there anymore.

Tired from work. Depressed. Don't feel like doing anything really.

7/20 11 am

Kit finally called! Voice mail from her when I woke up! Heading over there now!!!!!

Life. Is. So. Weird. Weirder than weird.

Been sitting at the park, drinking coffee all day, trying to figure out all of this weirdness. Couldn't be at home. Couldn't be at work. Couldn't be anywhere that anyone would see me, except Dad, who has jogged by twice, dropping off donuts on our park bench. Turned off my phone. Just need to think.

Kit's house yesterday. It was awkward at first, but awkward IS SO MUCH BETTER THAN NOTHING. I really missed her. Missed us just being us.

"I'm so happy to see you," I said, hugging her tightly, right when she opened the door. I felt like I was going to fall into her. She returned my hug, but pulled back a little.

"Let's go to my room," she said. "My mom is taking a nap and we have to be quiet."

Being with her was going to make everything better, I just knew it. It already was a little bit.

As we walked down the hallway, something smelled familiar and different: paint.

"I want to know everything going on! We haven't talked in forever! I miss you! I have so much to tell you! Oh my gosh!" I said. "Your room!"

All of her prints and mood boards were stacked/rolled in a corner. Her bed was pulled into the center of her room. The walls weren't white anymore but mossy, deep yellow-green, like

Galveston algae. Behind her bed, she had painted a goth-black and silver trompe l'oeil metal fence on the wall, as a headboard.

"That's awesome!" I said. I started to touch the edge of one of the spikes.

"Don't! It's not completely dry yet. I got inspired by all of the ironwork in New Orleans, and I had to go for it."

"It's amazing," I said. "What are you calling it?"

"Swampy Vampire."

She was barely saying anything and I was saying everything, like a bad first date. I sounded like such a dork. I had never felt so awkward in front of Kit before.

I sat on her bed, which had a new dark gray comforter on it. It looked like threaded steel.

"I miss you," I said again. I couldn't keep it in any longer. I didn't feel pissed at her, even though I knew she was lying to me about her phone. I felt scared. Sad. Lonely for Kit. She was looking at me like I didn't belong in her room, like I didn't match.

"I know you're mad at me and I'm sorry. I don't think C.J. is more important than you. You are my best friend in the entire world. And I don't know what I'd do without you."

"Piper. You don't have to be so dramatic."

She tapped her speaker and Solange came on, trying to block out the obvious big, weird silence between us.

"You sound like your mom," I said.

"What? You make a big deal out of everything, Piper. You always have."

"I have to!" I said. "We are big fucking deals."

"I'm not," she said, narrowing her eyes at me. "Can we please just be real."

"I can just leave if you don't want me here," I said. "I'm having a crappy month anyway."

"I know," she said, and for a second I saw the old Kit. "I don't want you to leave. I invited you over because Enzo called yesterday and said you were in a really bad place. He told me something that I didn't think could be true, unless you guys just planned it to get me to talk to you again. Tell me it's not true, Piper."

"Tell you what's not true?"

"That you're not going to New York. That you don't have enough money saved up and your parents don't either because of Marli. Enzo said, Piper said she may wait for a year, but I think if she doesn't go now, she never will."

"He said that?"

"Yeah."

I felt embarrassed, and sick. Enzo thought I would never go? He told Kit that?

I couldn't face each day I was stuck here if I didn't truly believe I was going to leave soon.

ENZO IS WRONG. I can't believe him, I won't.

"Well. It's true," I finally said. "About the money. My parents never really thought I'd get in, apparently."

"My parents could help you," she said. "You know that. Especially now that I'm not going anywhere."

Her back was turned toward me when she said it and I wasn't even sure I'd heard her right. The last part was muffled like she was swallowing and crying.

"I didn't even think of that," I said. Um, YEAH RIGHT would I let Kit's parents pay for my college. "But I'm pretty sure my parents would kill me if I talked about it with your parents. I don't think that would be a very good idea."

"But you should leave," Kit said. "You don't belong here anymore. Everyone at school, everyone our whole lives knew you had something special. I know you have something special. You can't waste it here." She spit it out, and I remembered how much Houston could feel small and closed-minded. She had dealt with her fair share of that kind of thinking, way more than me.

"That's why you wanted to talk to me? Is that the only reason?"

"Isn't that reason enough?"

"Are you still mad at me about C.J. and the dumb review?"

"That review wasn't dumb!" Kit exploded. "That review was everything! It changed everything about us, about me, about my art! It was bad enough to not get into school, but this? The first person who looks at it who doesn't know me hates it? And THAT'S how people find out about it?" She was shaking. "He was the only one to point out how stupid my whole site was. My whole big PLAN!"

I jumped over to her computer and pulled up her site as fast as I could, before she could stop me.

"Stop," I told her. "And just look. That," I pointed at her screen, "is brilliant, Kit Bash. And you can't listen to one dumb amateur reviewer who doesn't know art from his asshole. Look what you did there. Look how you curated every single thing about it, from the background art to the shape of the letters. And you've been updating it! It looks even cleaner, more you. . . . His review meant nothing, absolutely nothing!"

We were both quiet. She didn't believe me, or didn't agree.

"I worked so hard on it," she said under her breath. "I've BEEN working so hard on it."

"For months! Every day! This is not just your senior project, Kit. You know that, right? Everyone thinks it's easy to make something, anything, until they try to do it themselves, and then they fail totally miserably. Well, you didn't fail, Kit. You made what could have been just another website into something beautiful and something functional! Bash Labs is LIFE-CHANGING for the art world, for creators and artists, people who never had a chance to show their art before you introduced them into the world, and now they have customers and people buying their pieces! This could only come from YOU—not me, not Sam, not Enzo, not anybody else. You INVENTED this . . . this like, specific connection. You're the only one of us who's changing how the world actually experiences art. You're giving art back to people who can't go to galleries, or museums, or don't want to buy their outfits at the same basic-ass sites. You are changing people's points of view and showing people how to BE WITH ART. That's a big fucking deal."

"Nobody . . . nobody here thinks it's a big deal, at all. Even my parents."

"Since when have they been any kind of authority on art? They look at blood tests and broken-bone X-rays all day! Besides, they're letting you work on this for a year as an internship, so

333

they have to believe it's at least a little bit of a big deal. Come on, let's look at your comments."

I clicked over to her comment page.

There were so many. Of course, a few of the Little Freshies were on there, but most of the comments were from people I didn't know, asking how they could submit their work to be shown on her site, and there were a bunch of fan notes, with one girl proposing a meet-up with Kit so that she could interview Kit for her podcast. C.J. was so completely wrong. There was no doubt Kit was a genius.

There were a couple of comments with attached photos. I clicked on one, a coupon for discounted art supplies. Another was for "enlargements." And then there was another photo.

One of me.

Standing in front of my heart.

The night of the showcase.

I expanded on the comment.

Hello Ms. Bash or To Whom It May Concern,

My name is Carlyle Campbell.

I feel compelled to reach out to you. I found your website via an announcement link on the NYSCFA alumni website: one of your featured artists will attend the school in the fall. As an alumnus, I like to review the incoming class's portfolios. I pride myself on staying aware of the up-and-coming artists at my alma mater as I continue my work in the contemporary art world.

The concept of this website is incredibly compelling. Rare are the things I meet that restore my hope in the future of fine art. But a site like yours, created by a young person and clearly very successful—I feel secure with the future of art, fashion, and commerce in your hands.

I need to know who this girl is, Piper Perish, the one in the cobalt dress, standing in front of the art sculpture/painting, and I need to know more about this arresting work. Did she create this piece? Who styled her look? Is it possible that she is artist, designer, model, and stylist—all in one?

No matter the answer, I would very much like it if you would put her in contact with my assistant, Kennedy McEnroe, as quickly as possible. His email is CarlyleSKennedyGallery@gmail.com. He will take it from there.

Blessings!

Carlyle

"Have you seen this?"

I was reading the comment over and over again. Kit looked over my shoulder.

"Oh. Yeah."

"Why . . . why didn't you tell me?"

"I thought he sounded like a creep. 'Blessings'??"

I didn't say anything.

"He also seems to think you're a model, so yeah, really not trusting this dude."

"You could have told me about it, at least," I said. "I could have googled his name to find out more about him. If I thought he was creepy, I wouldn't respond. Plus, listen to what he says about your site!"

"I don't know, Piper. You kind of like creeps."

"What? No, I don't! You mean C.J.?"

Kit sighed. "We really do not need to talk about C.J. anymore. He's taken up enough space in my life."

"You sound like you went to your shrink," I said.

"I did," Kit said. "And a voodoo priestess in New Orleans. And they both told me I need to practice damage control, not let him get to me, grow a thicker skin."

"Well, okay then. But that's no reason not to tell me about this."

"What was I supposed to do? Call you up and tell you some guy wants to meet you off the internet? Who am I, your pimp?"

"I just wish you had told me, that's all. Did YOU google him? He sounds kind of . . . intriguing."

"Well, I figured you probably would have met him in person in August, but I didn't know until yesterday that you weren't going to New York."

"UM, I was texting you and calling you and emailing you!" I said. "I felt like I was stalking my best friend. I would have told you sooner if you had just called me back. I didn't even get to ask you about the new guy on the 4th of July."

"He's just temporary until DJA gets back from Paris. No one special."

"What's his name?"

"Paul."

"I tried to talk to him that night but he was pretty wasted. And you seemed kind of not interested in hanging out, like . . . at all."

"Like I said"—she smiled this chill smile that only made her look less chill—"he's temporary. And you and I are hanging out now. That night was just, weird." She picked at her nails.

"Does DJA know?"

Kit shook her head.

"He's gone for the summer, and I just felt like . . . maybe I needed to meet some new people. People who didn't know the old me."

"But . . ."

"I need to know people who don't know my failure. Who don't know what happened to me. It hurts too much to be around people who know . . . you know?" She tilted her head at me.

I nodded. My heart hurt for her. I hated to be someone she felt was part of the problem. I didn't "know her failure" since to me she hadn't failed. But I could see it didn't really matter. Because she felt like she had. This really wasn't about me, it was about her.

"I'm sorry, Kit. Really."

We didn't say anything to each other for a while, just listened to the music, which was now uncomfortably upbeat, almost like it was making fun of us. I wasn't sure what would make Kit feel better. I glanced at her laptop one more time, memorizing the email address that I would write to as soon as I got back home, and sat down by her on the floor. We leaned against the end of her bed, covered with its new bedspread, the way we had been doing since first grade. Instead of pulling out magazines or art books or messing around with her vintage jewelry boxes, we both stared up at her desk that was facing us. The laptop looked back at us like some kind of evil overlord.

"Now that I'm not going to New York, things don't have to change so much," I said.

"That's not good," Kit said. "Things are supposed to change, y'know."

"But maybe you won't be so mad at me if things stay the same."

Kit sighed.

"What?"

"I wish I could make you understand," Kit said, looking at everything but me. "I'm not mad at you. I mean, I was about C.J. for sure, but it was never just about him. Do you know how hard it's been for me to not be jealous of you . . . of what you make?"

Then I didn't say anything. Was she kidding? (I still half think she was.) I love making my art, and I want people to like it, but I've never thought I was as good as Kit. I thought I was good enough to get into NYSCFA, but I thought she was, too.

"You make it look easy, like you never really have to try, and then something amazing just comes out of you."

"But you know that's not true," I said. "You SEE how many times I have to start over. Just like you." Didn't she know she was the one I was jealous of? At the same time though, Silas's words were coming back to me.

"It's not the same, Piper. Maybe you can't see it, but just . . . trust me. You're good, Piper. Real-world good. Good enough to get out of here. And I just don't want to be the one who works and works forever and ever because no one will ever just tell me straight that I'm not good enough. I just want someone to tell me straight."

338

"You ARE good enough," I said. "It will always be me who tells you straight. And it will never be me who tells you to stop."

Then Kit started crying. Not trying to hide it at all, really crying. Messy crying.

"You . . . have . . . to . . . go. . . ."

"Okay!" I said and started to stand.

She flapped her hands at me.

"Don't interrupt!"

I sat back down.

"YouhavetogotoNewYork," she said all in one breath between cries. "Forbothofus. We both can't be stuck here. You have to do this for us."

Us?

"I didn't want to go without you anyway. That wasn't in the plan," I said. "So maybe staying here is for the best. I can go to U of H or HCC and then we'll still hang out on the weekends with E and Philip and DJA and make cool stuff."

For a second, it really didn't sound so bad.

"If you don't go," she said, "I won't hang out with you. Not anymore."

"What? Why?"

"Because then none of us will have made it. Because I don't want to run into anyone from school or anyone else and hear them say I told you so. Because I'm still going to get out of here as fast as I can. It may not be New York, but it will be somewhere. Somewhere new. I'll start over."

"Then why not New York? You could go. You could be the one who's made it! And I'll stay here. And then there will only be one of us in town."

She shook her head.

"Seriously," I said. "You can afford to go. You should go."

"I don't think I can talk about this anymore," she said.

We both sat there quietly, and then I started crying.

"I'm sorry?" I tried. "For all of it?"

I saw Kit's mouth turn up just a little, not quite a smile, but like her mouth moved before she had time to stop it. Is that what she wanted this whole time? For me to break down crying, to just say I'm sorry?

"Just be sorry for C.J. Don't be sorry for being awesome and talented."

We both cried and laughed at the same time.

I really am sorry I said to her and then she said it back to me and then we hugged really hard, crying and laughing on each other.

"We're okay?"

Kit nodded. Then she went to her desk, pulled out an index card and a Sharpie, and wrote something down. She handed the paper to me. It was the email address I had already memorized.

"Email this guy," she said. "He's legit."

I stood, holding the paper between us. She had looked him up after all. And she would never have given me the email address if he wasn't the real deal. I was sad she hadn't told me about him sooner. But I thought I understood now.

340

"I will," I said.

When I left her house, something had changed between us. I could feel it, the same way I could feel it when the sky was about to pour.

7/22 10 am

Going to email Carlyle later today. Everything I started writing yesterday was a mess. Sent a quick email to Silas, asking him if he knew him or about him, or anything. Have to go to work, last place on Earth I want to be today.

7/23 7:42 am Why the hell am I AWAKE o'clock

Made $27 yesterday. Note to self: never work another Monday ever. Also, don't spill freshly brewed coffee. Burnt left hand. Ouch.

Was talking to Enzo last night about what happened over at Kit's—not mad at him, just telling him I wish he had let me tell her—when Marli appeared in my doorway.

"I thought you were leaving," she said, very quietly.

"I'm on the phone," I said. "Please get out."

Enzo said, Oh shit and asked if he should come get me.

"I'll call you later," I said to him, clicking my phone off.

"This room was going to be the nursery. Now what are we supposed to do?"

"I don't know, Marli, maybe get an apartment? Maybe stop living at home?"

Her big blue eyes were crazy wide, there was white all around the edges of her pupils.

"How. Dare you."

I knew I should have been scared, but I wasn't. There was nothing she could do to me that was worse than what this entire freaking summer had already done. Even with my burned hand, I was ready to fight. Maybe I even wanted to. Maybe I had always been waiting for this and she had, too.

She took a step toward me.

"Once again, you have found a way to interrupt my life."

"How, Marli? How am I interrupting your life?"

She let out a long exhale.

"It's time you know the truth, little sister."

"Oh yeah?" I said.

"You know why you were born, right?"

Ugh, this again. I waited, knowing that whatever she was going to say was going to be downright berserk.

"You should really ask Mom and Dad," she said.

"No, Marli, why don't you tell me? You've obviously been holding back." I gave her the meanest eyes I could.

Marli literally rubbed her hands together, like she had been waiting for just this moment all her life. She seriously looked like some sort of Doctor Evil. She was savoring it.

"Okay, you asked for it." She took another step forward and stared me down. "You were supposed to be my fix."

"What?"

"I overheard it all, a long time ago. You were supposed to be Mom and Dad's fix, my fix. To teach me responsibility and caring. To help me develop emotionally. I heard all the conversations. Their shrink thought you would teach me empathy. I had to look up what that word meant when I was old enough."

"You're lying," I said.

"Nope. I'm not."

"When did this happen?"

"Years ago. Obviously."

"Bull," I said. "You were barely one when she got pregnant."

"Mom got pregnant because they didn't like me enough. Their shrink was on board. Having one normal kid always fixes a messed-up kid. Get it?"

"No . . ."

"I heard the conversations, over and over again, in the therapist's office. I was 8 by the time they'd figured out it wasn't worth me going anymore. They'd been taking me to doctor's appointments (she made air quotes when she said doctor's appointments) since I was 4. Ms. Sharon would ask me questions and shit to figure out how I was quote-unquote progressing, and then talk to Mom and Dad about it. Too bad Mom and Dad didn't know I could hear THEIR whole sessions from the playroom. 'All of Piper's positive traits will have a favorable influence on Marli. Research with children has shown that siblings serve as

socialization agents for each other's socioemotional develop-
ment. Give Marli time.'" She was rolling her eyes. "But nope! I
was TOO BAD. Or you weren't POSITIVE enough. Either way,
didn't work. Sorry Mom and Dad." She was back in perky/scary
mode. "Piper, you were always supposed to be the savior, not
just of me, but of this whole goddamn family. And every single
time I see you, oops!" She tapped a finger against her head, like,
doy! "I remember I'M the mistake that almost cost Mom and
Dad their marriage, I'M the mistake that made their lives so
freaking horrible. The Mistake. That's me in a nutshell."

I was stunned. I don't think I was breathing.

"So, you know, it would be helpful if you would move the fuck
away. Because for once, I would like to not be considered incapable of basic humanity. For once maybe I would like to NOT be
compared to YOU."

"Is any of this true?" I asked her.

"Yep," she said. "Every word."

It felt real. She wasn't playing. She couldn't make up stuff that
quickly, could she?

"I WANT to leave," I said quietly. "And I'm sorry. I never knew."

"You say that, but you don't act like it. If you did, you would
have started saving money a long time ago. You would have
gotten a job a long time ago."

My eyes dropped from her face to her stomach. I felt for my
little unsuspecting niece. What kind of world was she coming
into? Her mom and her aunt were just monsters and savages to
each other. I hoped she would be an only child, for her sake.

"Maybe you should get out of here," she warned me. "Maybe you should just go."

"Why? Where? Where should I go, Marli?"

She folded her arms over her belly and didn't say anything else. I could see how swollen her arms and wrists had become, which I hadn't noticed before. Her skin looked like it was about to split apart at any minute.

"Fine," I said. And I left her in my room. Probably not the smartest choice, but what could she really do in there? Tear everything up? Break stuff? It's not like I didn't want to do that myself anyway. She could be the monster.

I stayed in the garage until 7 this morning. Painted oversized swirling moons. Each time I started painting another one I started thinking of my niece. I want to tell her, whenever she appears, Welcome to Earth. We're going to have some real fun.

But I don't want to lie.

And Marli. Was it true what she said? Has she always hated me because of Mom and Dad? Was all this fighting all of our lives because of them? And if so, who am I supposed to be mad at now? All of them? Because maybe not everything is Marli's fault? I feel like hating everyone right now, but that's too much for me. I can't hate that much. I'm so fucking confused. No wonder I drive her crazy. Did I make her crazy?

My heart hurts. My head hurts. Maybe I should take one of Mom's fucking Klonopins so my whole body can be out of this pain and I can float around blissed-out like her.

Have to sleep now. Exhausted.

Dropping another postcard I have for Adams today. I feel weirdly better. "Talking" to other people outside of home—even if it's over email and postcards—is pure relief. Now it's like I can only be the most real me with everyone but my family. I've been avoiding Mom and Dad, don't know how to talk to them since Marli's "revelation," don't want to know if it's true.

C.J. and I are supposed to go out tonight, to talk about "us." All I want to do is make out with him and not-talk about the way he didn't react the right way when I told him I might be staying here.

I kind of could not care less about C.J. right now.

Just got an email from Silas:

Yes, I know who Carlyle Campbell is. Tell me you emailed him right away—if you didn't, stop reading this and do it right now. Don't wait.

Doing it!

Dear Mr. McEnroe,

My name is Piper Perish and I just read an email from your boss, Mr. Carlyle Campbell, asking me to please contact him through you. So, I guess that is what I am doing!

I'm not exactly sure what to say, but I would like to thank Mr. Campbell for his comments about my senior project, and I guess, me. He seems very nice. Please tell him I said thank you. The piece he mentioned in his email, which I got an A on, was one of my favorites I have ever made.

Well, now you have my email address if you or Mr. Campbell wants to write me back. My phone number is 713.555.8023.

Thank you,

Piper Perish, Artist

I keep rereading it, wondering if I should change anything, but I didn't know what else to say. I didn't want to mention I wasn't going to NYSCFA anymore. I didn't want to tell him I would have responded sooner if Kit had actually told me about it because I didn't want her to get in trouble with anyone.

Have to be at work in 30 for lunch shift and already running late.

7/25 11:45 pm

So this just happened on my date with C.J. BTW, I thought I would be home around 2, not like, 11. Even Dad looked up from his book and asked, Early night???, which is code for MY DAUGHTER IS A LOSER.

Anyway, this:

At C.J.'s apt., making out, he asks me if I'm done being mad at him. I nod at him and keep kissing his neck and then basically he pulls out the holier-than-thou I don't want to be this guy.

Me: What guy?

Him: The guy who falls in love with you and wants you the way I want you right now.

Me: But I want you, too. It's okay.

347

We made out some more.

Him: We can't.

He pulled back from me and pressed down on his pants, like he could stop what was happening from happening.

(I'm so glad girls don't get boners.)

Me: We're safe. Don't worry.

The thing was, now I WANTED to have sex with him, not only because he looked incredibly hot tonight even in just a white T-shirt and jeans, but because everything else was just so fucking . . . bleak. I wanted something new, something fun, something real. And I wanted to forget, just for a minute, that everything in my life was basically a mess. Maybe if we did it, I could forget the other stuff.

Him: Look, there's like . . . a reason we can't do it. If you were going to New York still, that might be one thing. But you're not.

Me: So? What does New York have to do with us right now?

I waved my hands over us, like some kind of weirdo magician of sex. Why did I flail so much around him? Why did I turn into a clumsy Girl Explosion? I felt hot. Why didn't I act it?

"Here," I said, kissing him again, "maybe I can help you change your mind." Lame. Especially because it didn't even work.

He kissed me back for a second before he jumped off the couch and ran his fingers through his hair and walked to the window that overlooked his driveway and the street. I could see the skyline of downtown behind him.

"Just tell me what's wrong. I promise I won't get pregnant if that's what you're worried about."

"That's not what I'm worried about! I'm not thinking about you, Piper! I'm thinking about Lisa!"

"Who's Lisa?"

"Lisa . . . Lisa is my . . . girlfriend."

"Your what?"

"My girlfriend."

?!?!!?

He kept looking out the window, refusing to turn to me, resisting me pulling his shoulder, trying to get him to face me.

"Who is Lisa Your Girlfriend?" I asked, which was kind of a dumb thing to say because I was answering my own question as I asked it but I was so mad I couldn't think straight.

"Lisa goes to school with me. She went home to Dallas over summer break. I didn't expect to meet you this summer. I didn't expect to fall so hard for . . ."

"Did you tell her we were hanging out?"

He shook his head no.

"Why not?"

"I thought you wouldn't be here when she got back. I didn't know things were going to happen. . . . I'm trying to be honest. I'm a nice guy."

"Fuck your honesty!" I said. "Fuck nice guy!"

"Dude, Piper."

"You're being honest NOW because you got caught. You weren't honest the first night you talked to me because you knew I wouldn't be down if I found out you had a girlfriend."

349

"That's not true! I didn't know we were going to get together. I didn't know I would get so into . . . you. You're not even my type."

"You're not my type either!" I said. "Man, they were so right."

"Who?"

"My friends. They all warned me about you. I should have listened. You basically fucked up everything between me and my best friend."

"I didn't do that," he said, holding his hands up. "Those cards were on the table."

"Your review—"

"My review didn't do anything but tell the truth!"

"Did it?" I asked. "Or was it another lie? To get me?"

"Don't flatter yourself, Perish."

And that's when I slammed the door of his apartment and hightailed it to the diner. The night manager, Stanley, was there. Nadia was gone and Marli wasn't working. It was my old diner again, without me having to answer to anyone. I got a cup of coffee and a piece of pecan-fudge pie with vanilla ice cream. C.J.'s smell was on the collar of my shirt and on my hands. I pulled out my notebook and sketched, trying not to inhale any more of him. I doodled closed and open doors all over the pages and onto the napkins. I really wanted Dad for some reason, but 2-weeks-ago Dad, Dad before Marli's BIG REVELATION. I wanted Kit, but normal Kit, who wouldn't make me feel completely lame for not having my life together. And I didn't want to call Enzo again, but I wasn't sure what else I should do.

This time when he picked me up, I announced it was over, before he could ask me anything.

"Good," he said. "Finally."

List of Shit:

- C.J. and I "broke up."

- Marli is screaming at Ronnie to make her breakfast. Ronnie is screaming back at her. This isn't going to be good.

- My left hand now has a blister on it from that coffee spill. Gross.

- Still not going to New York

List of OMG Non-Shit:

- Emails!

- Postcards!

From Silas:

Piper,

Have you heard back from him yet? What did he say? Don't leave me hanging.

You're going to meet him, right?

Thinking about you meeting him when you get here. Send me the date and time you get in.

I still don't know how to tell Silas I won't be coming to New York.

Then this arrived from Carlyle's assistant, Kennedy:

Dear Piper,

We're so happy to hear from you. Carlyle doesn't really understand emailing and tries to stay off the computer as much as possible so he can keep his creative focus, but he couldn't stay away from the photos of your work online once I showed them to him. You have me to thank for his interest and following up on his alumni emails. I saw under your artist bio that you're arriving in New York in August. You'll buy me a coffee when you get here, won't you? ;)

Carlyle would like a phone call with you. He will be calling you tomorrow, 7/27, at 3 pm (ET), 2 pm (CT). Please confirm you are available to speak to him. His schedule, as you can imagine, is ridiculous this time of year. Fashion Week is about to kill us.

Yours in Insanity,

Kennedy

My hands were shaking just now as I typed him back:

Yes, I will be able to talk at 2 pm tomorrow and Thank you and Can't wait to hear from you.

Just opened the Bash Lab website again and found an About the Artists page that Kit made—I had no idea it was there. Kit wrote it. So good. So much better than anything I could have written. She made me sound so professional and so . . . real. And she used a photo of me from Philip's shoot. I had forgotten about it. There I was, looking hungover and sleepy and my eyeliner was smudgy . . . and kind of cool.

Have to call diner. Must get my work schedule changed for tomorrow. Have to text Kit and thank her, text Enzo this amazingness. Have to email Silas for any intel and google everything I can on Carlyle so I don't sound like a total dipshit tomorrow.

But before I do anything else, have to tape the latest Adams postcard to my mirror, which is almost totally covered with all of the amazing postcards she has sent so far. It's like she knows everything, always. This one is painted with a little boat set in the corner of an all-watercolor blue sea. On the back it reads:

Piper—

Catching up on my reading at night. Such a delight. This reminded me of you. I look forward to hearing all about your travels.

"Travel far enough, you meet yourself."
—David Mitchell, Cloud Atlas

Alice Adams

7/27 4:30 pm

Holy shit. I'm going to New York. I think I'm going to New York.

7/28 Midnight

I didn't have time after the phone call to write everything down. Had to get to the diner. (Made $96.50.) Hustled my ass off because now I need to, like really need to. I'm. Going. To. Fucking. New. York.

✦ ✦ Best conversation of my life yesterday ✦ ✦

Him: Is this Piper Perish?

Me: Yes.

Kennedy (apparently): Hello, doll. So nice to hear your voice. This is Kennedy McEnroe. Hold for Carlyle, please.

(Then there was hold music. Interpol. Cool.)

Carlyle: Piiiiiiper?

Me: Yes?

Carlyle: This is Carlyyyyyle.

Me: Thank you so much for calling me, uh, sir.

Carlyle: Don't call me sir. Call me Carlyyyyyle.

(I wasn't sure if that meant I should call him Carlyle or Carlyyyyyle.)

Me: Okay. Thank you for calling me.

Carlyle: Who are you and where do you come from? You're like some vision from outer space. Your creation was alien. I loved it. You.

Me: Oh? Well, thank you.

Carlyle: Sold it yet?

Me: No. Not yet. (At least I didn't think I had. Kit would have told me if she sold it on her website, right? Yes, she definitely would.)

Carlyle: Are you planning to?

Me: I'm not sure.

Carlyle: I hope you know what it's worth. When do you arrive?

Me: Sir?

Carlyle: Don't call me sir.

He sighed and sounded irritated and then I heard a bunch of noise in the background and he shouted, I'm on a call, you'll have to wait, take your drama back to Jersey, you amateur!

Carlyle: Apologies. Where were we?

Me: You told me not to call you sir, again.

Carlyle: Yes, that's right. Don't. Now. You'll be here soon?

Me: Well, I mean, I want to be, but school isn't going to work out how I planned. I'm not sure. No, I think.

Carlyle: WHY NOT?

Me: Because it's too, we're too . . .

Carlyle, roaring: I'M SORRY?

Me: Expensive! We, my family . . . (My throat was throbbing and thick.) We can't do it.

Carlyle: How does this happen?

I felt worse.

Me: We just didn't . . . plan right. I'm working though. And I have a bunch of money saved up.

Carlyle: I'll call you in 2 hours. This number?

I didn't want to tell him I would be at the diner, but I also didn't want to miss his call.

Carlyle: Pick up your phone in 2 hours.

Then he hung up.

2 hours later, I took his call by the recycling in the diner parking lot.

Kennedy: Piper doll, this is Kennedy McEnroe, hold for Carlyle please. (All in 1 breath.)

(More music. This time: the Clash. A sign?!?!?)

Carlyle: Piper, it's Carlyyyyyyle. Have you had time to think?

Me: About?

Carlyle: Our call, of course.

Me: Yes, of course, I'm so happy you called me.

I wasn't sure what I was supposed to say.

Carlyle: You won't be staying in—where is it? Where are you now?

Me: Houston.

Carlyle: You won't be staying in Houston. Kennedy will arrange it. You'll come to New York. You'll unravel the school situation . . . when you get here. In the fullness of time. In the meantime, I need you for my show.

There was so much traffic by me and noise on his end that I wasn't sure I was hearing him correctly. My brain was spinning faster than when I drank too much beer.

Me: What do you mean? My work? For your show?

Carlyle: I need YOU for my show. How much clearer need I be? You'll fly up here, Kennedy will take care of establishing you in an apartment. We'll need to ship your piece, the one on the website.

Me: Ship it?

Carlyle: Oh, gracious me. I don't have time to explain all of this. I'm putting you back on with Kennedy. We'll see you soon.

Me: You will?

Carlyle: Piper, talk to Kennedy. Kennedy, talk to Piper.

And then I was talking to Kennedy again. Or rather he was talking to me.

Kennedy: Piper, listen up. Carlyle has taken an interest in you, as you must've gathered. So, we need to make Carlyle happy. You'll need to be here by August 10th.

Me: August 10th?

Kennedy: We'll have you set up with an apartment, and you can work in our studio.

Me: Studio?

Kennedy: Yes. We're going to need more, you know. One piece isn't going to cut it.

Me: Cut what? I'm sorry, this is going so fast. I don't know what you're talking about.

Kennedy: We need you and your work for our runway.

Me: I've never modeled!

Kennedy: I know. I've seen your posture.

Me: Then . . . ?

Kennedy: We're going to use your art for Carlyle Campbell's Hearts on Fire show for his spring collection at New York Fashion Week; we're using it for set design because honestly,

Carlyle hasn't found major centerpieces he has really liked—no, LOVED—until yours. The models will appear from behind it, as if bursting forth in a gush of fashion! It's perfect for the line, we've been searching and searching and nothing has been right. Carlyle's collection is red-hot, it's on fire, you'll understand when you see it in person. So. We need you to bring the piece you've created, and then we'll pay for your materials that you need up here, and you can continue to create our background pieces. We only have about a month to prepare. Oh, and you'll be compensated, naturally.

Me: But . . . but . . . (My heart! Exploding!)

Kennedy: But, what. Do you really want to disappoint Carlyle Campbell?

He said the name like I should understand who I was dealing with.

Me: Of course not.

Kennedy: Then you'll be here?

Me: Yes. (I didn't know if I was lying or telling the truth.)

Kennedy: Good. You can call me direct with any questions, but I prefer email or text. Understood?

Me: Yes.

Kennedy: Carlyle will be unavailable to speak again until you get here. Understood?

Me: Yes.

Kennedy: Good. I'll be in touch soon to figure out your flight, et cetera. We can't wait to meet you, Piper Perish. It's going to be a MAJOR MOMENT.

Me: It is?

Him: It is. Ciao, doll.

And then he hung up before I could hang up, before I could breathe, before I could do anything but fall backward and stare at the sky, wondering how the hell I just landed two Fairy Godfathers.

✳

This is the morning of the night that never ended. I haven't gone to sleep yet. Going to start at the beginning. Total fucking chaos.

Asked Mom and Dad if we could go out after dinner, just the three of us, no Marli or Ronnie. We did. I told them everything that had happened, the phone call, Kit's website, the money Dr. and Dr. Bash had given me, that I could afford a ticket to get to New York and that everything else would be covered by Carlyle.

"So you just want me to let my daughter go stay with some man who claims to be an artist in New York?" Dad said. "Have you ever watched the news? Don't you know what happens to people who do that? Do you want to end up in a ditch?"

"I don't think there are any ditches in New York City," I said. "Besides, I looked him up. Here."

I handed them printed-out articles of his work as an artist, how he had been featured in the Whitney Biennial, which was a huge deal, and of all of the publicity surrounding his upcoming big fashion show, comparing him to a young Karl Lagerfeld. Even Dad knew that name. And my artwork would be used in his very first show!

359

"You understand why we think this is very . . . sudden, don't you? You've never even mentioned this guy before and now suddenly you want to fly up there because he sounds like a hotshot? It makes me question your judgement, Piper." Mom's eyes turned down. She looked sad for me, like I was a kid on crutches.

"I know what I'm doing," I said. "And I'm not asking you for anything—not money, not new clothes, you don't even have to pay for textbooks."

"That hurts," Dad said, stopping. "You know we would have paid for your schoolbooks if you were still . . . going."

"But I'm not," I said. "I'm not going to school, at least right away, anyway. So why not go to New York? Why not at least try it out? Nothing says I have to stay there, or here, for that matter. And I have the money to get there. I looked at tickets last night online. I can get there for under $500. The rest of my diner money could be spending money."

"Some kids backpack across Europe," Mom said.

It was the same voice she used when she tried to reason with Dad over some mistake Marli had made.

"And you're saying that's the same thing as sending our kid to some creep, someone we've never even met, someone who can rip her off and use her art and maybe not even give her credit or pay her, and that's okay with you? Want to go ahead and marry her off as well?"

"Jesus, Hank," Mom said, and her voice got all twangy. She was pissed.

"Dad!" I said. "I'm pretty sure he's not going to creep on me! And he IS paying me for my art!"

"Really?" Mom froze in place.

"Of course he's saying that NOW," Dad said. "Did you get anything in writing, Piper? It just worries me, honey. This really puts you in a vulnerable position. You can't seriously be okay with this, Donna?"

"I'm thinking," she said. "This is brand-new information to me, too. Piper, how long have you known about this option? About Carlyle? About being paid?"

"I told you already. I just spoke with him and his assistant on Saturday. Kit got comments from them on her website a couple of days after she posted photos from the gallery showcase back in June. I didn't know until last week, when I saw Kit."

"Why wouldn't she tell you something like that?" Mom said. "That doesn't sound like Kit."

"Uh, we've kind of been in a . . . fight . . . I guess."

"You didn't tell me that," Mom said, 100% concern in 1 second flat. "What happened?"

"Nothing, it's fine. It'll be fine. I just don't want to talk about it if that's okay. By the way." I needed to distract her. "Marli told me something super weird a couple of days ago." Might as well get it over with.

"You're kidding," said Dad, super sarcastic.

"For all I know, she could be lying," I said, "but it would be one big fat ugly lie, even for Marli."

"Tell us," Mom said.

"She told me why I was born."

"No secrets there," said Mom.

"We had you because we wanted another baby," Dad said. "Clear and simple."

"Really?" I asked. "Not because you thought I'd FIX everything?"

"I don't know what you're talking about, Pipes," Mom said. She looked like she really didn't.

"Marli told me everything that she remembers—or made up? About some therapist's office," I said. "The way you had me to FIX her? According to her, she—well, you all—saw a therapist when she was just a kid, and she heard and remembered all kinds of stuff. That I'm supposed to be her emotional fix, that you guys were WORRIED about her and you had me because your therapist was on board! So, I don't know, no wonder she's hated me all her life!"

Mom looked like I'd knocked the wind out of her.

Dad leaned against a nearby tree in the Robichauxes' yard.

"Kiddo," he said.

"WHAT?" A fire engine passed us with its lights flashing and siren blaring. Mom covered her ears. "Why would you take a little kid to therapy? How bad could she have been? Didn't you think that would make her feel bad?"

"We wanted to help Marli," Mom said. She turned to me. "Therapy was key to helping her, that's what we were told at the time. I am sorry you had to find out this way, but . . . we're not perfect. We love you both the best we can. Parenting is a learning process, kiddo."

We stared at each other. Nobody moved. I knew what that meant. If they weren't saying it wasn't true, they were saying it was.

"This is a discussion for a different day," Dad finally said.

I was furious and fuzzy, quiet and churning.

"Right now we need to figure out: if you are going to New York—"

My heart 100% exploded! Who cared if he was trying to distract me if it meant he'd let me go!

"—we need to make a plan. And I'm going to need to speak to Carlyle himself."

I almost choked on the sip of water I had just taken.

"OH MY GOD NO! You can't speak to him!" I said.

"Really?" Dad said, smirking at me. "You think I'm not going to talk to the guy who is insisting my daughter move to New York on her own dime?"

"I told you, Dad, he's paying for the apartment. And I'm using their art studio."

"Great! A sugar daddy!" Dad said, but obviously he was softening.

"Gross, Dad. He's not KEEPING me, I'm working for him!"

"Until I talk to him, you don't go. That's final."

"I have enough money," I said quietly. "I can book a ticket if I want to. You can't stop me. I graduated."

Another firetruck passed us, this one with just the flashing lights.

363

"This is my chance, guys. If I don't go now, I'm stuck." I hadn't been able to stop thinking about what Enzo said. Still haven't. "I'm stuck forever. And I can't be here forever."

Mom tried to put her arm around my waist, to pull me to her. I let her for a few seconds until it was too awkward to walk that way.

When we turned the corner to our block, Dad took off running toward our house. It was like he had known what we were about to see. The firetrucks were parked in front of it, blocking our view. Mom grabbed my arm and we both started running, fast. It was hard to tell what was going on until we got close.

Our garage. The car. Marli and Ronnie. Firefighters. Neighbors. But no smoke. No fire. Just confusion.

While Mom and Dad and I were out walking, Ronnie and Marli had been fighting. Marli threatened to leave Ronnie and leave the house for good. She threw a bunch of her clothes into a suitcase and everything, breaking stuff of his on her way out and smashing a couple of framed pictures Mom had put up of the two of them together to make Ronnie feel welcome in our (fucking crazy nuthouse of a) home.

Then she'd gotten into Dad's car and threw it into drive when she meant to reverse it, and put the pedal to the metal. The roof of the garage fell onto the car. Marli was pinned in for a few minutes—we didn't see that part. The firefighters had gotten her out. When we got home, the whole back of the garage was on a slant, falling in pieces into our backyard.

Marli, covered in a blanket and sitting in an ambulance getting her blood pressure taken, was crying hard.

"Is my baby okay? You have to save my baby!" she was screaming.

She had a huge cut on her forehead.

"Your baby is fine," the firemen kept telling her, "the baby's heartbeat is fine."

She was being so loud I could tell she wasn't hearing them. Mom was trying to get her to drink some water and I was wishing I could have pulled my niece from Marli then and there, taken the baby and just run away.

I looked back at the garage. The roof had broken Dad's windshield into a million pieces. Next to it, the police were talking to Ronnie. Dad was standing with him, his arm on Ronnie's back, literally supporting him. Ronnie was crying and Dad looked more like his actual dad than his father-in-law-to-be. Dad kept patting his back, telling him it was all going to be okay. Some of the firemen were hosing down the car and the garage. All of the neighbors were out, watching us: The Perish Family Freak Show.

I went into the backyard. I wanted to see what the back of the garage looked like, what the car looked like jutting out of it.

And then I saw it. My art. My heart. My heart my heart my heart. The remains of it.

Some of it was stuck into the garage itself. Half of it was shredded and splintered into the backyard. Little pieces, like confetti, like how I imagined snow, suspended in the air, still falling to the ground in slow motion.

I limped to the toolshed. I couldn't breathe. I couldn't scream. I opened my mouth and tried. I tried to cry. I dry-heaved. I wish I could have cried until my lungs fell out of my mouth. I wish I could have emptied myself of all of this, of all of them. Of Marli. But I couldn't. It was like my entire insides were scraped out and hollow already.

The family circus continued. Nobody noticed me go back to my room. Nobody cared that I wasn't there. I am barely here. I went online and bought a ticket. A one-way ticket. No return.

7/31 Diner 9:30 am

Waiting for Enzo to get out of the bathroom.

I told him everything.

"Do I look like somebody beat me up?" I asked him first. "I'm tired as fuck."

"For someone who hasn't slept, you look amazing."

"I haven't told my parents about the ticket. I don't even care."

"But—"

"I'm not fixing their problems for them anymore."

"I just don't think this is like, the time to start believing what Marli says." He blew on his coffee. "There's got to be more to it than her weird-ass story."

"Whatever," I said. "I don't know if I want to know any more. I know some of Marli's side. Some of Mom and Dad's side. But, fuck it. It's too much, I just can't, right now. . . ." The lump in my throat was almost too big.

Enzo took the hint. "WHATEVER is right," he said. "We have major issues to attend to right now. As in, what are we going to do about your piece?"

"I dunno. I'm not sure it can be fixed. The bigger pieces are soaked from the hoses, the smaller pieces are all over the grass. How do I tell Kennedy that?"

"You don't. Not yet. We need to think. We need to rebuild it."

"I don't know if I can do it in a week."

"You don't have a choice, missy. You have to. And I'll help you."

He's coming back now. More later.

Just got off my shift. ($58) Told Nadia that 8/8 is going to be my last day.

"One week's notice?" she asked. "I thought you were leaving at the end of the month."

"I need to be up there earlier than I thought."

"Okay, champ. Well, I'm glad I had you this summer."

"Are you mad? I know I was supposed to give you 2 weeks, but things happened really fast. I'm really sorry."

"You think I've never had someone quit on me before? At least you're giving me a week." She rolled her eyes and winked at me. "Now go get your tables."

I took care of my three 4-tops, surprised that Nadia wasn't mad, and honestly fucking happy to just concentrate on the customers. I was happy to not be at home, where I am now, feeling nervous and sick. Sitting in the backyard, looking at the complete freaking mess, wondering how Mom and Dad are planning on fixing any of this. Not sure where you begin when half your garage is trashed and your backyard looks like a junk-yard. The insurance guy was out yesterday, talking to Dad and Mom about the car and how Marli's rate was going to go up. He brought a tow truck to pick up the car. I was going to tell them about my plane ticket but I've been feeling so awkward and weird since the last conversation and they looked so bummed-out I didn't think it was the right time.

Marli's been in her room a lot. Ronnie's creeping around, trying to stay out of everyone's way. I don't think Mom and Dad are mad at him, but they haven't had a chance to tell him that because he's really making himself scarce. He probably feels guilty. But he shouldn't. Around midnight, I looked out my window and saw him stacking pieces of wood and chunks of my art by the side of the garage. I think he was trying to clean up, apologize in his own way. I almost ran out to make him stop touching my pieces, but he was moving so slowly, so quietly, I just watched him instead.

I have to talk to Mom and Dad tonight.

Not going to stare at the backyard anymore. Going to start a list of what I need to bring with me. How do I pack when I don't know how long I'm actually going to be there? How do I know what's enough?

369

8/2 11:55 pm

Tonight was actually good.

Ronnie and Marli went out on a date. Mom ordered pizza. Dad was having a glass of wine and pouring one for Mom before the pizza arrived, and that's when I told them.

"I know this is going to come as a surprise to you, and I don't want to make everything worse, but I'm still going to New York."

Mom sighed, "We know you will one day, honey. We still believe in you."

"No," I said. Even though I was about to make them more upset, and I felt bad, a part of me couldn't help but be annoyed at that "still." They hadn't believed in me yet! "Still," please.

"I am going. Next week."

"Don't start, Piper," Dad said. "You can't right now."

"I am, Dad. I bought a ticket."

I put my printed ticket on the dining room table. Mom picked it up. They took big slugs of their wine. I watched Mom's hand start to shake.

"Piper," she said, "What have you done?"

"You can get a refund," Dad said.

"I know what I've done." Jeez, drama much? "And I know it's a risk. And I know you're worried about me. But I've been saving my money, just like you wanted me to do. I have to take this chance."

"What about school?" Mom said.

"I'll still go to school," I said. "Just not right away. Not when we thought."

"You have to go to school," Mom said. "College isn't optional!"

"I'm not trying to make it optional! I'm trying to figure this all out. If I want to go to NYSCFA in the spring, this will give me time to apply for grants, loans, and work-study, and I'll be able to keep working on the side."

"Look," said Dad. "We're proud of you trying to figure this all out, Piper, and saving your money, too. . . . But I told you I didn't want you going up there to stay with some guy we've never even met . . . who you won't even let me talk to on the phone."

"I can barely talk to him on the phone, Dad!" (Wrong answer.)

"So you're not important enough to talk to, just steal art from?"

"Dad!" I said. "He's in the middle of prepping for Fashion Week. He's busy. That's why he can't talk. I've been talking to his assistant. If you want to talk to Kennedy, you can talk to Kennedy."

"Nobody's talking to anybody yet until we figure this all out," Mom said, taking the wine bottle from Dad and topping off her glass.

The doorbell rang and I ran to get the pizzas from the delivery guy (paid for FROM MY TIPS, BTW). When I came back to the kitchen, Mom and Dad were hugging, and Mom was patting his back.

"I have the pizzas," I said, which was obvious. I didn't know what else to say to them.

Dad's face was red.

"Are you okay? Dad?"

Mom pointed to the island and I put the pizzas down and got plates for the three of us.

"I'm not hungry," Dad said, and got up.

"Dad? Are you mad at me?"

He shook his head no, but he left the kitchen.

I looked at Mom and was immediately crying. "I didn't mean to upset him. I didn't mean to upset you. This should have been a really happy thing, me finally going to New York. It's not like you guys didn't know I was going. I'm going, Mom!" I said. "Aren't you happy? Or proud?"

She picked up a slice and dumped an amazing amount of crushed red pepper on it, the way she always does, and held it up to her mouth before she said, "We know, honey. We both know. And of course we are so proud of you. But that doesn't mean this doesn't make us nervous."

She took a bite, and tears ran down her face.

"Mom."

"It's the pizza," she said.

I brought a slice to Dad out in the backyard. We sat next to each other, looking at the huge hole in what used to be the top of our garage.

"It's like a meteor hit it. Just gone. Worse than a hurricane. Not supposed to rain for a bit, which I guess is a good thing. Gives me time to get it covered this weekend."

"I'll help you fix it," I said.

"We need the professionals for this and the shed, too," he said, "but I appreciate it. We'll hold off on the big repairs. Do it after you're gone."

He said it. He actually admitted I was going. My stomach is swirly just thinking about it. I think there was some secret part of me that liked it when Dad didn't want me to go away.

Mom joined us with the bottle of wine and we all sat outside, even though it was humid and we were sweating and the mosquitos were trying to bite us. Dad turned on the zapper and lit the bug candle and we all just talked and Mom even poured me my own glass. They took turns tearing up, talking about me leaving while the sounds of flies being fried—pop, fizz—filled the backyard.

"You've always been our special girl, Piper," said Mom. "You've always done things your way, always been so strong, so creative and brave." I could tell she meant it even though she was definitely tipsy.

"Mom and I have been wanting to finish our conversation from last night," Dad said. "You were never our <u>fix child</u>. It's very important to me, to us, that you know that. You are your own person, our daughter. We had you because we wanted another child, regardless of what the therapist would have encouraged us to do. Our therapist did tell us a second child usually helps stabilize the moods of the first child, but we'd already had you at that point. We didn't have you to FIX Marli. We only hoped you would help."

"You were such a happy little camper. You slept through the night your third week on Earth. So happy and content with your binky-bink." Mom touched my cheek.

"But Marli is"—Dad took a breath—"her own person. She always has been and she always will be. We wish she hadn't overheard all that . . . or remembered it"—he and Mom shared a look—"but the REASON we had you? Easy. We wanted to have you. We only found out about the studies and such later."

My breathing was so light, I was barely taking in breath. Thank god. It was like until then I hadn't really been able to think about how sad it would be, if Mom and Dad had just had me for like, a reason, to solve a problem—to think about if that was actually true. And it wasn't. Thank god x a billion. I didn't know what to say, I was so relieved/weird-happy.

"But didn't that just drive her crazy? Being in therapy?" If I was supposed to be the good cop to her bad cop, I'd hate me too. "Like, did I drive her crazy?"

"Piper, you are not responsible for your sister, then, now, or in the future," said Dad.

"The way Marli was progressing, taking her to a therapist was a very important thing for us to do. WE decided to have her see someone because our doctor thought it would be best for her. You did not hurt your sister. You did not drive her crazy. And anyway," Mom said, catching herself. "She isn't crazy. She's complicated." Classic Mom.

"Look," Dad said. "We knew we wanted another baby, plain and simple. And thank god we had this one." He put his hand on my knee. His voice was catching every so often, like someone was stringing beads down his throat. "You have made us so proud. You are such a success, Piper, despite your mom and me failing you in . . . so many ways."

"Dad!" Jeez, this was turning into a total emotioncon. "How could you have failed me if I'm still going to New York? If I'm still following my dream?" I asked. "You guys always told me to be good at what I do, whatever I do, and to follow my passion, my dream. Well, I am. Maybe not exactly the way we thought, but it's happening. Doesn't that mean you didn't fail?"

"It's just so soon," Mom said. "You're still our baby, Pipes. I'm not ready to let you go."

"We just want the best for you, kiddo," said Dad. "We love you, and with love comes worry. We're happy for you, of course. Of course we want you to follow your dreams. Maybe your Mom and I, well, we just didn't know your dream was going to arrive so soon. Maybe we thought we'd have a little more time with you."

We were silent for a few seconds. He had made it all sound really dire.

"Dad!" I said. "I'm not dying!"

And then we lost it. Couldn't stop cracking up. For the first time since my NYSCFA acceptance, since all of the shit that had gone down this year, things didn't feel hyper/crazy/tense. It just felt normal, laughing with them for the first time in a long time, not freaking the fuck out.

"I am your daughter," I finally said, "but I'm not a baby. Soon you'll have another one of those around here anyway. So you need the room. And Marli needs the room, too."

We kept talking and watched the sun set behind our broken garage, the sky turning lilac, then violet, then gray, and finally just dark, all the colors I stayed away from when I painted—careful and mute. Now they would be my Houston colors.

I kissed them both and hugged them hard before I told them good night and came up here. Mom hadn't wiped her tears off and I could feel a few smear on my neck.

They're still sitting outside and I'm sure still talking about me and Marli. How could they not?

My head is buzzing.

The pit in my stomach is huge. It's the Grand Canyon.

I'm so scared and so nervous and so excited, I can't sleep and I need to sleep.

Enzo said he's planned a surprise that will take all day and is coming over in the morning. I even took off work for it. I wonder what we're doing. All-day shopping trip?

I emailed Silas.

Hey Silas,

It's happening. I arrive August 9th at 6:10 am at LaGuardia Airport.

I'm not going to school this semester, but I'll explain everything when I arrive. Counting the days until I see New York, until I meet you.

Piper

Suddenly, so tired. Night.

Enzo told me he was coming at 9 am. Figured it was going to be the ultimate shopping trip, the biggest trip before the biggest trip of my life. I was ready.

- my red and white mod shift dress

- black Doc Martens

- black headband

- red lipstick

While I waited for Enzo, I got an email from Silas:

Piper—No school? Please explain. Silas.

I wanted to write back and explain everything—but it wasn't the time. Enzo texted right then: *Meet me in your backyard now.*

I went back there.

Enzo was way underdressed I thought, just wearing jeans and an old T-shirt, his lucky navy one he always wore whenever he was sewing. And then around the corner came Philip, in overalls that had paint stains all over the knees. He had a cute little white cap on that only he could pull off and cream-colored Converse also splattered with paint.

"What the—?" I said.

And then Kit walked out in yoga pants and a T-shirt and tennis shoes. She was wearing a turban and she had on her cat-eye sunglasses. She took a sip from her giant to-go coffee mug and yawned. "Morning, sunshine."

"Hi," I said. "What are you doing here?"

377

She tilted her sunglasses at me.

"I mean, hi! I'm happy you're here." Something was very up and very weird. "You guys?" I asked.

Then Sam Chang! (He was wearing shredded denim overalls.)

"Sammy?"

He just said, "9, right?"

Enzo nodded at him.

"Enzo, what's happening?" I asked. "Are we all going shopping?"

"Shopping?" Enzo asked. "I never said we were going shopping."

"I just assumed."

"Hold on," he said.

Then he ran around the side of the house and I heard him talking, trying to whisper, which he is really bad at, and as he turned the corner, so did she.

Adams.

He had Adams with him!!!

I ran over and hugged her so hard. "WHAT ARE YOU DOING HERE?"

"Well, Enzo flashed the Bat Signal," she said.

"Huh?"

"He called all of us to come help you," Adams said. "We heard about the . . ." (She pointed to the garage.)

"We're gonna help you rebuild your piece for the show in New York," Sam said. "Enzo said you couldn't do it alone."

"You shouldn't do it alone," Kit said.

"So, I came in for the day," Adams said. "I'd only come in for you guys, you know. A few weeks away and you forget how shitty the Houston traffic is, even at 6 am."

We laughed.

"What?" Adams said. "You're all graduates, I can say shitty. . . ."

"I can't believe this, you guys! I can't believe it! I guess I should go get changed," I said. "I didn't know we were—" I felt so beyond everything.

"You change," Philip said. "I'll serve breakfast."

"Breakfast?"

"We brought kolaches and donuts," Enzo said. "It's going to be a long day."

"Dad!" I said, coming up to the house as he was walking out.

"Hey, everyone," he said.

"Dad," I started.

"He knows everything," Enzo said. "I texted him last night to get permission to come over with everybody."

"As long as you all stay away from the inside of the garage and work in that part of the yard"—he pointed over to the toolshed—"it's fine. I just don't want anyone getting hurt. You guys shouldn't even be out here, you know. Please be careful. There's still glass in the grass. No bare feet!"

"We'll be careful," Enzo promised.

"Thanks, Dad," I said.

"Now I know I don't know the first thing about fashion," Dad said, "But I have to say, that doesn't look like such a great painting outfit."

"Just going to change," I said. "Kit, come with me."

Kit and I ran upstairs and I threw off my dress and put on a pair of jean shorts and my David Bowie T-shirt.

"I cannot believe how awesome you guys are," I said. "I'm so glad you're here!"

"Well, it was all E's idea."

"Yeah, but you're here. I don't care who came up with it."

"It's kind of hilarious that you thought you were going shopping."

"Why else would E want to hang out with me on a Saturday morning?"

"Right?" Kit laughed.

Then we heard Marli's bedroom door shut.

Kit whispered, "What's her deal? Is she grounded?"

"Grounded?" I asked. "She's pregnant. I don't think you can get grounded anymore when you're pregnant."

We both thought about this. We didn't know what the rule was there.

"Have you talked to her about what happened? What were they fighting about anyway?"

"I dunno," I said.

"Well, did she say she was sorry?" Kit asked. "She destroyed your fucking project, for fuck's sake."

"Not yet," I said. "We haven't really talked. We've been avoiding each other. If I'm in one part of the house, she's in the other part. If I'm outside, she's inside. I don't really think she cares at all."

"Really?"

"I honestly don't even know if she knows what she's done."

"She's not dumb, Piper."

"Right," I said, "but she was pretty upset that night. I don't think she was thinking the whole thing out."

Enzo yelled from downstairs to hurry up and stop making myself pretty.

"Hold on, loverboy," I called out the window.

Right before leaving my bedroom, Kit licked her thumb and pressed it across my chin, wiping off lipstick I had smeared.

"There," she said. "Now you're perfect."

"Thanks," I said.

"Friends don't let friends wear chin-stick," she said.

"Thanks, friend," I said. I couldn't help it, I grabbed her and hugged her.

"C'mon," she said. "We need to get started."

Then we worked all day, reassembling the larger pieces we could find without the mini pieces that had been mowed over or blown somewhere by the wind or moved by Ronnie. Mom and Dad surprised everyone with barbecue for dinner. While we ate, Mom asked Adams about Paris.

"It's really just my home away from home," Adams said. She took a slug of iced tea. "It's amazing when you find the place you're supposed to be, as opposed to the place you are."

Kit shot me a look.

"You don't think you're supposed to be in Houston?" Sam asked.

"It's a good job," she said. "And I love my students. How could I not love you guys?"

"We are very lovable," Enzo agreed, leaning against her.

"My paycheck is here," she said. "But my heart is in Paris. And as long as I get my 2- to 3-month fix every year, I'm good. Besides, my son would kill me if I kept him out of the BIG CITY. He hates living in Paris for the summer."

"How is he?" Kit asked, I guess to be polite—I knew she'd been texting him.

"He's certainly been missing you," Adams said. "But you probably know that." She winked at Kit. "He wanted to come with me today, but he couldn't get a day off. The Paris community pool needs him!"

"Sure," Kit said.

Adams had no idea that Kit was hooking up with other guys while DJA was out of town. I could feel me and Kit both vibrating with the weirdness.

"I'd like to propose a toast," Dad said. He was holding his beer high over his head.

"Since we're all here and you all know that Piper is indeed . . . going away—that's why you're here to help her after all—why not cheers our girl, who is going to make us all proud? You're all so very talented, I'll be damned if I know where any of you got it from, I guess it's from Ms. Adams here, but I'm just as proud of each and every one of you graduating and making all that . . . art. . . ." He waved his hand toward the big knot that was supposed to be my project.

I could tell Dad had maybe had a little too much beer because he was getting the glossy eyes.

"My little Piper has always known what she's wanted to do, and her mother and I"—he pulled Mom over to him—"have always trusted that she knows best. Course we're scared that she's going all the way to New York City, but we know she'll be okay and that she knows her home, her first home, is always ready to welcome her back. Texas will always be waiting for you, Piper!"

Enzo was letting me squeeze his hand as hard as I wanted. He nudged my hip with his elbow, reminding me I should say something.

"You guys . . ." I tried. But I just didn't know what to say and my throat was really tight.

Part of me wanted to cry. Part of me wanted to laugh. Part of me couldn't stop staring at my still-broken piece. No matter how we tried to repair it, to mend it, it was now just a thing with stitches. It didn't look like art and it didn't look like a heart. It looked like a doll out of a Tim Burton movie. It looked like one of those blood clots we studied in bio. An alien. A tumor. A really bad Chuck Close. How would I explain this to Kennedy? How would he explain this to Carlyle?

"Here's to our Piper," Kit said, pulling me out of my nightmare daydream.

Everyone held up their half-full glasses. "Cheers," they said, and I looked around at them, my people in my not-place, and when Kit and I made eye contact, that's when the tears started to fall, mine and hers.

"Cheers to y'all," I said. I held up my cup to them. But all at the same time everyone's smiles fell and they started to send weird looks around. Kit was focused over my shoulder, and when I turned around, I saw why. It was the first time Marli had shown her face since the accident. It was the first time she'd been in the same space with me, and now she was standing there in front of my friends, in my moment.

"What are we celebrating?" she asked.

"Piper!" Sam Chang answered. "You want some tea?"

Even though we were outside, it felt like there was no air left.

"I'm okay," she said. She looked over at my project and then back at everyone standing around, but not directly at me, not in the eyes.

"It's nice to see you again," Adams said, and nodded at Marli's belly. "Congratulations are in order to you!"

"Thank you," Marli said.

Nobody else was moving really. Even Mom and Dad were keeping their distance from Marli right at that moment. You don't wake a sleeping snake.

I just watched Marli, even though she wouldn't make eye contact. What was she planning? I held my breath. Kit placed the corner of her foot on top of mine to stop me from twitching.

"I could hear you guys from my room and it was kind of loud and I was just wondering when you were going to finish up," she

384

said, really faint, quiet-like, like it was too hot and too hard for her to even speak.

"You're due soon, right?" Adams asked Marli.

"Middle of the month," Marli said, nodding.

"Well of course you need your rest," Adams said. "We'll be finishing up very soon. We just need to clean up the mess we've left. Don't think your parents would like it if we left your yard like this." She nodded at Mom and Dad, trying to break the tension—Adams, always the peacemaker.

But it worked. Marli left, like a ghost.

"She's still there," I said to Kit as we washed out the paint-brushes with the garden hose. Marli was peeking from her bedroom window.

"Of course she is. She's always going to be there." Kit flicked the paintbrushes to toss off the excess color and water. "Even with Ronnie, you think they're ever going to leave? Unless your parents kick them out, they'll be here when their kid goes to college."

"You're the one who said they'd move out!"

"Yeah, well." Kit rolled her eyes. "Wishful thinking. They haven't even tried to find a place yet, right? And your parents do everything for her."

Kit was the only person who could get away with talking shit about my parents to me. Also, she was right, but for some reason I felt like defending Marli AND Mom and Dad, which was confusing.

"So were you surprised?" Enzo said, bouncing up behind us.

"You outdid yourself, sir," I said, and did a silly curtsy in front of him. "Seriously, thank you."

"We couldn't let you do this alone." He swung my hands in his back and forth.

I said goodbye to Sam and Philip, and Adams, who had to get back on the road to Paris.

"My duckling," she said before leaving, "I'm thrilled that you are making this adventure your own. I'm thrilled that you are going to New York in this unexpected way. I'm thrilled to find out what comes next for you. You will write me?"

"Yes," I said. "Of course!"

"Write, not email."

"Of course."

"And no matter what happens up there, you must not stop. You must pay attention to detail. Remember, just walking down the street is a cultural experience. Don't get tied up in what you think you SHOULD do; do everything. Try everything. Be everything. Don't be afraid to get lost in the world. Don't be afraid to be you. Remember that. Promise me that."

"I'll be me," I promised her.

She gave me a huge hug and whispered in my ear, "Remember, Piper, fear is the enemy of creativity."

"Who said that?" I asked her.

"I did." She tilted her head up toward the little snippet of moon rising in the sky, as if she was receiving some mystical sign. "You're going to be okay."

"Okay, then," I said.

She hugged me one more time before she drove away. I was sad. I was happy.

Sammy wished me good luck and told me I could email him, I didn't have to write him, and then Philip said bye too, and that he was leaving Enzo with me for tonight, and that he was really, really relieved that I had dumped C.J.

"That guy was a piece of shit and no girl of mine dates a piece of shit." Philip smiled at me.

"I'm your girl?"

"Well, you're his"—he pointed to Enzo—"so you're my girl-in-law." He gave me a kiss on the cheek and then in his best gay Southern voice he told me to "give 'em something to remember."

Then it was just Enzo, Kit, and me in the backyard.

"How can I thank you guys?" I asked them.

We turned around and looked at my heart. It was still an over-sized mess. I knew Enzo and Kit were thinking the same thing.

I figured I still had a few more days to work on it before I left. Besides packing and getting together my money, I didn't have to do much else.

"Come dancing with us tonight," Enzo said.

"Really?"

"The outfit you had on this morning? Perfect," said Kit.

"What about you guys?"

"Our stuff is in Enzo's car. We're spending the night."

"But?"

"We cleared it with your folks," Enzo said. "Don't worry! Now, we have, like, an hour to get our amazing on. Let's do this!"

We got ready.

Enzo in a leather jumpsuit.

Kit in a black tank top, gold sequin pants, and gold sequin platforms.

My outfit I had on this morning, but no Docs—hologram metallic heels instead.

We danced. We raided the photo booth. Philip showed up and got us free drinks.

We came home because Kit got wasted, but it's all good.

We're here. We're together.

8/4 9 pm

Worked today. Earned $102.80 on brunch shift! WOO-HOO! Even though I have 4 more days I could work, Nadia told me it was my last day and gave me an extra $50 for my trip. $152.80!

Sent emails before brunch to Silas and Kennedy asking them what I should bring.

Piper—

It's New York. You can get anything you need here. Bring what makes you happy.

Still want to hear what's up with you and school.

I'll be at the airport when you land.

We're finally going to meet. It's about time.

Silas

P.S. Do you like Indian food?

and—

Piper,

Bring:

Your art, of course. (Let me know if you need a mailing label.)

Supplies, equipment

At least two dresses suitable for galas

Protein bars and water bottle

Your everyday things

(Could have used a little more help here. Duh.)

Here's your new address: 419 West 34th Street. It's the best we could do on short notice. All the interns live around here. You'll adore it. Not the Village or Williamsburg, that's played out anyway, but you'll be near trains, and can get up/downtown easily. Besides, you'll only be sleeping there and you won't be doing much of that.

Carlyle will send a car to the airport. In the baggage claim area, look for one of the drivers with a sign with your name on it. He'll take you to your place. You'll get your apartment keys at the front desk in the lobby.

Heads up, there's no air-conditioning. So also bring a fan.

Yours in Dior,

Kennedy

So excited I'm packing now. Wasn't planning on bringing a fan. I'm sure it won't be that bad. After all, I've survived 18 Houston summers.

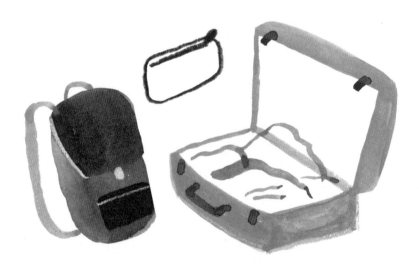

Stared at my art in the backyard this morning. Thought it would dry by now. It's still wet in places, I guess because of the humidity. I have nowhere else to keep it but out there. It doesn't look good. Maybe when it's dry it will look better. I'm not sure what I'm going to do. It looks like a big red lump of mud. How am I supposed to pack this before I leave and send it out?

Mom and Dad are at work. Mom is going to take off the rest of the week to be with me. I still have a lot to pack. I'm supposed to get everything I need into two suitcases? Not gonna happen.

Dear Silas,

How will I know what you look like? I know your elbows. I know your eyelashes. I know your knees. How will I piece you together? I wish I had a photo of the full you, but I suspect I will know you because there is only one you.

Kennedy, Carlyle's assistant, told me they are sending a car for me. Neat! Do you think we could ride together into Manhattan?

Even though we won't be going to school together at first, I'm so happy that you're there. Do you believe in fate?

—Piper

All day I literally watched the paint dry on my art, except for when I sent emails and talked to Enzo on the phone. I can't take my piece. It's horrible. I wrote to Kennedy. I hope he'll understand. I hope he doesn't say I can't come.

Mom and I went out for a Ladies' Day. First, we got our hair cut at Pam's, of course, since Mom's been going there forever. Mom even treated me to a fancy facial and a manicure because she said they wanted to send me off being the best Piper I could be. While we were still at the spa, Mom pulled out a little navy box and placed it in my lap.

"What is it?"

"Open it." Her smile was huge and her face was extra shiny from her mud mask.

Inside the box was a tiny silver watch, kind of a 1920s Great Gatsby Art Deco thing. It was thin and beautiful and sharp in my hand.

"Mom? This is really cool."

"You don't have a watch," she said. "And we'll be in different time zones. And even though we'll be in different places, I just want you to know . . ."

The tears popped into her eyes.

"I just want you to know that no matter where you are, no matter what time it is, no matter what you're wearing or what you're doing or what you're making, you can always call me. This was your grandmother's watch," she continued, "and it is a bit fancy. But you deserve something fancy. Something good. Something that reminds you how unique you are, Piper. Because in that great big old city, you might forget sometimes. So even though this may not go with every outfit you own, wear it. Keep being uniquely you, Piper. And know I'm here for you at any and all times."

395

She took in a breath, finally. Then she said, "Try it on."

I slipped it onto my wrist. It was perfect.

"Mom," I said, and then we hugged each other and I couldn't stop crying and neither could she.

"Nice way to undo all of that relaxation we just got." Mom dabbed her eyes and handed me a Kleenex. We were both red, snotty messes.

"Piper," she said as we were getting into the car. "There is one thing. I'd really like it if you made amends with your sister before you leave."

"Mom. She won't even be in the same room with me. She won't even apologize."

"She has a lot on her mind." Mom put her hand up to stop me from interrupting. "Wait. She has a lot on her mind, BUT YOU DO, TOO. So, do me this favor. Be the BIGGER sister this one last time. Be the sister I know you ALWAYS are. Make peace with Marli. Don't leave town like this. I think you'll look back and wish you hadn't."

Mom's eyes were soft and pink and puffy.

"Okay," I said.

It wasn't for me. It was for Mom.

At home, Dad was grilling in the backyard and Mom's nose and my nose were up in the air like dogs at dinnertime. Steaks!

We ate, me, Dad, and Mom. It was nice, telling Dad about the day. None of us mentioned New York or that Marli and Ronnie weren't at the table or that tomorrow was my last official day in Texas. It was so normal that it wasn't normal at all. It isn't till now that what Dad said, that I might never come back, or at least not be the same, is really hitting me. Was this my last "normal" night at home with them? When am I going to have another one? I was trying to memorize every detail, take a picture in my head, just the entire dinner in one shot: Dad laughing, his chin on his right hand, elbow on the table; Mom looking fancy with her glass of wine, her plate so clean it looked like she had never been served; and me, just watching them.

I'm excited. I'm exhausted. No emails tonight. Bedtime.

8/8 10:43 pm

Nothing is ever normal. I think we're going to be here forever. I fly to NY on a red-eye tonight, but now we are here, at the hospital.

Day started off not normal, but sane. Two emails.

Kennedy's freaked me out hard:

Your art piece falling apart is between you and me. We will settle this when you get up here. You will not tell Carlyle, and you will be responsible for making a replacement piece as well as the other pieces. Understood? This is between us.

Oh my god, so freaky. Should I bring my green-gold-monster piece? I love it, but it's very different from my heart and they've never seen it. Yikes.

And then, Silas's email:

Of course we will know each other. You're Piper. I'm Silas. We could have blindfolds on and know each other. I'll find you, I promise. Happy flying, Piper Perish.

I read his email over and over. I'm Piper. He's Silas. I love how he called me by my first and last name. All of me. And soon I would see all of him.

Then, met Enzo and Kit for last coffees this morning.

Enzo gave me a spiky bracelet and Kit gave me the password to her website so I could post photos about the New York art/fashion scene on it. I gave them pictures of us standing outside the gallery the night of our showcase, before all the shit went down, when we just looked cool. I painted our hair fluorescent colors on both photographs, so our hair would look 3-D and fireworky. We hugged hard and promised never, ever to let anything come between us again. I promised to send them sample-sale stuff and they promised to send me gossip. Had to leave sooner than I wanted but it was better than all of us crying in the diner.

When I got home, all of my luggage was already in the back of Mom's car. If there was anything I'd forgotten, it would now have to fit in my backpack. Mom was on the phone with a work call in the kitchen, so I headed back to my room to see if Silas had emailed again.

My bedroom door was open and Marli was sitting on my bed. She was so motionless I almost didn't realize she was there. She looked like a still life.

I waited in the doorway. No way was I going all the way in there.

"Hi," I said.

She didn't say anything.

"Marli? Do you need something?"

"Shut the door," she said.

398

"It's too hot," I lied. "We need the cross-breeze."

"I wish I could feel a breeze," Marli said. "I'm like a stuffed pig. So damn hot. Breeze or no breeze, doesn't matter."

"I'll just keep it open for me then," I said. "You okay?"

"No," she answered quickly. "No, I'm not okay. What makes you think I'm okay?"

"I dunno." I shrugged. I noticed my feet were turning inward, like when I was a kid, and I straightened them out. "Do you want to . . . talk about anything?" I asked. I was nervous, but trying to play it cool, thinking of Mom, trying to be the bigger sister, the nicer sister. "Or . . . just hang out in here?"

"This is going to be the nursery. I'm just figuring out where I'm going to put everything as soon as your stuff is gone."

"Gone?" (That stung a little bit. Where were Mom and Dad going to put my stuff? They weren't just going to get rid of it, right?)

"And by the way, you need to move that big old red chunk out of the yard. Your art thingy."

"That big old red chunk"—I started to get pissed—"that big old red chunk will be moved," I said. "And you know it isn't just an art thingy. I know you don't care, or didn't care when you hit it with Dad's car, but it meant—means—something to me."

"Don't make it into a big deal, hotshot."

Again I thought of Mom, asking me to be nice, of "complicated" and why she was, and took a breath.

"It's okay," I said, partly to myself. She was never going to get it. "You don't understand, that's all."

399

"No, you don't understand, Piper. You made a thing, I'm making a human. I'm making someone real, someone who will outlive you, me, and everything we ever do. THAT'S art Piper. I'm making something that matters."

"PLEASE GET OUT OF MY ROOM," I said. Mom was going to flip, I didn't care. She was freaking me out.

"Don't yell at a pregnant woman," she snarled. "You're not even thinking about my baby."

"I'm not yelling at the baby! I'm yelling at you!"

Marli shot me such a dark look, she looked supernatural.

"You should go," I said. "Please. Please just leave my room. You can have it as soon as I leave."

She stood up and I wasn't sure if she was going to leave or hit me and I stepped back. But she reached to her lower stomach and made a little whimpering, weird sound.

"Oh my god," she said. "My water. My water broke."

I looked at my carpet and her legs.

"What do I do?"

"Get Mom," she said. "Mom! Mommmmm! Mom! Mommy!"

I ran to the kitchen. Mom had her fingers over her lips, signaling me to hush while she was on her call. "MARLI'S WATER BROKE! WHAT DO I DO?"

She didn't even hang up, just threw the phone down on the counter and we ran to my room.

"How are you feeling?" Mom asked.

"Wet!" Marli said, "and crampy!"

400

"Okay," Mom said. "Piper, call your dad and Ronnie and tell them what's happened. Marli, I'll get your bag and put it in the car. Piper, tell them we're headed over to Methodist."

Then they were gone and the house was so quiet. Just like Marli, to make silence so scary.

"Already?" Dad asked me on the phone.

"I don't know, I thought she wasn't due for 2 more weeks," I said. "But her water broke."

"She's like your mother. She's gonna go early. Nothing to worry about, sweetheart."

"I'm not worried," I said.

"I'm on the way," he said, and hung up. He sounded worried.

The last 5 hours have been hanging around the hospital. Enzo and Kit stopped by for a while after I texted them what was happening. Nadia came from the diner. Mostly, there's been a lot of waiting around in the lobby, with Mom going in and out of Marli's room.

Mom just told me to go in for a few minutes. I was terrified. The last thing I wanted to see was Marli all screwed up in pain. But Mom assured me it was a good time to see her. I tiptoed to her door and hoped she wouldn't see me, but she waved me over. Her face was covered with sweat and she looked like a wet rat.

"Mom said I was supposed to come see you but I can leave you if you want. I don't want to upset you anymore, Marli."

"Come here." She reached out a hand, IV attached.

I wasn't sure I should touch her when she took my forearm and held on to it.

"I want you to know something, Piper."

I didn't say anything out of fear. Whatever she was going to tell me was going to be it: the last words, the final fuck-yous.

"Piper, if something happens to me during this delivery, make sure Ronnie takes care of our baby. And you better"—she paused and seized up in cramps—"you better do right by my baby. She's your niece."

"Of course," I said. I was stunned. Why would she think I'd do anything else? I was so happy and kind of surprised that Marli had even thought about me in her baby's life, wanted me in it at all.

"I'm sorry I broke your—" (More cramps.) She tried to roll to her side but she couldn't. She gripped the sides of the hospital bed. "Holy fuck this hurts," she said. "I guess I should have said yes to the epidural!" She squeezed my hand and we both inhaled, nervous.

"Pipsqueak, I don't mean to be such a shit to you. I don't know what's wrong with me. I really don't."

"I don't know what's wrong with me either," I said. "And I'm just really sorry for everything." Was this amends? It really felt like it, actually. I squeezed her hand again. Possibly the last time that will ever happen.

"Get out of here and go get the doctor and Mommy, okay?"

"Okay," I said to her. "I'll be in the lobby if you need me. I'll be here to meet my niece, I promise."

"Savannah," Marli said through gritted teeth. "Her name is Savannah Jolene."

"Perfect," I said.

402

I left the room and got Mom and Ronnie and the doctor to go in.

As of now, we're still waiting for Savannah to arrive. Ronnie's freaking out. We're all kind of freaking out.

Some last night in Houston.

8/9 3 am

I got to meet her—my niece!—before Dad drove me to the airport for my red-eye. She is the most perfect person in our wackadoodle family. She is squiggly and wiggly and pink, and if someone as crazy as Marli could invent someone as beautiful as Savannah, the world is a miraculous place.

Mom kissed me goodbye at the hospital. She wanted to come to the airport, but I told her to stay with Marli. Whether Marli ever knows this or not, I don't care. I just want Marli to be happy, whatever that means anymore.

Dad walked me into the airport and helped me check my luggage. He hugged and kissed me about a million times and after a while it got a tiny bit embarrassing, but I didn't really mind.

I sent texts to Enzo and Kit that I was at the airport and on my way. They both sent me emojis of airplanes and kisses and champagne bottles.

On the plane, I've been drawing in my sketchbook. Sleeping. I looked at photos of everyone on my phone. I looked at sweet Savannah, 30 minutes old. I watched the sky grow even darker outside my window.

I took a plane selfie to send to E and K and then I watched myself watch myself in the camera. The silver in my hair is gone. My hair is almost as dark as my eyebrows again. I didn't end up dyeing it before I left because I didn't have time and wasn't thinking much about it. But I like what I see now. Now, buckled into 23F on my way to the greatest city in the world, I feel like The Most Me I have ever been.

8/9 7:50 am EASTERN TIME! OFFICIALLY ON NY TIME!

The plane landed a little late and then we had to sit on the runway for a while, but now I'm finally off. Texted Mom and Dad and let them know I made it.

I'm in the airport.

I'm in New. York. City.

I'm hiding and writing behind the luggage carousel in the baggage claim.

I want to see Silas before he sees me.

I want to see if I can spot him the way he thinks I can, the way I think I can.

I see a man wearing a fancy black suit and hat holding a sign with my name on it. He must be the driver.

A guy with dark blond hair and the most perfect face I have ever seen walks up and stands next to the man. It's definitely him.

The eyes.

The elbows.

The knees and neck.

All undoubtedly his.

He sees me.

He's walking toward me.

My heart is pounding so hard I think it's going to set off airport alarms.

No more writing now.

Only this.

Only the beginning.

———————————

ACKNOWLEDGMENTS

Thank you to my agent, the unstoppable, insightful Molly Jaffa at Folio Literary Management, for taking a chance on me and plucking Piper from the slush pile. I could not have wished for a better dream to come true for my debut novel. Thank you for everything.

Thank you to Taylor Norman, my funny, razor-sharp editor and now friend. From our very first phone call, I knew you were The One. I remain in awe of everyone at Chronicle Books, especially the hyper-talented Ginee Seo, Amelia Mack, Sally Kim, Hannah Moushabeck, Lara Starr, and the entire crew.

Thank you to Luke Choice and Maria Ines Gul. These two artists helped bring Piper to life—Piper herself would be so impressed!

Thank you to my family, who has always supported my wacky creative life, and to Josh's family, who has loved me as one of their own from the beginning. My mom, Carolyn Solomon, taught me that the best life is one filled with art, and for that I will always be grateful. My grandmother took me to museums as a kid, and I remember her fondly whenever I visit one now.

This book would not have been written, rewritten, queried, sold, or published without the help of my close friends and writing critique partners in crime, Vanessa Napolitano and Leila Howland. Thank you for being honest, devout, and accountable readers. Thank you for your sense of humor and cheering me up when I felt lost. Big thanks as well to clinical psychotherapist Stacey Datnow for helping me with research on sibling relationships. The insight I got from this research was invaluable.

Special thanks to the brightest creative lights in my life: Richard Robichaux, Meredith Mundy, Sherine Gilmour, Tiffany Hodges and Marshall Mintz, Deborah Hetrick and Matty Groff, Paul Davis, Sharon and Manuel Gonzales, Tress Kurzym, Karen Sommers, Jordana Oberman, Maggie Klaus, Amy Spalding, Andrea Adams, Brandy Colbert, Bryan Mason and Holly Reeves, Lori McLeese, Mike Monteiro and Erika Hall, Adam Savage and Julia Ward, Hope Larson for hosting the original Writing Nights (with homemade ice cream), my JoCo LadyBros, and the LA Brunch Crew, including Jen Leavitt and Lorna MacMillan.

Thank you to the readers for picking up my book and committing your time to reading it. I'm a reader, too, and I value your experience. I hope you enjoy reading the journey of Piper Perish as much as I enjoyed writing it.

And lastly, thank you to my husband, Josh. The words thank you feel way too small for all that you do for us. You are my favorite human, my favorite writer, and my favorite Banjo co-owner. Thank you for always being the funniest man in the room, a force of good in humanity, and the love of my life. I became a better me when I met you.

QUOTATIONS IN ORDER OF APPEARANCE

Sources are provided where available.

page 2: "Everyone winds up kissing the wrong person goodnight." —Andy Warhol
Warhol, Andy. *The Philosophy of Andy Warhol: From A to B and Back Again.* United States of America: Harcourt Books, 1975.

page 16: "The idea of waiting for something makes it more exciting." —Andy Warhol
Warhol, Andy. *The Philosophy of Andy Warhol: From A to B and Back Again.* United States of America: Harcourt Books, 1975.

page 18: "People should fall in love with their eyes closed." —Andy Warhol
Warhol, Andy. *The Philosophy of Andy Warhol: From A to B and Back Again.* United States of America: Harcourt Books, 1975.

page 43: "The best love is not-to-think-about-it love." —Andy Warhol
Warhol, Andy. *The Philosophy of Andy Warhol: From A to B and Back Again.* United States of America: Harcourt Books, 1975.

page 45: "A picture means I know where I was every minute. That's why I take pictures. It's a visual diary." —Andy Warhol
Baldwin, Neil, and William V. Ganis. *Andy Warhol: through a glass starkly.* Published in conjunction with the exhibition of the same name, shown at the George Segal Gallery, Montclair State University. Montclair, NJ: Montclair State University, 2009. Exhibition catalog.

page 66: "The best thing about a picture is that it never changes, even when the people in it do." —Andy Warhol

page 68: "It does not matter how slowly you go so long as you do not stop." —Andy Warhol

page 70: "Fantasy love is much better than reality love." —Andy Warhol
Warhol, Andy. *The Philosophy of Andy Warhol: From A to B and Back Again.* United States of America: Harcourt Books, 1975.

page 74: "A friend of mine always says, 'Women love me for the man I'm not.'" —Andy Warhol
Warhol, Andy. *The Philosophy of Andy Warhol: From A to B and Back Again.* United States of America: Harcourt Books, 1975.

page 81: "Art washes away from the soul the dust of everyday life."
Commonly attributed to Pablo Picasso.

"The Wisdom of Pablo Picasso: the world's foremost living artist puts forth a credo for creativity." *Playboy*, January 1964.

page 94: "Art is what you can get away with." —Andy Warhol
Warhol, Andy. *The Philosophy of Andy Warhol: From A to B and Back Again.* United States of America: Harcourt Books, 1975.

page 95: "Making money is art and working is art and good business is the best art." —Andy Warhol
Warhol, Andy. *The Philosophy of Andy Warhol: From A to B and Back Again.* United States of America: Harcourt Books, 1975.

page 95: "Art is the only way to run away without leaving home." —Twyla Tharp
Tharp, Twyla. *Push Comes to Shove.* New York: Bantam Books, 1992.

page 114: "As soon as you stop wanting something, you get it." —Andy Warhol
Warhol, Andy. *The Philosophy of Andy Warhol: From A to B and Back Again.* United States of America: Harcourt Books, 1975.

page 121: "During the 1960s, I think, people forgot what emotions were supposed to be." —Andy Warhol
Hodge, Susie. *How To Survive Modern Art.* London: Tate Publishing, 2010.

page 142: "For every action there is an equal and opposite reaction." —Isaac Newton

page 142: "Great things are done by a series of small things brought together." —Vincent van Gogh
Vincent van Gogh. Letter to Theo van Gogh. October 22, 1882. Translated by Mrs. Johanna van Gogh–Bonger, edited by Robert Harrison. URL: http://webexhibits.org/vangogh/letter/11/237.htm.

page 157: "Try again. Fail again. Fail better." —Samuel Beckett
Beckett, Samuel. *Worstward Ho.* United States of America: Grove Press, 1982.

page 164: "Only put off until tomorrow what you are willing to die having left undone."
Commonly attributed to Pablo Picasso.
Centre Daily Times (State College, PA), December 10, 1973.

page 184: "When it is working, you completely go into another place, you're tapping into things that are totally universal, completely beyond your ego and your own self. That's what it's all about." —Keith Haring
Sheff, David. "Keith Haring, An Intimate Conversation." *Rolling Stone*, August 1989.

page 187: "I think everybody should like everybody." —Andy Warhol

page 187: "Isn't life a series of images that change as they repeat themselves?" —Andy Warhol

Bockris, Victor. *Warhol: The Biography.* New York: Da Capo Press, 2003.

page 187: "Sometimes people let the same problem make them miserable for years when they could just say, *So what.* That's one of my favorite things to say. *So what.*" —Andy Warhol

Warhol, Andy. *The Philosophy of Andy Warhol: From A to B and Back Again.* United States of America: Harcourt Books, 1975.

page 190: "I'm afraid that if you look at a thing long enough, it loses all of its meaning." —Andy Warhol

page 207: "Inspiration is for amateurs." —Chuck Close

Finch, Christopher. *Chuck Close: Life.* New York: Prestel Publishing, 2010.

page 216: "A picture is a secret about a secret. The more it tells you the less you know." —Diane Arbus

Bosworth, Patricia. *Diane Arbus: A Biography.* New York City: Open Road Media, 2012.

page 256: "They always say time changes things, but you actually have to change them yourself." —Andy Warhol

Warhol, Andy. *The Philosophy of Andy Warhol: From A to B and Back Again.* United States of America: Harcourt Books, 1975.

page 267: "When ordinary life shackles me, I escape, one way or another. No more walls." —Anaïs Nin

Nin, Anaïs. *The Diary of Anais Nin, Volume Two (1934-1939).* New York: Houghton Mifflin Harcourt, 1970.

page 320: "The real voyage of discovery consists not in seeking new landscapes but in having new eyes."

Commonly attributed to Marcel Proust, shortened variant of the following: "The only true voyage of discovery, the only fountain of Eternal Youth, would be not to visit strange lands but to possess other eyes, to behold the universe through the eyes of another, of a hundred others, to behold the hundred universes that each of them beholds, that each of them is."

Proust, Marcel. *Remembrance of Things Past: Volume II.* Translated by C.K. Scott Moncrieff and Stephen Hudson. London: Wordsworth Editions, 2006.

page 353: "Travel far enough, you meet yourself." —David Mitchell

Mitchell, David. *Cloud Atlas.* New York: Random House, 2004.